ECONOMISTS IN PARLIAMENT IN THE LIBERAL AGE (1848-1920)

Economists in Parliament in the Liberal Age

(1848-1920)

Edited by
MASSIMO M. AUGELLO
MARCO E.L. GUIDI
Università di Pisa, Italy

Routledge
Taylor & Francis Group
LONDON AND NEW YORK

First published 2005 by Ashgate Publishing

2 Park Square, Milton Park, Abingdon, Oxon OX14 4RN
711 Third Avenue, New York, NY 10017, USA

Routledge is an imprint of the Taylor & Francis Group, an informa business

First issued in paperback 2017

British Library Cataloguing in Publication Data
Economists in parliament in the liberal age (1848-1920)
1. Economists - Political activity - History - 19th century
2. Economists - Political activity - History - 20th century
3. Economics - Political aspects - History - 19th century
4. Economics - Political aspects - History - 20th century
5. Legislators - History - 19th century 6. Legislators - History - 20th century 7. Economists - Biography
8. Legislators - Biography
I. Augello, Massimo M. II. Guidi, Marco E. L. (Marco Enrico Luigi), 1958-
330'.0922

Library of Congress Control Number: 2005929793

ISBN 978-0-7546-3965-7 (hbk)
ISBN 978-1-138-25887-7 (pbk)

Contents

List of Contributors

Salvador Almenar, born 1949, is Professor of History of the Economic Thought at the University of Valencia, Spain. He has recently published several works on classical, industrialist and Keynesian economics, and on the history of econometrics in Spain. He is co-editor and contributor of the important collection on the history of Spanish economic thought entitled *Economía y economístas españoles* (Galaxia Gutenberg – Funcas, Barcelona 1999-2000), and member of the Advisory Board of *The European Journal of the History of Economic Thought.*

António Almodovar, born 1953, is Professor of History of Economic Thought at the University of Porto, Portugal. He is a specialist of the history of economic thought in Portugal. He has published *A Institucionalização da Economia Política Clássica em Portugal* (Edições Afrontamento, Porto 1995), co-authored *A History of Portuguese Economic Thought* (Routledge, London 1998), and edited *Estudos sobre o pensamento económico em Portugal* (Facultade de Economia, Universidade do Porto, Porto 1990). He is a member of the Editorial Board of *The European Journal of the History of Economic Thought.*

Massimo M. Augello, born 1949, is Professor of History of Economic Thought at the University of Pisa, Italy. He has published books and articles on the French industrialist school and the Italian economic thought. He is also the author of *Joseph Alois Schumpeter. A Reference Guide* (Springer, Berlin 1990). He has recently co-edited *The Spread of Political Economy and the Professionalisation of Economists* (Routledge, London 2001), *La scienza economica in Parlamento 1861-1922* (Angeli, Milan 2002), and *Gli economisti in Parlamento 1861-1922* (Angeli, Milan 2003). He is the managing editor of *Il pensiero economico italiano* and member of the Advisory Board of *History of Economic Ideas* and *Storia del pensiero economico.*

Roger E. Backhouse, born 1951, is Professor of the History and Philosophy of Economics at the University of Birmingham, England. He has recently published *The Penguin History of Economics* (Penguin, London 2002, available in the USA as *The Ordinary Business of Life*, Princeton University Press), and co-edited *Toward a History of Applied Economics* (Duke University Press, Durham, NC 2000) and *Macroeconomics and the Real World* (Oxford University Press, New York 2000). He is currently editing (with Bradley Bateman) *The Cambridge Companion to Keynes*. He has been review editor of the *Economic Journal*, and editor of the *Journal of Economic Methodology*, and is associate editor of the *Journal of the History of Economic Thought.*

Bradley W. Bateman, born 1956, is Gertrude B. Austin Professor of Economics at Grinnell College, Iowa, USA. For many years, his research focused on J.M. Keynes. Currently, most of his work focuses on the influence of religion in the formation of professional economics in America. Among his recent publications there are *Keynes's Uncertain Revolution* (Un. of Michigan Press, Ann Arbor 1996), 'Clearing the Ground: The Demise of the Social Gospel Movement and the Rise of Neoclassicism in American Economics' (*History of Political Economy*, 1998), 'Bringing in the State?: The Life and Times of Laissez-Faire in the 19th Century United States' (*History of Political Economy*, 2005).

Yves Breton, born 1942, is Research Director at CNRS, Centre Auguste et Léon Walras, University of Lyon 2, France. He is a specialist in the history of French economic thought (1800-1940). He co-edited *L'économie politique en France au XIXe siècle* (Economica, Paris 1991), and *La longue stagnation en France. L'autre grande dépression (1873-1897)* (Economica, Paris 1997). With Gérard Klotz and other researchers of the École Nationale Supérieure des Ponts et Chaussées, he is working to the critical edition of Jules Dupuit's works (1804-1866).

José Luís Cardoso, born 1956, is Professor of Economics at the Technical University of Lisbon, Portugal. He has published several articles and books on the history of economic thought in Portugal: *O pensamento económico em Portugal nos finais do seculo XVIII* (Estampa, Lisboa 1989); *Pensar a economia en Portugal: digressões históricas* (Difel, Miraflores 1997). He is co-author of *A History of Portuguese Economic Thought* (Routledge, London 1998). He is the general editor of the series *Classics of Portuguese Economic Thought*, and managing editor of *The European Journal of the History of Economic Thought*.

Guido Erreygers, born 1959, is Professor of Economics at the University of Antwerp, Belgium. He obtained his PhD from the Université Paris X - Nanterre. His main fields of research include the history of economic thought, linear production models, and basic income/basic capital. He widely published on international journals such as *The European Journal of the History of Economic Thought*, *Journal of Economics* and *The Manchester School*.

Marco E.L. Guidi, born 1958, is Professor of History of Economic Thought at the University of Pisa, Italy. He has published books and articles on Bentham and classical utilitarianism and the Italian economic thought. He has recently co-edited *The Spread of Political Economy and the Professionalisation of Economists* (Routledge, London 2001), *La scienza economica in Parlamento 1861-1922* (Angeli, Milan 2002), and *Gli economisti in Parlamento 1861-1922* (Angeli, Milan 2003). He is chief-editor of *Il pensiero economico italiano* and member of the Editorial Board of *The European Journal of the History of Economic Thought*, and of the Advisory Board of *Storia del pensiero economico*.

Harald Hagemann, born 1947, is Professor of Economic Theory at the University of Hohenheim, Stuttgart, Germany. He is also a Life Member of Clare Hall, University of Cambridge and Research Professor at the German Institute for Economic Research DIW in Berlin. His main areas of research are growth, structural change, new technologies and employment and the history of economic analysis. He is editor of *Business Cycle Theory. Selected Texts 1860-1939* (4 vols, Pickering & Chatto, London 2002) and co-editor of *Growth Theory and Growth Policy* (Routledge, London 2003). He is a member of the Council of the European Society of the History of Economic Thought and of the Editorial Board of *The European Journal of the History of Economic Thought.*

Jiro Kumagai, born 1938, is Professor of Economic History at St Andrews University, Osaka, Japan. He has published many works on the economic history and on the history of economic thought in nineteenth-century Japan. He also contributed to S. Sugihara and T. Tanaka (eds), *Economic Thought and Modernization in Japan* (Elgar, Cheltenham 1998).

Bert Mosselmans, born 1969, is Associate Professor of Economics and Philosophy at the Roosevelt Academy in Middelburg, the liberal arts and sciences honours college of the University of Utrecht. His main field of research is the history of economic thought. He prepared his PhD on William Stanley Jevons at the Free University of Brussels, published widely in international journals and books and held previous positions at the Universities of Bristol, Antwerp and Utrecht.

Michalis Psalidopoulos, born 1950, is Professor of History of Economic Thought at Panteion University of Political and Social Sciences, Athens, Greece. His research focuses on national traditions in the history of economics, especially in Greece and the relation between economic thought and economic policy. He co-edited *Economic Thought and Policy in Less Developed Europe. The 19th Century* (Routledge, London 2003). His most recent article is 'The Society for the Freedom of Trade in Greece, 1865-67. Rise, Activities, Decline' (*Journal of the History of Economic Thought*, 2005).

Matthias Rösch, born 1973, is Ph.D. of Economics at the University of Hohenheim, Stuttgart. His doctoral thesis concerning investment wage and profit sharing schemes was published in 2004. In 2000 he made postgraduate studies at the University of Bologna. Together with Harald Hagemann he contributed an article on 'The Reception of Italian economic thought in Germany and Austria from 1900 to the Second World War' to P.F. Asso (ed.), *From Economists to Economists. The International Spread of Italian Economic Thought, 1750-1950* (Polistampa, Firenze 2001).

Adamantios Syrmaloglou, born 1974, is a Ph.D. candidate at the Department of Sociology, Panteion University of Political and Social Sciences, Athens, Greece.

He holds a B.A. in Sociology from Panteion University and an M.A. in Sociology and Political Science from the University of Athens. His research has focused on the history of economic and sociological ideas, specifically of the nineteenth century.

Foreword

This book represents one of the steps of a long-term project in which we have been engaged for more than twenty years. At the beginning of the 1980s, a group of scholars launched an international research project on the academic institutionalisation of economics, a conception that was embraced by groups of scholars from various European countries, the US and Japan. The idea of studying the history of economics from the viewpoint of the economists' relationships with the institutional and professional environment appeared to us to offer a highly innovative approach. Therefore we enthusiastically participated with a study on the Italian case.[1] The international project culminated in a conference held in San Miniato (Italy) in the spring of 1986.

The San Miniato conference provided all the participants with an opportunity to examine the results of their analyses in the light of the experiences of other countries and areas of the world. However, the decision by the organisers not to gather together in a single collection the studies presented at the conference, leaving national groups free to publish their papers in their own country and in their own language,[2] was in our view disappointing. What we felt was lacking was a moment in which a systematic and meditated comparison among national cases was attempted by those who had animated the research in different contexts, so that the interpretive framework of each might be enriched by cross-fertilisation.

Even more crucially, we believed that continuation should be given to the project of studying the history of economic science not merely from the canonical standpoint of doctrinal or paradigmatic evolution. Rather, awareness should be fostered that economics was rooted in institutional contexts and had itself over time become an *institution*[3] – a doctrinal corpus of knowledge which permeates and frames the mind of the student body, scholars, professionals and public opinion at large. Previous research on the professionalization and spread of economics had already revealed that this field of research promised to disclose many still unexplored phenomena whose knowledge would improve our understanding of the public role of economic science and also of its 'internal' theoretical evolution.

We thus outlined a long-term project articulated in a series of stages in which the phenomena concerning the institutionalisation and spread of political economy

---

1 The collective results of the research of the Italian group have been collected in Augello *et al.* (1988).

2 See Levan Lemesle (1986); Augello *et al.* (1988); Barber (1988); Sugiyama and Mizuta (1988); Waszek (1988); Kadish and Tribe (1993).

3 This notion of 'institution' is largely based on the classical work by Berger and Luckman (1966).

in different institutional contexts would be studied. Furthermore, we decided that at each stage an effort to provide international comparison should be made. In 1990, working jointly with Marco Bianchini of the University of Parma, we created a 'permanent seminar' in which an extensive group of historians of economic thought regularly met to debate on these topics. From these wide-ranging discussions there sprang a research project on the 'national styles in political economy',[4] and a collective study on economic periodicals, which represented the second step of our original design.[5]

While this work was in progress, we had a series of meetings with groups of scholars in other nations who were setting up similar research projects. Among others, the contacts with the Centre Alexandre Vandermonde pour l'histoire de la pensée économique at the Ecole Normale Supérieure de Fontenay-St. Cloud, the Centre Auguste et Léon Walras (Lyons), the Centro de Investigaçao sobre Economia Portuguesa (ISEG, Lisbon), and the group of historians of economics of the University of Valencia, proved very fruitful. Projects were suggested such as that of an international data base of biographies of economists and of the literature on economics. This project was not pursued at that time, although the Portuguese have since provided their precious repertoires,[6] and a dictionary on the biography and bibliography of the Italian economists of the nineteenth century is forthcoming.[7] These contacts, however, created a network that offered the opportunity to propose the comparative analyses to which we felt it was most important to address. A first occasion in this sense was provided by the research on economic periodicals.[8]

A similar integration between research on the Italian case and international comparison was obtained in the third stage of our project: the research on economic associations which we brought to completion at the end of the 1990s.[9] A further step – the study of economic dictionaries and encyclopaedias, and of the role played by economists in various works of divulgation – was partially achieved thanks to an initiative taken by our colleagues of the University of Florence.[10]

4 On which see Albertone and Masoero (1994). This line of research was inspired by Coats (1988) and has been discussed since, as to the Italian case, by us in the introductions to the works mentioned in notes 5, 9 and 11, as well as by Guidi (1994) and Faucci (1994). Our project on this issue was partially related to, albeit distinct from, the other on institutionalisation and spread, since the best way of reconstructing a 'national style' of thought in one discipline consists in examining the plurality of voices that contribute to economic discourse, especially in these contexts in which dissemination, popularisation and the teaching of this discipline are implied.

5 See Augello (1995); Augello, Bianchini and Guidi (1996).

6 See Cardoso (1998) and (2001).

7 See Augello (forthcoming). See also the recently edited dictionary of British economists: Rutherford (2004).

8 See Bianchini (1996).

9 See Augello and Guidi (2000) and Augello and Guidi (2001), respectively on the Italian case and on international comparison.

10 See Roggi (2001). We participated in this initiative with a contribution on Italian dictionaries and encyclopaedias in the nineteenth century.

Finally came the investigation on the economists in Parliament, which forms the subject of this book.

This research, in the part dedicated to the Italian case, involved around 50 scholars and was accomplished between 2000 and 2001. It was crowned by a conference held in Pisa and San Miniato on 15-17 October 2001.[11] Again, we were convinced it would be beneficial to promote international comparison. We thus invited those who had already participated in our former initiatives and several other colleagues to provide synthetic papers in which the presence of economists in different national Parliaments and attention to political economy in parliamentary debates was analysed. Some of the methodological difficulties that arose in assembling cases which in some aspects proved to be rather heterogeneous are discussed in chapter 1 of this book. These problems were at first the subject of intense discussion among contributors and thereafter were debated during a session organised at the HES Annual Meeting held at Duke University on 4-7 July 2003, marvellously organised by Roy Weintraub. We thereby reached a consensus on the idea that each contribution should present and discuss the role played by economists and political economy in parliamentary debates and legislation against the background of the political and social evolution of each country, and of the development, spread and institutionalisation of economics. It was in fact understood that the sometimes active role played by economists in the political sphere was an essential part of a broader process of dissemination of economic ideas and of institutional consolidation of economic science that took part in the nineteenth century and continued in later periods, although at various speeds and encountering obstacles of varying degree in different local circumstances.

Such a consensus proves that in the last two decades historians of economic thought – or at least a growing number among them – have gradually appreciated that the study of the spread and institutionalisation of economics and a focus on the sociology of the economists' 'profession' are of fundamental relevance for an understanding not only of the 'external history' but also of the 'internal history' of the given discipline. It is now clear that since the very outset, dissemination, the conquering of the public sphere, formation of the 'social capital', civic and patriotic commitment, philanthropy, and institutional innovation have been part and parcel of the inner core of political economy as a scientific discourse, and not only of the 'vision' of economists: much less are they merely an offshoot of the non-scientific side of their intellectual and public activity.

This may explain why studies on these and related aspects of the evolution of economic ideas, conducted by both groups and individuals, have recently multiplied.[12] And an indirect demonstration is also offered by the latest editorial

11 The papers presented at that conference are collected in Augello and Guidi (2002) and (2003).

12 See, *inter alia*, and besides the above mentioned works, the studies on French economic journals coordinated by Luc Marco (1996), and other initiatives taken to celebrate the first 50 years of the *Revue économique* (Lapidus 2000), and the 80 years of the *Rivista di*

initiatives aiming at reconstructing the overall evolution of economic science in single national areas, which make room for an analysis of the phenomena of institutionalisation and dissemination of economic ideas,[13] as well as by studies on the international circulation of economic ideas[14] and on the relationships between political economy and policy-making in 'peripheral' countries and in 'neglected' schools of economic thought.[15] All these works share the assumption that studying not only the most influential economists, but also the plurality of less eminent scholars and intellectuals who debated, spread and taught their ideas, or simply elaborated other fragments of discourse on economic topics from different perspectives, and investigating the institutional context that surrounded economic thinking, may contribute to highlighting the nature and evolution of economic theorising and its transmission to different spheres of social life, including politics.

It would not be hazardous to conclude that the studies listed above have progressively favoured the emergence of a field of studies which certainly draws inspiration from historical research on the sociology of the economist's profession[16] and on economic discourse, although it is independent of either of them. This field of study might be defined 'the history of the institutional contexts surrounding the discourse on political economy' or, more briefly, 'the institutional history of political economy', where institutions are both of a formal (universities, academies, journals, debating societies, scientific associations, Parliament, government agencies, etc.) and an informal type (schools and traditions of thought, national styles of theorising, paradigms, ideologies, mentalities, etc.).

This book aims at developing one of the facets of this field of study, that of the spread of economic science into the sphere of politics in different areas of the world through the activity of economists and the development of economic debates in Parliaments. It is our intention to pursue other themes in the near future. A research project is currently in progress in Italy under our coordination on the manuals of political economy and other economic disciplines and the consolidation and spread of economic paradigms in the nineteenth and early twentieth centuries, while we have already planned a further project on the economists and the daily press. We will not refrain from stimulating our colleagues from other countries to join our investigation in an internationally comparative approach. We hope they will not feel embarrassed by our enthusiasm.

---

politica economica (Bini 2004). A wealth of histories of economics faculties and economic societies, which it would be tedious to enumerate, have been provided in the last few years.

13 See Almodovar and Cardoso (1998); Fuentes Quintana (1999-2004); Dockès *et al.* (2000); Faucci (2000); Breton and Lutfalla (1991).

14 See Demals *et al.* (1995); Bianchini (2000); Asso (2001); Barucci (2003); Steiner (2004).

15 See Samuels (1998) and (2003); Psalidopoulos and Mata (2002).

16 See Coats (1993).

This work opens with a chapter which presents an overview of the methodological assumptions and problems underlying the research on the economists in Parliament and attempts a comparative evaluation of the phenomenon in different areas of the world. The opening chapter is followed by a series of contributions focusing on single national cases.

The succession of the latter has been organised following a geographical and a chronological criterion. We have first grouped together all the chapters concerning Europe, since they constitute the majority of cases observed in the present book, and also because in these countries the evolution of constitutional arrangements, electoral systems and the institutionalisation of political economy follows similar pathways, although with differences and temporal gaps. Within this group, we have adopted a strictly chronological order, respecting the starting date chosen by single contributors.

The latter decision requires some justification. When we first launched the project of this book almost three years ago, we asked contributors to focus on what appeared to us as a sufficiently homogeneous period, that between the revolutionary events of 1848-1849 and the aftermath of WW1. Some authors reacted by suggesting a different starting date for their country, justified by the specific political evolution in the given nation. Others accepted our proposed dates with reasoned compliance. The result is somewhat paradoxical, since nations that first established elected representative Assemblies, for instance Britain and France, are actually placed after those that did not adopt a parliamentary system until the first half of the nineteenth century. This outcome can however be justified by considering, as Roger E. Backhouse and Yves Breton argue at the beginning of their chapters, that the period approximately following 1848 was for both countries a sufficiently homogeneous stage, and that study of this period allows interesting comparisons with other national cases.

The two chapters concerning Japan and the United States have been placed at the end. In this case a strictly chronological order has been avoided for a simple reason. Kumagai's chapter on Japan describes a succession of events that in many ways is connected to European history. When the Meiji era commenced, Japan attempted at first to imitate the British model, and soon thereafter the German model, not only with regard to political order but also in the organisation of intellectual and social life.[17] On the other hand, as discussed in chapter 1, Bateman's considerations on the United States, although covering the whole of nineteenth-century American history, represent a sort of counterpoint *vis-à-vis* the other contributions, describing a surprising example of radical absence of economists from legislative assemblies and more generally from political life. Setting this contribution at the end of our book does not mean that we intend to marginalise it. On the contrary, Bateman's chapter shows how relative is the European evolution and why in many areas of the world the post-WW2 internationalisation of

17 See Kumagai (2001).

economics[18] may have produced an attitude situated midway between American absenteeism and European over-commitment.

The editors wish to thank Bill Barber and Bob Coats for their most valuable advice when the project was started. They are also indebted to all the contributors to the volume not only for the quality of their papers, but also for having shared the methodological and substantive problems that were raised at every step of the research and for cross-reading and commenting on the drafts of chapters sent by their colleagues. A special word of gratitude goes to Roger E. Backhouse, who accepted to join the project at a later and quite uncomfortable stage and provided a thought-provoking contribution and many useful suggestions for the whole work.

During the last two years, we have had many opportunities to discuss the first results of our research with numerous colleagues, especially thanks to those who accepted to organise seminars, meetings and thematic sessions on our topic. The fact that they are acknowledged in individual chapters does not exempt us from thanking them collectively on the present occasion.

We owe thanks to Rachel Costa and Adriana Basta for their invaluable help respectively in revising the English of the texts included in this volume and in copyediting it. We are indebted also to Fabrizio Bientinesi and Rosaria Adriani for their collaboration in the indexing of the work, and to Melissa Riley-Jones, Brendan George and Maureen Mansell-Ward for their careful and competent revision of the text.

Finally, this book would not have been possible without the financial support provided by the Italian Ministry of Education, University and Research (Miur) for the collective research which preceded it.

MASSIMO M. AUGELLO
MARCO E.L. GUIDI

References

Albertone, M. and Masoero, A. (1994) (eds), *Political Economy and National Realities*, Fondazione Luigi Einaudi, Torino.

Almodovar, A. and Cardoso, J.L. (1998), *A History of Portuguese Economic Thought*, Routledge, London and New York.

Asso, P.F. (2001) (ed.), *From Economists to Economists. The International Spread of Italian Economic Thought, 1750-1950*, Polistampa, Firenze.

Augello, M.M. (1995) (ed.), *L'economia politica nell'Italia di fine Ottocento. Il dibattito sulle riviste*, special issue of *Il Pensiero economico italiano*, **3**(2).

Augello, M.M. (forthcoming), *Gli economisti italiani dell'Ottocento. Storiografia e bio-bibliografia.*

Augello, M.M., Bianchini, M., Gioli, G. and Roggi, P. (1988) (eds), *Le cattedre di economia in Italia (1700-1900). La nascita di una disciplina 'sospetta'*, Franco Angeli, Milano.

18 See Coats (1996).

Augello, M.M., Bianchini, M. and Guidi, M.E.L. (1996) (eds), *Le riviste di economia in Italia (1700-1900). Dai giornali scientifico-letterari ai periodici specialistici*, Franco Angeli, Milano.

Augello, M.M. and Guidi, M.E.L. (2000) (eds), *Associazionismo economico e diffusione dell'economia politica nell'Italia dell'Ottocento. Dalle società economico-agrarie alle associazioni di economisti*, 2 Vols, Franco Angeli, Milano.

Augello, M.M. and Guidi, M.E.L. (2001) (eds), *The Spread of Political Economy and the Professionalisation of Economists. Economic Societies in Europe, America and Japan in the Nineteenth Century*, Routledge, London.

Augello, M.M. and Guidi, M.E.L. (2002) (eds), *La scienza economica in Parlamento 1861-1922. Una storia dell'economia politica dell'Italia liberale - I*, Franco Angeli, Milano.

Augello, M.M. and Guidi, M.E.L. (2003) (eds), *Gli economisti in Parlamento 1861-1922. Una storia dell'economia politica dell'Italia liberale - II*, Franco Angeli, Milano.

Barber, W.J. (1988) (ed.), *Breaking the Mould. The Development of Academic Economics in XIX Century America*, Wesleyan University Press, Middletown, CT.

Barucci, P. (2003) (ed.), *Le frontiere dell'economia politica. Gli economisti stranieri in Italia: dai mercantilisti a Keynes*, Polistampa, Firenze.

Berger, P.L. and Luckmann, Th. (1966), *The Social Construction of Reality. A Treatise in the Sociology of Knowledge*, Doubleday, New York.

Bianchini, M. (1996) (ed.), *Political Economy in European Periodicals, 1750-1900*, special issue of *History of Economic Ideas*, **4**(3).

Bianchini, M. (2000) (ed.), *La Francia, l'Italia e la formazione dell'economia politica (secc. XVIII-XIX)*, special issue of *Il Pensiero economico italiano*, **8**(2).

Bini, P. (2004) (ed.), *I novant'anni della 'Rivista di politica economica' 1911-2000. Teorie economiche, scelte politiche e cultura d'impresa nell'Italia del Novecento*, Sipi, Roma.

Breton, Y. and Lutfalla, M. (1991), *L'économie politique en France au 19ème siècle*, Economica, Paris.

Cardoso, J.L. (1998) (ed.), *Pensamento económico português. 1750-1960. Fontes documentais e roteiro bibliográfico*, Cisep, Lisboa.

Cardoso, J.L. (2001) (ed.), *Dicionário histórico de economistas portugueses*, Tema e Debates, Lisboa.

Coats, A.W. Bob (1988), 'National Styles in Contemporary Economics: Some Introductory Remarks', *History of Economics Society Bulletin*, **10**(2), pp. 145-6.

Coats, A.W. Bob (1993), *The Sociology and Professionalization of Economics, British and American Economic Essays*, Routledge, London and New York.

Coats, A.W. Bob (1996) (ed.), *The Post-1945 Internationalization of Economics*, annual supplement to Vol. 28 of *History of Political Economy*, Duke University Press, Durham, NC, and London.

Delmas, B., Demals, T. and Steiner, Ph. (1995) (eds), *La diffusion internationale de la physiocratie (XVIIIe-XIXe)*, Pug, Grenoble.

Dockès, P., Frobert, L., Klotz, G., Potier, J.-P. and Tiran, A. (2000) (eds), *Les traditions économiques françaises 1848-1939*, Cnrs éditions, Paris.

Faucci, R. (1994), 'The Development of an Italian Economic Style from Ferrara to Pantaleoni (1835-1890)', in Albertone and Masoero (1994), pp. 239-54.

Faucci, R. (2000), *L'economia politica in Italia dal Cinquecento ai nostri giorni*, Utet Libreria, Torino.

Fuentes Quintana, E. (1999-2004) (ed.), *Economía y economistas españoles*, 1. *Una introducción al pensamiento económico*; 2. *De los orígenes al mercantilismo*; 3. *La Ilustración*; 4. *La economía clásica*; 5. *Las críticas a la economía clásica*; 6. *La modernización de los estudios de economía*; 7. *La consolidación académica de la economía*; 8. *La economía como profesión*; 9. *Cronología e historiografía*, Galaxia Gutenberg – Funcas, Barcelona.

Guidi, M.E.L. (1994), 'Stili nazionali nell'economia politica', *Prometeo*, **12**(47), pp. 159-61.

Kadish, A. and Tribe, K. (1993) (eds), *The Market for Political Economy. The Advent of Economics in British University Culture, 1850-1905*, Routledge, London.

Kumagai, J. (2001), 'Orchestrating Economic Ideas: the Formation and Development of Economic Societies in Modern Japan', in M.M. Augello and M.E.L. Guidi (eds), *The Spread of Political Economy and the Professionalisation of Economists. Economic Societies in Europe, America and Japan in the Nineteenth Century*, Routledge, London, pp. 200-15.

Lapidus, A. (2000) (ed.), *Revue économique 1950-2000. Un demi-siècle en perspective*, special issue of *Revue économique*, **51**(5).

Levan-Lemesle, L. (1986) (ed.), *Les problèmes de l'institutionnalisation de l'économie politique en France au XIX siècle*, special issue of *Economies et sociétés*, série *Oeconomia*, **PE 6**.

Marco, L. (1996) (ed.), *Les revues d'économie en France. Genèse et actualité (1751-1994)*, L'Harmattan, Paris.

Psalidopoulos, M. and Mata, M.E. (2002) (eds), *Economic Thought and Policy in Less Developed Europe. The Nineteenth Century*, Routledge, London.

Roggi, P. (2001) (ed.), *Le grandi 'voci' nei dizionari specializzati (e non) di economia*, special issue of *Storia del pensiero economico*, **41-42**.

Rutherford, D. (2004) (ed.), *Biographical Dictionary of British Economists*, Thoemmes Continuum, Bristol.

Samuels, W.J. (1998) (ed.), *European Economists of the Early 20th Century*, **1**, *Studies of Neglected Continental Thinkers of Belgium, France, The Netherlands and Scandinavia*, Edward Elgar, Cheltenham.

Samuels, W.J. (2003) (ed.), *European Economists of the Early 20th Century*, **2**, *Studies of Neglected Continental Thinkers of Germany and Italy*, Edward Elgar, Cheltenham.

Steiner, Ph. (2004) (ed.), *L'économie politique néo-smithienne sur le continent: 1800-1848*, special issue of *Economies et sociétés*, série *Oeconomia, Histoire de la pensée économique*, **PE 34**(2).

Sugiyama, C. and Mizuta, H. (1988) (eds), *Enlightenment and Beyond: Political Economy Comes to Japan*, University of Tokyo Press, Tokyo.

Waszek, N. (1988) (ed.), *Die Institutionalisierung der Nationalökonomie an deutschen Univertitäten*, Scripta Mercaturae Verlag, St. Katharinen.

Chapter 1

Economists in Parliament in the Liberal Age: A Comparative Perspective

Massimo M. Augello and Marco E.L. Guidi*

Introduction

Since the pioneering works of Roger Church, Bob Coats, and William Barber[1] on the sociology of the profession of economics, the problem of economists' involvement in politics has attracted the attention of historians of economic thought. In a broader perspective, the evolution of this connection from the age of Antoine de Montchrestien's *Traicté de l'oeconomie politique* (1615)[2] to the era of professional economics seems crucially related to the changing nature of economic science, which has gradually been transformed from an ingredient of legislators' and bureaucrats' wisdom to a formalised science, with rigorously defined distinctions between pure and applied economics, or between science and art.

In this evolution, the nineteenth and early twentieth century represent an age of crucial changes. Classical political economy spread into different areas of the world, enlightening public opinion and the ruling elites with what was presented as a scientific analysis of market mechanisms and the benefits of free competition. Anti-market visions based on archaic moral and religious values did not disappear altogether, although they were endorsed only by a conservative minority. In many European countries, in the United States and Japan, the message of political economy – itself often associated with religious views – became the banner of groups of intellectuals who founded associations, journals and political movements in favour of free trade.[3] At the same time, the importance of the science of political economy

* Early drafts of this chapter were presented at two seminars, respectively at Phare, Paris, on 29 September 2004, and at Iseg, Lisbon, on 22 October 2004. The authors wish to thank the participants in these events and the contributors to the present volume, and especially Y. Breton, J. Kumagai, and M. Psalidopoulos, for their precious comments. The usual disclaimers apply.

1 See Church (1974); Coats (1968-1973); Barber (1985, 1988, 1996).

2 For an appraisal of the nature 'political economy' in the age of Montchrestien and until the rise of classical political economy see Perrot (1988).

3 See the papers collected in Bianchini (1996) and Augello and Guidi (2001).

as part of the education of future bureaucrats and politicians was recognised by the governments of many countries, leading to its institutionalisation in the legal and philosophical curricula of universities.[4] Furthermore, the new approaches that emerged in the second half of the nineteenth century, despite their critical stance towards deductive reasoning and *laissez-faire*, insisted on the scientific character of economic science, while its political implications became more evident thanks to the prevailing interventionist attitude. Finally, the marginalist revolution of the 1870s definitively imposed the scientific canons the majority of economists still adopt today, but the attempts to construct a pure, *wertfrei* theory inaugurated by Stanley W. Jevons and his contemporaries clashed with the strong political commitment of many neo-classical economists, who seemed to deduce their policy recommendations directly from the theoretical constructions they had elaborated. Thus the scientific status that political economy acquired over the century increased, rather than reducing, the political implications of economic knowledge and expertise, providing political debate with new powerful arguments.

This process was accompanied by a parallel evolution affecting the galaxy of experts on economic questions. This evolution was conditioned by two crucial changes: the new status of economic science and transformations in the political scenario. In the seventeenth and early eighteenth century, the vast majority of economic authors were philosophers and bureaucrats who aimed at influencing the decisions of absolute monarchs in favour of the interests they supported, or simply for the sake of their own career at court. By contrast, the chapters collected in this book, focusing on the second half of the nineteenth century, unveil a fascinating and polymorphous world of specialised experts in the new science of political economy, whose training and professional background was only partially a result of the ongoing process of academic institutionalisation of economic disciplines. From Portugal and Spain to Germany, the rise of constitutional regimes favoured the emergence of pre-professional figures of politicians with a solid scientific and technical background who specialised in economic questions, while the expansion of the State machinery and the rise of central banks and other national and international institutions of economic governance[5] promoted the creation of specialised economic and statistical services, in which a new generation of civil servants received a comprehensive and original economic training. As to the growing number of academic economists, the osmosis between scientific and political activity was intense. On the one hand, the proportion of members of parliament and ministers out of the total number of university professors of economics was in some cases very high,[6]

4 See Levan Lemesle (1986); Augello *et al.* (1988); Barber (1988); Sugiyama and Mizuta (1988); Waszek (1988); Kadish and Tribe (1993).

5 The International Institute of Statistics was founded in London in 1885 with the participation of a large number of eminent economists and statesmen; while the International Institute of Agriculture (later FAO) was founded in Rome in 1905, likewise thanks to the activity of some economists. Another important episode was the creation of the Society of Nations in Geneva after WW1.

6 See S. Almenar's study of the Spanish case in this book, and Augello and Guidi (2005).

and in others considerable;[7] on the other hand, especially at the early stages of institutionalisation, there were cases of members of the establishment who were appointed professors of political economy and public finance after a brilliant political career.

The study of economists' political activity in the period of consolidation and spread of economic science is therefore a very promising subject. The role played by economists in Parliament is interesting for at least two reasons. First, in mid-nineteenth-century Europe, and some decades later in Japan, Parliament became the centre of the political life and the starting point of careers in government. Even in the British 'mixed constitution' and in the American federal organisation, both enjoying a more ancient parliamentary tradition, the mid-nineteenth century represented an age in which Parliament wielded a greater power than before (and after). Second, lawmaking was in Parliament the last act of a long chain of events starting with the introduction of bills and proceeding with lengthy debates, which are recorded in the volumes of parliamentary reports. Debates demand issues, and it is interesting to explore whether or not political economy provided consistent arguments for discussion, and how these arguments interacted with other questions of a political or social nature.

Despite this, studies on the role of the economists in Parliament and in government are still a rarity. The British case is probably the only exception,[8] but the two remarkable studies by Barry Gordon (1976, 1979) cover the period preceding the Reform Bill of 1832, focusing on the cases of Ricardo and Joseph Hume, while Frank W. Fetter's (1980) famous book arrests its analysis in 1868. Other works on political debates involving the participation of economists are also limited to the golden age of classical political economy, and focus on the typical issues discussed by classical economists: colonies, the Corn Laws, the Poor Laws, the machinery question, etc.[9] An important comparative study on the *Economists in Government* was coordinated by Bob Coats,[10] including research on Britain, Australia, India, Norway, the US, Israel, Hungary, Japan, Italy and Brazil. However, this work covers the period after WW2 and focuses on the activity of 'professional' economists employed as government consultants. Introducing the issue of *History of Political Economy* that contained the results of this research, Coats significantly stated that: 'Although "economists" of one sort or another have tendered advice to governments from time immemorial, the practice of employing any significant number of professional economists in government did not become widespread until World War II':[11] an assertion that the present book contributes to reconsidering, unless a very narrow notion of 'professional economist' is adopted.

A recent collective research project has delved into the role of economists in

7 See the chapters on Belgium, France and Germany in this book.
8 See however the two studies on Spain by Mateo del Peral (1974 a and b).
9 See, e.g., Coats (1971); Berg (1980); Hilton (1980); Howe (1997).
10 See Coats (1981).
11 Ibid., p. 342.

the Italian Parliament in the period between the political unification of Italy (1861) and the rise of the Fascist regime (1922),[12] and an analogous investigation is now in progress in Portugal. The present collection presents an overview of this phenomenon in these and other six countries of Europe (Spain, France, Belgium, the United Kingdom, Germany and Greece), as well as in the United States and Japan. In each chapter, the contribution of economics to parliamentary debates and the role played by different categories of economic experts in Parliament and in government during the so-called 'liberal age' is interpreted in the light of the relevant social, political and intellectual evolution and of the path followed by the institutionalisation and early professionalisation of economics. These contributions raise a number of interesting questions and aim at stimulating more detailed research on the relationships between economic science and politics and on the consequences, both for the development of economic legislation and the evolution of economics, of the political commitment displayed by economists.

The present chapter attempts a first comparative analysis of the cases examined in the volume. The next section presents the interpretive questions which prompted the research project on the economists in Parliament and the contributions this study may make to the advancement of research on the history of economic thought. The remaining three sections discuss some methodological problems related to research on this topic, and specifically:

- the definition of 'liberal age', its periodisation and applicability to different countries;
- the definition of 'economist' that is chronologically and geographically most appropriate to the cases in question, against the backdrop of the relationships between economics and politics;
- the contribution of the discourse on political economy to parliamentary debates and to legislation.

A concluding section highlights some further research developments that may be stimulated by this book.

The economists in Parliament and the history of economics

The chapters that compose this book have been written by historians of economic thought, and inevitably the questions they raise are those most relevant for their research. This may be viewed as a limit, which calls for further interdisciplinary attempts to assess the relationships between the economists' activities in Parliaments and, to cite only two examples, the evolution of political discourse or the formulation of economic policies in different countries or areas.

12 See Augello and Guidi (2002, 2003 and 2005). See also the chapter of this book on the Italian case.

At the most elementary level, this book answers a basic need for documentation. In some cases, a first inventory of the main economic debates in Parliaments had to be attempted, while in other cases it was necessary to extend already existing knowledge of single important episodes to attain a more systematic level of understanding on the role played by political economy in parliamentary debates. The typical questions raised at this level of analysis concern the continuity, extent and depth of parliamentary debates on economic issues; the nature of economic arguments employed by the protagonists of these debates; the presence or absence of significant references to current economic literature and to the classics of economics, and the interrelations between economic analysis and arguments of a political or ideological nature.

A parallel cluster of questions is of a more sociological character and concerns the protagonists of economic debates, their social and professional origins, their knowledge of the scientific literature on political economy, their political stance, their affiliation to different schools of economic thought and the consequences of these characteristics for the issues to which they devoted their parliamentary activities. Another relevant problem is that of the degree of specialisation and proficiency of eminent members of parliament in the science of political economy, as revealed both by the content of their public speeches and by their writings on political economy, as well as by their involvement in the institutionalisation and spread of political economy.

A third important group of questions has to do with the activities and behaviour of economists and experts of economic problems in Parliament. The papers published in this book investigate the intensity of their commitment in political debates and lawmaking, exploring whether they focused exclusively on issues related to economic policies or on other non-economic topics, and to what extent they differentiated themselves from their parliamentary colleagues. In some cases useful information can be gleaned on the parliamentary economists' political career and the ways in which they were recruited into the political class, the compromises they were compelled to accept, their relations with their constituencies, etc. Finally, the economists' behaviour in Parliament is also a crucial subject of inquiry, since it is interesting to ascertain whether they adopted a particular attitude, preferring some activities rather than others, or simply acted like any other politician. This question invests the extent to which the message of political economy was transmitted to the political debate and the compromises that were established between the point of view of economic science and the ordinary logic of politics.

Clearly, a basic assumption of our work is that documenting economic debates in Parliament and the role played therein by economists is not a matter of pure curiosity. It answers a more fundamental purpose, that of understanding the nature and inner evolution of economic discourse in a crucial age of consolidation, spread and transformation. From this point of view, the analysis of the presence or absence of political economy in parliamentary debates and of the role played in such debates by more or less 'professional' experts of economics can be considered a litmus test for revealing some essential features of the discourse on political economy.

To begin with, the fact that some eminent classical economists such as David Ricardo and John Stuart Mill sat in the British Parliament, and that their example was followed by other leading economists in France, Germany, Belgium, Italy, and Spain is a signal of the strong political implications of their conception of economics. More specifically, it reveals that classical political economy implied as an essential part not only a general *laissez-faire* recommendation in foreign trade, the poor laws or the regulation of labour and production, but also a precise programme of institutional reforms aiming at radically transforming the attitude of government *vis-à-vis* economic regulation. The decisive encouragement James Mill gave to Ricardo's election in 1818 and the daily discussions between the former and Jeremy Bentham on parliamentary agenda[13] may be taken as a symbolic example of the close connection between classical political economy and institutional reform. In the British case the main problem was represented by the power of monopolies and by the system of 'old corruption' which coexisted, albeit conflictually, with a developed commercial and industrial society. But in other areas, as the examples of the liberal revolutions of the 1820s in Spain and Portugal reveal, this message of political economy interacted with a more radical need to overcome the feudal remains of the *ancien régime*, a task that the enlightened reforms of the eighteenth century and the Napoleonic regimes had at least started to perform in other countries. Moreover, especially on the Continent, it was a common view that this programme of institutional reform was to be accompanied by an equally indispensable plan of structural interventions directed to facilitating the functioning of market mechanisms and promoting the spread of knowledge and innovations.

Another interesting feature of the discourse on political economy highlighted by the study of economists in Parliaments concerns the close connection between theorising on the one hand, and the spread of economic ideas and the enlightenment of public opinion on the other hand. Classical economists – and in this they were not alone – constantly felt such a task to be an essential element of their intellectual mission. The cases examined in this volume reveal an interesting continuum between the activities of economic associations for free trade or social reform, economic journals and economists who were elected to Parliament. The leaders of the Société d'Economie Politique in France and of the Association Belge pour la Liberté Commerciale or the Association Internationale pour les Réformes Douanières, for example, were among the main promoters of the *Journal des économistes* and headed the troop of liberal economists in their Parliaments. The cases of the *Escuela Economista* in Spain, of Francesco Ferrara and the Società Adamo Smith founded in Italy in 1874 together with a journal entitled *L'Economista*, of John Prince-Smith, who founded in 1847 the Deutscher Freihandelsverein, and that of Aristides Economos' journal *Oikonomiki Epitheorissis* in Greece show many similarities. But the examples of Bruno Hildebrand, one of the most eminent representatives of the old German Historical School who founded in 1863

13 See Bentham (1838-1843), **10**, p. 498.

the *Jahrbücher für Nationalökonomie und Statistik*, and that of Gustav von Schmoller, who was the chairman of the Verein für Sozialpolitik from 1890 until his death, reveal that this attitude was by no means limited to the followers of classical economics. Throughout the period under review, the legislative chambers were considered as an important arena from which the message of political economy could reverberate with increased energy on public opinion.

But even the cases in which the economists were absent from Parliament and government have significant implications. In Britain, for example, the number of economists who entered Parliament in the second half of the nineteenth century and early twentieth century was much lower than in the golden age of classical economics. The reasons suggested by Roger Backhouse to explain this phenomenon are interesting on both sides of the 'market for members of parliament'. On the demand side, the increasing opposition in the public mind between the necessary expansion of State activities in social and economic policies and the *cliché* of political economy as intrinsically associated with *laissez-faire* reveals the difficulties encountered by the economists of this period – who included the main protagonists of the marginalist revolution – in 'seeking to distance themselves from this position whilst avoiding any association with socialism'.[14] On the supply side, the efforts made by Alfred Marshall and others to re-establish the scientific credentials of economics and to promote economic studies in the main British universities created the preconditions for a more modern vision of professional economics, based on prudent retreat from direct political commitment, concentration on academic research and teaching, and development of scientific standards of excellence.[15] In this framework, the choice made by Alfred Marshall to limit his political activity to involvement with Royal Commissions paved the way to the typical attitude of modern economists, who prefer consultancy and 'persuasion' to direct political activity, considering the former more consistent with their scientific and academic status.[16] Nevertheless, the fact that Jevons, Sidgwick or Marshall felt an impellent necessity to contribute (although with unequal degrees of success) to political debate and decision-making confirms the point highlighted by recent studies on these authors: there was a strong political and social *pathos* in their decision to devote their life to the study of economic science.

A comparison with the Italian and the German cases reveals two interesting differences. On the one hand, the existence in the Peninsula of a deep-rooted tradition of moderate liberalism dating back to the Italian Enlightenment and to the school of Gian Domenico Romagnosi in the early nineteenth century, which stressed the role of institutions in promoting economic development and mitigating the most disruptive effects of market competition, favoured the development of an interventionist approach in the 1860s and 1870s. A similar outcome was produced in the German area by the evolution of the Historical School, which embodied some

---

14 See below, p. 121.
15 See Maloney (1991).
16 See Coats (1981).

aspects of the older Cameralist tradition.[17] In both these cases, the economists were able to provide theoretical arguments in favour of increasing State intervention and political economy was not discredited as in the British case. The fact that the leading figures of these schools of thought sat in Parliament and became in some cases influential ministers is another demonstration of the popularity enjoyed by their theories in the public mind.

On the other hand, the strong involvement in Italian parliamentary politics of Maffeo Pantaleoni and Antonio De Viti de Marco, two major protagonists of the marginalist revolution, reveals a radically different strategy from that adopted by Marshall, although it corresponded to a similar need to consolidate the credentials of 'theoretical' economics against public attacks. Here, however, the context was different, and this may explain the peculiarity of their response. First and foremost, Italian marginalist economists were unable to find a comfortable ground for their scientific activities in universities, since academic economics was dominated by the main exponents of the interventionist school who employed their political power and influence to consolidate their monopoly over university recruitment. And second, unlike the welfarist overtures of the Cambridge school and Fabianism in Britain, their approach to economic policy was more in line with the Italian (minority) tradition of radical *laissez-faire.* Their parliamentary experience mirrored the difficulties of their academic career: they sat on the benches of the opposition and campaigned against corruption and State inefficiency, while after 1900 they fought against the coalition between interventionists and Socialists. After WW1, they looked favourably on the rise of Fascism. A comparative history of the political behaviour of marginalist economists in different national contexts, as the present book suggests, would reveal interesting features of the transformations of economic discourse at the turn of the twentieth century.

The vicissitudes of Italian marginalist economists have some features in common with those of American institutionalists and early marginalists at the end of the nineteenth century, though for opposite political reasons and with opposite outcomes. As reported in Bradley Bateman's chapter, John Bates Clark, Richard T. Ely and Simon Nelson Patten were forced to relinquish their early commitment to some forms of Christian socialism, for which they 'were put under tremendous pressure by the boards of trustees at their respective universities and by the popular press'.[18] In essence they were obliged to choose between an academic career and political commitment. The price for professionalisation was that, similarly to, but more radically than, their British colleagues, they had to forsake any kind of *vita activa.* As suggested by Bateman, there may be institutional and sociological reasons accounting for this situation: European economists enjoyed a public status as members of the civil service, and generally had tenure. Although from time to time they were exposed to the will of governments that might decree individual sanctions or even collective purges, as happened in France at the beginning of the

17 See Tribe (1995).
18 See below, p. 298.

Second Empire (1852), they were relatively free to expound their ideas and to take an active part in politics. Their American colleagues, with no tenure until the third decade of the twentieth century and with a decentralised and largely private university system, were obliged to submit themselves to the censure of their employers. This negative case offers a further illustration of how fascinating it is to delve into the connection between professional activities, political commitments and the inner evolution of economic thought in different national contexts.

But the late nineteenth century was not the only period in which American economists remained at the margin of political life. Attempting an explanation of this abstention, if not marginalisation, in the first half of the nineteenth century entails in-depth analysis of the interactions between economic discourse, institutionalisation of political economy and political paradigms. Anti-intellectualism and the self-sufficiency of the republican ideology are persuasively invoked by Bateman as possible explanations. The role contemporarily played in Europe by political economy as a bourgeois progressive ideology and as the foundation of the political and social discourse in the 'public sphere' was here endorsed by an autochthonous political ideology that magnified the virtues of self help and the 'free market'. Moreover, although political economy was considered an element of the education of the learned classes, it remained a part of the teaching of moral philosophy rather than becoming an independent subject. This aspect was not surprising as such, nor was it strange that the teachers of economic topics and authors of economic textbooks were religious ministers. The most interesting fact was that in the United States of the nineteenth century a religiously founded economic discourse remained confined to the level of education, crushed as it were by the monopoly exerted by republican ideology in the public sphere and in active political life.

This situation was different from that of Britain, where Evangelical political economy was not only very popular,[19] but encouraged figures like John Howard and Elisabeth Fry to take an active part in political campaigns for social and economic reform.[20] But Frédéric Bastiat's extolling of 'economic harmonies' was also largely based on religious arguments,[21] and his engagement in campaigns for free trade and in parliamentary politics were a direct consequence of his profound Christian beliefs. Once again the study of the economists' political activity reveals unexpected connections with a deeper understanding of the discourse on political economy.

In other contexts, for instance in Portugal, Spain, Italy, Greece and Germany, the moral and religious content of economic education and political-economic based ideologies was directly connected to the fundamental political goal of nation building. This connection explains the commitment of many economists in favour of the reform and enlargement of primary, technical and secondary education.

19 See Hilton (1988); Howe (1997).
20 See Ignatieff (1978); Cooper (1981).
21 See Bastiat (1850).

Looking at their writings and parliamentary speeches on this topic with a retrospective eye would be disappointing. It is striking to what extent no nineteenth-century economist – with the possible exception of the French industrialists and their followers abroad – conceived of education as an investment in human capital or as a factor of economic growth.[22] Rather, they took these economic effects for granted, since they believed that economic development was a natural consequence of the civilising effects of education. However, for many of them, the most urgent problem was creating a strong national identity and solid networks of 'social capital' at a national level, in countries that had been for centuries under foreign domination or divided into small States subject to external influences and incapable of solving the basic needs of their populations. To quote a phrase pronounced by an eminent Italian statesman after the unification of the country (Massimo d'Azeglio), 'now that Italy has been created, we must create the Italians'. This example makes it clear that study of parliamentary debates can reveal some interesting aspects of the changing scope and content of economic discourse in different periods and different areas.

Those who turn to this book in search of some 'measure' of the success of economists in Parliament and of the influence they exerted on important political decisions will be largely disappointed. Even leaving aside the cases in which such influence was totally absent, an overall assessment would be impossible, since it is difficult to evaluate globally whether the political success of economists depended on the persuasive force of their economic arguments or on other sociological and political variables. Equally difficult would be the attempt to disentangle, in the framework of parliamentary debates and the path leading to political decisions, the role of economic expertise and advice from the pressure of the interests at play and from the inner logic of political action. Despite this, the chapters that compose this book deal extensively with the influence of economists and the political prestige they enjoyed, as well as the cases of total failure and neglect. Nevertheless, the focus is less on policy results than on their meaning for the history of economic thought. On the one hand, as Almodovar and Cardoso argue in their chapter, knowledge of 'the bases and the doctrinal and theoretical justifications behind constitutional and legislative measures' is necessary in order to understand a crucial aspect of 'the process involved in the affirmation, formation and dissemination of the scientific discourse of political economy';[23] on the other hand, the role awarded to economists by different institutional arrangements is partially responsible for favouring the expansion of some schools of thought at the expense of others or determining different paths toward the institutionalisation of political economy and the professionalisation of economics.

A further crucial issue which at times emerges in this book is the reverse question of the influence, if any, of the political experience of many eminent economists on the nature, content and evolution of economic discourse. No clear-cut

22 See Teixeira (2004).
23 See below, p. 27.

'demonstration' of such an effect is obviously possible. In many circumstances, however, it is evident that the connection between parliamentary and political debates and political decisions on the one hand and, on the other hand, discussions in scientific journals, in the press and in economic associations, was so strong that it can be concluded that the political debate was at one and the same time a source of inspiration and a repository of the global evolution of economic ideas. Perhaps there was no significant influence of political militancy on questions of pure economic analysis. Nor was there any bi-unique relationship between political ideologies and economic 'visions'. But legislation and policy making constituted the natural ground of 'verification' for applied theories concerning trade regulation, money issue, credit, population, industrial organisation, labour, etc., and it is obvious that for economists interested in these questions political debates offered a rich source of evidence and a fertile wellspring for their reflections. More than that, it is essential to grasp to what extent political discussions on the 'wealth and poverty of nations', on such urgent problems as famines, the grinding poverty of rural or urban areas, emigration, the conditions of labourers, etc., no less than those on customs tariffs or the banking system, provided the motivational bases for the scientific calling of so many economists, revealing that political economy was exactly the reverse of the 'dismal science' depicted by Thomas Carlyle.

A liberal age

The above examples show that one of the complexities underlying the present collection consists in identifying a period with sufficiently distinctive and similar characteristics in all countries to allow useful comparisons. The obvious requirement is the existence of a liberal constitution conferring the legislative power on an assembly of deputies elected by the people, or at least by the upper classes. Now, as is well known, this process was significantly asynchronous in different areas of the world. In the British case a liberal constitution and a Parliament had existed since the Glorious Revolution. The Reform Bill of 1832, which created a more balanced system of representation, might constitute a useful starting point for comparison with 'late comers' in this liberal evolution. Unfortunately however, as the cases of David Ricardo and Joseph Hume can illustrate, the unreformed Parliament of the early nineteenth century had been the theatre of interesting debates involving the most outstanding economists of the time, and their exclusion from the scope of our research entails a clear cost. In the United States, a democratic constitution, with a peculiar system of 'checks and balances' which conferred great power on the President elected by the people, had existed since the American Revolution of 1776, and no significant break in this institutional equilibrium and in parliamentary practice can be detected until at least the Civil War.

The case is different with most countries of continental Europe, which after the fall of the Napoleonic Empire were subjected to the starkly illiberal discipline of the Holy Alliance. The pace at which these countries disengaged from the hold of reactionary governments varied from case to case. The Cadiz Constitution of 1812 that Spain and Portugal revived during the revolutions of 1820-1823 became a model which was partially imitated by France in 1830, although the limits of the institutional order established by the Orléans monarchy led to the February 1848 revolution and the establishment of a short-lived republican constitution, which paved the way to the *coup d'état* by Louis Napoléon Bonaparte. The new regime, however, did not suppress the liberal institutions altogether, although a new start in parliamentary life was represented by the establishment of the Third Republic in 1871.

Focusing again on the Iberian peninsula, while in Portugal the liberal constitution adopted in 1820 lasted until 1910, when a republican regime was instituted, in the case of Spain a parliamentary system was definitively consolidated only between 1837 and 1845, the year of the new constitution. In Belgium a statement declaring Belgium to be a constitutional, parliamentary monarchy was approved in January 1831 by the National Congress elected some months before as a result of the struggle for independence from the Low Countries. Analogously, in Greece the introduction of a liberal constitution was a gradual outcome of the independence from Ottoman rule obtained in 1829-1830, although a Parliament was not elected until 1844 and was endowed with significant legislative powers between 1864 and 1874.

In other countries, for instance in Germany and Italy, the creation of a parliamentary regime was paralleled by a process of national unification which, despite the essentially liberal and bourgeois revolutionary movements of 1848-1849, was the upshot of successful military campaigns led by Prussia and Piedmont respectively. The process of unification was virtually concluded in the Peninsula by 1861. When the Kingdom of Italy was proclaimed, however, it adopted the liberal constitution the Kingdom of Sardinia had obtained in 1848. In contrast to the ephemeral Parliaments elected in Italy between 1848-1849, the National Assembly gathered in Frankfurt in 1848 was already a Pan-German Parliament elected by virtually universal suffrage. However, after its suppression *manu militari* in June 1849, a new period of reaction was ushered in, and the rise to power of Bismarck in Prussia after 1862 created a regime in which, despite the existence of a Landtag and – after 1867-1871, when unification was concluded – of a Reichstag elected by universal suffrage, power was firmly in the hands of an independent executive.

Finally, the case of Japan differs significantly from that of European countries, although its inclusion in the present collection is fully justified by the opening of permanent relations with the Western world and by the gradual adoption of Western political institutions, a process initiated in 1868 with the shift of the capital from Kyoto to Tokyo and the inauguration of the 'Meiji era'. Here, the announcement of the opening of an Imperial Diet would not be accomplished until 1881, and indeed it was not opened until 1890.

In the light of this picture, it seems natural to assume that 1848 is little more than a conventional date, an Aristotelian *via media* between liberal revolutions that took place some decades before and those which followed a few years later. But this date had also an important symbolic meaning, since the liberal-democratic revolution that took place in France, Germany, Italy, as well as in the Netherlands, Austria, Bohemia, Hungary and in other areas under the Habsburg monarchy (unfortunately, these countries and the Scandinavian area remain outside the scope of the present work) left in the public mind of the so called civilised world the impression that progress towards liberal institutions was inexorable. Similarly in the British case the decades that followed the repeal of the Corn Laws in 1846 may be considered, from a political and social point of view, as a sufficiently independent period marked by a gradual transition towards more democratic institutions.

Less controversial is the *terminus ad quem* chosen for the studies collected in this volume. In most cases, the aftermath of WW1 seems to be a convenient date, as all of the countries concerned were involved in the war and in the dramatic political and economic events following the Treaty of Versailles. The ideological confrontations that considerably changed the political scene of Europe and the consequences of the Great Crisis of 1929 definitively closed what Stefan Zweig called *die Welt von Gestern*, which from our point of view represented the golden age of liberal institutions. Some countries moved towards totalitarian regimes, whereas the political atmosphere was radically transformed in those that conserved a liberal-democratic constitution. This was mainly due to the rise of ideologically oriented mass political parties, which organised political life and constituted an indispensable intermediary between individuals and government, while from an economic point of view, the new attitudes towards public intervention which followed the 1929 crisis heralded the modern structures of the Welfare/Warfare State. As a consequence, while the formal Constitution of these States often remained unchanged, the material *Verfassung* underwent radical alterations.

Even the choice of a final date, however, is not devoid of problems. In the areas of the world that were not affected by Fascism, the continuity of parliamentary life might call for interesting comparisons between the pre-WW1 situation and the interwar period, as the chapter on Belgium in this book clearly illustrates. Moreover, the pace at which the elitist liberal regimes of the nineteenth century were transformed into democratic constitutions varied from case to case. Britain seems to have anticipated by some decades what in other countries occurred before the World War or immediately in its aftermath: the rise of modern parties and the gradual dissolution of the social compromises which had characterised the life of nineteenth-century governments. Different speeds of transformation, however, do not entail that comparison is impossible or less telling.

On the whole, it is beyond doubt that a liberal age did exist and that the political organisation of different States had a common ground and similar features. There is therefore only one answer to the questions 'why this age' and 'why Parliament': with the partial exception of the US, this was an age in which the Parliament was the centre of both political decisions and political debates. If one seeks to assess the relationship between the spread and institutionalisation of economics and the evolution of politics in this age, one must turn to the analysis of parliamentary debates and lawmaking.

Amongst the common features that characterise this period the most significant factor is that the government was placed under the more or less strict control of an initially limited elite of wealthy citizens of aristocratic or bourgeois origin, with agrarian and commercial interests or connected to the world of professions. This control was enacted through the suffrage, but also through public opinion and the organisation of complex networks of urban sociability and patronage in which there emerges the role of those who in neo-Latin languages are called '*notables*': those 'leading citizens' who based their social and political power on conspicuous consumption, charity and dynastic hegemony over local administrations.[24] The obvious result of their strong hold over electoral mechanisms was that Parliaments were inhabited by *notables* from the different provinces of each State. For similar reasons, as recalled by Backhouse, the British House of Commons was called 'the best gentleman's club in London'.

An interesting consequence of this state of affairs was that the local networks dominated by *notables* involved frequent contacts with the learned and academic world, and especially with jurists, whose expertise was useful both in private and in public affairs. With the exceptions noted above, the close connection between law and political economy in most European educational systems favoured the parallel social rise of the economists, whose public profile was already evident. These connections, coupled with the frequent absence of census limits on eligibility for learned people, largely explain why men of letters and academics were so over-represented in early liberal Parliaments (significantly, the Frankfurt National Assembly was called a '*Professorenparlament*'), and why jurists and economists were the largest groups among them.

These social and political equilibria gradually evolved towards an enlargement of the franchise as a response to pressure from the popular classes involved in industrialisation, and particularly to the danger represented by the advent of Socialism. This enlargement at first incorporated the middle classes and the petty bourgeoisie, until male universal suffrage was obtained, in many cases in the early years of the twentieth century. Corresponding to this political involvement came increasing State intervention in economic and especially social affairs, justified with arguments ranging from national emulation to paternalism and the need to avoid the tyranny of uneducated majorities influenced by revolutionary ideologies. Thus – with the exception of the US and Britain as regards custom tariffs – the age of political liberalism is far from corresponding to an age of economic liberalism.

These political and economic processes called for technically refined economic expertise at all levels of government. As we have seen in the former section, there were very different attitudes vis-à-vis economists' involvement in public decisions. On the whole, however, the interface between economists and public affairs was increased by these transformations.

24 See Agulhon (1979); Best and Cotta (2000).

This conclusion raises another crucial question that this book attempts to answer in different ways: who were the economists who sat in Parliament? This issue is discussed next.

Identifying the economists who sat in Parliament

It is not surprising that the consensus among the authors of the present collection on the range of the notion of 'parliamentary economist' is far from being general. The use of different definitions evidently mirrors both diverse national evolutions of the institutionalisation and 'professionalisation' of economics and different historical conditions of the economy and society, which corresponded to parliamentary debates of variable content and level of analysis. However, it would be a mistake to take this variety as proof of the impossibility of identifying a distinct, albeit multifaceted, figure of 'economist in Parliament'. Indeed, perhaps it is this very variety that offers the most useful result of the research behind this book.

In his work quoted above, Frank W. Fetter[25] suggested a quite broad range of criteria, which were certainly appropriate for the period he was referring to. Two of these criteria can be easily accepted as the standards that could identify an economist in the early decades of the nineteenth century: *profession* and *authorship*. The very limited number of scholars who taught political economy at university, and the larger number of authors – very often bankers and businessmen like David Ricardo, but also enlightened aristocratic or bourgeois landlords, as in continental Europe – who regularly published books and articles on economic topics, were certainly among those who could claim the title of 'economist' in the world of learning. These activities sometimes preceded their accession to Parliament, but it was not unknown for members of parliament to engage in such activities following their terms of office, in which case it was their political activity that stimulated deeper enquiry into the science of political economy. In both circumstances these 'objective' characteristics relating to social and intellectual activities might be coupled with more 'subjective' criteria, like *self-conscience*, *self-definition* and *reputation*, which strengthen the possibility of distinguishing the figures of economists from those of their parliamentary colleagues.

But Fetter additionally suggested a third criterion, arguing that a parliamentary economist could be a member of parliament who systematically participated in economic debates linked with economic legislation. As Roger Backhouse points out in his chapter, there is a clear risk of circular reasoning in using this definition. A related risk is that such a criterion makes it impossible to perform a comparative evaluation of the weight of the economists in different national Parliaments. As noted above, all the countries considered by the present inquiry faced similar problems, and no marked difference among these countries can be observed as regards the quantity of economic legislation discussed in Parliament. It is therefore

25 See Fetter (1980), pp. 12-13.

natural that some members of parliament specialised in predominantly economic and social questions. If applied to the second half of the nineteenth century and early twentieth century, Fetter's third criterion generates the paradoxical result that the number of 'parliamentary economists' appears to be similar, if not larger, in countries in which the institutionalisation of economics was at its very beginning and the literature on political economy was still limited, than in countries with an old-established tradition of studies in this field. The sociological analysis provided by Psalidopoulos and Syrmaloglou on the Greek case, however, shows that many parliamentary economists selected according to this criterion had a substantial economic background or practised professional and intellectual activities connected in various ways to the study of political economy.

There is however another reason for not dismissing Fetter's 'third criterion' as simply tautological. Until the last decades of the nineteenth century, there were no 'professional' economists in the sense suggested by Bob Coats,[26] who argued that in order to be professional an economist should have had specialised training in economics.[27] Nevertheless, political economy was an important ingredient of the education of the higher classes, and many members of the political elite had graduated in the faculties of law where this subject was taught along with public finance and statistics. Their profound knowledge of the classics of economic science and the clear understanding of the functioning of economic mechanisms they revealed were therefore the result of an educational pattern they shared with those who had chosen to devote their life to economic studies or to the teaching of economics in universities. Economic specialisation in government and Parliament was thus one of the possible vocations generated by this common background, and there is no reason why these members of parliament or government could not aspire to the title of economists like their academic colleagues. The fact that many of them published significant contributions in learned journals and participated in economic debating societies shows how difficult it is to separate them from those who, after a phase of intellectual achievements in the field of economics, decided to enter upon a political career.

A similar case was that of the large groups of jurists and lawyers who sat in many Parliaments during the period examined in this book. A considerable number of them had received some economic training – albeit not specialised – in law schools and law faculties, and those who devoted themselves with continuity to economic debate and economic legislation might equally deserve a title of 'economist' not merely as the result of *ex-post* reasoning. Here too, publications, participation in economic societies and in the institutionalisation of political economy are additional elements that allow such identification.

A third interesting group of members of parliament who constantly applied themselves to economic issues is represented by former members of the economic

26 See Coats (1991).

27 On the problems raised by this definition see our 'Introduction' to Augello and Guidi (2001).

departments of the civil service, originating especially from the statistical, accounting and legislative services of the Ministries of the Treasury, Finance, Agriculture and Trade. In the Italian case, for example, the enlightened effort of a number of heads of these Ministries had created something very similar to a modern research centre in the department of statistics of the Ministry of Agriculture, Industry and Trade. Numerous brilliant young employees received very technical and up-to-date training not only in statistics and accountancy, but also in economics. Their expertise rivalled, and in some cases surpassed, that of many academic economists, as demonstrated by the fact that some of them became university professors at a later date. Those among them who sat in Parliament not only revealed a high level of economic expertise, but also displayed special attitudes in their political commitment. Their activity was inspired by the values of loyalty, truth and backstage persuasion vis-à-vis statesmen and policy-makers. It would be tempting to extend to them Schumpeter's definition of 'consultant administrators'[28] that Psalidopoulos and Syrmaloglou attribute to most Greek members of parliament. And this case is likely to be similar to that of other economists in Parliament with a background in central banks, large private financial companies and other organisations of economic governance.

Only at the end of the period under review were there cases of members of parliament who had acquired specialised training in economics during their graduate and postgraduate studies. There is no reason why their constant interest in economic questions in Parliament should not earn them the title of 'economist' independently of any other merit.

On the whole, it seems impossible to define a parliamentary economist, and more generally an economist, by referring only to such criteria as authorship and profession. The present research on the economists in Parliament reveals that eminent economic experts existed outside universities or academies and even outside the group of the most prolific economic writers, and politics was the natural receptacle of their activism. This demonstrates a truth that in some measure is still valid today: there is no rigid monopoly on the economics profession by those who hold positions in universities and research institutions, or have an outstanding curriculum of publications.

On the positive side, the present book contributes to disclosing two pathways towards attainment of the status of economist that were typical of the social and intellectual position of economics in nineteenth and early twentieth-century societies. One of these pathways was connected to the then ongoing process of professionalisation of politics which resulted in the constitution of modern political parties. The other is related to the growth of bureaucracy within ministries, large private companies and international institutions, and particularly to the creation of statistical and economic research departments in many of these organisations. Some of these concrete 'modes of upward mobility' disappeared at a later time as a

28 Schumpeter (1954), p. 159.

consequence of the crisis of institutions created for political and social contexts that had been superseded by the course of history. However, they became a model for other, more recent, endeavours.

Spain, as shown by Salvador Almenar in this book, provides a noteworthy example of the relationship between the professionalisation of politics and the professionalisation of economics. The development of an endogenous economic specialisation within the '*caciquist*' political-parliamentary system at the beginning of the twentieth century resulted in expulsion from Parliament of the group of academic economists who had played an important role in the second half of the nineteenth century as representatives of the Economist School favourable to free trade. And similar cases are present in Belgium, France, Italy, Germany and other countries.

Nevertheless, such a broadening of the scope of professional (or pre-professional) economics still implies some risks of circular reasoning and all-inclusiveness. A notable ambiguity stems from the fact that some 'economic experts' were in Parliament not as representatives of scientific reasoning, economic competence and intellectual vocation, but as agents of powerful economic or social interests, which they defended by employing theoretical arguments in an instrumental manner. Analogously, members of the State bureaucracy could at times be elevated to Parliament as a result of Cabinets' attempts to keep the legislative power under control.

However, no criterion of identification is devoid of ambiguities. Even that of academic professionalisation is not immune from defects: especially at the earliest stages of institutionalisation of political economy, those who obtained an academic post as professor of economics sometimes had a rather scanty economic background and had published no noteworthy contribution to economic science. Among their ranks, one might find professors of law or philosophy who were appointed in order to fill a gap in the academic staff of their faculties; there were also cases in which a professorship of economics was a consequence of a brilliant political career. However, in countries in which the institutionalisation of economics had already made substantive advances, it is important to verify whether academic economists with a sound economic training did or did not accept to participate in parliamentary and government activities, and why they chose a particular strategy rather than another.

Even the criterion of significant economic publications – which is certainly the most universally appropriate for the period under review – has its own ambiguities, since it is very difficult to assess the meaning of 'significant', no less than that of 'economic' writing. There may be general agreement that the mere publication of parliamentary speeches and reports on economic questions does not constitute sufficient proof of a member of parliament's economic vocation and proficiency, especially if such publications were only a portion of those authored by the given politician. However, many recognised economists likewise wrote on non-economic topics, among which one may cite literature, music and fine arts, while the period in question also includes figures who are known above all for articles, pamphlets and memoirs that were strictly related to their political activity. So what is the threshold between significant, or genuine, and occasional economic publications?

Fortunately in many cases help comes directly from parliamentary debates. Official reports often contain indications suggesting that some members of parliament enjoyed the reputation of being an 'economist'. This reputation was on occasion accompanied by respect, but in other cases it revealed irritation at the manner of behaving and arguing of those who were acknowledged by their 'honourable colleagues' as economists. This rather telling picture provides an eloquent illustration of the way those who applied a purely political logic very often had little patience with members who stood up and dogmatically explained, in lengthy interventions and quoting the authorities of economic science, the tenets of economic theory with regard to the feasibility and consistency of measures that were the result of political compromises and tactical decisions.

On the other hand, it seems indisputable that many academic and non-academic economists 'betrayed' their scientific calling when they entered Parliament, either by acquiescing in political decisions that were inconsistent with their theoretical *credo*, or by taking an interest in topics and goals that bore little or no relation to economic questions, even in the broadest meaning of this term that might be accepted at that time. To some extent this apparent incoherence may have reflected the political beliefs of economists as citizens of their times and members of their class or party: industrialism or agrarianism, nationalism, Social Catholicism, Socialism, conservative paternalism, etc. But it may also have resulted simply from a change in life perspectives, which implied abandoning a former interest in literary and academic achievements and focusing on political ambition, the ultimate goal being that of achieving authority and influence in politics. In the light of the present reluctance by economists, especially in the Anglo-American area, to become directly involved in government or parliamentary office, such a 'vocational crisis' seems to be an indicator of a still weak degree of specialisation and professionalisation of economics. On the other hand, it also confirms the strong political nature of political economy. Study of this useful 'art (and science) of the statesman and legislator' was often considered as a preliminary step towards a *cursus honorum* in Parliament and government. The fact that in many areas of the world this is still so today shows how illuminating is the perspective adopted by the present research.

A final question that may be raised with regard to the identity of parliamentary economists concerns the scientific prestige enjoyed by the economists who sat in Parliament. The appropriate question is whether it was the most famous economists of the time who were attracted by a parliamentary and ministerial career or whether such a prospect lured only some 'minor' figures. The answer depends on the perspective adopted. If one starts from a canonical reconstruction of the history of economics focusing on Anglo-American standards, the only outstanding names that come to the mind are those of Ricardo and John Stuart Mill. If, instead, other national contexts are considered, the result is more encouraging. Taking France as the most widely known example, Frédéric Bastiat, Michel Chevalier, Louis Blanc,

Frédéric Le Play, Léon Say, Albert Aftalion, and, among the Socialists, Pierre-Joseph Proudhon, Pierre Leroux and the Christian liberal-socialist Félicité de Lamennais, represent some of the most important economic authors in the nineteenth and early twentieth century French context. And the same could be said of the German classical economists Friedrich von Hermann and Johann Heinrich von Thünen, and the historicist economists Bruno Hildebrand and Karl Knies, who took part in the 1848-1849 local or national Parliaments, or of Eduard Bernstein, Carl Friedrich Wilhelm Launhardt, Friedrich Naumann, Johann K. Rodbertus, Gustav von Schmoller, and Adolph Wagner, who sat either in the Reichstag or in the Prussian Parliament after 1867. Finally, prominent economists were Adolphe Le Hardy de Beaulieu in Belgium, Álvaro Flórez Estrada in Spain, or Francesco Ferrara, Antonio De Viti de Marco, Angelo Messedaglia, Maffeo Pantaleoni, Luigi Einaudi, Achille Loria and Antonio Graziadei in Italy. Comparing this situation with more recent times, a sharper split in the community of economists between economists-scientists and economists-politicians can be perceived today than in the period between 1848 and 1920.

Economic debates in Parliament and the expanding scope of political economy

The main focus of our research is the role played by economists of different descriptions in Parliament. However the presence of economists in Parliament is significant because it reveals that they favoured in some way the spread of economic science in the sphere of politics.[29] A study on economists in Parliament is therefore simultaneously a study on political economy in Parliament. This correspondence fully justifies the perspective adopted by some of the contributors to this volume,[30] who – independently of enquiry into the presence or absence of economists – have sought to evaluate the contribution of arguments deriving from political economy to parliamentary debates and to the ensuing legislation.

Adopting this point of view implies, as argued by Almodovar and Cardoso, looking at economic legislation not as a reflection of certain classes or sectors of society, or as the basis of economic policies, but as a result, albeit partial, of analytical and normative theorising stemming from the literature on political economy.

An extensive and varied array of cases are examined in this book, ranging from the above mentioned example of total absence represented by the United States to episodes of intense debate in which the 'voice' of political economy echoed distinctly in the halls of parliament. In many circumstances – especially in countries that stood in an unstable equilibrium between tradition and modernity – the arguments deriving from economic science contributed, not without opposition, to

29 See Colander and Coats (1989).

30 See especially the chapters on Portugal by António Almodovar and José Luís Cardoso, and on Japan by Jiro Kumagai, in this volume.

sweeping away archaic visions concerning commerce, money, credit and technological change, and encouraged a more favourable vision of the market and free enterprise. Especially in the central decades of the nineteenth century, they disseminated a faith in economic development that became the gospel of the 'age of improvement'.[31] At a later stage, when the enthusiasm raised by Cobdenism declined under the pressure of the 'social question' and socialist movements, arguments deriving from the new economic approaches suggested measures that became a permanent part of the economic and social policies of modern States, from the promotion of saving banks to compulsory life insurance for workers and public housing, not to mention the permanent debate on custom tariffs, tax allocation and public debt. Conversely, parliamentary debates contributed to modernising the language of political economy and favouring its spread in society; by the same token, one should not overlook the role played by Parliaments in promoting the academic institutionalisation of political economy.

It should be borne in mind, however, that nowhere did the language of political economy become the official or dominant idiom of the ruling class. What dominated in nineteenth-century Parliaments was a system of political representation based on negotiation between local demands and economic, social and institutional interests, couched in a rhetoric focusing on the ideals of national power, civilisation and economic progress. Only in a minority of cases or in exceptional times was this interest-based political activity superseded by a *super partes* conception of politics which attempted to direct partial interests towards more general goals.

Nor did political economy provide its acolytes with a single, neutral and uncontroversial strategy of policy making. Although those who defended its principles often affected an impartial attitude in the name of the 'true' interest of the nation and even of humanity as a whole, their views were partisan and lay at the core of ardent controversies both of a theoretical and political nature. There were not only contrasts between political and economic arguments in economic debates, but the use of economic arguments itself revealed how political economy as a science of legislators was the battleground of passionate controversies. When the socialist movement developed in Europe at the end of the nineteenth century, the fiction of impartiality and universality was challenged by a clearer understanding of conflicting class interests, although the Socialists themselves declared they were acting in the ultimate interest of mankind.

Nevertheless, divisions of a political and of a theoretical nature did not exclude the possibility that

- battles were fought with arguments drawn from the 'tool box' of economic science;
- there might be sound economic reasons for defending both sides of a controversy (as the debates on gold standard vs. bimetallism, or on free vs. central banking showed); and

31 See Briggs (1959).

- *bona fide* lay on both sides of disputes.

Parliamentary debates demonstrate *inter alia* that no economist possessed a magic wand in matters of economic policy, and that very often the divisions on this ground ran through member of one and same school thought, as the case of marginalist economists clearly reveals.

Nevertheless, theoretical differences mattered. The overviews provided by this book confirm what recent publishing initiatives[32] have contributed to highlighting: the methodological pluralism of the late nineteenth century – which may best be appreciated by taking into consideration some 'neglected' national traditions of economic thought – produced a wealth of ideas, approaches and interpretive tools which enhanced the understanding of the functioning of economic relationships and provided useful instruments of policy intervention. By adopting judicious critical tools the German Historical School, American institutionalism, the various currents of Socialism, French and Belgian Social Catholicism, together with other less renowned schools of thought such as the already mentioned Romagnosian School in Italy and Krausism in Spain,[33] discovered and analysed economic phenomena that had escaped the view of classical and neo-classical economists, and propounded new and viable instruments of regulation. The economists who adopted these approaches felt a strong mission to engage in politics in order to foster their proposals, while at the same time benefiting from the stimulus of political activity that prompted them to undertake more in-depth economic analysis. Seen from the point of view of parliamentary history, the economic pluralism of the late nineteenth century appears very rich and significant, and political economy a useful science.

Concluding remarks

The chapters that follow provide many answers to the questions discussed above. In no respect, however, is their contribution limited to the suggestions put forward here. Nor are their conclusions unanimous. This was probably unavoidable at the pioneering stage in which research on the topic of this book finds itself in many countries. Nevertheless, all contributors share the belief that pluralism of interpretations and approaches is an advantage in scientific debate, since it prompts further questions that stimulate new research and generate new and more profound knowledge.

As already mentioned, there are questions which in large measure remain outside the scope of the present book. Interdisciplinary research on the role played by

---

32 See Samuels (1998) and (2003); Psalidopoulos and Mata (2002).

33 Krausism was a neo-Kantian current of thought which was unsympathetic to the social effects of modernisation. See the chapter on Spain by Salvador Almenar in this volume and Almenar and Llombart (2001).

economists and political economy in parliamentary debates and legislation may in the future produce greater understanding not only of the policy orientations they contributed to constructing and of the relation between debates, policy making and different political and economic contexts,[34] but also of the incidence of political-economic discourse on parliamentary history. It would be interesting to know whether the scientific arguments employed by the economists in parliamentary debates remained a *vox clamans in deserto* or helped to create models of thought that permanently migrated into the political discourse. Equally interesting would be to understand the difference, if any, between 'scientific rhetoric' and 'parliamentary rhetoric' in economic discourse, and the connections between such concepts and different intellectual contexts or different interests at stake in political dialectics.

Other questions that further research on this topic may help to answer concern, for example, the repercussions of the political experiences of so many economists in different contexts on the evolution and social and professional identity of the economists. It can plausibly be speculated that in those countries in which the presence of economists in Parliament and in government was continuous, not only did this presence enhance the prestige of economists as an essential component of the political elite and favour the institutionalisation of economic studies, but it also created a system of expectations and a permanent channel of social upwards mobility which made economic expertise a harbinger of a political career. But even in countries where the majority of economists turned to consultancy as the typical interface with political institutions, the economics profession was permanently marked by this closeness between economics and politics.[35]

Moreover, as already suggested, this book may stimulate further research on the contribution that the political experience of economists, on the one hand, and economic debates in Parliament, on the other, may have made to economic research in some specific areas. It is known that parliamentary debates were the object of discussion and commentaries by economists in scientific journals. It would be interesting to explore whether in some cases the experience accumulated by economists in Parliament generated specific advances in the knowledge of economic mechanisms.

But a more obvious expectation is that other national cases remaining outside the scope of the present research will be studied and that the questions which are likely to arise from such studies will shed new light on the work already accomplished. Particularly promising seem to be the cases of the Netherlands, Denmark, Norway, Sweden, and the Habsburg Empire, all of which have important traditions of economic thought and whose most renowned economists, including Carl Menger, Eugen von Böhm-Bawerk, Freidrich von Wieser and Joseph A. Schumpeter,

---

34 The study by Martorell Linares (2000) on Spanish public finance is an outstanding example of the potential of such an interdisciplinary approach.

35 Another question which should be studied concerns the relationship between political journalistic activities by the economists and the role they played in influencing public opinion.

participated in political life. But equally interesting would be the cases of Russia after the outbreak of the Populist movement and of some Latin American countries.

What this research clearly indicates is that in the period examined, which was a decisive period of strengthening, spread and institutionalisation of political economy, economic debate flourished in the context not only of policy making but also of political passions of a generally noble and disinterested nature. It provided a language to examine some of the most dramatic questions of the time and taught many to cultivate political ambitions. The controversies that interested economists were sometimes of a theoretical nature, but very often of more practical origins and consequences. Part of this history is still ours.

References

Agulhon, M. (1979), *La République au village. Les populations du Var de la Révolution à la IIe République*, Seuil, Paris.

Almenar, S. and Llombart, V. (2001), 'Spanish Societies, Academies and Economic Debating Societies', in Augello and Guidi (2001), pp. 109-25.

Augello, M.M. (1989), 'The Societies of Political Economy in Italy and the Professionalisation of Economists (1860-1900)', *History of Economics Society Bulletin*, **11**(1), pp. 99-112.

Augello, M.M., Bianchini, M., Gioli, G. and Roggi, P. (1988) (eds), *Le cattedre di economia in Italia (1700-1900). La nascita di una disciplina 'sospetta'*, Franco Angeli, Milano.

Augello, M.M. and Guidi, M.E.L. (2000) (eds), *Associazionismo economico e diffusione dell'economia politica nell'Italia dell'Ottocento. Dalle società economico-agrarie alle associazioni di economisti*, 2 Vols, Franco Angeli, Milano.

Augello, M.M. and Guidi, M.E.L. (2001) (eds), *The Spread of Political Economy and the Professionalisation of Economists. Economic Societies in Europe, America and Japan in the Nineteenth Century*, Routledge, London.

Augello, M.M. and Guidi, M.E.L. (2002) (eds), *La scienza economica in Parlamento 1861-1922. Una storia dell'economia politica dell'Italia liberale - I*, Franco Angeli, Milano.

Augello, M.M. and Guidi, M.E.L. (2003) (eds), *Gli economisti in Parlamento 1861-1922. Una storia dell'economia politica dell'Italia liberale - II*, Franco Angeli, Milano.

Augello, M.M. and Guidi, M.E.L. (2005), 'The Italian Economists in Parliament from 1860 to 1922: a Quantitative Analysis', *The European Journal of the History of Economic Thought*, **12**(2).

Barber, W.J. (1985), *From New Era to New Deal. Herbert Hoover, the Economists, and American Economic Policy, 1921-1933*, Cambridge University Press, Cambridge and New York.

Barber, W.J. (1988) (ed.), *Breaking the Mould. The Development of Academic Economics in XIX Century America*, Wesleyan University Press, Middletown, CT.

Barber, W.J. (1996), *Designs within Disorder. Franklin D. Roosevelt, the Economists, and the Shaping of American Economic Policy, 1933-1945*, Cambridge University Press, Cambridge and New York.

Barucci, P. (2002), 'L'economista in Parlamento: alcune riflessioni', *Il Pensiero economico italiano*, **10**(1), pp. 7-15.

Bastiat, F. (1850), *Harmonies économiques*, Guillaumin, Paris.

Bentham, J. (1838-1843), *Works*, J. Bowring ed., Tait, Edinburgh.

Berg, M. (1980), *The Machinery Question and the Making of Political Economy*, Cambridge University Press, Cambridge.

Best, H. and Cotta, M. (2000) (eds), *Parliamentary Representatives in Europe. 1848-2000*, Oxford University Press, Oxford.

Bianchini, M. (1996) (ed.), *Political Economy in European Periodicals, 1750-1900*, special issue of *History of Economic Ideas*, **4**(3).

Briggs, A. (1959), *The Age of Improvement*, Longmans, Green, London.

Church, R. (1974), 'Economists as Experts. The Rise of an Academic Profession in the United States, 1870-1920', in L. Stone (ed.), *The University in Society*, **2**, Princeton University Press, Princeton.

Coats, A.W. Bob (1971) (ed.), *The Classic Economists and Economic Policy*, Methuen, London.

Coats, A.W. Bob (1981) (ed.), *Economists in Government*, special issue of *History of Political Economy*, **13**(3).

Coats, A.W. Bob (1991), 'Economics as a Profession', in Coats (1993).

Coats, A.W. Bob (1993), *The Sociology and Professionalization of Economics, British and American Economic Essays*, Routledge, London and New York.

Colander, D.C. and Coats, A.W. Bob (1989) (eds), *The Spread of Economic Ideas*, Cambridge University Press, Cambridge.

Cooper, R.A. (1981), 'Jeremy Bentham, Elizabeth Fry, and English Prison Reform', *Journal of the History of Ideas*, **42**, pp. 675-90.

Fetter, F.W. (1980), *The Economists in Parliament, 1780-1868*, Duke University Press, Durham, NC.

Gordon, B.L.J. (1976), *Political Economy in Parliament, 1819-1823*, Macmillan, London.

Gordon, B.L.J. (1979), *Economic Doctrine and Tory Liberalism, 1824-1830*, Macmillan, London.

Hilton, B. (1980), *Corn, Cash, Commerce: the Economic Policies of the Tory Government, 1815-1830*, Oxford University Press, Oxford.

Hilton, B. (1988), *The Age of Atonement: the Influence of Evangelicalism on Social and Economic Thought, 1795-1865*, Clarendon Press, Oxford.

Howe, A. (1997) *Free Trade and Liberal England, 1846-1946*, Clarendon Press, Oxford.

Ignatieff, M. (1978), *A Just Measure of Pain. The Penitentiary in the Industrial Revolution 1750-1850*, Macmillan, London.

Kadish, A. and Tribe, K. (1993) (eds), *The Market for Political Economy. The Advent of Economics in British University Culture, 1850-1905*, Routledge, London.

Levan-Lemesle, L. (1986) (ed.), *Les problèmes de l'institutionnalisation de l'économie politique en France au XIX siècle*, special issue of *Economies et sociétés*, série *Oeconomia*, **PE 6**.

Maloney, J. (1991), *The Professionalization of Economics. Alfred Marshall and the Dominance of Orthodoxy*, Transaction Publishers, New Brunswick and London.

Martorell Linares, M. (2000), *El santo temor al déficit. Política y Hacienda en la Restauración*, Alianza Editorial, Madrid.

Mateo del Peral, D. (1974a), 'Aproximación a un estudio sociológico de las autoridades económicas en España (1868-1915)', in G. Tortella Casares (ed.), *La banca española en la Restauración*, Banco de España, Madrid, **1**, pp. 15-106.

Mateo del Peral, D. (1974b), 'Autoridades económicas. Presidentes del Consejo de Ministros, Ministros de Hacienda, de Fomento y Gobernadores del Banco de España', in G. Tortella Casares (ed.), *La banca española en la Restauración*, Banco de España, Madrid, **2**, pp. 75-97.

Perrot, J.-C. (1988), 'Economie politique', in R. Reichart and E. Schmitt (eds), *Handbuch politisch-sozialer Grundbegriffe im Frankreich 1680-1820*, heft 8, R. Oldenbourg Verlag, München; French translation in J.-C. Perrot, *Une histoire intellectuelle de l'économie politique (XVIIe-XVIIIe siècle)*, Editions de l'EHESS, Paris 1992, pp. 63-95.

Psalidopoulos, M. and Mata, M.E. (2002) (eds), *Economic Thought and Policy in Less Developed Europe. The Nineteenth Century*, Routledge, London.

Roggi, P. (2001) (ed.), *Le grandi 'voci' nei dizionari specializzati (e non) di economia*, special issue of *Storia del pensiero economico*, **41-42**.

Samuels, W.J. (1998) (ed.), *European Economists of the Early 20th Century, **1**, Studies of Neglected Continental Thinkers of Belgium, France, The Netherlands and Scandinavia*, Edward Elgar, Cheltenham.

Samuels, W.J. (2003) (ed.), *European Economists of the Early 20th Century, **2**, Studies of Neglected Continental Thinkers of Germany and Italy*, Edward Elgar, Cheltenham.

Schumpeter, J.A. (1954), *History of Economic Analysis*, Oxford University Press, New York.

Stigler, G.J. (1965), 'Statistical Studies in the History of Economic Thought', in Id. *Essays in the History of Economics*, The University of Chicago Press, Chicago.

Subacchi, P. (1997) (ed.), *Les associations économiques et groupes de pression en Europe XIXe-XXe siècles*, special issue of *Histoire, économie et société*, **16**(2).

Sugiyama, C. and Mizuta, H. (1988) (eds), *Enlightenment and Beyond: Political Economy comes to Japan*, University of Tokyo Press, Tokyo.

Teixeira, P. (2004), 'The "Human Capital Revolution" in Economics', paper presented at the 2nd Siena Meeting in the History of Economics, Pontignano, 26-27 November 2004.

Tribe, K. (1995), *Strategies of Economic Order. German Economic Discourse, 1750-1950*, Routledge, London.

Waszek, N. (1988) (ed.), *Die Institutionalisierung der Nationalökonomie an deutschen Univertitäten*, Scripta Mercaturae Verlag, St. Katharinen.

Chapter 2

Political Economy in Portuguese Parliamentary Debates (1820-1910)

António Almodovar and José Luís Cardoso*

Introduction

Parliamentary debates provide considerable material for historical research. In the specific case of debates on economic and financial affairs, understood in very broad and general terms, these represent one of the most useful sources for studying decision-making processes in matters of economic policy and, naturally, for studying the bases and the doctrinal and theoretical justifications behind constitutional and legislative measures. In the Portuguese case and for the period considered here, 1820-1910, corresponding to the period of the constitutional monarchy, parliamentary debates on the issues under consideration are crucial for improving our understanding of the process involved in the affirmation, formation and dissemination of the scientific discourse of political economy.

Based on this series of premises, certainly shared by the other contributions in this book, this chapter seeks to provide a synthetic view of the significance of Portuguese parliamentary debates on economic and financial matters. We begin by providing a brief historical framework, both of the period under consideration and of the state of the art regarding the institutionalisation of economic and financial studies in Portugal. We then analyse one of the most frequent and significant themes in Portuguese debates, namely the opening up of the economy to the outside world and the protectionist and free-trade stances adopted in regard to this matter. Next, we discuss other equally relevant issues mentioned in parliamentary debates, such as monetary circulation and banking organisation, as well as consumption and taxation. At the end, we present some concluding remarks.

In the analysis put forward here, we have opted for a solution of illustrative exemplification, without any concern for undertaking an exhaustive treatment or a quantitative and systematic survey of parliamentary debates and the economic and financial matters they covered. The examples highlighted function as possible forms for illustrating the variety of matters that aroused the interest of Parliament.

* We are grateful to the comments and suggestions provided by Harald Hagemann, Roger Backhouse and the editors of this book. The usual disclaimer applies.

However, we believe that, from amongst the range of possible choices, we have chosen to focus on the most suitable themes for achieving our aim of highlighting the importance of this area of study.

Thus the aspects discussed here represent the first major crystallisation of our interest in these matters. At the same time, they also form the starting point for new and more detailed avenues of research. In this perspective, the invitation to take part in this collective work became a decisive factor prompting us to embark on a research project that will seek to catalogue and analyse in greater detail this important group of historical sources, for the same period under analysis here.[1] The results presented at this stage are therefore only a first revelation of the heuristic potentialities of this research theme.

The historical and political context

The period under consideration begins with the liberal revolution of 1820, which put an end to the political regime of enlightened despotism, and closes with the republican revolution of 1910, which represented the ushering in of a new political era in Portugal. The substantial changes that occurred in the aftermath of the establishment of the republican regime created a new political agenda and implied a considerable modification of the very nature and contents of parliamentary debates. The sudden end of the Portuguese monarchy, together with the participation in WW1 a few years later, represented an opportunity and a challenge to set the role of Parliament at the forefront of political debate devoted to an enormous variety of political, religious and educational subjects, as well as economic and financial matters. It therefore seems advisable to differentiate this republican period and to leave it out of the present survey. One should bear in mind, however, that it was this lively political period that served both as a pretext for pointing out the shortcomings of a parliamentary regime, whose animated debates did not result in real changes to the well being of the population, and as a justification of the coup d'état of 1926, which lay at the origin of the dictatorial, fascist-like regime that would not be quashed until the democratic revolution of 1974.

We will thus focus our attention on the period of the constitutional monarchy (1820-1910), a period of utmost importance for the construction of a modern liberal State in Portugal.[2]

From a political point of view, this was a period riddled with dissidence and conflict, reaching the extremes of two civil wars (in 1832-1834 and 1846-1847), besides an untold number of revolts, rebellions and minor coups d'état. For some,

1 This project is entitled 'Economic and Financial Parliamentary Debates (1820-1910)', coordinated by José Luís Cardoso and financed by the Fundação para a Ciência e a Tecnologia, through the POCTI programme, and the Banco de Portugal.

2 For a general overview of the historical context corresponding to this period See Almodovar and Cardoso (1998), ch. 3 and 4.

what was at stake was the staunch defence of the liberal values and political principles enshrined in the first Portuguese Constitution of 1822, undoubtedly the most important outcome of the parliamentary work begun in January 1821. For others, discontent with the furious pace of the reforms set in motion during this initial phase of liberalism, the main goal was to reconcile the new regime with the old tradition of the power and authority of the monarch, who sought to exercise his political legitimacy by granting the Constitutional Charter of 1826.

The struggles waged in defence of the Constitution or Constitutional Charter represented a parting of the political waters, with its inevitable impact on the country's administrative, economic and financial organisation. The dispute not only involved disagreement as to the nature of the constitutional and legal bases of the liberal regime. Also at stake were economic and social interests linked to the most resolute political parties and groups, as well as the outside support provided by European powers, for whom the course taken by decisions on matters relating to domestic and foreign policy was a cause of some concern. As far as the subject matter of this essay is concerned, what was at stake was also the range and depth of the debates on matters for which the executive power might or might not be subject to the vigilance and control of Parliament. Which, in turn, directs our attention to the actual dynamics of the work of specialist parliamentary committees, and to the assessment, at each moment considered, of the political relevance of the work of a second chamber of representatives (the Senate or Chamber of Peers).

An institutional and political lull occurred in 1851, as a result of yet another military coup that put an end to doubts about the legitimacy of the Constitutional Charter of 1826 (later ratified by the Additional Act of 1852) and marked the beginning of the so-called Regeneration period. Besides achieving political agreement on the Charter and thus guaranteeing the indispensable political peace, the Regeneration meant accepting the urgency of pursuing a programme of material improvements with the aim of modernising the country. The development of a policy of public works, especially in relation to the creation and improvement of equipment and transport infrastructures, required heavy investment by the State. This necessarily had implications and consequences on both the economic and financial levels, matters about which the civil society and Parliament were obliged to express their opinions. Budgets, taxes and fiscal policies, the public debt, internal and external loans, credit instruments provided by the banking and financial structure, customs regimes, industrial or agricultural development schemes, colonial administration problems, all these matters came into and out of Parliament, being discussed amongst the enlightened public opinion makers and highlighting the concerns of a country seeking to rediscover a path to progress and growth.

But this path also led to areas in which the vicissitudes of the economic cycle were discussed, as well as the causes and consequences of financial crises, the advantages and disadvantages of a greater openness to the outside world, the poverty and misery to which the less-favoured social groups were condemned, the revolts provoked by climates of dissatisfaction with taxes, a sense of dissatisfaction that spread and seemed to determine the failure of premeditated policies.

The parliamentary debates on these different subjects became more and more intense from the 1850s onwards, although these same matters had been under discussion since the first parliamentary sessions of 1821. There should consequently be no doubt about the importance of parliamentary structure in the institutionalisation of debate on themes relating to economic and financial policy. Furthermore, in addition to Parliament's duties of supervision and control, mention should also be made of its role of legitimising the processes of political choice and decision-making on matters that bore a direct relation with the functioning of the economic and financial system.

It is therefore essential to understand the actions of the members of parliament who showed themselves to have the highest level of doctrinal and theoretical background in economic matters. Just as it is important, generally speaking, to understand the extent of the Portuguese Parliament's susceptibility to the concepts and proposals for political, economic and fiscal action arising from political economy. The discourse of economists and the language of political economy are undeniable features of the minutes of parliamentary meetings and sessions. Examining their meaning and revealing the purposes behind their use are therefore aims that we will attempt to pursue here, without overlooking the role played by parliamentary debates themselves in modernising this language and making it increasingly acceptable to the general public.

Further proof of the strategic importance of political economy is provided by the actual debates that took place in Parliament whenever the subject of the creation of lessons and courses for the teaching of this science was discussed. We therefore propose to look at the way in which parliamentary activity can also be a useful element for understanding the process of the institutionalisation of political economy in Portugal throughout the period under consideration here.

The institutionalisation of political economy in nineteenth-century Portugal

With rare exceptions, the main representatives of economic thought in Portugal also undertook significant political activity, whether as mouthpieces for the interests and projects of national reorganisation or as agents of a State seeking to reform itself, or even as active members of parliament. It is easy to understand why. Faced with a relatively backward teaching structure, controlled by the pontifications of Coimbra University, the academic professionalisation of economists was either difficult or even impossible; and, naturally, there was as yet no room for the development of the profession amongst companies and in private economic activities.

It is therefore not altogether surprising that the cultivation of political economy was itself closely linked to the cultivation of an activity of pamphleteering and indoctrination. By the same token, many of the speeches were concerned with discussing the main guidelines of economic policy, namely the choice between protectionism or free trade, the liberalisation and construction of the internal market, the defence of industry or agriculture, etc.

The development of the process leading to the institutionalisation of political economy in Portugal was therefore inextricably linked to the main cycles of political activity. The typical discourse of political economy emerged amidst the crisis and the *ancien régime*'s last attempts at reform in the late eighteenth-century and the first few decades of the nineteenth-century, thereafter establishing itself as a fundamental form of knowledge in the early years of the newly-introduced liberalism after the 1820 revolution. It then became muted for quite some time during the period of political stability and for as long as the financial model of Regeneration introduced from 1851 onwards continued to inspire confidence. Thereafter, and once again coinciding with the beginning of a crisis, political and social economy re-engaged in its controversial arguments with socialism, enjoying a new lease of life as a result of the controversy between the supporters of the various doctrinal schools that marked the transition from the nineteenth to the twentieth century.

Despite its proximity to political economy – a fact that sometimes blurs the existence of a differentiation in approach, themes and even in the pace of institutionalisation – the discussion of monetary, financial and fiscal matters gained a more stable and more rapidly accepted public forum. In other words, besides the doctrinal divergences of political economy and the agitated waters of the passions peculiar to the schools, we find discussion venturing into the deeper waters of budgetary equilibrium, even addressing such questions as the amassing of the public revenue necessary to ensure the country's development and attempt to guarantee a political and social equilibrium that would be at least minimally satisfactory. Here, as well as the controversy about the most suitable tax collection system, there was general agreement about the decisive importance of this issue for the survival of the regimes and of the country itself, thereby revealing one of the most distinctive features of the balanced budget policies that were later adopted.

José Ferreira Borges symbolised the starting point for the systematisation of this line of thought, a reflection that was continued (as, in fact, were the various reflections of an economic nature) and developed amongst the legal classes. Indeed, reflection on taxation gained a more constant and influential presence in political and legal discourse than had so far been the case for political economy, allowing various nineteenth-century Portuguese politicians to establish their authority and gain respect. The decisive importance of these themes was foreshadowed in an announcement by Ferreira Borges himself, when he stated that it was to the 'members of both hemispheres that we mainly address ourselves: may they remember that the law largely entrusts them with the initiative of taxation and the calculation thereof, and that it would be shameful if they were to ignore that for which they have been specially elected'.[3]

The main issues from the political point of view, of the kind that decide the fate of governments and even of regimes, were as follows: the conception and collection of taxes, the use of such revenue in development and public works, the attempt to control the public debt, the almost permanent negotiation with investors and

3 Borges (1831), p. 55.

external creditors, the preparation of State budgets and the discussion of public accounts.[4] This provides a key for understanding why political instability was associated with financial speculation and why, years later, these adverse examples served to warn against the negative effects of excessive political ambitions in regard to the economic development of the country. It also offers insight into why, on the private level, the very notion of political economy was associated with the practices of usury and speculation, as it was depicted by Eça de Queiroz and other nineteenth-century writers:[5] since Portugal was a country lacking in resources, it was natural that capital and capitalists should end up being more easily associated with speculative investments and less with the undertaking of significant productive investments in agriculture or even industry.

Indeed, the economic history of the large nineteenth-century enterprises and entrepreneurs is laden with examples that clearly highlight the increased profitability of tax-contracting companies and a vast series of large-scale capitalists jointly dedicated to financial speculation.

The references found in parliamentary financial discourse are close to those of economic discourse, and there is specific recognition of the proximity and interconnections that must exist between these spheres.[6]

References to 'old financial economists' such as Vauban, Boisguilbert and Melon and to German cameralism strike the eye immediately. Naturally, references to contemporary authors, both Portuguese and foreign, are also prominent; the list of figures of authority was regularly reviewed, with periodic replacement of certain names.

One should note the hybrid nature of these references, where theoreticians rub shoulders with practical statesmen, thus revealing the eminently duplicitous nature of the 'science of finance'.

Just as was the case at the level of political economy,[7] the progressive consolidation of the teaching of finances in the Law course at Coimbra University spread awareness of the existence of new authors and schools – French, Italian, German and Spanish – thus giving rise to conceptions of greater or lesser amplitude as regards the sphere of action peculiar to the science of finance.[8] Now, foreign authorities gained this status basically through the publication of manuals – manuals that could be adopted by a legal universe that was clearly interested in the development of modern economic and financial regulation. By the same token, and as in the case of political economy, the credibility of the legal universe in which the Portuguese authors moved and established themselves was important, as was the proximity between the legal system of the respective countries and the Portuguese legal system. So it is natural that the traditional French reference should be

4 See Lobo (1871).
5 See Cardoso (2001).
6 Jardim (1904), part 1, pp. 26-7.
7 See Almodovar (1995).
8 Jardim (1904), part 1, p. 4 and following.

embodied by Paul Leroy-Beaulieu, and that, in the case of the vaster and better organised Italian school, reference should be made to the names of Ricca Salerno (University of Modena), Luigi Cossa (University of Pavia), Garelli della Morea and Augusto Graziani. Moreover, German scholarship also played a major role, embodying one of the most influential references for the Portuguese legal universe. Here one finds the figure of Rau (University of Heidelberg) whom Adrião Forjaz de Sampaio had already adopted as a model for his lectures in political economy,[9] as well as the contemporary representatives of the German historical school, Adolph Wagner (University of Berlin) and L. Stein (University of Vienna). Finally, Spain is represented by Piernas Hurtado (Madrid Central University), the liberal Krausist author who distinguished himself precisely through his contributions to law, political economy, and finance.[10]

The above-mentioned details demonstrate that the institutionalisation of the economic and financial sciences took place in parallel fashion in the context of both the university and the political activities of parliamentarians, many of whom began their careers on the benches of Coimbra University. However, the rates of progression were different. In Coimbra (and later in Lisbon), even though the teaching of these sciences may have been marked by the charisma and the analytical and doctrinal preferences of the professors, it can still be said that, generally speaking, those teaching in the university were genuinely concerned with painting a reasonably favourable and up-to-date picture of the great doctrinal guidelines that were being developed and perhaps pursued abroad. By contrast, there was no reason to expect great sophistication at the theoretical and doctrinal level in Parliament, which was the quintessential political organ and one that was consequently governed by different rules and functional responsibilities. The natural importance assumed by political questions was further enhanced by the role of rhetoric and debate between factions and groups with divergent interests, and the conditions were created whereby the discourse used might incorporate – but only incorporate – some authoritative arguments in which the names of foreign financiers and economists were mentioned.

The arguments put forward by the members of the government and the members of parliament whose credits were at least to some extent established in the field of economic and financial sciences inevitably became watered down by the rapid flow of ideas springing forth during parliamentary debates. This can be attributed, first and foremost, to the fact that political discourse is not, at least in essence, a discourse whose efficacy and credibility derives basically from the scientific nature of the reasons put forward. But it should also be taken into account that many of the questions under analysis, even when appearing to be naturally 'economic' or 'financial', did not cease to be eminently political and practical, and were consequently capable of being addressed from perspectives other than those of the economic and financial schools. In other words, depending

9 Sampaio (1839).
10 See Malo (1998).

on the circumstances the teachings from books were regarded as dispensable, in view of the wide range of concrete problems that needed to be resolved. Effectively, in the light of this practical, political and legislative concern one might go so far as to dub a real waste of time some of the more specious discussions about the correct significance to be attributed to the concepts being debated.

Finally, it should also not be forgotten that the ambiguities and disagreements between the different authors and schools of economics made it fairly difficult to adduce authoritative arguments that could not be almost immediately contradicted.

Protection and free trade in the first Constituent Assembly

The debates on economic and financial issues that took place in the Constituent Assembly (1821-1822) offer a first insightful example of the relevance of this source for studying the process involved in the formation and use of the discourse of political economy.[11]

The Portuguese liberal revolution of 1820 was made possible by the combination of a wide variety of factors of a contingent and structural nature. Among these, perhaps the most important was the dissatisfaction felt by different social sectors, not only in relation to the state of economic dependence in which Portugal and its dominions found themselves, but also in relation to the continuing blockades that prevented the nation's productive capacities from developing in accordance with their full potential.

The establishment of a new regime based on a constitutional monarchy and a new form of the exercise of sovereignty created appropriate institutional and political conditions for dismantling the bases on which the economic and social edifice of the *ancien régime* had been built, whilst at the same time leading to the belief that it was possible to create a new model of development.

Although its fundamental aim was to draw up a constitution, the 'Sovereign Congress' both discussed and legislated upon the most diverse areas of social life, seeking to give a legal framework to everything that needed regulation, as well as to respond to the series of requests emanating from an effervescent civil society that was eager for solutions to its individual and collective problems.

As well as the requirement to manage barely reconcilable economic, social and political interests – resulting in different attitudes and rhythms being displayed in relation to the regenerative process – the members of the Constituent Assembly were faced with two circumstances that considerably limited the scope of the reforms they sought to introduce. On the one hand, there was the Portuguese-British trade agreement of 1810, which greatly restricted any attempts to restructure productive activities, particularly in the manufacturing and industrial sector; on the other, the illusion was still cherished that it might be possible to revise the terms of the Brazilian colonial pact (interrupted by the opening of the ports in

11 For an extended discussion of the arguments presented here see Cardoso (1997), ch. 7.

1808), on which the main hopes for commercial and financial regeneration had been staked.

Such circumstances implied the definition of a markedly protectionist strategy, with instruments being sought and policies being sketched out that would breathe new life into what had been diagnosed as a depressed state of agriculture, atrophied industry and paralysed trade. Consequently, the ideals of liberalism and economic free trade were stifled and relegated to a more subordinate position, even though they were apparently more in keeping with the prerogatives and rhetoric of freedom that permeated the discourse being developed at the political level.

The ephemeral nature of this first Portuguese liberal experiment (extending between August 1820 and April 1823) may be explained through the difficulty of resolving tensions and contradictions that had proved to be of greater significance than the main protagonists and mentors of change had imagined. However, what remained were the lessons that could be drawn from a political experiment that would later be consolidated; and, in particular, the main legislative measures had taken root which (in spite of their somewhat hesitant and moderate nature) would lead to the dismantling of the structures of the *ancien régime*.

In the parliamentary work of the Constituent Assembly (which met between January 1821 and November 1822), one particular concern of a political nature stands out more than any others: the establishment of rules and precepts relating to the definition of the individual rights and duties of citizens and the institutionalisation of the new practices for the exercise of sovereignty. But although the drafting of the Constitution, which absorbed the main energies of the members of the 'Sovereign Congress', did prove to be a rather slow process, it should also be stressed that their attention was directed towards a wide range of different areas, which not only afforded the Assembly's work a broad legislative mission, but also conferred upon it unexpected executive powers and duties.

The need to regulate by law what had previously been regulated by convention or tradition, the demand for the creation of a legal framework that would establish the prerogatives of the new political regime emerging from the 1820 Revolution, the lack of confidence shown by the supreme parliamentary authority concerning the way in which the Regency was acting, and above all the pressure exerted by an excitable public opinion directing its complaints, petitions and demands to Parliament (channelled through the various parliamentary committees set up for this effect): these are just some of the factors that provide insight into the perfectly justified 'absent-mindedness' of the members of parliament in relation to their primary mission.

Thus, in the study of the legislation produced at the time, attention should be paid both to the variety of areas on which it had an impact (dealing with themes that were the responsibility of the different parliamentary committees: agriculture, fisheries, arts and manufactures, trade, public finance, overseas affairs, diplomacy, criminal justice, civil justice, constitution, education, public health, statistics, ecclesiastical matters, military affairs, etc.) and to the diversity of its forms (laws, decrees, resolutions, opinions, orders, ministerial decisions and official letters).

As far as economic legislation itself is specifically concerned, it should immediately be stressed that the same attributes of diversity should be applied in relation to both content and form. More important than this, however, is the difficulty of establishing the precise limits of what can or should fall within this category. For the sake of the argument to be discussed here, we will consider only the legislation that explicitly contemplated the problems of organising and restructuring the supply and demand for goods and services. We will therefore seek to analyse the series of measures decreed by the Constituent Assembly of 1821-1822, in which an obvious intention of imposing direct regulation and control over agricultural, industrial and commercial activities can be discerned. Our main objective is to clarify some of the doctrinal and theoretical grounds for the measures and policies that were put forward (regardless of whether or not they were approved), seeking to explain how the discourse of classical political economy was assimilated and instrumentalised by the members of the Constituent Assembly.

In this sense, economic legislation resulting from Parliamentary debates will cease to be seen as an expression or reflection of the contradictions between the interests of the sectors or social classes involved, or as the structuring element of the economic policy to be pursued. It will instead be seen as testifying to the different normative and analytical stances adopted in relation to the laws and principles that are presumed to regulate economic life.

As noted earlier, the economic legislation produced during the period of 1821-1822 points to economic policy measures of a markedly protectionist nature. Customs barriers, through the prohibition of imports or the establishment of high import duties, and industrial protection were the instruments brought into play with the aim of recovering sectors of activity threatened by foreign competition. But the success of such instruments necessarily depended on the national market's capacity to provide both a stimulus and a response. The members of parliament showed their concern in this regard by approving various opinions, channelled through the Trade Committee, seeking to eliminate tax obstacles to internal circulation and giving a greater margin of freedom to trading agents. Particularly significant in this area were the Decrees of 18 September and 13 November 1821, which abolished the duties on the transhipment of wines, eaux-de-vie and olive-oil between national ports, and the Decree of 5 July 1821, which abolished the charges and penalties levied by the municipal inspectors. The preamble to this decree stated that: 'Only free competition between buyers and sellers can produce abundance, and regulate the price of goods'.[12]

From these brief notes, we are however led to conclude that the legislation produced by Parliament does not in itself provide sufficient information to delineate the characteristic lines of force of the economic policy followed during the period in question. Many of the measures that were decreed resulted from special guidelines laid down as a result of individual requests, so that it is not possible, from the arid wording of the decrees, to ascertain whether or not these were connected to

12 *Colecção dos Decretos*, 1822-1823, p. 190.

any previously established principles or criteria. Thus the account briefly sketched out here concerning the policy of economic regeneration adopted by the members of the Constituent Assembly is based on our interpretive approach, which attributes significance to a process of casuistic decision-making, so that when the individual measures are analysed separately they do not reflect the existence of a concerted strategy.

Yet beyond the strictly legislative scope of action, additional information can be gleaned that confers some kind of unity on the clauses of the many decrees, opinions and orders issued by the 'Sovereign Congress', which also represented a forum where different theoretical and doctrinal concepts referring to the interpretation and management of economic mechanisms were compared and contrasted. Seen from this perspective, it is important to discuss to what extent the prevailing guidelines regarding economic policy did (or did not) represent choices grounded in the field of economic ideas, taking the discourse of classical political economy as the frame of reference.

In several debates reproduced in the Parliamentary Proceedings, it is very clearly shown that references were made to the doctrinal and theoretical sources of political economy. The minutes of the parliamentary session of 9 March 1821, which discussed the ban on the importation of foreign eaux-de-vie, provide an excellent summary of the essence of the controversy centring on whether the abstract principles of political economy should be adopted:

> Senhor Brito was of the opinion that the importation of foreign goods, far from impoverishing a nation, enriches it because the exports from one country are the same as its imports. He was opposed by other members, saying that the maxims of Say, Chaptal, Smith, Ricardo, and other economists were excellent in theory; yet they were inapplicable in practice in the current state of affairs, and in the general system adopted by all nations.[13]

In fact, the Member of Parliament João Rodrigues de Brito was almost always alone in his defence of a policy of free trade, despite the fact that he felt protected by the authority that he invoked in his own support:

> The science of political economy has been much debated: let these authors be consulted and they will say that trade slows down agriculture. The importation of foreign goods leads to the importation of our own goods: the amount of the imported foreign goods will have to be paid for with our industry, they cannot take anything other than an equal value in goods. It will be said that they can take money; but this cannot be anything other than the equivalent of goods: they cannot take this money except through our products.[14]

---

13 *Diário das Cortes*, 1821, p. 231.
14 Ibid., p. 312.

In the previous extract, Brito clearly inserts his proposals of economic openness to the outside world within the analytical framework of Say's law, defending the idea that the increase in the supply of imported goods would spontaneously generate a corresponding increase in the supply of goods produced internally, which would be given in exchange. And he confidently assumes that:

> These are not vain theories of Jean-Baptiste Say, as they are called by those who do not read them. They are clear and indisputable principles, which long before him were demonstrated with clear proof by Adam Smith..., which Say developed and proved with tried and tested facts... And it was not only him, but all the scholars who, after him, wrote about that science that is as important as it is unknown. Authors such as David Ricardo...; Sismondi ... and about them all, with his inimitable clarity, the great Storch.[15]

We may therefore defend the idea that the member of parliament Brito attempted to justify, at the level of economic theory, the free-trade options that he so vigorously defended. His opposition to manufacturing protectionism, as well as his firm belief in the advantages of complete freedom in the allocation of resources and productive factors, are also aspects for which Brito tried to find justification in the principles of political economy. The speeches he delivered in Parliament clearly reveal this blend of doctrine, politics and theory, demonstrating an overall coherence of thought.

João Rodrigues de Brito did not win over many supporters to his cause. Some speeches seem at times to have supported his ideas, but even so there was a clear minority of members adopting positions in defence of economic liberalism when applied to foreign trade.

The members of the Constituent Assembly refused to adhere to the theoretical discourse of political economy, in so far as the adoption of such a discourse implied the acceptance of supposedly universal laws and principles which, given the particular circumstances that affected the country, would necessarily involve a worsening of the situation of economic backwardness. As the member of parliament Francisco de Lemos Bettencourt explained so clearly: 'When we have imports equal to exports, or better, even more exports, then we will realise these principles of political economy'.[16] The sympathies aroused by political economy were heavily restricted, being filtered through the sieve of criteria that invoked the national interest.

As a conclusion, it can be said that the victory of the protectionist economic policy (embodied in the legislation approved by the Parliament between 1821 and 1822) did not constitute a defeat for liberal political economy, even though it was achieved at the expense of the latter's subordination and the demonstration of its inapplicability. Within the historical context of the first experience of political liberalism, the frequent use of the arguments provided by both Smith and the

15 Ibid., p. 2514.
16 Ibid., p. 313.

Physiocrats, with regard to internal *laissez-faire*, was by no means original, since it represented the continuation of a discursive practice that had been in use since the last quarter of the eighteenth century as an instrument for protesting against the structures of the *ancien régime*. For this reason, the most prominent aspect of the parliamentary debates of the time is the refusal to assimilate the free trade dimension of economic liberalism that classical political economy consolidated in the first few decades of the nineteenth century, especially through the analytical contributions of Say and Ricardo.

The members of parliament who were most intransigent in their protection of the market against the threat of external competition devoted little energy to putting theoretical arguments alternative to the models of Say's law of markets or Ricardo's theory of international trade. All they needed to do was invoke the specificity of the national economic situation and criticise the abstract content of principles that benefited the interests of the most favoured nations.

This debate illustrates a particular situation corresponding to the historical context of the first parliamentary experience, which was a period of special importance for the constitution and strengthening of political economy as a scientific discipline. Hence the emphasis given here to the arguments addressed in these debates, which effectively act as an archetype of situations of debate having a natural follow-up. Naturally, similar arguments can be found in other periods of the Portuguese Constitutional Monarchy. The fight between protectionists and free-traders was a permanent feature of the debates taking place during the second half of the nineteenth century. By the same token, the arguments handled by both parties did not significantly differ from those discussed above.

Apparently everything was working in favour of an increasing use of political economy as a rationale for economic development and modernisation: there had been a substantial political change; the opportunity had been created for taking decisions as to the best use of resources and capacities; the improvement and growth in the supply and demand of goods and services had been outlined as an aim; the ideas of progress and change had been turned into the essence of the movement for 'regeneration' of the country. Nevertheless, there were many who contended that the changes prompted by political economy could be tested only provided that national interests were not at stake. There was little likelihood of political economy being a success unless its principles were made compatible with the superior aim of achieving a reasonable performance for the national economy and a satisfactory solution to the interests of national economic agents.

Monetary circulation and banking organisation

A second example of parliamentary debates that served to structure economic reasoning relates to a discussion that displayed constant cut and thrust in the Portuguese Parliament, namely that centring on the organisation of the banking system and the issue of banknotes.

The problem was first raised in 1877 with a proposal for the regulation of the issue of banknotes presented by the minister António Serpa, immediately seconded by Oliveira Martins, one of the most influential and important Portuguese economists, as well as a remarkable historian and important opinion maker in his own right in the last quarter of the nineteenth century.

The subject was a fascinating one and allowed Oliveira Martins to demonstrate how situations of crisis and financial disequilibrium, largely caused by speculation and money-lending activities, could be overcome. Countering the arguments of the opponents of António Serpa's proposal – conveyed, above all, through the Porto-based periodical press – Oliveira Martins defended the legality, opportunity and usefulness of a measure which, in his view, would allow for the effective 'constitution of a bank, in which all credit services will be centralised, without them being joined by the spirit and practice of usury that has thrived under its shadow. Reconstituting the Bank of Portugal and putting an end to banking anarchy (this is how we must describe the current system) means once again directing Portuguese economic life towards the examples provided by the great European states'.[17]

The immediate casualty was the right to issue banknotes enjoyed at that time by the Porto banks. However, in view of the scarce use made of that entitlement – in 1876 those 5 banks had been responsible for only 6 per cent of the total issue of banknotes, the rest being issued by the Bank of Portugal – what was really at stake was the need to conceive new forms for the whole exercise of banking activity in Portugal.

For Oliveira Martins, it was essential to pursue a policy of moralising and regularising the trade in paper money, thereby avoiding the 'giddiness of stock market games, of speculations with funds' and, above all, ensuring the 'organisation of credit as a social function'.[18] The main question under discussion was therefore the justification of the State's central role in organising the credit system, as well as, generally speaking, in the supply of goods of a public nature. It was Martins' opinion that in order for credit to be able to act as an instrument for the development of the real sphere of the economy, it would be necessary to set up an independent national bank, one that was not at the mercy of private speculative interests. Only in this way could such a bank be classified as the provider of a public credit service.

And so it was that, aided by his incisive and suggestive writing style, Oliveira Martins launched an attack on the system of *laissez-faire* and free competition, stating unequivocally that 'not all individual activity is useful, and therefore not all freedom is convenient'.[19] Showing signs of excessive optimism, resulting from his finely-honed rhetoric of propaganda, he centred his opinion around the general consideration that 'the fatal Manchester school already has its days numbered', that

17 Martins (1877), pp. 35-6.
18 Ibid., pp. 58 and 62.
19 Ibid., p. 62.

'the beneficial omnipotence of competition is no longer a dogma' and that 'everywhere there is a reaction against free trade'.[20]

Oliveira Martins never called into question the need to issue banknotes or the usefulness of the circulation of fiduciary currency in general. The role played by the circulation of such currency in causing financial crises was due exclusively to its maladministration. Hence, on a number of occasions, he defended the need for a rational and effective system for the circulation of paper money, based on four main ideas.

Firstly, the principle that it was indispensable to have banknotes in circulation in contemporary economies, in view of the need to diversify the instruments which, especially in the short run, make it possible to fulfil the functions of money and to produce its effects as a stimulus to the economy. Secondly, the idea that crises are 'diseases of the social economic organism' whose main symptom is 'immoderation in relation to the amount of money in circulation',[21] which would justify extra care on the part of the State in ensuring the suitable functioning of the sphere of circulation.

A third idea to be found in Oliveira Martins' writings upon these matters relates to the framework the author provides for the crises in circulation, stating in concrete terms that:

> If the problem of the organisation of circulation is immediately connected to that of the organisation of credit, both of them together are connected to the problem of the organisation of the national finances; and it will always be fanciful to wish to solve the first one whilst the second one continues along the road to damnation that it has been following.[22]

For Oliveira Martins, the reorganisation of the financial system mainly involved eliminating the costs incurred with the (internal and external) public debt, thereby overcoming the budget deficit. Only in this way would the conditions be created for the country to enjoy an effective economic development, allowing an increase in production and better distribution of wealth. The fourth and last idea, which was of a more general kind and was based on a philosophical principle that governed his economic and financial reflections, concerns his comparison between protectionist and free-trade systems, from which he deduced the model of development best suited to the characteristics of the Portuguese economy and society. For Oliveira Martins, it was imperative that such a model should be based on a powerful stimulus and control exercised by the State.

These ideas re-emerged in the debate that was to return to Parliament ten years later, once again in relation to António Serpa's proposal for centralising the issuing of money. And once again it was Oliveira Martins who climbed up onto the rostrum to defend the idea that the Bank of Portugal should have a monopoly over the

---

20 Ibid., pp. 58-9.
21 Martins (1878), p. 48.
22 Ibid., p. 210.

issuing of money, countering and refuting the opinion of those who, through the mouthpiece of Júlio de Vilhena, amongst others, believed in the virtues of a model based on free competition between banks with the right to issue banknotes.

The debate dragged on for several days in June 1887. Under discussion were some questions of a technical nature that were relevant for a Bill on matters requiring specialised knowledge. Most important in this regard was the problem of the limits on the issue of paper money, its relationship with the coins in circulation and with the production of gold and silver, the question of the metallic reserve fund and the guarantees of convertibility, the rules to be established as well as the precautions to be taken in order to fix the interest rates for banking operations and the taxes to be charged by the State in return for granting the right to issue money. As it was a subject for which knowledge of similar experiences was felt to be advantageous, the debate was not short of examples of banking organisation and legislation in other countries, nor did it fail to evoke the words of foreign economists who might vouch for the opinions expressed in the Portuguese Parliament.

But the debate also served to reaffirm the doctrinal principles which, in the case of Oliveira Martins, ten years after his first defence of the centralising model for the issue of banknotes, still maintained intact the premises for criticising 'those traditions of free trade and capitalism that have had such tragic consequences for the economy of the Portuguese nation over the last thirty years'.[23] Set against the 'system of unbridled capitalism in force in the United States' there stood a model of 'unity and cohesion of the social body, and never the deplorable establishment of rivalries, oppositions and class struggles that spell the certain ruin of societies'.[24] It can therefore be seen that the parliamentary debate on the issuing bank provided Oliveira Martins with the pretext to denounce a model of social organisation (liberal and individualistic capitalism) which, in his view, did not make it possible to obtain collective benefits or to realise the common assets of citizens.

The exemplary nature of this debate is further revealed by the final intervention of the member of parliament João Pinto dos Santos, less well known for his qualities as an economist, but undoubtedly deserving of praise for his skilful defence of a political compromise solution for the problem under discussion. After summarising the gist of the polarised positions adopted by the members of parliament Júlio de Vilhena (the model for the competitive issue of banknotes) and Oliveira Martins (the model for the monopoly issue of banknotes), and after weighing up the pros and cons of the opposite positions and legitimising the validity of both approaches in the light of the contradictory arguments put forward by different masters of political economy, João Pinto dos Santos opted for a clever compromise solution: lamenting the lack of information and proposing that any decision upon the matter should be postponed until it could be better clarified through the holding of an inquiry or a report on the situation of the circulation of banknotes.

23 *Diário da Câmara*, session of 8 June 1887.

24 Ibid.

Moreover, through the solution that was found, this case highlighted one of the most important lessons provided by the debates on economic and financial problems in the Portuguese Parliament. In concrete terms, it can be seen that no matter how powerful the doctrinal and theoretical justifications for adopting a particular orientation in economic policy, political imperatives would sometimes arise that delayed the realisation of reforms considered to be suitably ready for implementation. In the case examined here, not even ten years sufficed for the question of the issuing bank to be regulated through Parliament.

Consumption and taxation

This last section looks at some of the recurrent uses made of political economy during the course of almost one hundred years of Portuguese parliamentary life. In the references made by Portuguese parliamentarians to such apparently diverse questions as the concept of consumption, savings banks, money and banking, public finance, roads, railways and other public works, monopolies and the exclusive rights over new inventions, the colonies and the colonial system, and even the most diverse schemes for protecting the various sectors of national economic activity, these politicians were invoking arguments drawn from their readings of classical authors, Adam Smith, David Ricardo and Jean-Baptiste Say, for instance, as well as fairly fashionable reviews and journals such as *The Economist*, the *Journal des Economistes* and the *Revue des Deux Mondes*.

As a complement to the examples given earlier, there is room here for the exploration of another group of parliamentary debates, in which economic science and the science of finance were repeatedly used – sometimes even wielded like weapons – to substantiate the positions adopted by either the government or the opposition. Overall, the discussions analysed in this section were centred upon many different aspects of the same basic problem, namely the problem of finding the best fiscal and financial means for accomplishing the previously stated economic policy options, and thus improving the standard of living of the Portuguese people.

As far as the main programmatic guidelines were concerned, there was always solid, widespread agreement. In particular, there was no disagreement about the need to develop the State's overall activities as a generic instrument for stimulating a national economy that was almost unanimously classified as decadent and backward, and all the parliamentarians subscribed to the need to stimulate the sources of wealth and encourage its fair and equitable division. However, Parliament was also responsible for managing the tensions between the interests of the various types of producers and between these and the interests of consumers, seeking to ensure a reasonably stable social, economic and political balance. This management of what amounted to diversified and sometimes incompatible interests was found expressed not only in the discussions of the successive State budgets, but also in the everyday management of the petitions originating from the most varied groups and sectors, who, as a general rule, called upon the services of parliamentarians to obtain better conditions for exercising their activity – which most often was expressed in either a reduction of, or exemption from, taxation, or in a request for subsidies and extraordinary aid.

Despite the diversified range of interests, the reading of the *Diários da Câmara dos Senhores Deputados da Nação Portuguesa* (1822 to 1910) does allow identification of some recurrent patterns, both at the level of the problems touched upon and also of the actual arguments used in parliamentary debates on economic and financial questions.

We can immediately note the recurrence of a systematic awareness of a contrast between the general principles of political economy, normally quoted from the works of the most authoritative authors, and a whole series of arguments relating to the effective possibility and appropriateness of their immediate application to the country. To some extent, as Fontes Pereira de Melo said in 1849,[25] this disparity had arisen because Portugal still lagged behind on the scale of civilisation, preventing most people from genuinely realising their true interests and acting appropriately, but it could also be attributed to the fact that the country was underindustrialised, with a scanty population and a depressed agriculture,[26] together with an inflexible and economically inefficient colonial system,[27] with trade clearly declining and without the necessary road and rail infrastructures. Thus, despite the constant assertion of the importance to be given to economic science and the science of finance as basic sources of knowledge for the profitable exercise of government and parliamentary activity,[28] the fact remained that sometimes there prevailed the political fear of provoking a revolt of significant strata of the population (farmers, traders, industrialists). Furthermore, and perhaps even more systematically, there were financial and fiscal difficulties clearly advising against adopting any measure that might result in a loss of duties and revenue for the State.[29]

Parliamentary liberalism therefore took on a fundamentally political guise, seeking to distance itself from the more authoritarian model of the *ancien régime*, and striving to demonstrate that, despite its high fiscal costs, freedom was the best way to achieve the greatest good for the greatest number of people and to promote justice and genuine economic and social equity. But in the continued absence of any significant increase in national wealth, the full and consequential application of principles such as free competition or the opening up of the economy to international trade was repeatedly postponed until such a time as the country had reached a stage of greater development and would thus potentially be better equipped to support the effects of the liberal principles enshrined in economic science. In the same way, the basic principles of the science of finance relating to the need to

25 *Diário da Câmara*, session of 1 February 1849.
26 Ibid., session of 20 December 1870.
27 Ibid., session of 30 February 1849.
28 Ibid., session of 16 March 1827, discussion of Bill No. 129.
29 Ibid., session of 6 April 1837.

alleviate the excessive and complex burden of taxation inherited from the *ancien régime*, to achieve a healthily balanced budget, and, at all costs, to avoid the heavy burden of an uncontrolled public debt, were in effect given no practical expression: the difficulties of the Portuguese economy were too severe, and there was keen awareness that immediate application of radically new measures might jeopardise the survival not only of governments but also of the very parliamentary system itself. Whenever cuts were proposed in customs duties on imports or exports, whenever suggestions were made to reduce taxes on the circulation of products or on consumption, whenever it was proposed that taxes should be reduced on agriculture or industry in order to stimulate domestic economic activity and to endow national products with greater international competitiveness, there immediately arose the spectre of the lack of revenue necessary for government activity. And, in turn, whenever it was proposed that public works should be undertaken to facilitate the circulation of products and the consequent development of agriculture and industry, there inevitably arose the barrier of the impossibility of establishing new sources of revenue.

In view of this apparently vicious circle, from which the country was seemingly unable to emerge throughout the nineteenth century, the technical and conceptual superiority of the specialists in economic and financial matters did not succeed in asserting itself in a clear and consequential manner. Therefore, in spite of the fact that parliamentary activity enjoyed the committed and active participation of members of both Parliament and government with firmly established reputations in the field of economic and financial sciences – amongst whom mention should be made of João Rodrigues de Brito, Ferreira Borges, Agostinho Albano da Silveira Pinto, Carlos Morato Roma, Oliveira Marreca, Oliveira Martins, Rodrigues de Freitas and Anselmo de Andrade[30] – their skills were blunted by the tangled webs of political debate and rhetoric. Thus although one may note some fairly carefully planned speeches and even some conceptual depth in the arguments – as was the case with the explanation of Ricardian rent,[31] the analysis of the concept of consumption,[32] or even the enumeration of the various points of view on credit[33] – these examples were by no means characteristic of the vast majority of speeches in which economic and financial sciences were mentioned.

Rather, the numerous appeals made to good economic and financial principles, as well as the recurrent use of references to the works of Jean-Baptiste Say and other French economists such as Joseph Garnier and Leroy-Beaulieu, must be seen more as a routine that was gradually becoming institutionalised in the midst of parliamentary speeches, a routine that eventually allowed a speaker to ironically note that certain expressions were 'very much in fashion, because for everything

30 For a general presentation of the writings of these economists who were members of the Parliament See Cardoso (2001).

31 *Diário da Câmara*, session of 15 February 1827.

32 Ibid., session of 18 April 1837.

33 Ibid., session of 18 August 1869.

that one wishes to be approved, it is said that it is in accordance with science (laughter)'.[34]

Conclusions

In Portugal, the analysis of parliamentary debates during the phase of the constitutional monarchy (1820-1910) shows itself to be a fundamental instrument for insight into the process of the rise, formation and dissemination of the discourse of political economy.

Throughout this chapter, we have observed the decisive role played both by the members of parliament and the members of government in promoting the formal beginning of the process leading to the institutionalisation of economic and financial knowledge in Portugal. One can go so far as to say that it was Portuguese parliamentary activity that emphasised the importance of economic science and enabled the science of finance to gain public acceptance, not only because the members of parliament were responsible for introducing the first lessons in these subjects at the University of Coimbra, but also because many of them took it upon themselves to repeatedly invoke some of the basic concepts and principles of economic science, regularly pointing out that it would be senseless to oversee the nation's destinies without taking into consideration the suggestions made by economic science.

We have also seen that, as was to be expected, not all members of parliament enjoyed the same level of economic knowledge and not all economic and financial questions were approached with the same depth and intensity in the course of parliamentary debates. Hence the selection that we have made, choosing to highlight recurrent issues and those issues in which the debates were notably more lively. One of these themes was precisely the question of opening up the economy to the outside world, where the defence of more openly protectionist positions against the principles of free trade gave rise to many interesting exchanges of arguments. Similarly, the questions relating to the circulation of money and the need to promote a modern banking organisation were also the root cause of lengthy and fairly heated debates, of which some salient examples have been provided here. Finally, the problems inherent in the need to promote the external competitiveness of the Portuguese economy, without calling into question either the well-being of the people or the actual financing capacity of the liberal State, were the subject of analysis in the last section, which illustrated the extreme difficulty faced by the Portuguese members of parliament in reconciling the desire to reduce taxes and the price of labour with the imperative need for fiscal and customs revenue designed to subsidise and protect the development of economic activity.

The subjects analysed in this chapter illustrate the variety of economic and financial problems that aroused the attention of the Portuguese Parliament through-

34 *Diário da Câmara dos Pares*, session of 14 April 1880.

out the period 1820-1910. Together with the contributions on other national experiences, they undoubtedly show the immense heuristic potential of historical and comparative research in this field.

References

Almodovar, A. (1995), *A Institucionalização da Economia Política Clássica em Portugal*, Afrontamento, Porto.

Almodovar, A. and Cardoso, J.L. (1998), *A History of Portuguese Economic Thought*, Routledge, London and New York.

Borges, J.F. (1831), *Princípios de Sintelologia*, Bingham, London.

Cardoso, J.L. (1997), *Pensar a Economia em Portugal: Digressões Históricas*, Difel, Lisboa.

Cardoso, J.L. (2001), 'Progresso material e civilização: a economia política e a "Geração de 70"', *Penélope*, **25**, pp. 65-86.

Cardoso, J.L. (2001) (ed.), *Dicionário Histórico de Economistas Portugueses*, Temas & Debates, Lisboa.

Colecção dos Decretos, Resoluções e Ordens das Cortes Gerais, Extrordinárias e Constituintes da Nação Portuguesa, desde a sua instalação em 26 de Janeiro de 1821 (1822-1823), Imprensa da Universidade, Coimbra, Parts I, II and III.

Diário da Câmara dos Senhores Deputados da Nação Portuguesa (1822-1910), Imprensa Nacional, Lisboa.

Diário da Câmara dos Senhores Pares do Reino de Portugal (1842-1910), Imprensa Nacional, Lisboa.

Diário das Cortes Gerais e Extraordinárias da Nação Portuguesa (1821-1822), Imprensa Nacional, Lisboa.

Jardim, A. dos Santos Pereira (1904), *Sciencia e Legislação Financeira*, Imprensa da Universidade, Coimbra.

Lobo, F. (1871), *As Confissões dos Ministros de Portugal 1832-1871*, Tipografia Lisbonense, Lisboa.

Malo, J.L. (1998), *Pensamiento economico y filosofia social en la España del siglo XIX. Liberalismo, Krausismo y reformas sociales*, Mimeo, Zaragoza.

Martins, J.P.O. (1877), *A Reorganização do Banco de Portugal*, Guimarães & C^{a}, Lisboa.

Martins, J.P.O. (1878), *A Circulação Fiduciária*, Parceria A. M. Pereira, Lisboa.

Sampaio, A.F. (1839), *Elementos de Economia Política*, Imprensa da Universidade, Coimbra.

Chapter 3

Economists in the Belgian Parliament (1831-1918)

Guido Erreygers and Bert Mosselmans*

Introduction

The leading politicians who ran the country and forged Belgium's new constitution during and after the struggle for independence in 1830 numbered one economist among their ranks: Charles De Brouckère. He was also the only economist who obtained a seat in Parliament following the first general elections in 1831. After his resignation in 1832, economists would not return to the Belgian Parliament until 1848, but since then economists have been present in the Belgian Parliament without interruption.

Our main aim in this chapter is the identification of the members of the Belgian Parliament who can be described as economists. We focus primarily on the period between Belgium's independence and the end of WW1. Towards the end of the chapter, we also briefly consider the period 1919-1939, in which the situation changed considerably. In addition, we provide a few very preliminary indications of the impact of economists upon the economic policy of Belgium, emphasising, however, that by no means should this paper be seen as a fully-fledged analysis and assessment of the contribution of Belgian economists to law-making and economic policy.

We begin with a short overview of important characteristics of the Belgian political system in the period under consideration, together with a brief sketch of the development of economic thought in Belgium. The core of the paper consists of the identification of economists among the members of the Belgian Parliament, and attention is drawn to a few areas where the impact of economists may have been crucial. We then offer a somewhat broader perspective by briefly discussing the role of economists in the Belgian Parliament in the period between the two World

* We are grateful to both Lutgarde Aerts of the Archive of the Belgian Chamber of Representatives and Véronique Laureys of the Archive of the Belgian Senate for their kind assistance in tracking the biographical information on the Belgian economists in Parliament. We also thank Massimo Augello and Marco Guidi for their valuable comments on a previous draft of the paper. All errors are due to the authors.

Wars. In our conclusion we point to the need for detailed research that can take into account the more general context of public debate.

The political system in Belgium

In order to clarify the context in which the economists of the Belgian Parliament were working, it seems useful to highlight a few significant facts in the history of the Belgian political system.[1] On 4 October 1830 the 'Temporary Government' of Belgium declared the country independent. Very soon thereafter, on 3 November 1830, elections for a National Congress were organised. Already in January 1831 the National Congress approved a constitution which declared Belgium to be a constitutional, parliamentary monarchy.

The constitution created a Parliament with two 'houses', designated respectively as the Senate and the Chamber of Representatives. Although the members of both houses were appointed by direct elections, the Senate was the more elitist of the two: only those above the age of 40 and paying at least 1000 florins per year in direct taxes were eligible for the Senate, whereas the only eligibility condition for the Chamber of Representatives was that of being at least 25 years old. For both houses, the constitution placed restrictions on the right to vote, which was limited to male, Belgian citizens who paid at least 20 florins per year in direct taxes. This system of census suffrage severely limited the number of voters.

The first general elections for both houses were held in August 1831. The Senate was dominated by the Catholic, land-owning aristocracy; in the Chamber of Representatives, on the other hand, there was no clear majority of either Catholics or Liberals. In the years following Belgium's declaration of independence, political party structures hardly existed. The Government was appointed by the King, who ensured that it was composed of protagonists of both tendencies. This situation of 'unionist' rule lasted until 1847.

During the 1840s, tensions between Catholics and Liberals increased considerably. In 1846 the Liberals organised a first national congress, which paved the way for the creation of a Liberal Party. The notable success of the liberal candidates in the 1847 elections left King Leopold I with no other choice than to accept the formation of a homogenous liberal government headed by Charles Rogier. The 1848 elections brought a new victory for the Liberal Party, which obtained a clear majority of seats in both houses of Parliament. Between 1852 and 1857 there was a brief return to unionist rule, with governments led by Henri De Brouckère and Pierre De Decker. But in 1857 the Liberal Party again gained the upper hand, and held power throughout the 1860s with governments led by Charles Rogier and Waltère Frère-Orban. This long period of liberal domination was interrupted in 1870, when the Catholic Party emerged victorious from the elections. Between

1 This paragraph is based upon Witte, Craeybeckx and Meynen (1997), Laureys *et al.* (1999), and Gerard, Witte, Gubin and Nandrin (2003).

1870 and 1878 Catholic governments ruled the country, but the Liberals returned to power between 1878 and 1884.

The June 1884 elections marked the beginning of a period of 30 years of homogeneous Catholic governments. Prime Ministers with long terms in office were Auguste Beernaert and Paul De Smet De Naeyer. During this period substantial changes occurred in the electoral system of the country. Previous governments had already amended the tax requirements for voter eligibility, with liberal governments seeking to enlarge the pool of liberal-minded voters and Catholic governments attempting to achieve the opposite. But during the 1880s and 1890s the labour movement increased the pressure for political reforms and demanded the extension of the right to vote to the whole population (or at least to every man). 1885 saw the creation of the Belgian Working Men's Party. A series of strikes and demonstrations in the 1880s and 1890s led to the replacement of census suffrage by the system of the general plural voting right for men in 1893. The effects were immediately visible in the 1894 election results: the Catholics retained a huge majority, but the Socialists entered into Parliament, even obtaining more seats than the Liberals in the Chamber of Representatives. In 1899 the majority system – in which one seat per district was allocated to the candidate with the most votes – was replaced by a proportional system. This allowed the Liberals to regain part of what they had lost, but the Catholic majority remained intact. Finally, in 1919 the general singular voting system for men ('one man, one vote') was adopted. Women, however, did not gain the right to vote until after WW2.

During WW1 the Catholic Cabinet headed by Charles De Broqueville was enlarged with Liberals and Socialists. After the end of the war this *union sacrée* was continued until 1921, with governments of 'national union' headed by the Catholic politicians Léon Delacroix and Henry Carton De Wiart. Between 1921 and 1939 fifteen different governments succeeded one another. All of these cabinets – with the exception of the very short-lived government headed by Alois Van De Vyvere (May 1925), which was homogeneously Catholic – were coalition governments. But the Catholics were always part of the coalition and usually provided the Prime Minister, in particular Paul Van Zeeland, who formed two governments of 'national union' in the period 1935-1937. Also worth noting is the considerable input of the Socialists in these two governments, symbolised by the presence of Hendrik De Man, author of the famous Labour Plan launched in 1933.

Economics in Belgium

Economic thought in Belgium was strongly influenced by French economic thought and to a lesser extent by British, German and Dutch economics. No separate Belgian tradition emerged, but Belgian economists were usually part of larger international networks, and often stimulated international cooperation.[2]

2 There is no standard reference work on the history of economic thought in Belgium.

Separate academic programmes in economics slowly emerged from the end of the nineteenth century onwards. Prior to that time, the four main universities (the State Universities of Liège and Ghent, the Free University of Brussels, and the Catholic University of Louvain) tended to have only one economist, who taught a course in political economy in the Faculty of Law (sometimes in the Faculty of Arts and Humanities). The most important university for economics in the nineteenth century was the University of Liège, thanks to the presence of the Dutch scholar Jan Ackersdijck in the 1820s, and of Emile De Laveleye between 1864 and 1892. The former introduced French and British classical political economy to the students in Liège, many of whom would become influential statesmen. The latter was an internationally recognised scholar in the historical tradition of economics, and without doubt the most important Belgian economist of the nineteenth century. The University of Brussels hosted several liberal economists, including Charles De Brouckère, who advocated economic liberalism in academics as well as politics. The University of Louvain rejected the new science of economics from a Catholic point of view, arguing that it restricted the image of man to a selfish being, leaving no room for 'higher' motives. Economics in Ghent remained strongly within the framework of law and statesmanship. Overall, academic economics between 1830 and 1890 was not well developed at Belgian universities and depended strongly on the qualifications of a few individuals. In spite of that, Belgian economists played a major role in the establishment of an international free trade movement, with the organisation of the Congrès des Economistes (Free Trade Congress), the very first international economics conference that was organised in Brussels in 1847. In the late 1850s they were instrumental in creating an international free-trade association, the Association Internationale pour la Réforme Douanière, which had its seat in Brussels.

A major impetus for the development of economics came from business schools that emerged in the middle of the nineteenth century, upon the request of industry and trade, where the need for qualified business economists was making itself felt. Gustave de Molinari, editor of the French *Journal des économistes*, was a professor of economics in one of the two business schools that emerged in Antwerp in 1852. Partly in response to the growing success of these business schools, the universities began to offer separate ('master') programmes in economics from the 1890s onwards. However, these programmes at universities tended to be more theoretical and devoted to the education of statesmen and diplomats, in contrast to the programmes at business schools which tended to be more practical and devoted to the training of 'managers'. Moreover, universities sought to distinguish themselves from business schools by emphasising academic aspects. Ernest Solvay and his followers at the University of Brussels can be seen as pioneers in this respect.

The result of these tendencies was that a 'professionalisation' emerged in early twentieth century economics in Belgium. In Liège, the historical tradition of De

Mahaim (1895) and Michotte (1904) are outdated, but remain useful for the history of the nineteenth century.

Laveleye was continued by Ernest Mahaim, who also played a major role in the establishment of international labour legislation. The University of Brussels had several liberal (such as Maurice Ansiaux) and socialist economists (such as Hector Denis). In Louvain Victor Brants attempted to reconcile the historical tradition in economics with Catholicism.

After WW1, division of labour and specialisation occurred and greater attention was devoted to specific subjects such as banking and finance, colonial economics, economic crises, agricultural economics, etc. Important names include Van Der Smissen and Dechesne (in Liège), Bigwood, Chlepner and De Leener (in Brussels), and Goffart, De Lannoy and Dubois (in Ghent). In the 1930s truly separate ('undergraduate') programmes in economics emerged. In Louvain the first germs of quantitative economics were visible, with Baudhuin and Dupriez. Most other economists in Louvain (such as Eyskens, Van Zeeland, Janssen) were actively involved in politics, which may have hampered their scientific output.

As early as 1895 Mahaim complained that truly scientific economics had not emerged in Belgium, a major reason being the attitude of the population who tended to reject everything that had no immediate direct practical purpose. Economic thought in Belgium between 1830 and 1940 was never *l'art pour l'art*, but instead maintained close links to specific business purposes, as well as to law, statesmanship and political interests. It is therefore hardly surprising that numerous economists were also active on the Belgian political scene.

'Economists' in the Belgian Parliament, 1830-1918

It is no self-evident task to identify the 'economists' among the members of the Belgian Parliament. Especially in the nineteenth century, very few thinkers in Belgium would have qualified themselves as economists. The criteria used here to label members of parliaments as 'economists' are either education (e.g. those who graduated in economics), or profession (e.g. professors of economics), or publication output (e.g. authors of books or articles on economics). Such criteria inevitably result in fuzzy categories, and we do not deny that our designation of some members of parliament as economists might be challenged, although it seems impossible to completely rule out all borderline cases. In the first instance, we have limited ourselves to those who were active in the Belgian Parliament up to 1918.

On the basis of biographical information from different sources, but mainly relying on information documented by the Belgian Parliament itself, we have drawn up a list of 20 economists (see Appendix, Table 3.5).[3] For each economist, this table gives the name, year of birth and death, the assembly to which this figure

3 We have used the information taken from the biographical records conserved in the Archive of the Belgian Chamber of Representatives and in the Archive of the Belgian Senate. Where necessary, we have complemented this information with data from Van Molle (1969) and De Paepe, Raindorf-Gérard, Gillard and Brion (1996).

belonged, the period during which he was a member of parliament, and his political affiliation.

Perhaps the most striking feature of this list is that it is dominated by members of the Liberal Party. With thirteen economists among their ranks, the Liberals clearly outnumbered both the Socialists, with four economists, and the Catholics, who counted only a meagre three economists. In the case of the Socialists it must be added that they were not present in the Belgian Parliament before 1894. It seems that throughout the nineteenth and the beginning of the twentieth century, the Catholic Party exerted only a very limited power of attraction upon economists. As we will see later, this changed drastically in the interwar period. It is also interesting to note that the majority of economists were active in the Chamber of Representatives, and not in the more elitist Senate.

A quarter of the economists who were members of parliament also became ministers, although they did not always occupy economic or financial posts. In Table 3.1 we give an overview of the ministerial positions held by these five economists. It must be concluded that in this period economists apparently had a rather limited presence in the country's governments; this does not imply, however, that economists played only a marginal role in the political system.

Table 3.1 Elected economists serving as ministers (1830-1918)

Name	Function	Period
De Brouckère, Charles	Finance [Provisional Government]	1831
	Internal Affairs	1831
	War	1831-1832
Franck, Louis	Colonies	1918-1924
Pirmez, Eudore	Internal Affairs	1868-1870
Thonissen, Joseph	Internal Affairs and Public Education	1884-1887
Vandervelde, Emile	Minister	1916
	Intendance	1917-1918
	Justice	1918-1921
	Foreign Affairs	1925-1927
	Minister	1935-1936
	Public Health	1936-1937

Liberal economists

At least in the nineteenth century, the Liberal Party was by far the preferred environment for economists working in Parliament. Perhaps not surprisingly, this domination ended in the twentieth century, when increasing numbers of economists were joining the Socialist and Catholic Parties. In the order in which they first entered Parliament, the following were the liberal economists.

The first of them was Charles De Brouckère, who played a major role in the struggle for the independence of Belgium in 1830 and in the establishment of the relatively liberal Belgian constitution. He was one of the founding fathers of the

Free University of Brussels, where he taught a course in political economy from 1835 to 1838, but he was also a banker and a businessman. He was a proponent of free trade and presided over the Congrès des Economistes in 1847, and the Congrès International des Réformes Douanières in 1856. His publications include *Principes généraux d'économie politique* (1831). His brother Henri, also a liberal, was Prime Minister from 1852 to 1855.[4]

De Brouckère's successor in the chair of political economy at the Free University of Brussels was Auguste Orts, who lectured there from 1838 until his death in 1880. As a lawyer who graduated from the University of Liège, he may have been influenced by the teachings of Jan Ackersdyck. He published mainly in the fields of law and history. As far as economics is concerned, he was a moderate liberal. His course notes on political economy have survived but remain unpublished.[5]

After a short career as an entrepreneur and founder of a cotton factory in the neighbourhood of Brussels, Eugène Prévinaire became a banker. He resigned from Parliament to become Vice Governor (1864-1870), and then Governor (1870-1877) of the National Bank of Belgium. With Auguste Couvreur, who replaced him when he resigned from his seat in Parliament, and together with others, he co-founded the Association Internationale pour le Progrès des Sciences Sociales.[6]

Another liberal parliamentary economist was Eudore Pirmez, a lawyer and banker. He was a liberal politician and a strong proponent of free trade. He did not hold academic positions, but became a minister and was director of the Banque de Belgique and the National Bank. In Parliament he delivered a number of speeches on monetary policy, labour legislation and free trade. In 1884 he gave a remarkable talk before the Société Belge d'Economie Politique, which was published later under the title *La Crise* (1894).[7]

Prévinaire's brother in law, Frédéric Fortamps, was a prominent merchant and banker. Like Charles De Brouckère before him, he was for some time president of the Banque de Belgique, one of Belgium's main banks in the mid-nineteenth century. In 1878 he was sentenced to one year's imprisonment for his role in the fraudulent bankruptcy of this bank, which also signalled the end of his parliamentary career. He served on the boards of the Association Belge pour la Liberté Commerciale and the Association Internationale pour les Réformes Douanières.[8]

An outstanding figure was (Jean-) Adolphe Le Hardy de Beaulieu. He received a degree in law at the Free University of Brussels and studied engineering at the Ecole Centrale in Paris. He promoted the cause of free trade and was one of the

---

4 Juste (1867); Ramaer (1933); De Paepe, Raindorf-Gérard, Gillard and Brion (1996), pp. 115-16.

5 Mesdach De Ter (1901); De Paepe, Raindorf-Gérard, Gillard and Brion (1996), pp. 447-8; Van Dijck (2004), pp. 107-8.

6 N.B.B. (1960), p. 245; De Paepe, Raindorf-Gérard, Gillard and Brion (1996), pp. 472-3.

7 Discailles (1903); N.B.B. (1960), p. 239; De Paepe, Raindorf-Gérard, Gillard and Brion (1996), p. 464.

8 Laureyssens (1975), pp. 525, 633; De Paepe, Raindorf-Gérard, Gillard and Brion (1996), pp. 310-11; Erreygers (2001), pp. 92, 99.

founders of the Association Belge pour la Liberté Commerciale. At the end of his career in Parliament, this prominent liberal served as vice president of the Chamber of Representatives. He was responsible for several engineering projects in Belgium and abroad (especially Spain). As a progressive liberal and a notorious freemason, he advocated a strict separation of State and Church, a diminution of the military budget, the extension of public education for the poorer classes of society, and the further economic development of the country. He was president of the Société Belge d'Economie Politique until his death in 1894.[9]

After studies in philosophy at the University of Ghent and in Paris, Auguste Couvreur worked for some time as a journalist, and among other things he was a correspondent of *The Times* newspaper in Brussels. But his true vocation in life was that of organiser: he founded, co-founded and managed several societies and conferences, often with a strong international component. As such, he was strongly involved in the Association pour la Réforme Douanière, the Association Internationale pour le Progrès des Sciences Sociales, and the Société d'Etudes Sociales et Politiques. Over a period of about 40 years he was a member of the Société Belge d'Economie Politique, and even served as its vice-president.[10]

Hubert Brasseur was one of the first professors of political economy in Belgium. From 1850 to 1852 he taught natural law and political economy at the University of Liège, and from 1852 to 1865 at the University of Ghent. In 1855 he was at the centre of a fiery controversy due to accusations by students that he had denied the divinity of Christ. He resigned from university in order to be able to work in the financial sector. His career as a politician lasted less than two years, and he spoke only rarely in Parliament. His main publication is *Manuel de l'économie politique* (2 Vols, 1860-1863).[11]

Georges Montefiore-Levi, born in Great Britain, graduated as a civil engineer from the University of Liège. He was an important businessman, with interests in many areas of Europe, but mainly in Belgium and Italy. In 1882 he was awarded Belgian nationality, and immediately thereafter he was elected to the Belgian Senate. Towards the end of his life he became involved in international monetary issues. He was president of the International Monetary Conference held in Brussels in 1892, and represented Belgium at the Conference of the Latin Monetary Union in Paris in 1893.[12]

Then came the lawyer Oscar Deprez, of whom we know that he was a professor of industrial economics at the Ecole Industrielle of Châtelet.[13]

More famous was the next liberal economist to be elected to Parliament: the

9 De Paepe, Raindorf-Gérard, Gillard and Brion (1996), p. 388; Tordoir (1999).

10 De Paepe, Raindorf-Gérard, Gillard and Brion (1996), pp. 79-80; Erreygers (2001), pp. 98-9, 101-3.

11 De Ridder (1913); De Paepe, Raindorf-Gérard, Gillard and Brion (1996), p. 40.

12 Coosemans (1958); N.B.B. (1960), pp. 221-2; Stockmans (1973-1974); De Paepe, Raindorf-Gérard, Gillard and Brion (1996), pp. 429-30. On the International Monetary Conference of 1892, see de Molinari (1892) and Foster (1893).

13 De Paepe, Raindorf-Gérard, Gillard and Brion (1996), p. 205.

entrepreneur Ernest Solvay, founder of the chemical concern Solvay & Cie and one of Belgium's wealthiest citizens. Although he lacked a formal scientific education, he devoted a substantial part of his time, especially in the second half of his life, to scientific investigations. Moreover, he used his personal fortune to finance individual scientists and to found scientific institutions. His interests included both natural and social sciences. With the help of Hector Denis, Guillaume De Greef and Emile Vandervelde he proposed to replace the existing monetary system by that of 'social comptabilism', which led to a debate with Léon Walras. Later in life he developed the idea of 'social energetics'. During his two terms in Parliament, Solvay attempted to convince his fellow members of the necessity of the reforms he proposed, but with little success. During WW1 he organised and financed the Comité Nationale de Secours et d'Alimentation. His main writings are collected in the *Notes, lettres et discours d'Ernest Solvay* (2 Vols, 1929).[14]

The last two liberal economists were elected to Parliament after 1900. Louis Franck studied law at the Free University of Brussels, and later became a professor at this university. He played a prominent role in the Flemish movement. After WW1 he was placed in charge of Belgian colonial policy; he subsequently resigned from Parliament in 1926 when he was appointed Governor of the National Bank, a position which he held until two months before his death in 1937. Soon after his move to the National Bank he published *La Stabilisation monétaire en Belgique* (1927).[15]

Finally Albert Devèze, another lawyer from the Free University of Brussels, became one of the protagonists of the Liberal Party. His parliamentary career lasted 46 years, during which he held several ministerial positions and was president of the Liberal Party (1927-1933). He published on different social and economic issues, and advocated a liberal view on economic policy, for instance in his book *Aujourd'hui. Etude pour l'après-guerre économique* (1919).[16]

Socialist economists

When the first wave of socialists entered the Belgian Parliament after the 1894 elections, the new entrants included a strong delegation of economists. Among the 28 socialist delegates in the Chamber of Representatives there were no fewer than four economists. What is also particularly remarkable is that all four retained their seats for prolonged periods of time (respectively 19, 32, 42 and 46 years).

The first socialist economist was Emile Vandervelde, who was the *patron* of the Belgian Socialist Party in the early decades of the twentieth century, and played an important role in the international socialist movement. He obtained a PhD in law, a PhD in social sciences, and a special PhD in political economy, all at the Free University of Brussels. In the 1890s he was a professor at the Université

---

14 Despy-Meyer and Devriese (1997); Erreygers (1998).
15 N.B.B. (1960), pp. 137-8; Kauch (1966); Van Molle (1969), pp. 148-9; Mertens (1985).
16 Van Molle (1969), p. 121.

Nouvelle in Brussels and also worked with Ernest Solvay, before obtaining an appointment at the Free University of Brussels, where he lectured on the history of social doctrines. In his scientific work he combined insights from sociology, economics, biology and Marxism; he published prolifically. His most important contribution to socialist economic theory lay in an analysis of the role of the State in a socialist society, as illustrated by his *Le Socialisme contre l'Etat* (1918). He belonged to the left wing of the Socialist Party and played a prominent part in the campaign for 'one man, one vote', although later in life he gradually abandoned the hard line of socialist struggle and instead espoused a more 'reformist' approach, hoping to achieve reforms through parliamentary action. In contrast to many other socialists, Vandervelde supported Belgium's annexation of Congo, arguing that exploitation would continue in any case, but annexation would allow parliamentary control. During and after WW1 he held the office of minister, and many reforms were undertaken under his guidance: reform of the penitentiary system, the struggle against alcoholism, the recognition of labour union rights, and the protection of children and women. He remained a socialist, internationalist and pacifist throughout his life.[17]

Next there was Hector Denis, who held academic degrees in both the natural sciences and in law and should be seen as a founding father of labour statistics in Belgium. He was a professor of economics and rector (1892-1894) at the Free University of Brussels, where he was known for his well-documented lectures and his extensive use of diagrams. He published widely on socialism, economics and labour relations, his major work being entitled *Histoire des systemes économiques et socialistes* (2 Vols, 1904-1907). During the 1890s he joined Ernest Solvay and Emile Vandervelde in research on monetary reform. The amelioration of the condition of labourers was his main concern in Parliament.[18]

A third interesting personage was Louis Bertrand, a marble worker who had turned to journalism and eventually became director of the main socialist newspaper *Le Peuple*. He was one of the founders of the Belgian Socialist Party (Parti des Ouvriers Belges) in 1885. A prolific writer on a wide variety of social and economic issues, he will be remembered most for his monumental *Histoire de la démocratie et du socialisme en Belgique depuis 1830* (2 Vols, 1906-1907).[19]

Finally, Jules Destrée studied law at the Free University of Brussels, but is mainly known for his writings on art and socialism. He also founded and was the first president of the Walloon Assembly, which affirmed the Walloon identity in Belgium. With Max Hallet he published a compendium of labour legislation, *Code du travail* (1904), and with Vandervelde a book on the socialist movement in Belgium, *Le Socialisme en Belgique* (1898).[20]

17 Van Molle (1969), pp. 344-7; Abs (1973); Polasky (1995).
18 Vandervelde (1938); Julin and Chlepner (1957); Van Molle (1969), p. 102; Sirjacobs (1997), p. 26.
19 Van Molle (1969), p. 15.
20 Van Molle (1969), p. 117-19; Dumont (1999).

Catholic economists

Despite the fact that throughout the nineteenth century the Catholic Party often dominated political life in Belgium, there were very few economists among its ranks in Parliament.

One of them was the industrialist Auguste Royer De Behr, whose interests were mainly in the railway sector. He was a defender of free trade and *laissez-faire* policies. Although he was influenced by the French liberal tradition of Say and Bastiat, he did not belong to the group of liberal economists centring around De Brouckère, de Molinari and Le Hardy de Beaulieu. In 1854 he published a *Traité élémentaire d'économie politique*, which appeared in several editions.[21]

A second Catholic economist was (Jean-) Joseph Thonissen, who studied law in Liège and Paris. From 1848 to 1884 he taught criminal law at the University of Louvain. His publications range over a wide variety of subjects, but he is best known for his works on the history of law and the history of socialism. Some of his writings on economics can be found in *Mélanges d'histoire, de droit et d'économie politique* (1873). He was a member of the Société d'Economie Politique of Paris.[22]

Lastly, the list of Catholic economists includes Count Arnold T'Kint De Roodenbeke, who studied law in Louvain and became a lawyer in Ghent. During his 37 years in Parliament he served on many committees dealing with economic matters. From 1922 to 1928 he was president of the Senate; in addition, he was also president of the Société Belge d'Economie Sociale and the Société Belge d'Economie Politique.[23]

Economic issues in the Belgian Parliament, 1830-1918

It would be beyond the scope of this short contribution to give a complete overview of the economic issues dealt with in the Belgian Parliament. A general outline of the Belgian economic policy debates can be found in the standard sources on Belgian economic, social and political history.[24] We will restrict attention here to some of the major debates addressing issues felt to be of vital importance within parliamentary debate during the period in question.

21 Brouwers (1908-1910); De Paepe, Raindorf-Gérard, Gillard and Brion (1996), p. 495; Van Dijck (2004), p. 66.

22 Terlinden (1930-1932a); De Paepe, Raindorf-Gérard, Gillard and Brion (1996), pp. 536-7.

23 Terlinden (1930-1932b); Van Molle (1969), pp. 318-19; De Paepe, Raindorf-Gérard, Gillard and Brion (1996), pp. 539-40.

24 See, for instance, Witte, Craeybeckx and Meynen (1997), or the older works of Baudhuin (1928, 1946) and Chlepner (1972).

The development of train infrastructure

In the 1830s and 1840s Belgium's ruling class was dominated by the landed nobility, which crafted economic policies tailored to its interests. But at the same time opportunities were created for new entrepreneurial initiatives, and the country proved to be a fertile ground for new industrial and financial projects. A host of metallurgic and coal firms were founded, often with the substantial aid of the two leading financial institutions, the Société Générale and the Banque de Belgique. The first Belgian governments supported this process by awarding high priority to the modernisation of the country's infrastructure, such as roads and canals. As early as 1833, Prime Minister Rogier submitted to Parliament an ambitious project to construct a network of railways, in order to facilitate transport and reduce costs. The project led to an intense debate in Parliament, focusing in particular on the choice between Rogier's proposal for a fully State-operated railway system and that of a mixed public-private system, in which the State would be the owner of the infrastructure but the exploitation would be placed in the hands of private concessionaries. In April 1834 Rogier's project was approved.[25]

Protectionism and free trade

Another early preoccupation of the Belgian governments was the external trade policy. In the 1830s and 1840s the textile cottage industry increasingly suffered from competition from England's more modern and mechanised firms, and from France's restrictive trade barriers. In order to preserve at least the domestic market for the local producers, a protectionist policy was adopted. The law on differential tariffs adopted in July 1844 serves as an illustration of the protectionist tendency. But the policy could not avert a gradual deterioration of the economic situation in the Flemish region, culminating in the agrarian crisis of 1845-1847. The textile cottage industry collapsed, while crop failures threatened large parts of the rural population with starvation. But significant policy changes were not introduced until the late 1850s and early 1860s, when protectionist policies were gradually abandoned or reformed. In the end, however, the Belgian Parliament played only a small role in this change of policy, since the government decided to move towards free trade by diplomatic means. The treaty Belgium signed with France in 1861 was very similar to the Cobden-Chevalier Treaty signed between Britain and France in 1860.[26]

The National Bank

In the early years of Belgian independence the creation of money was largely in the hands of two private banks, the Société Générale and the Banque de Belgique. But

25 Michotte (1904), pp. 7-10.
26 Ibid., pp. 29-52.

more than once their activities were threatened by their massive engagements in the upcoming Belgian industry, and the Belgian government was obliged to come to their rescue. By the end of the 1840s a consensus had arisen around the creation of a mixed public/private National Bank, which would be in charge of monetary creation but would not be involved in any industrial activity. The National Bank was founded in 1850. Throughout the second half of the nineteenth century, the debate on the functions and scope of the National Bank would continue, since it was necessary for its 'privileges' to be renewed at regular intervals by Parliament.[27]

The social question

The protection of workers, the freedom of association, the development of social security: these are all issues that became increasingly prominent in the second half of the nineteenth and the first half of the twentieth century. In Parliament the interests of the labouring population were voiced by the members of the Socialist Party, and by the representatives of the Christian labour movement in the Catholic Party. Over time, their activity gradually changed the structure of society and shaped the contours of the modern Welfare State.

The colonial policy

Belgium was not one of the traditional colonial powers. But towards the end of the nineteenth century a serious problem arose in connection with the position of Congo. With the help of Henry Stanley, King Leopold II had acquired large parts of Central Africa in the 1870s. In 1885 the international community recognised these claims, and King Leopold II became sovereign of the Congo Free State, at which point Congo was the personal property of the King, not an appendage of the State of Belgium. Not long thereafter, however, the possibility was mooted that the King would transfer Congo to the Belgian State. This led to prolonged and intense debates on Belgium's colonial policy, with remarkable shifts in position and internal divisions in the political parties, not least in the wake of rumours and reports on the atrocities committed in Leopold's Free State. In 1908 the Belgian Parliament approved a law annexing Congo to Belgium.

The interwar period

It seems useful to briefly compare the situation of the period 1830-1918 to that of the period between the end of the First and the beginning of the Second World War. A different picture emerges, reflecting not only substantial changes in the economic structure and political forces in Belgium, but also in the influence of economics upon public policy.

27 Ibid., pp. 55-64.

Undoubtedly the most important economic issue of the inter-war period was the economic depression of the 1930s. The depression was characterised by a sharp decline in industrial activity and high unemployment. The elaboration of a coherent economic policy was, however, seriously hampered by the unstable political situation: coalition governments succeeded one another, while extreme right-wing parties entered Parliament. The Socialist Party advocated more active intervention by the State, and finally rallied around De Man's Labour Plan. Although the economic policy did undergo a change under Prime Minister Van Zeeland, it was but a faint shadow of the Labour Plan. Nevertheless, this was a period in which economic issues ranked high on the politicians' agenda.

During the period 1919-1939 a total of 17 economists were elected in the Belgian Parliament. The list of these economists is given in the Appendix, Table 3.6 (since six of them were already active in the period 1830-1918, there is some overlapping with Table 3.5). In comparison to the previous period, it can be noted that the domination of liberal economists (only four) no longer endured, with the Liberals outnumbered both by Catholic (six) and socialist economists (seven).

In addition to the 17 elected economists, five unelected or 'extra-parliamentary' economists also form part of this group (see Table 3.2). These were economists appointed as ministers without being elected to Parliament. Even though the phenomenon of extra-parliamentary ministers already existed in the nineteenth century, it is striking that in the inter-war period crucial economic positions like the Ministry of Finance were quite often held by non-professional politicians. These 'technocrats', as they might be called, were chosen because of their competence in financial and economic issues when the country was in need of new and sometimes painful economic policies. This was especially the case in the troubled economic waters of the 1930s.

Table 3.2 Extra-parliamentary ministers (1919-1939)

Name	Life	Function	Period
Gérard, Max-Léo	1879-1955	Finance	1935-1936
		Finance	1938
Gutt, Camille	1884-1971	Finance	1934-1935
		Finance	1939-1940
		Finance, National Defence, Economic Affairs and Communications	1940-1942
		Finance and Economic Affairs	1942-1943
		Finance	1943-1945
Heymans, Paul	1895-1960	Economic Affairs, Middle Classes and Agriculture	1938-1939
Janssen, Albert	1883-1966	Finance	1925-1926
		Finance	1938-1939
		Finance	1952-1954
Mahaim, Ernest	1865-1938	Industry, Labour and Food Supply	1921

Some of the elected economists also served as ministers (see Table 3.3). The list includes two Prime Ministers (Van Zeeland and Eyskens), and one Vice Prime Minister (De Man). This suggests that despite their small number, Belgian economists left their mark on the government of the country, especially in the twentieth century.

Table 3.3 Elected economists serving as ministers (1919-1939)

Name	Function	Period
Barnich, Georges	Middle Classes and Economic Affairs	1939
De Man, Hendrik	Public Works and Labour Creation	1935-1936
	Finance	1936-1938
	Vice Prime Minister	1939-1940
Destrée, Jules	Sciences and Arts	1919-1921
Devèze, Albert	National Defence	1920-1923
	National Defence	1932-1936
	Internal Affairs	1939-1940
	Economic Affairs	1946
	National Defence	1949-1950
Eyskens, Gaston	Finance	1945
	Prime Minister	1949-1950
	Economic Affairs and Middle Classes	1950
	Prime Minister	1958-1961
	Finance	1965-1966
	Prime Minister	1968-1973
Franck, Louis	Colonies	1918-1924
Sap, Gustave	Public Works	1932
	Public Works, Agriculture and Middle Classes	1932-1934
	Finance	1934
	Economic Affairs	1939-1940
	Economic Affairs and Food Supply	1940
Vandervelde, Emile	Minister	1916
	Intendance	1917-1918
	Justice	1918-1921
	Foreign Affairs	1925-1927
	Minister	1935-1936
	Public Health	1936-1937
Van Zeeland, Paul	Minister	1934
	Prime Minister; Foreign Affairs and Foreign Commerce	1935-1936
	Prime Minister	1936-1937
	Foreign Affairs and Foreign Commerce	1949-1954
Wauters, Arthur	Public Health	1937-1939
	Labour and Social Providence	1939
	National Information	1939-1940
	Agriculture	1946

Following the same procedure as adopted above for the period 1830-1918, we will now provide some biographical information on both the elected and the unelected economists in Parliament in the period 1919-1939, the elected economists being grouped by political party.

Liberal economists

In addition to Louis Franck and Charles Devèze, two other economists of the Liberal Party were elected to Parliament.

One of them was Louis Strauss, who graduated in economics at the Institut Supérieur de Commerce d'Anvers (one of the precursors of the University of Antwerp) in 1862. He served in the Belgian consulates in Germany, the USA, Canada and Japan, and was appointed by the Belgian government to study the establishment of steam boat lines between Antwerp and the transatlantic ports. He was politically active in the Werkersverbond, the liberal worker's party. His importance for the history of economic thought in Belgium lies primarily in his editorship of the *Revue économique* (1890-1904), and in his organisational role in different associations of economists.[28]

The second liberal economist was Jules Ingenbleek, who specialised in fiscal issues after obtaining a PhD in political and administrative sciences. The Institut de Sociologie of the Free University of Brussels published his comparative study *Impôts directs et indirects sur le revenu. La contribution personnelle en Belgique, l'Einkommensteuer en Prusse, l'Income-Tax en Angleterre* (1908). He resigned from Parliament to become governor of the province of East Flanders (1935-1938), a post which he left when he was appointed Vice Governor of the National Bank (1938-1944).[29]

Socialist economists

Apart from Louis Bertrand, Jules Destrée and Emile Vandervelde, the Socialist Party had four other economists in the Belgian Parliament.

Although a physician by education, Georges Barnich published mainly on sociology and economics. From 1916 to 1923 he co-directed the Institut de Sociologie which had been founded by Ernest Solvay at the Free University of Brussels. He published an extensive study on Solvay's doctrine of 'social energetics': *Essai de politique positive basé sur l'energétique sociale de Solvay* (1919).[30]

The second socialist economist was Max Buset, who studied economic and social sciences at the Free University of Brussels. He enjoyed a long career as a socialist member of parliament, holding the presidency of the Socialist Party from

28 Schreiber (1992), p. 328; Van Molle (1969), pp. 308-9; Lenders (2002). In the parliamentary records and archives his name is given as 'Straus'.

29 Van Molle (1969), pp. 191-2; Vandewoude (1981).

30 Van Molle (1969), p. 7.

1945 to his death in 1959. With G. Koulischer he published the booklet *L'Action pour le Plan* (1933) in support of Hendrik De Man's Labour Plan.[31]

The third in the list is Arthur Wauters, who obtained a PhD in economics in 1928. Initially a journalist for the socialist newspaper *Le Peuple*, he embarked upon a political career in 1932, and taught a course on 'agricultural economics' at the Free University of Brussels from 1935 onwards. He published widely on socialism, agriculture and colonialism, writing works such as *La Réforme agraire en Europe* (1928). After WW2 his political career had a more international dimension.[32]

But the most famous figure was certainly Hendrik De Man, one of the most important politicians of the 1930s. After studies in history and philosophy at the University of Leipzig, he became a professor of social psychology in Frankfurt. Strongly influenced by Marxism in his youth, he criticised Marx and Marxist thought in his *Zur Psychologie des Sozialismus* (1926), better known under its French title *Au delà du Marxisme* (1927). Returning to Belgium in the beginning of the 1930s, he became vice-president of the Socialist Party and elaborated a new socialist economic policy which was launched under the name *The Labour Plan*. In 1935 De Man became minister in Van Zeeland's first government. Although achieving a substantial reduction in unemployment, he met with stiff resistance with regard to the more radical proposals of *The Labour Plan*. Disillusioned, he resigned in 1938. When Vandervelde died in 1939, De Man became president of the Socialist Party. During WW2 he followed a course which many considered to be pro-German. After the war a military tribunal sentenced him to 20 years of imprisonment for collaboration with the enemy, but he had already fled to Switzerland where he found asylum as a political refugee.[33]

Catholic economists

In stark contrast to their marginal influence throughout the nineteenth century, economists linked to the Catholic Party became quite influential in the twentieth century, with two Prime Ministers coming from their ranks. While many liberal and socialist economists had strong connections with the Free University of Brussels, the Catholic economists were predominantly linked to the Catholic University of Louvain.

Gustave Sap was among the first to teach a course of economics in Dutch at the Catholic University of Louvain. His academic career was overshadowed by his political activities as a representative of the Boerenbond, the agricultural lobby, within the Catholic Party. Through the newspaper *De Standaard*, which he controlled, he advocated right-wing and strongly Flemish-oriented policies. His

31 Ibid., pp. 31-2.
32 Ibid., pp. 380-1; Sirjacobs (1997), p. 51.
33 Van Molle (1969), pp. 94-6; Claeys-Van Haegendoren (1970), Brélaz and Rens (1973-1974).

political career was marked by incidents and quarrels with other members of his party.[34]

Also connected with the University of Louvain was the Dominican father Georges Rutten, who had obtained a PhD in theology and an additional PhD in social and political sciences at that university. He was one of the ideologues of the Christian (anti-socialist) labour movement in Belgium. One of his many publications was *La Doctrine sociale de l'Eglise résumée dans les encycliques Rerum Novarum et Quadragesimo Anno* (1932).[35]

Charles Dejace was instead a professor and rector (1921-1924) at the University of Liège. He taught courses on natural law, political economy, and labour legislation. His publications focused mainly on labour legislation and social economics, although during his term in Parliament he focused mainly on issues of education.[36]

Paul Van Zeeland studied law, philosophy, and political and diplomatic sciences at the University of Louvain, but his student career was interrupted during WW1, when he spent four years as a prisoner of war in Germany. In 1920 he crossed the Atlantic and studied economics at Princeton University, where he obtained a master of arts in economics. The result of his research on the American monetary system can be found in his book *La Réforme bancaire aux Etats-Unis d'Amérique de 1913 à 1921. Le Système de la Réserve Fédérale* (1922). After his return to Belgium he became a professor of economics at the University of Louvain, where in 1928 he founded the Institut des Sciences Economiques, the precursor of the Institut des Recherches Economiques et Sociales (IRES). At the same time, he pursued a career at the National Bank, of which he was appointed Vice Governor in 1934. Although not a member of parliament, but with a clear Catholic designation, Van Zeeland became Prime Minister of a government of 'national union' in 1935, a government that enacted some drastic measures to reverse the economic situation, devaluing the Belgian franc by 28 per cent and launching an ambitious program of public works. The economic situation improved, but the political situation remained unstable. In 1936 Van Zeeland crushingly defeated the fascist leader Léon Degrelle in a partial election in Brussels. In 1937, however, he was forced to resign as Prime Minister after a 'scandal' stirred up by Gustave Sap over the conditions under which Van Zeeland had left his job at the National Bank. His activities after WW2 fall outside the scope of this chapter.[37]

Gaston Eyskens studied economics at the University of Louvain and spent two years in the United States, at Columbia University in New York and at the University of Chicago. In 1931 he was appointed professor in economics at the University of Louvain. Starting with his election as a member of parliament for the Catholic

34 Van Molle (1969), p. 294; Gerard (1987).
35 Van Gestel (1964); Van Molle (1969), p. 290.
36 Van Molle (1969), p. 79.
37 N.B.B. (1960), pp. 309-10; Van Molle (1969), pp. 363-4; Baudhuin (1973); Snoy (1973); Eyskens (1974).

Party in 1939, he combined an academic career with political commitments. He was several times Prime Minister, but this falls outside the scope of this chapter as his terms of office came after WW2.[38]

Extra-parliamentary economists

In the unstable economic and political climate of the interwar period the economically sensitive post of minister of finance was more than once occupied by a 'technician', usually a figure with roots in the financial sector. Their terms in office were without exception short.

Ernest Mahaim was a minister for less than a month. He held a PhD in law and another in political and administrative sciences, and was the successor of the economist Emile De Laveleye at the University of Liège. Following the tradition of De Laveleye, he produced an impressive amount of publications. He was especially interested in labour regulations, as shown by his dissertation *Etudes sur l'association professionnelle* (1891), and in this context he was one of the driving forces behind the International Association for the Legal Protection of Labourers. Subsequently he was strongly involved in the International Labour Organisation, of which he became president in 1930. He represented the Belgian government at the 1919 Peace Conference, and contributed to the Versailles Treaty.[39]

Albert Janssen became minister of finance three times without being a member of parliament, twice before WW2, and again in the 1950s. He had obtained a PhD in law and a similar qualification in political and diplomatic sciences from the Catholic University of Louvain. In 1911 he became a professor at this university, where he taught courses on banking and monetary economics. During this period he published *Les Conventions monétaires internationales* (1912). Only at the end of his life was he a member of the Senate.[40]

Camille Gutt, who studied law and social and political sciences, was a businessman and a banker. He became minister of finance in the short-lived government headed by Georges Theunis (1934-1935). In 1939 he returned once more as minister of finance. During WW2 he was one of the major figures in the Belgian Government in exile in London, where he prepared the so-called 'Gutt operation' aimed at bringing about monetary stabilisation after the war. From 1946 to 1951 he was the first Managing Director of the IMF.[41]

The civil engineer Max-Léo Gérard was the secretary of the Belgian King in the period 1919-1924, and a prominent banker. He had specialised in public finance, and published several articles on the Belgian situation in the *Revue économique internationale*. In the 1930s, he was twice appointed as minister of finance

38 Van Molle (1969), p. 142; Smits (1996).
39 Van Molle (1969), pp. 230-1; Rey (1983-1984).
40 Van Molle (1969), p. 196; De Voghel (1976).
41 Van Molle (1969), pp. 164-5; Crombois (2000).

without being a member of parliament. After WW2 he was president of the International Institute of Public Finance (1948-1950).[42]

Finally, Paul Heymans graduated as a mechanical engineer in Ghent. He obtained a PhD in sciences at the Massachusetts Institute of Technology, where he was an assistant professor in the period 1922-1926. When he returned to Belgium he became a professor in Ghent as well as head of a public bank. Before and after his short term as Minister of Economic Affairs, he published several articles on economic issues.[43]

Assessing the influence of economists in the Belgian Parliament

The data presented so far suggest that economists played a relatively minor role in the Belgian Parliament throughout the nineteenth century, but enjoyed an increasingly important function in the first half of the twentieth century. The view that a number of economists in the Belgian Parliament were quite influential is confirmed by noting that 13 out of a total of 36 economists considered in this chapter received the title of 'Minister of State' (see Table 3.4). This is an honorary title awarded by the King to distinguished politicians who have rendered particularly valuable services to public life. The ratio of 13 to 36 seems exceptionally high, given the fact that the title is awarded rather sparingly.[44]

Table 3.4 Economists appointed as Ministers of State

Name	Year of nomination
Bertrand, Louis	1918
Buset, Max	1948
Deveze, Albert	1930
Eyskens, Gaston	1963
Franck, Louis	1926
Gutt, Camille	1945
Janssen, Albert	1949
Pirmez, Eudore	1884
Solvay, Ernest	1918
Thonissen, Joseph	1884
Vandervelde, Emile	1914
Van Zeeland, Paul	1948

But a proper evaluation of the role played by economists in Parliament and of their impact on economic policy in general calls for a more thorough investigation. Firstly, a careful reading is required of the minutes and records of the Belgian

42 Van Molle (1969), p. 154.
43 Ibid., p. 78.
44 Between 1830 and 2004, 216 persons were awarded the title of Minister of State.

Chamber of Representatives and Senate.[45] The parliamentary discussions should then be compared with the economic policies actually implemented by the Belgian government, and moreover be set within the broader context of public debate in Belgium, including newspapers, meetings, conferences, etc.

To illustrate the relevance of the wider context, let us take the example of the free-trade debate. In Belgium, the free-trade movement was predominantly a matter of economists *outside* the Belgian Parliament. Inspired by the examples of Richard Cobden in England and Frédéric Bastiat in France, the campaign in favour of free trade was launched by a group of economists and businessmen led by Adolphe Le Hardy de Beaulieu. In October 1846 they founded the Association Belge pour la Liberté Commerciale, of which Charles De Brouckère, then mayor of Brussels, became the president. At that time, neither Le Hardy de Beaulieu nor De Brouckère was a member of parliament. In 1847 the association organised an international free trade conference in Brussels, the Congrès des Economistes. However, the influence of the association upon government policy was negligible. It was not until the mid 1850s that any significant change came about, when, in 1855, Charles Le Hardy de Beaulieu and Gustave de Molinari re-launched the free trade campaign on the pages of the journal *L'Economiste Belge*, and by means of the Société Belge d'Economie Politique. In January 1856 the Association pour la Réforme Douanière was founded, with Michel Corr-Vandermaeren as president, and with Gustave de Molinari and Auguste Couvreur among the members of the board of directors. In September 1856 the association organised a new international free trade conference, this time under the title Congrès International des Réformes Douanières, which led to the foundation of the Association Internationale pour les Réformes Douanières. Throughout the country meetings were organised in favour of free trade, this time apparently achieving considerably greater impact on both Parliament and government, since in the 1850s protectionist policies were gradually abandoned or reformed.[46]

However, it cannot be ruled out that other forces may also have been at work in bringing about a gradual shift in approach. Therefore insight into the precise impact of economists upon law making and economic policy requires a detailed analysis springing from the painstaking research of economic historians, to complement the general context sketched above. This will be a task for future research.[47]

---

45 These can be found in *L'Union Belge* (1830-1831), *Moniteur Belge – Belgisch Staatsblad* (1831-1845) and *Annales Parlementaires – Parlementaire Handelingen* (Est. 1845).

46 For more information on the free-trade campaign, see Mosselmans and Erreygers (2003).

47 An excellent recent example is the PhD thesis by Van Dijck (2004) on the influence of classical political economy on Belgium's agricultural policy in the period 1830-1884, which complements Van Molle's (1989) study on agricultural policy in the period 1884-1914.

Conclusion

Three tentative conclusions emerge from this chapter. First, in the period 1830-1918 a relatively limited number of economists were active in the Belgian Parliament, but during the inter-war years their presence increased considerably. Second, in view of the high proportion of ministers and ministers of State among these economists, their impact upon economic and social policy seems to have been substantial. And third, more detailed and contextualised research is needed in order to appraise their true influence upon parliamentary and governmental activities.

References

Abs, R. (1973), *Emile Vandervelde*, Labor, Bruxelles.

Baudhuin, F. (1928), 'Histoire économique de la Belgique', in *Histoire de la Belgique Contemporaine. 1830-1914*, Albert Dewit, Bruxelles, **I**, pp. 233-348.

Baudhuin, F. (1946), *Histoire Economique de la Belgique. 1914-1939*, Emile Bruylant, Bruxelles, 2 Vols.

Baudhuin, F. (1973), 'Paul Van Zeeland tel que je l'ai connu', *Revue Générale*, **9**, pp. 11-17.

Brelaz, M. and Rens, I. (1973-1974), 'Man (Henri de)', in *Biographie Nationale, Publiée par l'Académie Royale des Sciences, Lettres et des Beaux-Arts de Belgique*, Emile Bruylant, Bruxelles, **38**, cols. 535-54.

Brouwers, D.-D. (1908-1910), 'Royer De Behr (Auguste-Nicolas-Maximilien)', in *Biographie Nationale, Publiée par l'Académie Royale des Sciences, Lettres et des Beaux-Arts de Belgique*, Emile Bruylant, Bruxelles, **20**, cols. 297-9.

Chlepner, B. (1972), *Cent Ans d'Histoire Sociale en Belgique*, ULB, Bruxelles.

Claeys-van Haegendoren, M. (1970), 'Man, Hendrik de', in *Nationaal Biografisch Woordenboek*, Koninklijke Vlaamse Academiën van België, Brussel, **4**, cols. 528-41.

Coosemans, M. (1958), 'Montefiore-Lévi (Georges)', in *Biographie Coloniale Belge – Belgische Koloniale Biografie*, Académie Royale des Sciences Coloniales – Koninklijke Academie voor Koloniale Wetenschappen, Bruxelles – Brussel, **V**, cols. 606-7.

Crombois, J.-F. (2000), *Camille Gutt. Les Finances et la Guerre. 1940-1945*, Ceges, Bruxelles.

De Molinari, G. (1892), 'La Conférence Monétaire de Bruxelles', *Journal des Economistes*, **51**, Déc., pp. 337-9.

De Paepe, J.-L., Raindorf-Gerard, Ch., Gillard, P. and Brion, R. (1996) (eds), *Le Parlement Belge. 1831-1894. Données Biographiques*, Académie Royale de Belgique, Bruxelles.

De Ridder, R. (1913), 'Hubert Brasseur (1852)', in *Université de Gand. Liber Memorialis. Notices Biographiques*, I. Vanderpoorten, Gand, **I**, pp. 373-85.

Despy-Meyer, A. and Devriese, D. (1997) (eds), *Ernest Solvay et son temps*, Archives de l'ULB, Bruxelles.

De Voghel, B. (1976), 'Janssen (Albert-Edouard)', in *Biographie Nationale, Publiée par l'Académie Royale des Sciences, Lettres et des Beaux-Arts de Belgique*, Emile Bruylant, Bruxelles, **39**, cols. 499-505.

Discailles, E. (1903), 'Pirmez (Eudore)', in *Biographie Nationale, Publiée par l'Académie Royale des Sciences, Lettres et des Beaux-Arts de Belgique*, Emile Bruylant, Bruxelles, **17**, cols. 566-611.

Dumont, G.-H. (1999), 'Destrée, Jules', in *Nouvelle Biographie Nationale*, Académie Royale des Sciences, des Lettres et des Beaux-Arts de Belgique, Bruxelles, **5**, pp. 117-23.

Erreygers, G. (1998), 'The Economic Theories and Social Reform Proposals of Ernest Solvay (1838-1922)', in W. Samuels (ed.), *European Economists of the Early 20th Century*, **1**, *Studies of Neglected Thinkers of Belgium, France, The Netherlands and Scandinavia*, Edward Elgar, Cheltenham, pp. 220-62.

Erreygers, G. (2001), 'Economic Associations in Belgium', in M.M. Augello and M.E.L. Guidi (eds), *The Spread of Political Economy and the Professionalisation of Economists. Economic Societies in Europe, America and Japan in the Nineteenth Century*, Routledge, London, pp. 91-108.

Eyskens, G. (1974), 'Paul Van Zeeland (1893-1973)', *Yearbook of the American Philosophical Society*, pp. 212-18.

Foster, Ch. (1893), 'The Brussels Conference Reviewed', *North American Review*, **156**(437), pp. 493-501.

Gerard, E. (1987), 'Sap, Gustave Charles' in *Nationaal Biografisch Woordenboek*, Koninklijke Vlaamse Academiën van België, Brussel, **12**, cols. 642-56.

Gerard, E., Witte, E., Gubin, E. and Nandrin, J.-P. (2003) (eds), *Geschiedenis van de Belgische Kamer van Volksvertegenwoordigers, 1830-2002*, Kamer van Volksvertegenwooridgers, Brussel.

Julin, A. and Chlepner, B. (1957), 'Denis (Hector-Achille)', in *Biographie Nationale, Publiée par l'Académie Royale des Sciences, Lettres et des Beaux-Arts de Belgique*, Emile Bruylant, Bruxelles, **29**, cols. 542-50.

Juste, Th. (1867), *Charles De Brouckère. Bourgmestre de Bruxelles, etc. (1796-1860)*, C. Muquardt, Librairie Européenne, Bruxelles.

Kauch, P. (1966), 'Franck (Louis-Marie-François)', in *Biographie Nationale, Publiée par l'Académie Royale des Sciences, Lettres et des Beaux-Arts de Belgique*, Emile Bruylant, Bruxelles, **33**, cols. 335-54.

Laureys, V. *et al.* (1999), *De Geschiedenis van de Belgische Senaat, 1831-1995*, Lannoo, Tielt.

Laureyssens, J. (1975), *Industriële Naamloze Vennootschappen in België. 1819-1857*, Editions Nauwelaerts, Béatrice-Nauwelaerts, Leuven and Paris.

Lenders, P. (2002), 'Strauss, Louis', in *Nationaal Biografisch Woordenboek*, Koninklijke Vlaamse Academiën van België, Brussel, **16**, cols. 734-9.

Mahaim, E. (1895), 'Economics and Social Science in Belgium', *Economic Journal*, **5**, pp. 462-71.

Mertens, J. (1985), 'Franck, Louis', in *Nationaal Biografisch Woordenboek*, Koninklijke Vlaamse Academiën van België, Brussel, **11**, cols. 217-28.

Mesdach De Ter, K. (1901), 'Orts (Auguste)', in *Biographie Nationale, Publiée par l'Académie Royale des Sciences, Lettres et des Beaux-Arts de Belgique*, Emile Bruylant, Bruxelles, **16**, cols. 334-42.

Michotte, P. (1904), *Etudes sur les théories économiques qui dominèrent en Belgique de 1830 en 1886*, Charles Peeters, Louvain.

Mosselmans, B. and Erreygers, G. (2003), *What did Really Happen at the First International Economics Conference in Brussels in 1847?*, Paper prepared for the CHORD conference, Wolverhampton, 10-11 September.

N.B.B. (1960), *Notices Biographiques – Biografische Nota's. 1850-1960*, Nationale Bank van België, Brussel.

Polasky, J. (1995), *Emile Vandervelde. Le Patron*, Labor, Bruxelles.

Ramaer, J.C. (1933), 'Brouckère (Charles Marie Joseph Ghislain de)', in *Nieuw Nederlandsch Biografisch Woordenboek*, A.W. Sijthoff, Leiden, **9**, pp. 102-6.

Rey, J. (1983-1984), 'Mahaim (Ernest-Aimé-Joseph)', in *Biographie Nationale, Publiée par l'Académie Royale des Sciences, Lettres et des Beaux-Arts de Belgique*, Emile Bruylant, Bruxelles, **43**, cols. 501-9.

Schreiber, J.-P. (2002), *Dictionnaire Biographique des Juifs de Belgique*, De Boeck, Brussels.

Sirjacobs, I. (1997), *L'Economiste dans le temps*, Archives de l'ULB, Bruxelles.

Smits, J. (1996), 'Eyskens, Gaston', in *Nationaal Biografisch Woordenboek*, Koninklijke Vlaamse Academiën van België, Brussel, **15**, cols. 223-44.

Snoy, J.-Ch. (1973), 'Paul Van Zeeland, une figure de proue', *Revue Générale*, **9**, pp. 1-10.

Stockmans, F. (1973-1974), 'Montefiore Levi ou Montefiore (George Levi dit)', in *Biographie Nationale, Publiée par l'Académie Royale des Sciences, Lettres et des Beaux-Arts de Belgique*, Emile Bruylant, Bruxelles, **38**, cols. 596-618.

Terlinden, Ch. (1930-1932a), 'Thonissen (Jean-Joseph)', in *Biographie Nationale, Publiée par l'Académie Royale des Sciences, Lettres et des Beaux-Arts de Belgique*, Emile Bruylant, Bruxelles, **25**, cols. 112-19.

Terlinden, Ch. (1930-1932b), 'T'Kint De Roodenbeke (Henri-Marie, baron puis comte)', in *Biographie Nationale, Publiée par l'Académie Royale des Sciences, Lettres et des Beaux-Arts de Belgique*, Emile Bruylant, Bruxelles, **25**, cols. 376-8.

Tordoir, J. (1999), *Le Baron Jean-Adolphe le Hardy de Beaulieu (1814-1894). Châtelain de la Bawette à Wavre, Vice-Président de la Chambre des Représentants, Président de la Société Belge d'Économie Politique*, Incourt.

Vandervelde, E. (1938), 'Notice sur Hector Denis', *Annuaire de l'Académie Royale de Belgique*, **104**, pp. 1-32.

Vandewoude, E. (1981), 'Ingenbleek, Jules Jean François Marie', in *Nationaal Biografisch Woordenboek*, Koninklijke Vlaamse Academiën van België, Brussel, **9**, cols. 377-88.

Van Dijck, M. (2004), *De Wetenschap van de Wetgever. De Klassieke Politieke Economie en het Belgische Landbouwbeleid. 1830-1884*, PhD thesis, Katholieke Universiteit Leuven, Faculteit Letteren, Departement Geschiedenis.

Van Gestel, C. (1964), 'Rutten, Georges', in *Nationaal Biografisch Woordenboek*, Koninklijke Vlaamse Academiën van België, Brussel, **1**, cols. 793-97.

Van Molle, L. (1989), *Katholieken en Landbouw. Landbouwpolitiek in België. 1884-1914*, Universitaire Pers, Leuven.

Van Molle, P. (1969), *Het Belgisch Parlement – Le Parlement Belge. 1894-1969*, Erasmus, Ledeberg and Gent.

Witte, E., Craeybeckx, J. and Meynen, A. (1997), *Politieke Geschiedenis van België van 1830 tot Heden*, Standaard Uitgeverij, Antwerpen, 6th edition.

Appendix

Table 3.5 Economists who entered Parliament (1830-1918)

Name	Life	Sen./ Rep.	Period	Party
Bertrand, Louis	1856-1943	Rep.	1894-1926	Soc.
Brasseur, Hubert	1823-1890	Rep.	1870-1872	Lib.
Couvreur, Auguste	1827-1894	Rep.	1864-1884	Lib.
De Brouckère, Charles	1796-1860	Rep.	1831-1832	Lib.
		Rep.	1848-1856	
		Rep.	1857-1860	
Denis, Hector	1842-1913	Rep.	1894-1913	Soc.
Deprez, Oscar	1854-1921	Rep.	1890-1894	Lib.
Destrée, Jules	1863-1936	Rep.	1894-1936	Soc.
Devèze, Albert	1881-1959	Rep.	1912-1958	Lib.
Fortamps, Frédéric	1811-1898	Sen.	1859-1878	Lib.
Franck, Louis	1868-1937	Rep.	1906-1926	Lib.
Le Hardy de Beaulieu, Adolphe	1814-1894	Rep.	1863-1884	Lib.
Montefiore-Levi, Georges	1832-1906	Sen.	1882-1901	Lib.
Orts, Auguste	1814-1880	Rep.	1848-1880	Lib.
Pirmez, Eudore	1830-1890	Rep.	1857-1890	Lib.
Prévinaire, Eugène	1805-1877	Rep.	1848-1864	Lib.
Royer De Behr, Auguste	1824-1886	Rep.	1859-1876	Cat.
Solvay, Ernest	1838-1922	Sen.	1892-1894	Lib.
		Sen.	1897-1900	
Thonissen, Joseph	1816-1891	Rep.	1863-1890	Cat.
T'Kint De Roodenbeke, Arnold	1853-1928	Rep.	1891-1900	Cat.
		Sen.	1900-1928	
Vandervelde, Emile	1866-1938	Rep.	1894-1938	Soc.

Note: Sen. = Senate, Rep. = Chamber of Representatives
Cat. = Catholic, Lib. = Liberal, Soc. = Socialist

Table 3.6 Economists who entered Parliament (1919-1939)

Name	Life	Sen./ Rep.	Period	Party
Barnich, Georges	1876-1948	Sen.	1925-1946	Soc.
Bertrand, Louis	1856-1943	Rep.	1894-1926	Soc.
Buset, Max	1896-1959	Rep.	1932-1959	Soc.
Dejace, Charles	1856-1941	Sen.	1921-1925	Cat.
De Man, Hendrik	1885-1953	Sen.	1936-1944	Soc.
Destrée, Jules	1863-1936	Rep.	1894-1936	Soc.
Devèze, Albert	1881-1959	Rep.	1912-1958	Lib.
Eyskens, Gaston	1905-1988	Rep.	1939-1965	Cat.
Franck, Louis	1868-1937	Rep.	1906-1926	Lib.
Ingenbleek, Jules	1876-1953	Sen.	1931-1935	Lib.
Rutten, Georges	1875-1952	Sen.	1921-1946	Cat.
Sap, Gustave	1886-1940	Rep.	1919-1940	Cat.
Strauss, Louis	1844-1926	Rep.	1919-1926	Lib.
T'Kint De Roodenbeke, Arnold	1853-1928	Rep.	1891-1900	Cat.
		Sen.	1900-1928	
Vandervelde, Emile	1866-1938	Rep.	1894-1938	Soc.
Van Zeeland, Paul	1893-1973	Rep.	1937-1939	Cat.
		Sen.	1946-1956	
Wauters, Arthur	1890-1960	Sen.	1932-1936	Soc.
		Rep.	1936-1944	

Note: Sen. = Senate, Rep. = Chamber of Representatives
Cat. = Catholic, Lib. = Liberal, Soc. = Socialist

Chapter 4

Chair, Tribune and Seat: Spanish Economists in Parliament (1844-1923). An Exploration

Salvador Almenar

Introduction: the social uses of economic knowledge

A study of the participation of Spanish economists in Parliament during the liberal age can help clarify some relevant questions on the role of economic ideas and political strategies in the evolution of contemporary society. But the allusion to 'economists' immediately invokes a preliminary question that concerns their identity, which usually leads to investigation of a complex relationship among characteristics such as their education and background, their most frequent or continuous activities, economic publications and the subjective or social context.[1]

The Spanish writers of economic works in the nineteenth century themselves used a fairly broad concept to refer to those they considered their colleagues. The term 'economist' indicated the recognition of a special ability attributed by the nature of their publications and public interventions, or by virtue of specialist or expert knowledge. In an essay published in 1850 entitled, *Clave de los economistas en el poder y la oposición* (*A Key to the Economists in Power and in the Opposition*) a 'catalogue of Spanish economists' was included that featured works in political economy and public finance but also in neighbouring fields such as studies on administration, politics, statistics and international relationships.[2]

In order to build up a more clear-cut picture of this identity and to facilitate a detailed international comparison, this chapter studies the parliamentary participation of two groups of economists separately: professors of political economy and a group of economic 'experts' without academic posts.

The social uses of economic knowledge were very varied in terms of the authors' training and competence, the nature of economic discourse and the audiences (teaching, applied analysis and debate among specialists, education or persuasion of public opinion). In Spain, as in other European countries, professors of political economy, experts, politicians, editors and journalists often crossed the

1 See Augello and Guidi (2003).
2 See Bona (1850).

frontiers of a hypothetical professional specialty, addressing different audiences and with various purposes. The distinction between professors and experts in economic matters was not of major significance in the mid-nineteenth century, but the relative role carried out by both groups of economists inside Parliament was undergoing modification between 1844 and 1923.

The first section presents some basic features of Spanish political evolution, the distribution of power among institutions and their relationship with electoral systems and practices. The second section details an interpretive outline of the institutionalised teaching of political economy. The third section studies the participation of professors of political economy in Parliament. The fourth section presents some hypotheses regarding the role carried out by members of parliament who specialised in economic debates and their relationship with government initiatives.

An outline of the political evolution

A new historical cycle began in Spain with the Franco-Spanish War (1808-1814). The Constitution of 1812 had established a unicameral parliamentary monarchy. Fernando VII re-established the absolute monarchy between 1814 and 1820 and, after the parenthesis of the Liberal Triennium (1820-1823), he newly re-established absolutism until his death in 1833. Between 1836 and 1843 the revolutionary process completed a liquidation of the old social order. The 1837 constitution re-established the principle of national sovereignty that dated back to 1812 and introduced the bicameral system. It accelerated the disappearance of feudal institutions together with the government declaration that part of the possessions of the Church were to become national property.

After 1843 political confrontation concentrated particularly on the distribution of power between Crown and Parliament, the broad nature of the system of political representation and the demands for freedom of the press and the right of association and meetings. Three major political periods are usually distinguished: the moderate regime (1844-1868), the revolutionary process of 1868-1874, and the Restoration (1875-1923).

The moderate regime (1844-1868)

After a progressive military regency (1841-1843) a new constituent process arose that was controlled by the Moderate Party. The new Constitution of 1845 established a sovereignty shared by the Crown and the Spanish Parliament (Congress and Senate); it submitted the exercise of civil rights to special laws, reaffirmed the Catholic character of the State, and eliminated all means of progressive revolutionary power.

The essential feature of the moderate regime was the combination of the Queen's new discretionary power (faculty to nominate government and Senate members, power to veto legislation and to dissolve Parliament), the restriction of suffrage (approximately one per cent of the population), and the government's limitation of rights as stated in the Constitution. Isabel II administered this hegemonic power during the decade 1844-1854 with the appointment of cabinets inspired by influence groups of the Moderate Party, frequently not included in parliamentary majorities.

A military pronouncement supported by popular uprisings led to a brief revolutionary period (1854-1856) that multiplied the moves towards political and economic reformation. This was followed by a period of stability directed by the Liberal Union, a new centrist party composed of some moderates, progressives and part of the army. The decline of the Liberal Union starting from 1864 culminated in a new particularly authoritarian phase of the Moderate Party.

The 1868 revolution and the Republic (1873)

In September 1868 a revolutionary process began, supported by part of the army, which resulted in the exile of queen Isabel II, elections based on male universal suffrage (around 25 per cent of the population) and the formation of Constituent *Cortes* with a progressive majority but with strong representation of the Liberal Union, the Federal Republicans and the Democratic Monarchists. The 1869 Constitution established the primacy of national sovereignty represented in the *Cortes* (Congress and Senate) and the King's authority was restricted to the power of sanction in the framework of the parliamentary monarchy. The Constitution also separated the executive power from the judicial, while guarantees concerning individual rights were reinforced; in addition, the Constitution explicitly opened up a path towards decentralisation in the political organisation of the State.

The enthronement of a King from another dynasty, Don Amadeo of Savoy, in November 1870, was unable to establish effective bonds among parliamentary parties that would have allowed the formation of a solid government. Amadeo I's abdication in February 1873 resulted in the parliamentary proclamation of a Republic which, however, was subject from its outset to a profound political and territorial disintegration: local rebellions, conflicts in Cuba, the Carlist War (1872-1876), and growing social conflict. The *coup d'état* in January 1874 terminated the Republic, and a new *coup* at the end of that year restored the monarchy to Isabel II's son, Alfonso XII.

The Restoration (1875-1923)

The new political system endeavoured, from its start, to proceed toward a recovery of the moderate principles of 1845, yet basing its legitimacy on the alternation of two majority parties, the conservative and the liberal, which did not question the monarchy. The 1876 Constitution revived the principle of the shared sovereignty and the King's prerogatives to name ministers and to dissolve the Cortes. Formally, it incorporated some institutional and juridical guarantees but electoral rights were limited (to two per cent of the population), until male universal suffrage was introduced in 1890.

The habitual operation of the system was based on a peculiar combination of institutional regulations and political practices. The King's control over the appointment of the Cabinet and the dissolution of Parliament, together with the government's capacity to influence the electoral processes, led to a practice that allowed for the resolution of political crises (lack of trust in the government by the King or Parliament) by means of the dissolution of the Cortes and the appointment of a government from the opposition party that organised the new elections as it saw fit. Moreover, the existence of numerous electoral districts with a single deputy, the limitation of franchise, and a network of local, provincial and national powers allowed manipulation and electoral fraud with the support of the Ministry of the Interior.

The group of rules and practices governing bipartisanship was defined critically, at the end of nineteenth century, as a system of *caciques* (powerful local political figures) or *caciquismo*. This system provides insight into the mechanics of alternation (swing) between the two parties (conservative and liberal) and the greater stability of the Parliaments and governments in the first stage of the Restoration (1876-1902).

The second stage (1902-1917) is usually defined by the succession of King Alfonso XIII to the Crown in 1902 (after a period of regency from 1885), but also by the development of a new political scenario marked by the political, financial and moral crisis that implied the loss of Cuba, Puerto Rico and the Philippines in 1898, and the disappearance of the founders of the main parties. With the new century Conservatives and Liberals faced growing fragmentation and unstable leadership, while the spread of the vote favoured a reinforcement of political professionalisation and the incorporation of other forces into Parliament (Nationalists, Republicans, Radicals and Socialists). The 1907 electoral reformation did not modify the mechanisms of *caciques* system, thus contributing to prolonging a vast crisis of hegemony among the political elite.

During the final Restoration period (1918-1823) social conflicts increased as the two traditional parties, which were also divided into tendencies within Parliament, were unable to solve the absence of a defined leadership. The duration of successive governments between 1917 and 1923 decreased by half as compared to the two previous decades and the suspension of constitutional guarantees was almost permanent. In September 1923, general Miguel Primo de Rivera launched a *coup*, with Alfonso XIII's passive complicity, beginning a period of dictatorship that extended up to 1930.

Institutionalisation and professionalisation of political economy

This section presents an overview of institutionalisation and the paths on which professors of political economy embarked in the progression towards professionalisation between 1842 and 1923.[3]

3 This section is based on a provisional census of seventy professors. A complete analysis

From the end of the eighteenth century the teaching and diffusion of political economy gradually gained favour among Spanish liberals, although it was still taught only in very few institutions. From 1807 onwards, incipient and discontinuous educational experiences were initiated within universities, Economic Societies, Boards of Commerce and Athenaeums, which educated future politicians, professors of political economy and civil servants. Translations of classical economists and books by Spanish authors, sometimes published while in exile, contributed to expanding the prestige of political economy, thereby enriching the education of citizens and helping to guide economic reforms.

Between 1836 and 1845 three centralised reformations took place that jointly led to the consolidation of political economy in the syllabi of law faculties, while the teachings held in other institutions disappeared. From 1857 until the end of the century the teaching of 'political economy and statistics' was compulsory in law faculties, as was 'public finance' from 1868. After 1900 political economy (without statistics) and public finance continued to be compulsory in legal studies, with the same professor in charge of teaching both subjects, except for the universities of Madrid and Barcelona. The number of universities remained stagnant at ten throughout the whole period 1844-1923. From the second half of the century political economy was also included at the Royal Industrial Institute (1850-1867), in the schools of commerce, the schools of engineers and in the preparatory studies for the Faculty of Philosophy (1845-1857). The Higher Schools of Commerce increased in number from two to eight between 1887 and 1901, but in spite of some proposals, the creation of the first Faculty of Economics in Spain did not take place until 1944.

The professors of political economy between 1842 and 1868 were graduates or doctors of law, with the exception of some figures who had followed studies in philosophy, engineering or commerce. Some of the early professors had studied political economy previously. Frequently, they also taught other juridical subjects such as political, administrative or mercantile law. During the period in question

---

on economic studies in Spain does not yet exist, but is being undertaken as part of the research project directed by professor Enrique Fuentes Quintana (and coordinated by Jesús Astigarraga). Provisionally, my work has gathered basic information on professors of political economy and public finance in universities during the period 1840-1923. Some other professors from commerce schools and engineers schools have been added if they published textbooks or other economic monographs. The group amounts to nearly seventy professors in this period. This compilation comes from multiple sources, among which mention should be made of *Escalafón general de los catedráticos de las universidades* (from 1846) and *Documentos para la historia de la Educación* (CIDE), as well as valuable secondary sources, some of which unpublished: Anes (1986); Aracil Fernández (2000); Artal, Gabriel, Lluch and Roca (1979); Blanco Canales (1976); Bru Parra (2002); Cano Pavón (1998); Fuentes Quintana (1999-2004); Iparaguirre (1975); López Castellano (2002); Martín Rodríguez (1989, 2000); Perdices de Blas and Reeder (2003); Robledo (2004); Román Collado (2003); Sánchez Hormigo, Malo Guillén and Blanco Domingo (2003); Teixeira (2002); Velarde Fuertes (2002); Velasco Pérez (1990).

political economy became a complementary or accessory discipline relative to legal studies. In addition, some professors changed specialty in order to obtain stable chairs in another subject or university and, frequently, they taught while at the same time also practising other occupations, such as the legal profession and politics.

A considerable diversity is observed in the number and content of their publications. Between 1840-1850 many university professors composed no economic works as such, publishing at most some booklets in juridical or political fields. A commission named by the government specified a list of textbooks recommended for teaching political economy, but incentives were also given for professors to publish textbooks. The hegemony of the teachings of J.-B. Say came to an end in the 1840s with the rising influence of Ricardian political economy and the new 'eclectic political economy', which devoted attention to the differences between 'economic theory' and 'economic policy' and was critical of the 'chrematistic school'.[4]

Very soon however, an accelerated influence of Bastiat's writings and the *Journal des économistes* group took hold and spread, as a result both of debates on free trade, encouraged by Richard Cobden's tour of Spain in 1846, and of the teaching of political economy. Nine professors and former professors of political economy contributed decisively to the formation of a group called the Economist School in the mid 1850s. With a style similar to that of the Belgian and French free-trade economists, the Economist School founded debating associations in Madrid, started economic journals, promoted public debates and participated actively in Parliament and government, as we will see later on in more detail. The academic hegemony of the Economist School (1855-1874), concentrated in Madrid and focusing on the battle for economic freedom and for free trade in particular, encountered little resistance from other professors of political economy (with one exception in Barcelona). Their main opponents were economic (non academic) experts, managers, politicians and spokesmen of protectionist interest groups.

During the 1870s new professors who had been previously well educated in the law faculties were appointed to chairs of economics. They held their teaching posts for long periods of time, maintained a predilection for academic publications and did not participate in parliamentary activities. A group of these professors (José Manuel Piernas, 1843-1911, and Adolfo Álvarez Buylla, 1850-1927), influenced by 'Krausism' (a neo-Kantian current that enjoyed considerable favour in Spain), were particularly attentive to the criticism formulated by the Historical School, Chair Socialists and Cooperativists against the 'Optimistic School'. But these economists rejected the fundamental proposals underlying these critical approaches while not developing an alternative point of view. With time they became advisors in institutions of social policy during the Restoration. A second group showed greater adherence to the classical tradition (now including John Stuart Mill), with a

4 See Lluch Martín and Almenar (2004).

style similar to the works of Charles Gide, where the allusions to marginalist and neo-classical economists had no great relevance. This 'basic consent between Krausist economists and the Economist School'[5] guaranteed a slightly revised fundamental continuity of the classical economic programme in the teaching of political economy until the beginning of the twentieth century. A third group (five professors) oriented its teaching according to diverse versions of Catholic 'social economics' by means of translated manuals or with revisions and adjustments to those previously published. Some were especially active in Catholic Congresses and the so-called 'Social Weeks'.

Towards the turn of the century and during the first decade of the twentieth century a change in direction began to take shape in economic studies, coinciding with a new mentality of 'national regeneration' impelled by the moral crisis associated with the military disaster in Cuba (1898). The main novelty was a regular practice of post-graduation training in foreign universities. The new professors of political economy Antonio Flores de Lemus (1876-1941), Francisco Bernis (1877-1933) and José María Zumalacárregui (1879-1956) familiarised themselves with the Historical School, marginalism and neoclassical economics. Flores de Lemus imposed upon his pupils post-graduation studies in German universities as a requirement for the academic course, constituting – before 1925 – a hegemonic group in the teaching of political economy: Vicente Gay (1876-1949), Jaime Algarra (1879-1948), Ramón Carande (1886-1887), Luis Olariaga (1885-1976), Agustín Viñuales (1891-1959) and Gabriel Franco (1897-1972), among others.

However, the process of modernisation of economic studies was quite slow, and scientific production remained sluggish during the first three decades of the twentieth century. This paradox is a consequence of Flores' predilection for 'realistic' empirical studies applied to the Spanish economy and the severe criteria of originality that he imposed upon his pupils in their publications. In addition, from 1905 to 1936 Flores dedicated most of his time to the economic assessment of successive governments, establishing a professional profile of economists' 'silent' influence on economic policy that in part also affected Bernis and Zumalacárregui.

Finally, during the first two decades of the twentieth century some professors maintained a position favourable to Catholic 'social economics' (Sánchez Rubio, Teodoro Peña). Amando Castroviejo joined their ranks (from 1903 at 1934) and was an active diffuser of Giuseppe Toniolo's ideas in Spain. The presence of marginalist and neoclassical economics was insignificant inside lecture halls and in publications.

Professors of political economy in Parliament (1844-1923)

The study carried out on the participation of professors of political economy and public finance in Parliament presents a surprising quantitative balance. Out of

5 Malo Guillén (2001), p. 442.

seventy professors of political economy and public finance, approximately twenty had some parliamentary mandate during 1844-1923, which represents a proportion of 29 per cent.[6] This high proportion seems to indicate that during this period there was a close relationship between economic teaching and political activity. However, a detailed analysis will help to specify the historical meaning of this relationship.

Professional profile: (1) political economy

The professional profiles of academic members of parliament are strikingly diverse, if one considers indicators of specialisation and continuity, such as permanence in economic teaching, the specialisation of published works and the esteem enjoyed among their contemporaries.[7] A list of political economy professors and members of parliament, with relevant professional information, is presented in the Appendix (Table 4.1).

A quantitatively important group of professors, amounting to around half the total number, published either no works on economic matters (Álvarez, Arnau, Arriaga, Jiménez, Viñas), or only few works of minor impact (Guillén, Nougués, Moyano, Paso and Ponzoa). Their scanty contribution to economic literature can partly be ascribed to the relatively short period in which they were involved in teaching (with the exception of Jiménez, Nougués, Moyano and Ponzoa). This group includes some of the appointed professors or those in charge of teaching for a few years who came from other disciplines (Álvarez, Arnau, Moyano), and also numerous figures who left the teaching of political economy for other subjects, or for other activities (Arnau, Nougués, Paso).

The remaining group presents a more consistent academic profile with regard to permanence in teaching and publications in the economic field.[8] Although Colmeiro, Figuerola and Sanromá were no longer professors of political economy after 1847, 1853 and 1858 respectively, they continued publishing on economic subjects. The most outstanding figures of this academic group already belonged to the aforementioned Economist School (Figuerola, Colmeiro, Carreras, Diego Madrazo, Moret, Gabriel Rodríguez, Sanromá and Arnau) that enjoyed recognition by contemporaries inside and outside Parliament, in debating societies and in the

6 Basic parliamentary historical information in Spain is very scarce, especially on the Congress of Deputies. The main general repertoires and studies used here are: Cortes (1880); Mateo del Peral (1974a, 1974b); Rull Sabater (1974); Senado (2004); Urquijo Goitia (2004a, 2004b); Varela Ortega (2001).

7 The periods of effective teaching, based on sources mentioned in note 3, are still provisional. José Posada Herrera (1815-1885) has been excluded, as he held the position of professor of political economy at the University of Oviedo during a single course (1838) as well as Manuel Prado Tovía, who was a deputy in a previous period (1839-1840).

8 Ramón Anglasell should be included in this group, but he died soon after the term began and did not participate in the debates. See DSC-CD (1812-1923), 7 January 1864, p. 676.

Athenaeum. These authors entered into the Real Academia de Ciencias Morales y Políticas (except Carreras and Rodríguez).

Professional profile: (2) political participation

The activity carried out in Parliament can be appreciated, in a preliminary quantitative approach, by the number of mandates in which professors occupied a seat. This quantification is presented in Table 4.1, column 'Political activity', which integrates the mandates in both chambers. In Spanish parliamentary history the terms differed noticeably in duration up until 1876, but this irregularity was accompanied by different electoral systems and a different intensity in parliamentary activity.[9]

Three groups dedicated to politics can be distinguished. The first was formed by members of parliament with less than three mandates (Anglasell, Arriaga, Carreras, Guillén, Jiménez, Nougués, Ponzoa and Antonio Rodríguez), which could be considered as occasional participation in political activity.[10] Another intermediate group, with a frequency of between three and eight mandates, demonstrated significant continuity in political life. The Economist School members are included in this intermediate group, except for Carreras and Moret. Finally, Moyano and Moret were members of parliament with a prolonged activity extending over sixteen terms, a circumstance pointing to an unequivocal political professionalisation and which is in agreement with the absence or scarcity of their economic publications. The high degree of political dedication of these last two groups (between three and sixteen mandates) embraces sixty per cent of professors in Parliament, and this appears to be confirmed by the fact that a significant number of these professors assumed responsibilities in government (as president, minister or undersecretary).

This outline can be completed with a subjective perspective: professors who were non-elected candidates (for example, Benigno Carballo in 1863). It should also be kept in mind that in some cases prospective candidates explicitly declined to participate in electoral processes, as a result of the collective strategies of parties or internal groups, so-called periods of *retraimiento* or 'withdrawal' before changes in the political regime.

Historical evolution: a declining tendency

The participation of professors in parliamentary activities in terms of the chronology of periods in which Parliament was in office is shown in Figure 4.1. One can

9 A current notion of 'term' has been used as a parliamentary period between two elections. In the Spanish political vocabulary of the time 'legislatura' referred to the current denomination of 'period in which Parliament was in office'.

10 The exception is José Antonio Ponzoa, as his parliamentary mandates previous to 1844 have not been considered.

observe an irregular but persistent presence of professors, which peaked during the 1869-1872 term, subsequently disappeared during the constituent Republic (1873) and later reappeared with some regularity until 1891. From then on the presence of parliamentary professors tended to be quantitatively negligible until 1923.

Figure 4.1 Professors of political economy in the Spanish Parliament (1844-1923)

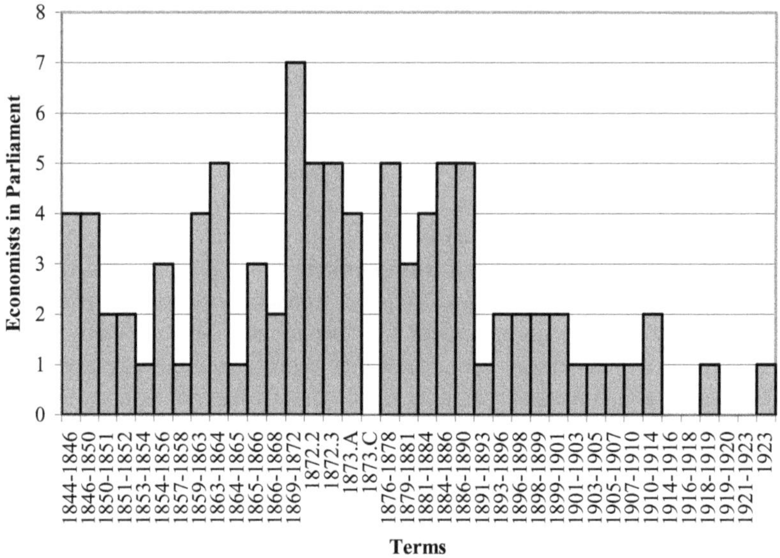

This evolution was subject to the influence of two general conditions. Firstly, successive regulations on the right to vote and the conditions for eligibility. Secondly, the true role attributed to members of parliament, that of political mediation, which was the result of a complex relationship involving the government's legislative initiative, the internal organisation of Parliament (commissions, plenary sessions, debates), and the particular professional or political characteristics (within the party) of deputies or senators.

The moderate regime (1844-1868). The first terms of the moderate regime incorporated into Parliament outstanding personalities from cultural life in consonance with the rules of doctrinal liberalism. Mandates were lengthened and *notables*' control over elections was reinforced by means of small electoral districts, in addition to a dominant presence of the aristocracy and bishops in the Senate. In fact, professors of political economy were not admitted to the Senate until 1869. The two main parties, the moderate and the progressive, were not autonomous centralised structures but groups of personalities and currents of opinion, so there were frequent internal discrepancies in economic matters.

The most important member of parliament and professor of political economy during the moderate decade (1844-1854) was Claudio Moyano, who was an odd moderate. He became well-known in debates on the tributary reform of 1845 and in the 1849 tariff reform for his opposition to the projects advanced by minister Alejandro Mon, who was also a moderate and enjoyed the support of two experienced economists, Ramón de Santillán and José Antonio Ponzoa. Paradoxically, in these debates and in his critique of the sale of towns' common lands in 1855, Moyano used an argument based on a Ricardian model formulated by the progressive democratic economist Álvaro Flórez Estrada (author of *Curso de economía política*, which Moyano recommended to his students).

The irregular presence of professors in Parliament during the period comprising the 1854 and 1868 revolutions is explained by the adaptive (and almost cyclical) political practice of the Progressive Party and the Liberal Union (which affected the Economist School), with an alternation of periods of 'withdrawal' (1857-1858) and participation (1859-1863, 1865-1866 and later periods). The term of 1863-1864 was initially one of participation, but the Progressives discretely gave up their seats a few months later.[11] The real balance of the presence of professors is much smaller than a first quantitative approach might suggest, above all if one considers the scarcity and relatively low impact of their interventions (mainly by Diego Madrazo, Colmeiro, Moret) in economic debates.

The 'glorious revolution' (1868-1874). Without a doubt, this represents the moment of the greatest quantitative significance of professors in Parliament. It was also the period of their greatest influence in economic policy because outstanding members of the Economist School directed, in government and Parliament, a process of economic reforms by adopting a programme in which two relevant sectors of the Progressive and Democratic Parties converged.

The main promoters of the so-called Economist School were the professors (or former professors) of political economy Laureano Figuerola (1816-1904), Manuel Colmeiro (1818-1894), Gabriel Rodríguez (1829-1901) and Luis María Pastor (1804-1872), the latter being a politician and financier and also well-known for his economic publications. Other professors immediately joined the group, Benigno Carballo (1826-1864), Segismundo Moret (1838-1913) and, a few years later, Joaquín Sanromá (1828-1895), Santiago Diego Madrazo (1816-1890) and Mariano Carreras (1827-1885).

This group of professors of political economy or public finance, together with colleagues from other specialties, lawyers, financiers and politicians founded the Sociedad Libre de Economía Política de Madrid in 1857, and two years later the Asociación para la Reforma de Aranceles de Aduanas, both in coordination with the initiatives by French and Belgian economists of the Guillaumin group. They also contributed to the foundation and development of the Abolitionist Society of

---

11 Figuerola's participation in 1865-1866 legislature was considered a betrayal by a section of progressive journals.

Slavery. Their analyses and proposals were circulated in specialised magazines such as *El Economista* (1856-1857), *La Tribuna de los Economistas* (1857-1858), and the *Gaceta Economista* (1861-1863). Finally, they planned a vast programme of activities in favour of free trade through a series of conferences in the Athenaeum and the Stock Exchange of Madrid, and also through their political participation in Parliament, especially during 1859-1863.[12] Considering these activities as a whole, one perceives a coherent strategy of influence directed towards the academic world, economic experts, Parliament, government and public opinion.

Their political victory has been interpreted in terms of opportunity: they were 'the only nucleus able to offer an alternative economic programme to the old system of economic policy, and were the group of men to put it into practice'.[13] Laureano Figuerola, treasury minister in 1868-1869, initiated a tributary reform that reduced taxes on consumption, declared a staggered tariff reduction and a liberalisation of economic activities (the elimination of interventions and monopolies, freedom in banking, the regulation of public works) that would be continued in part by other ministers of the Economist School up until 1874 (Madrazo, Moret, Echegaray). The greatest presence of members of parliament came during the first two years (1869-1871), in support of government reforms. During the following terms Figuerola and Madrazo assumed responsibilities in the presidency (or vice-presidency) of Congress or the Senate, which explains why their contributions to debates were only occasional. On the other hand, in this period a 'withdrawal' strategy was adopted among the moderates, and this extended to the professors of the Economist School during the Republic in 1873.

The Restoration (1) 1876-1902. The new Constitution of 1876 and its electoral development enabled university professors to enjoy a greater opportunity for parliamentary representation since their academic condition allowed them to avoid the income level restriction on eligibility. The notable presence of professors of political economy until 1891 was partly a response to the incorporation of Liberals leaning towards the Conservative Party (Arnau, Carreras, Colmeiro) and the assimilation of two professional politicians (Moyano and Moret) into the ranks of the majority parties. The 'withdrawal' shown by many Democrats of the Economist School, who refused to collaborate with the system, should also be borne in mind. However, analysis of the scanty contributions (mainly by Arnau, Carreras, Colmeiro, Antonio Rodríguez and Paso) reveals a parliamentary situation where only the leaders took a major role in debates.

The Restoration (2) 1902-1923. The abrupt decline of this marginal presence (except in the case of Moret) as from 1891 onwards can be interpreted as a consequence of the introduction of male universal suffrage in 1890 and the consolidation of *caciquismo* and political professionalisation. The presence of no more than a

---

12 See Almenar and Llombart (2001); Román Collado (2003).

13 Costas Comesaña (1988), p. 37.

few professors of political economy, who participated only marginally in debates, is also very revealing: Colmeiro (life senator), Jiménez (Marqués de la Merced) as a *notable* of a small electoral district, and Pío Suárez Inclán (professor in the High Army School), a member of a family dynasty of politicians and military officers.

However this political interpretation is incomplete. The scarce presence and participation of professors of political economy in Parliament during the lengthy period of 1891-1923 was also a consequence of the divorce between the academic currents of economic thought (economic 'Krausism' and revised classical political economy) and the newly arisen protectionist and interventionist tendencies that the majority parties adopted in order to engage with the new framework of international economic relationships (trade treaties, agricultural crises, revolution in transport, loss of the colonies, public debt, the gold standard, the 'social question', etc.).[14] In this double context of professionalisation and political fragmentation and of the relative divorce between the economic discourse of the academic world and the majority parties, professors of political economy were substituted by economic experts with experience in political mediation.

The political side of economic knowledge: experts in Parliament

The presence of economists in Spanish political life had been habitual from the first constituent Cortes of 1810. Thus numerous writers on political economy were prominent members of parliament or ministers between 1810 and 1844, and they used classical theories to expose or to refute their arguments in debates.[15] This presence was modified substantially between 1844 and 1923, as we will now see.

This evolution can be traced by starting from an inquiry into the existence of a sector of members of parliament who showed clear, outstanding protagonism in debates on economic matters (budgets, taxes, public goods, tariffs, transports, monetary and bank regulation, etc.). It can be observed that this economic specialisation coincided with a certain continuity in the form of members of parliament whose mandate extended over many terms. Furthermore, a very high proportion of these figures took charge of ministries with economic content, such as the Treasury Ministry or that of Encouragement (*Fomento*, with its different denominations), sometimes repeatedly. A selection of these experts is included in the Appendix (Table 4.2) to facilitate a rapid overview of the references in the text.

Further insight into the economic specialisation of some members of parliament can be gained by exploring the relations between different biographical, intellec-

14 See Serrano Sanz (2001a).

15 Ramón L. de Dou y Bassol (1742-1832), Juan Polo Catalina (1777-1813), Álvaro Flórez Estrada (1766-1853), José Canga Argüelles (1771-1842), Guillermo Oliver (1775-1839), Mariano Torrente, Eusebio María del Valle (1799-1867), José Antonio Ponzoa, José Manuel Vadillo (1777-1858).The list is not exhaustive. On economic thought in the first half of the nineteenth century see Lluch Martín and Almenar (2004); Smith (1968).

tual, professional and political features. The activity and influence of Spanish economists in Parliament and government have not been analysed systematically, although mention should be made of the pioneering study by Mateo del Peral on the economic authorities during the 1868-1915 period,[16] and some valuable studies dealing with relevant processes in the making of economic policy between 1844 and 1923.[17]

Economic training and specialisation

A very high proportion of parliamentary economic experts had carried out studies in law and, professionally, the majority had been practising lawyers. It should be remembered that law studies very soon incorporated some introductory teachings in political economy, statistics and public finance. During the moderate regime (1844-1868) there was still an appreciable presence of members o parliament who had acquired considerable experience in the Treasury Ministry, although this presence diminished slightly during the Restoration and practically disappeared by the beginning of the twentieth century. Parliamentary qualified engineers (linked to the railroad business) and managers (especially financial) represented less than 20 per cent of the economic experts in Parliament.[18] The specialised preparation of these economic experts was the result of self tuition, starting from a fundamentally legal university education, followed by experience in administration, Parliament, professional exercise, business, journalism and forums of civic discussion.

Economic publications by non-academic members of parliament were directly related to the economic debates taking place in Parliament, and together constitute a large proportion of Spanish economic literature during the period studied. However their composition also evolved significantly. With the process of institutionalisation of the teaching of political economy established in universities and schools, general treatises on political economy published by non-academic authors decreased drastically between 1840 and 1870.[19] As from 1860, publications by non-academic economists almost exclusively addressed the specific problems of the Spanish economy, and devoted greater attention to general or sectoral orientations of economic policy rather than to empirical economic analysis. On some issues, such as the problems associated with the potential incorporation of Spain

---

16 Mateo del Peral (1974a, 1974b).

17 See Comín Comín (2001); Comín Comín, Martín Aceña and Martorell Linares (2000); Comín Comín and Vallejo Pousada (2002); Martín Niño (1972); Costas Comesaña (1988); Serrano Sanz (2001b); Vallejo Pousada (2001): Martorell Linares (2000).

18 My preliminary estimate for the period 1844-1923 coincides with the results of the exemplary study by Mateo del Peral (1974a, 1974b) on the ministers of treasury and of encouragement in the 1868-1915 period.

19 There are significant exceptions: some members of parliament like Álvaro Flórez Estrada, Andrés Borrego, Ramón de la Sagra, José Manuel Vadillo, José Joaquín de Mora (1783-1864), Luis María Pastor and Alejandro Oliván published general and influential studies of political economy.

into the gold standard, the parliamentary contributions by some ministers or experts (Cos-Gayón, Fernández Villaverde, Navarro, Vázquez Queipo) constituted a reference point for all economists.

The intellectual recognition awarded by contemporary economists to the contributions of their own colleagues until the 1870s reveals a bias linked both to professional affinity and to the polemics regarding freedom of trade. Other institutions like the Real Academia de Ciencias Morales y Políticas showed a broader approach, welcoming among their members numerous economic experts who had shown special attention to economic matters in Parliament and government.[20]

The intellectual and professional paths of the spokesmen for associations or groups of economic interests that had arisen in the Spanish periphery, or in industrial regions like Catalonia and the Basque Country, constitute a special case until the end of the nineteenth century. These experts were less involved – when not faced – with the internal administrative process of the State, and they entered into Parliament with the explicit function of lobbying.[21] The proportion of jurists was less high than as a whole, and they included a greater presence of managers from the affected sectors. In addition, the duration of their presence in Parliament was shorter. In the protracted debate between protection and free trade both their publications as well as their parliamentary interventions reveal an analytical distance from the dominant version of classical political economy (from *Journal des économistes*) and show a predilection for statistical analysis to quantify the effects of legislation in production, sectors, markets and employment.

Economic experts: Parliament and government

During the period 1844-1923 the process of devising economic policy was transformed as a result of the reallocation of functions carried out by economic experts within Parliament. It should be noted, in this context, that Spanish governments had a very short mandate. Throughout the entire period studied more than 150 politicians held the treasury portfolio, although frequent repetitions also took place.

---

20 It has already been pointed out that the Academy welcomed seven of the eight professors and members of parliament of the Economist School. Professors Álvarez Buylla, Azcárate and Piernas Hurtado would later be admitted. As regards economic experts, the list of Academy members is overwhelming: Alzola, Argente, Bravo, Caballero, Calbetón, Cánovas, Cos-Gayón, Costa, Fernández Villaverde, García Barzanallana, Marichalar, Mon, Oliván, Pastor, Ruiz Gómez, Sánchez de Toca and Ventosa (selected in Table 4.2), to which one should add Ministers Gabino Bugallal (1861-1932) and Augusto González Besada (1865-1919).

21 The main institutions considered are the Confederación Mercantil Española, Instituto Industrial de Cataluña, Fomento del Trabajo Nacional, Fomento de la Producción Española, Liga Agraria, Cámaras de Comercio, Cámaras Agrícolas, Liga Nacional de Productores and the Unión Nacional. Special mention should be made of spokesmen and members of parliament with economic publications, among others: Andrés Borrego, Pascual Madoz, Juan Güell, Juan Illas, Pere Bosch, Pablo Alzola, and the peculiar types, Germán Gamazo and Joaquín Costa.

The average duration of their mandates was 6.2 months (1841-1868), 3.1 months (1869-1874), 12 months (1876-1900), 6.2 months (1900-1917) and 3.8 months (1917-1923). The average values for the ministers of encouragement were very similar and follow the same tendency.[22] These systematic changes endowed political life with a peculiar combination of discontinuity regarding parliamentary agenda and a certain political and institutional permanence.

During the moderate regime, the step preceding parliamentary discussion began with the creation of Bills by figures whom the minister of the treasury (or encouragement) had designated to leading positions in administration (a ministerial team composed of the undersecretary, general directors and subdirectors). The biographical and parliamentary information analysed reveals that the experts were also members of parliament with experience as officials in administration (Burgos, Santillán, Oliván, Salaverría, García Barzanallana), or had published previously on economic matters (Borrego, Peña Aguayo, Madoz, Pastor). Thus, when the Bill reached Parliament their authors were designated members of the parliamentary commission and they assured a controlled process of political mediation with the help of other members of parliament with political affinity, also participating in the plenary debates. Furthermore, it was a frequent occurrence for the current minister of the treasury or of encouragement to coordinate the ongoing creation of projects and parliamentary political mediation, at times when parliamentary support was especially divided and conflictual.

The system practiced by governments during the 1868-1874 period was, formally, very similar to the previous approach. However, ministers of treasury or encouragement of this period had ministerial teams that did not come from the administration itself but from the progressive, unionist, democrat and republican members of parliament with little government experience and from experts with a background in universities, banking and railroad companies (followers of the Economist School). Furthermore, there was a greater degree of open debate in Parliament, with MPs' initiatives and speeches.

The pact of alternation between the conservative and liberal parties during the first stage of the Restoration (1876-1902) contributed to a greater stability of governments. The most notable tendency in the period was to accentuate the endogenous nature of economic specialisation among members of parliament. It has already been pointed out that the presence of Treasury (or Encouragement) officials, or authors on political economy with a recognised position in the sphere of academic economics diminished vertiginously at this time, to below 2 per cent.[23]

22 My own estimate from the lists compiled by Urquijo (2004a) but eliminating the cases of interim or substitute ministers. The figures for the ministers of encouragement: 7.3 months (1847-1868), 3.2 (1868-1874), 12.2 (1875-1900), 6.2 (1900-1917), 4.6 (1917-1923). The standard deviation for the moderate period (1844-1868) is higher than the average value of mandates in both ministries.

23 Estimate from Mateo del Peral (1974a), p. 60.

The most habitual course was a political career that began with inclusion in electoral lists (within the complex system of powerful local political figures and families) after some experience in the offices of lawyers, in business or in local politics. Parliamentary experience or expertise and incorporation into a position forming part of economic teams became an intermediate step to becoming a minister. Finally, ministerial experience itself became, in political practice, a condition in order to be re-appointed to the position or to continue parliamentary activity in the Senate for life.

The progressive fragmentation of the majority political parties during the period 1902-1923 modified the parliamentary activity of economic experts in a new context of economic policy-making. The move towards protectionism initiated by the Conservative Party from 1890 onwards was continued by the Liberals at the beginning of the twentieth century, while the crisis of the Treasury showed up discrepancies between those in favour of regularisaton (budgetary equilibrium, practiced by Fernández Villaverde in 1899-1900, after the defeat in Cuba) and the 'Regenerationists' who sought the government's selective role in economic development by means of regulations, tax deductions, tariffs, and expansionist public expenditure. The fragmentation disabled government control over the parliamentary process in commissions and the plenary, disrupting the general trend that had been practiced by parliamentary economic experts from 1844 until the end of the nineteenth century. The ministers of treasury (or encouragement) sought to set up the preliminary stages of the legislative process by means of study commissions, whose results were subsequently re-elaborated at the intermediate levels of economic ministries, members of parliament and experts in administration itself. During the first two decades of the twentieth century the study commissions progressively integrated a larger formal representation of interest groups, in agreement with the advance of a mentality that drew increasingly closer to economic and social corporativism.[24]

Such a situation coincided with the appearance of a new generation of professors of political economy trained abroad (preferably in German universities) whose thought was more in tune with the economic orientations of the majority parties (for instance Flores de Lemus, Bernis, Zumalacárregui). This marked the birth of a new period where some economic projects launched by government's initiative were elaborated within the administration with the silent advice of the professors, maintaining the link between government and Parliament through the partial identity of the intermediate positions in ministries and parliamentary economic experts. However the government no longer had effective control over all members of parliament in its party. Within Parliament there was increased pressure by the swelling ranks of parliamentary minorities and by organised interest groups inside and outside Parliament.

---

24 See Comín Comín, Martín Aceña and Martorell Linares (2000); Martorell Linares (2000); Muñoz, Roldán and Serrano (1978); Roldán, García Delgado and Muñoz (1973).

Concluding remarks: economists as professors and experts

The quantitative study carried out on professors of political economy shows a very high degree of presence in Parliament between 1844 and 1923, nearly 29 per cent. Detailed analysis of their activities shows that, except for some personalities from political life (Moyano or Moret), the only noteworthy activity during the period 1868-1873 came from the combined activity of a few outstanding professors from the Economist School in Parliament and government. The presence of these professors decreased abruptly as from 1891 as a result of the modification of the political system and also due to the divorce of currents of academic economic thought (on the whole favourable to market liberalisation) from the tendencies of the majority political parties (of protectionist tendencies).

However this decline in the presence of academic economists in Parliament can be given a complementary interpretation. The specialisation of economic experts in Parliament during the period studied was quite high, but there was a tendency towards a modification of their profiles, which began to shift from a previous specialisation based on the study of political economy or administrative or managerial practice (during the moderate period) to an endogenous economic specialisation within the close relationships between Parliament and government that were favoured by the stability and alternation between parties during the Restoration. This process of endogenous specialisation running in parallel with the consolidation of *caciquismo* weakened the possibility of participation for those professors of political economy who were not involved in the mediation process between the government and the parliamentary majority or the opposition. From the beginning of the twentieth century the role played by economic experts in Parliament was reoriented more specifically to political mediation within a context of growing uncertainty; in parallel, the external influence of some academic economists over the formulation of government initiatives began to increase.

References

Almenar, S. and Llombart, V. (2001), 'Spanish Societies, Academies and Economic Debating Societies', in M.M. Augello and M.E.L. Guidi (eds), *The Spread of Political Economy and the Professionalisation of Economists. Economic Societies in Europe, America and Japan in the Nineteenth Century*, Routledge, London, pp. 108-25.

Anes, G. (1986), 'Los Amigos del País y las enseñanzas de economía', in *Homenaje a Pedro Sainz Rodríguez*, Fundación Universitaria Española, Madrid, **4**, pp. 451-60.

Aracil Fernández, M.J. (2000), *Los estudios de Hacienda Pública en España: nacimiento y evolución*, Doctoral Thesis, Universidad de Sevilla.

Artal, F., Gabriel, P., Lluch, E. and Roca, F. (1979) (eds), *Ictineu. Diccionari de les ciències de la societat als Països Catalans (Segles XVII-XX)*, Edicions 62, Barcelona.

Augello, M.M. and Guidi, M.E.L. (2003) (eds), *Gli economisti in Parlamento 1861-1922. Una storia dell'economia politica dell'Italia liberale – II*, Franco Angeli, Milano.

Blanco Canales, R. (1976), 'La enseñanza de la economía política en España en la primera mitad del siglo XIX', *Revista de Economía Política*, **74**, pp. 77-94.

Bona, J.E.D. (1850), *Clave de los economistas en el poder y en la oposición. Discurso económico-político*, Imp. Francisco García Arias, Madrid.

Bru Parra, S. (2002), *La enseñanza de la Economía en la Universidad de Valencia (1807-1937)*, University of Valencia, mimeo.

Cano Pavón, J.M. (1998), 'El Real Instituto Industrial de Madrid (1850-1867): medios humanos y materiales', *Llull*, **21**, pp. 33-62.

Comín Comín, F. (2001), 'Las modestas realizaciones de la nueva política económica intervencionista de la Restauración', in E. Fuentes Quintana (ed.), *Economía y Economistas Españoles*, Galaxia Gutenberg, Barcelona, **5**, pp. 197-239.

Comín Comín, F., Martín Aceña, P. and Martorell Linares, M. (2000) (eds), *La hacienda desde sus ministros. Del 98 a la guerra civil*, Prensas Universitarias de Zaragoza, Zaragoza.

Comín Comín, F. and Vallejo Pousada, R. (2002), *Alejandro Mon y Menéndez (1801-1882). Pensamiento y reforma de la hacienda*, Instituto de Estudios Fiscales, Madrid.

Cortes (1880), *Estadística del personal y vicisitudes de las Cortes y de los Ministerios de España desde el 29 de setiembre de 1833 ... hasta el 24 de diciembre de 1879*, Imp. de la Viuda e Hijos de J.A. García, Madrid.

Costas Comesaña, A. (1988), *Apogeo del liberalismo en la Gloriosa. La reforma económica en el Sexenio Liberal (1868-1874)*, Siglo XXI, Madrid.

Dsc-Cd (1812-1923), *Diario de las sesiones de Cortes. Congreso de Diputados*, J.A. García, Madrid.

Fuentes Quintana, E. (1999-2004) (ed.), *Economía y economistas españoles*: 1. *Una introducción al pensamiento económico*; 2. *De los orígenes al mercantilismo*; 3. *La Ilustración*; 4. *La economía clásica*; 5. *Las críticas a la economía clásica*; 6. *La modernización de los estudios de economía*; 7. *La consolidación académica de la economía*; 8. *La economía como profesión*; 9. *Cronología e historiografía*, 9 Vols, Galaxia Gutenberg – Funcas, Barcelona.

Iparaguirre, D. (1975), 'Historiografía del pensamiento económico español', *Anales de Economía*, **25-26**, pp. 5-38.

Lluch Martín, E. and Almenar, S. (2004), 'The Itineraries of Neo-Smithian Political Economy in Spain (1800-1848)', *Économies et Sociétés. Oeconomia*, **34**, pp. 267-97.

López Castellano, F. (2002), *La enseñanza de la Economía en la Universidad de Granada (1807-1936)*, Universidad de Granada, mimeo.

Malo Guillén, J.L. (2001), 'El pensamiento económico del krausismo español', in E. Fuentes Quintana (ed.), *Economía y economistas españoles*, Galaxia Gutenberg, Barcelona, **5**, pp. 389-451.

Martín Niño, J. (1972), *La Hacienda española y la Revolución de 1868*, Instituto de Estudios Fiscales, Madrid.

Martín Rodríguez, M. (1989), 'La Institucionalización de los estudios de economía política en la Universidad Española (1784-1857)', in M. Martín Rodríguez (ed.), *Marqués de Valle Santoro. Elementos de Economía Política con aplicación particular a España*, Instituto de Estudios Fiscales, Madrid, pp. ix-ccxxxiv.

Martín Rodríguez, M. (2000), 'La enseñanza de la economía en España hasta la Ley Moyano', in E. Fuentes Quintana (ed.), *Economía y economistas españoles*, Galaxia Gutenberg – Funcas, Barcelona, **4**, pp. 593-619.

Martorell Linares, M. (2000), *El santo temor al déficit. Política y Hacienda en la Restauración*, Alianza Editorial, Madrid.

Mateo del Peral, D. (1974a), 'Aproximación a un estudio sociológico de las autoridades económicas en España (1868-1915)', in G. Tortella Casares (ed.), *La banca española en la Restauración*, Banco de España, Madrid, **1**, pp. 15-106.

Mateo del Peral, D. (1974b), 'Autoridades económicas. Presidentes del Consejo de Ministros, Ministros de Hacienda, de Fomento y Gobernadores del Banco de España', in G. Tortella Casares (ed.), *La banca española en la Restauración*, Banco de España, Madrid, **2**, pp. 75-97.

Muñoz, J., Roldán, S. and Serrano, A. (1978), 'La involución nacionalista y la vertebración del capitalismo español', *Cuadernos económicos de ICE*, **5**, pp. 13-221.

Perdices de Blas, L. and Reeder, J. (2003) (eds), *Diccionario de Pensamiento Económico en España (1500-2000)*, Editorial Síntesis – Fundación ICO, Madrid.

Robledo, R. (2004), *La enseñanza de la economía política en la Universidad de Salamanca: de Ramón de Salas a Gabriel Franco*, Universidad de Salamanca, mimeo.

Roldán, S., García Delgado, J.L. and Muñoz, J. (1973), *La formación de la sociedad capitalista en España, 1914-1920*, Confederación de Cajas de Ahorros, Madrid.

Román Collado, R. (2003), *La Escuela Economista española*, Universidad de Cádiz – Universidad de Sevilla, Cádiz-Sevilla.

Rull Sabater, A. (1974), *Diccionario sucinto de Ministros de Hacienda (Siglos XIX y XX)*, Instituto de Estudios Fiscales, Documento n. 16, Ministerio de Hacienda, Madrid.

Sánchez Hormigo, A., Malo Guillén, J.L. and Blanco Domingo, L. (2003), *La cátedra de Economía Civil y Comercio de la Real Sociedad Económica Aragonesa de Amigos del País (1784-1846)*, R. Sociedad Económica Aragonesa de Amigos del País – Ibercaja, Zaragoza.

Senado (2004), *El Senado entre 1834 y 1923*, http://www.senado.es.

Serrano Sanz, J.M. (2001a), 'Economía y controversias de política económica a finales del siglo XIX', in E. Fuentes Quintana (ed.), *Economía y economistas españoles*, Galaxia Gutenberg, Barcelona, **5**, pp. 155-96.

Serrano Sanz, J.M. (2001b), 'Liberalismo e intervencionismo económico en Cánovas del Castillo', in E. Fuentes Quintana (ed.), *Economía y economistas españoles*, Galaxia Gutenberg, Barcelona, **5**, pp. 247-67.

Smith, R.S. (1968), 'English Economic Thought in Spain, 1776-1848', in C.D.W. Goodwin and I.B. Holley (eds), *The Transfer of Ideas: Historical Essays*, The South Atlantic Quarterly, Durham, NC, pp. 106-137.

Teixeira, J.F. (2002), *Los orígenes de los estudios de economía política en la Universidad de Santiago de Compostela (1807-1934)*, Universidad de Vigo, mimeo.

Urquijo Goitia, J.L. (2004a), *Diccionario Biográfico de los Ministros españoles en la Edad Contemporánea (1808-2000)*, http://www.ih.csic.es/lineas/jrug.

Urquijo Goitia, J.L. (2004b), *Elecciones parlamentarias 1808-1876*, http://www.ih.csic.es/lineas/jrug.

Vallejo Pousada, R. (2001), *Reforma tributaria y fiscalidad sobre la agricultura en la España liberal, 1845-1900*, Prensas Universitarias de Zaragoza, Zaragoza.

Varela Ortega, J. (2001) (ed.), *El Poder de la Influencia. Geografía del caciquismo en España (1875-1923)*, Centro de Estudios Políticos y Constitucionales – Marcial Pons, Madrid.

Velarde Fuertes, J. (2002), 'Los estudios superiores de Economía de 1857 a 1936', in E. Fuentes Quintana (ed.), *Economía y economistas españoles*, Galaxia Gutenberg, Barcelona, **6**, pp. 853-92.

Velasco Pérez, R. (1990), *Pensamiento económico en Andalucía (1800-1850). Economía política, librecambio y proteccionismo*, Agora, Málaga.

Appendix

Table 4.1 Spanish professors of political economy in Parliament (1844-1923)*

Name and life	Graduation and year	Training and previous occupations	Academic appointments: economic topics	Academic appointments: non-economic topics	Political activity (n. of mandates)	Councils
Álvarez Arenas, Domingo –	–	–	PE (1845-?)	–	Deputy (3)	–
Anglasell Serrano, Ramón 1821-1863	Law (Dr.) (1862)	Lecturer in Philosophy	PE-PF (1851-1863) PF (1863)	CN-AL (1851-1853?)	Deputy (1)	–
Arnau y Lambea, Víctor (?)-1893	Philosophy (?)	Lecturer in History of Philosophy	PF (1852-1857)	AL (1852-1853, 1861-1875) CN (1875)	Deputy (3) Senator (1)	–
Arriaga, José Higinio –	Law (Dr.) (1863)	–	PE-CL-AL (1849-1856) PF (1864)	AL	Deputy (1)	–
Carreras y González, Mariano 1827-1885	Medicine, Commerce (1857)	Teacher of English and Literature, Journalist	PE (1862-1884)	CL (1856-1884)	Deputy (1)	Statistics, International Exhibition
Colmeiro Penido, Manuel 1818-1894	Law (1838); Law (Dr.) (1841)	–	PE (1840-1847)	CN-AL (1847-1881)	Deputy (1) Senator (7)	Education, State Council, Supreme Court
Figuerola Ballester, Laureano 1816-1904	Law (1840, 1841) Law (Dr.) (1852)	Teacher, Director of Teachers School	PE (1842-1853)	CN-Comparate Law (1853-1861) AL (1861-?)	Deputy (4) Senator (3) Minister (2)	–

Name and life	Graduation and year	Training and previous occupations	Academic appointments: economic topics	Academic appointments: non-economic topics	Political activity (n. of mandates)	Councils
Guillén Tomás, Narciso –	Law (Dr.) (1863)	–	PE (1863-1868)	Civil Law (1878-1879)	Deputy (2)	–
Jiménez y Pérez de Vargas, Francisco J. 1846-1921	Law (Dr.) (1873) Philosophy (1894)	Assistant Prof. (1872-90): CN, PF, Law History	PE (1893-1919)	Law History (1890-1892) CL (1892)	Senator (2)	Agriculture
Madrazo Arroyo, Diego Santiago 1816-1890	Philosophy (Dr.) (1839)	Assistant Prof. (Logic, History, PE, CN)	PE (1840-1876)	History (1847)	Deputy (3) Senator (3) Minister	Education, State Council
Moret y Prendergast, Segismundo 1838-1913	Law (1860); Law (Dr.) (1861)	Assistant Prof.	PE (1857-1859?) PF (1859-1875)	Administrative Studies (1881-?)	Deputy (16) Minister (23) President (3)	–
Moyano Samaniego, Claudio 1809-1890	Philosophy, Law (Dr.) (1833)	–	PE (1836-1845)	–	Deputy (13) Senator (3) Minister (3)	–
Nougués Secall, Mariano 1808-1872	Law (1825); Law (Dr.) (1825)	Assistant Prof. (Law, Moral Philosophy, RL, CL), Judge	PE (1836-1847)	–	Deputy (1)	–
Paso y Delgado, Nicolás 1820-1897	Philosophy, Law (1840), Medicine	Teacher of PE, Law professor	PE (1841-1843)	Canonical Law	Deputy (1) Senator (3)	–
Ponzoa Cebrián, José Antonio –	–	Lecturer in Mathematics (1812-1820)	PE (1820-1834) PF (1836-1838)	–	Deputy (2)	–

Name and life	Graduation and year	Training and previous occupations	Academic appointments: economic topics	Academic appointments: non-economic topics	Political activity (n. of mandates)	Councils
Rodríguez Benedicto, Gabriel 1829-1901	Civil Engineer (1850), Law (1872)	Engineer, Lawyer, Mathematical studies	PE-AL (1853-1868, ?, 1887-1888)	PE (Lecturer at Atheneum)	Deputy (4) Senator (1)	Public Works (1859), Social Reforms
Rodríguez de Cepeda Garrido, Antonio 1814-1896	Philosophy, Theology (1831), Law (1837)	Lecturer in Philosophy and Law	PE-ST-PF (1837-1894)	RL-AL-CN	Senator (1)	Water Law Comm.
Sanromá Creus, Joaquín M. 1828-1895	Law (1850), Philosophy (Dr.)	Teacher; works on Literature and History	PE (1854-1858)	CN-AL (1854-1858) History of Commerce-IL (1858-1867)	Deputy (4)	State Council (1891)
Suárez Inclán, Pío –	Army	–	PE (High Army School 1894-1898)	–	Deputy (2) Senator (1)	–
Viñas, Juan José 1811-1881	–	–	PE (1845)	–	Deputy (4) Senator (1)	–

Note:
* List of acronyms.- AL: Administrative law; CL: Commercial law; CN: Constitutional law; IL: International law; PE: Political economy; PF: Public finance; RL: Roman law; ST: Statistics.

Table 4.2 Spanish economic experts in Parliament (1844-1923). A Selection

Name and life	Grades (a)	Previous and current occupations	Publications: economics or related fields	Parliament (b)	Government (c)
Alba Bonifaz, Santiago 1872-1949	L	Lawyer, Journal editor, Chamber of Commerce	Ministerial speeches, Spanish economic policy	Deputy (1901-1923)	Minister (9) (1916-1917, 1918)
Alzola y Minondo, Pablo 1841-1912	CE	Engineer, Local politics, Financier, Protectionist speaker	Industrial development, Customs duties, Social reform	Senator (1907)	–
Argente del Castillo, Baldomero 1877-1965	L	Lawyer	Social reform; Henry George	Deputy (1910-1923)	Minister (1918-1919)
Azcárate, Gumersindo de 1840-1917	PH	Professor of Comparative Law	Political economy, Politics, Free trade, Parliamentary system, Social reform	Deputy (1891-1896, 1898-1914)	–
Bergamín García, Francisco 1855-1937	L	Journalist, Professor of Mercantile Law	Economic consequences of war, Politics	Deputy (1886-1910), Senator (vit. 1914-1923)	Minister (4) (1922)
Borrego Moreno, Andrés 1802-1891	–	Exiled, Journal editor	Political economy (Principles), Public debt, Social reform	Deputy (1837-1840, 1847-1858)	–
Bosch y Labrús, Pere 1827-1894	L	Business, Protectionist speaker	Parliamentary speeches, Budget, Customs duties, Transportation	Deputy (1876-1891)	–
Bravo Murillo, Juan 1803-1873	TH, L	Professor of Philosophy (1825-1834), Lawyer, Public prosecutor, Journal editor	Public finance	Deputy (1837-1840, 1843-1854, 1857-1858) Senator (vit. 1845-1868)	Minister (6) (1847, 1849-1850, 1851-1852) President
Burgos, Francisco Javier de 1778-1849	L	Civil servant, Exiled, Journal editor, Treasury official	Administration, Public finance	Deputy (1834-1836, 1843-1846) Senator (vit. 1845-1849)	Minister (2)
Caballero Morgáez, Fermín F. 1800-1876	TH, PH, L	Teacher of Geography, Journalist	Agriculture, Statistics	Deputy (1834-1843, 1854-1856)	Minister (3) (1843)

Name and life	Grades (a)	Previous and current occupations	Publications: economics or related fields	Parliament (b)	Government (c)
Calbetón Blanchón, Fermín 1853-1919	L	Lawyer, Lecturer in Political Economy, Officer	Interventionist economic doctrines	Deputy (1884-1886, 1891, 1893) Senator (1898, 1901, vit. 1903-1919)	Minister (2) (1910-1911, 1918-1919)
Camacho, Juan Francisco 1813-1896	–	Banker	Public finance	Deputy (1853-1866, 1871-1872, 1876-1878) Senator (1871-1873, vit. 1877-1896)	Minister (5) (1872, 1874, 1881-1883, 1885-1886)
Cambó y Batlle, Francesc 1876-1947	PH, L	Financier	Banks, Money and rate of exchange	Deputy (1907, 1914-1923)	Minister (2) (1918, 1921-1922)
Cánovas del Castillo, Antonio 1828-1897	L	Lawyer, Manager	History, Politics, Trade policy, Social policy	Deputy (1854-1856, 1859-1872, 1876-1897)	Minister (2) President (8)
Cos-Gayón y Pons, Fernando 1825-1898	L	Lecturer in Political Economy	Administrative law, Gold standard, Public finance	Deputy (1876-1898)	Minister (5) (1880-1881, 1884-1885, 1890-1891)
Costa, Joaquín 1846-1911	L, PH	Lawyer, Notary	Agriculture, Politics	Deputy (1903)	–
Durán y Bas, Manuel 1823-1907	L (Dr.)	Professor of Commercial Law	Protectionism, Commercial law	Deputy (1863-1866, 1879-1891) Senator (1886, vit. 1891-1907)	Minister
Echegaray y Eizaguirre, José 1832-1916	CE	Engineer, Professor of Physics, Mathematics, Literature (Nobel Prize 1904)	Mathematical economics (unpublished), Free trade, Ministerial speeches	Deputy (1869-1873, 1877-1881) Senator (vit. 1900-1916)	Minister (10) (1869-1874, 1905)
Fernández Villaverde, Raimundo 1848-1905	L	Assistant Prof. of Mercantile Law, Lawyer, Director of Treasury	Money, Public finance	Deputy (1872-1873, 1876-1905)	Minister (6) (1899-1900, 1902-1903) President (2)

Name and life	Grades (a)	Previous and current occupations	Publications: economics or related fields	Parliament (b)	Government (c)
Flórez Estrada, Álvaro 1766-1853	L	Treasury Officer	Constitutional law, Political economy, Free trade, Money, Agricultural reform	Deputy (1820-1822, 1834-1843) Senator (vit. 1845-1853)	Minister
Gamazo Calvo, Germán 1828-1901	L (Dr.)	Lawyer	Parliamentary and ministerial speeches on budget	Deputy (1876-1901)	Minister (4) (1883, 1885-1886, 1892-1894, 1898)
García Barzanallana, José 1819-1903	L	Civil Servant, Director of Customs, Taxes and Public Debt	Public finance, Demography, Foreign trade, Politics	Deputy (1857-1858, 1864-1868) Senator (1876, vit. 1879-1903)	Minister (1876-1877)
Güell y Ferrer, Juan 1800-1872	–	Commercial and industrial business, Protectionist speaker	Manufactures, Business cycles, Customs duties	Deputy (1857-1862) Senator (vit. 1845-1868)	–
Illas y Vidal, Juan 1819-1876	L (Dr.)	Lecturer in Commercial Law	Customs duties	Deputy (1857-1858, 1864-1866)	–
López Puigcerver, Joaquín 1845-1906	L (Dr.)	Lawyer, Vice-minister (Treasury)	Ministerial speeches, Finance	Deputy (1872-1873, 1881-1905)	Minister (7) (1886-1888, 1894-1895, 1897-1898)
Madoz Ibáñez, Pascual 1805-1870	L, ST	Lawyer, Editor and Publisher	Geographic, Statistical and Historical Dictionary of Spain	Deputy (1836-1843, 1846-1856, 1859-1864, 1866-1867, 1869-1870)	Minister (1855) President (Revolutionary Deputy)
Marichalar Monreal, Luis de, Vizconde Eza 1872-1945	L	–	Economic policy, Social reform, Monetary policy	Deputy (1899-1914, 1916-1923)	Minister (3) (1917)

Name and life	Grades (a)	Previous and current occupations	Publications: economics or related fields	Parliament (b)	Government (c)
Mon y Menéndez, Alejandro 1801-1882	TH, L	–	–	Deputy (1836-1854, 1857-1867, 1876-1877) Senator (vit. 1877-1882)	Minister (5) (1837-1838, 1844-1846, 1846-1847, 1848-1849, 1857-1858) President
Navarro Reverter, Juan 1844-1924	CE	Civil engineer (Mountains), Entrepreneur, Business	Parliamentary and ministerial speeches, Monetary policy, Public finance, Income tax	Deputy (1886-1903) Senator (vit. 1903-1923)	Minister (5) (1895-1896, 1906, 1906-1907, 1912)
Oliván Borruel, Alejandro 1796-1878	Army Sch.	Statistics Commission	Political economy (Principles), Agriculture, Agronomics, Administrative law	Deputy (1836-1851) Senator (vit. 1845-1868, 1877)	Minister
Pastor Coxo, Luís María 1804-1872	L	Journalist, Lawyer, Financier (insurance, banks)	Political economy (Principles), Public finance: Taxes, Debt, Free banking, Free trade	Deputy (1847-1854, 1857-1858) Senator (vit. 1845-1868, 1871-1872)	Minister (1853)
Pedregal Cañedo, Manuel 1832-1896	L	–	Public finance, Politics, Free trade, Social reform	Deputy (1873, 1881-1896)	Minister (1873-1874)
Peña Aguayo, José 1801-1853	L	Lawyer	Spanish public finance	Deputy (1837-1840, 1844-1847) Senator (vit. 1846-1853)	Minister (1846)
Pi y Margall, Francisco 1824-1901	PH, L (Dr.)	Editor, Writer	Philosophy, Politics, Political economy	Deputy (1869-1873, 1891-1896, 1899-1901)	Minister (3) President
Ruiz Gómez, Servando 1821-1888	PH, L	Journalist, Director and Vice-minister (Treasury)	Monetary policy, parliamentary and ministerial speeches, Budget	Deputy (1854-1856, 1869-1873), Senator (1876, vit. 1877-1887)	Minister (3) (1871, 1872)

Name and life	Grades (a)	Previous and current occupations	Publications: economics or related fields	Parliament (b)	Government (c)
Sagra, Ramón de la 1798-1871	MA, ME	Botanist, Entrepreneur, Journal editor	Social political economy, Sociology, Statistics, History, Proudhon on credit	Deputy (1837-1841, 1854-1856)	–
Salaverría Charitu, Pedro 1810-1896	–	Civil servant, Treasury officer, Treasury director, Vice-minister of Treasury	Foreign trade, Budget	Deputy (1859-1866, 1872-1873, 1876-1878)	Minister (8) (1856, 1858-1863, 1874-1875, 1875, 1875-1876)
Salvador Rodrigáñez, Amós 1845-1922	CE	Engineer (Agriculture)	Parliamentary and ministerial speeches, Social reform, Budgets, Public education	Deputy (1891-1901, 1920) Senator (1901-1922)	Minister (6) (1894, 1905-1906, 1915-1916)
Sánchez de Toca, Joaquín 1852-1942	L	Lawyer	Economic policy, Protectionism, Agriculture, Money, Banks	Deputy (1884-1899) Senator (1898, vit. 1899-1923)	Minister (3) (1900-1901) President
Santillán González, Ramón de 1791-1863	L, Army	Official of Finance Ministry, Governor of Banks (S. Fernando, Bank of Spain)	Monetary policy, Fiscal policy, Banking regulation	Deputy (1837-1845) Senator vit. (1845-1863)	Minister (2) (1840, 1847)
Tutau Vergés, Joan 1829-1893	–	Commercial business, Exiled, Banker	Ministerial speeches, Finance, Theory of business cycles	Deputy (1869-1873)	Minister (1873)
Ventosa i Calvell, Joan 1879-1859	L (Dr.)	–	–	Deputy (1907-1923)	Minister (3) (1917-1918, 1918)

Notes:
(a) List of Acronyms.- L: Law, CE: Civil Engineer, PH: Philosophy, TH: Theology, MA: Mathematics, ME: Medicine, ST: Statistics.
(b) The abbreviation 'vit.' denotes senators for life.
(c) The first figure in brackets represents the amount of mandates as minister or president. The time periods in brackets make reference to years in charge in economic ministries only (Treasure, Encouragement, Provisions, Agriculture).

Chapter 5

Economists in Parliament in Britain (1848-1914)

Roger E. Backhouse*

The liberal age in Britain[1]

It would be natural for an economist to assume that the liberal age in Britain started much earlier than 1848, perhaps as early as the late eighteenth century when Edmund Burke, William Pitt and others were extolling the virtues of Adam Smith's *Wealth of Nations* (1776). Britain began the move towards free trade relatively early, a landmark being William Huskisson's dramatic reduction in the number of goods subject to tariffs in the 1820s. The monetary framework for a liberal capitalist economy was arguably laid down by the Bullion Debate, and policy was refined in the period leading up to the Bank Charter Act of 1844. During this period parliament was clearly sovereign and, in parliament, the House of Commons was clearly dominant, though not to the extent that it became in the twentieth century. Parliamentary debate was vigorous and could affect the fate of governments. In 1848 Britain experienced no revolution and did not even see any change in the franchise.

However, though Britain may have been moving towards a liberal economic system, the age of William Pitt was anything but liberal. Popular movements were forcibly repressed, the army being brought in where necessary (at Peterloo in 1819, troops killed eleven protestors and wounded 400). Trade Union activity was severely restricted and political movements such as Chartism were considered a

---

* I am grateful to Bob Coats and Marco Guidi for encouraging me to write this paper and for providing extensive helpful comments, which have led to significant changes. David Levy drew my attention to the *Punch* cartoon that is used. Bradley Bateman, Mark Blaug, Peter Cain and Denis O'Brien have also been sources of helpful ideas. None of these should be blamed for the use I have, or have not, made of their ideas.

1 Liberalism, as the term is used here, must be distinguished from the Liberal Party, one of the parties that dominated British politics during much of this period. There was, of course, enormous overlap – Gladstone, for example, pursued many policies that were liberal in both senses of the word – but they were not identical. The Conservative leader, Disraeli equally typifies the bourgeois dominance of politics, being responsible for some of the measures that might be considered generically liberal, such as extending the franchise. The meaning of Liberalism in the British context is discussed further below.

serious threat. The system was permeated by what came to be known as 'old corruption': there were many government appointments carrying salaries but few duties; political power could be bought and sold.[2] During the 1820s, 276 out of 489 English MPs were elected for seats controlled by an owner or patron – the so-called pocket boroughs.[3] For example, Old Sarum was notorious for returning two MPs even though it had only seven voters, at a time when Birmingham and Manchester were not represented. There was no uniformity to the franchise. It was a system in which political power, wealth and social status could be transformed one into another.

The big change came with the Reform Act of 1832, which standardised the franchise in the boroughs (householders owning or renting property valued at £10 per annum, a substantial sum) and extended it in the counties by giving large tenant farmers the vote. The political map was redrawn so as to represent the cities, and hence industrial and financial interests. Popular pressure, with rioting when it was thought that the Bill might not be passed, is believed to have been an important influence.[4] However, the franchise remained small – around one in five men could vote and corruption was not eliminated. To the contrary, because the 'rotten boroughs' had been eliminated, more elections were now contested, and because voting remained public, corruption was perhaps more widespread than before the Act. The working class remained firmly excluded from the formal political process. Parliament remained dominated by the wealthy, landed elite. Notwithstanding the fact that the system was hardly democratic by modern standards, the Reform Act of 1832 marked the end of the *ancien régime* in British politics and in this sense is comparable with the 1830 revolution in France.

In 1848, there was no revolution in Britain. Chartism, a popular movement that might have led to a revolution (or so the authorities feared) was kept firmly under control and Sir Robert Peel's government introduced many reforms to relieve the extreme economic distress of the 1840s. Income tax (introduced in 1842), though at a very low rate, was seen as an important measure, making it possible to reduce taxes on goods consumed by the poor and to remove protective duties that favoured particular interests. There was no change in the franchise. However, two years earlier, British politics had been transformed by repeal of the Corn Laws which split the Conservative Party and resulted in two decades when government was dominated by the Whig-Liberal Party.[5] These changes meant that the period from the late 1840s to WW1 was a distinctive period in British politics: the party system changed dramatically; the social structure of Britain changed; and the franchise was extended. It had many of the characteristics of what Guidi and Augello describe as the liberal age.

---

2 See Rubinstein (1987), ch. 9.

3 Rubinstein (1998), p. 36.

4 For a short discussion of the passage of the Act, see Rubinstein (1998), pp. 36-40.

5 The Anti Corn Law League was, unlike Chartism, a middle-class movement. Though it has been credited with changing views on the Corn Laws, it is arguable that this shift of opinion might have happened anyway. See Howe (1997).

The most obvious feature of this period was a complicated reorganisation of the political parties as they evolved from comparatively informal groupings into organisations more like modern political parties. The period saw important splits in the main parties, and it was far more common for politicians to move from one party to another than in the twentieth century. In the early nineteenth century, the Whigs were reformers, perhaps because, dominated by the very wealthy landed aristocracy, they were sufficiently wealthy that they could afford to do so. Against them were the Tories (Conservatives), who represented smaller landowners and businessmen. Throughout the period they were divided between the more pragmatic, liberal wing, led by Canning and Peel, and the reactionaries who resolutely opposed change. There was also a group of Radicals, led by Joseph Hume, who generally worked alongside the Whigs. These were reformers, including the Philosophic Radicals. After 1846, the Tories split between the protectionists, whose rising star was Benjamin Disraeli, and the free-traders, led till his death in 1850 by Peel. The Whigs, Radicals and some of the free-trade Tories coalesced, by the late 1860s, into the Liberal Party. It was from around this time that political parties began to become organised in the manner of modern parties. Apart from two short minority conservative governments, the period from 1846 to 1874 was dominated by Whigs and Liberals under Lord Palmerson and William Ewart Gladstone, a Peelite conservative who moved over to the Liberals after serving in Lord Aberdeen's coalition government in 1852. His major reforming government was from 1868 to 1874. Disraeli, who had formed a minority conservative government from 1866-1868, then formed an administration from 1874-1880.

In retrospect, the significant feature of the 1874 election was the return of 58 to 59 members of the Irish Home Rule Party, though the effects of this were not felt immediately. After Gladstone returned to office in 1880, the next decade was dominated by Ireland, the Home Rule Party switching its allegiance between liberal and conservative. Within the Liberal Party, strains between the Radicals, led by Joseph Chamberlain, and the more moderate Whigs developed. However, the party did not split until, in 1885, Gladstone became converted to home rule for Ireland. The drama surrounding the introduction of his Home Rule Bill, in 1886, was comparable with that surrounding the Reform Act of 1832. For the first time, Ulster was raised as a major stumbling block to home rule. A group of 93 Liberals, comprising both Radicals (most prominent among whom was Chamberlain) and Whigs, voted against the Bill, which was defeated. These Liberal-Unionists, as they quickly came to be called ensured a period of conservative dominance in British politics that lasted till 1906. However, their departure ensured that the Liberal Party became more committed to social reform than it might otherwise have been, with the result that when it came into office it was with a very radical agenda.

The late nineteenth century saw a slow increase in working men's representation. This came about through labour representatives within the Liberal Party through the Labour Representation Committee (LRC). When the Liberal Party eventually came to power in 1905, the Cabinet contained a majority of Radicals, of which David Lloyd George was most prominent. There were 29 labour MPs affiliated to the LRC and a further 24 members of the Independent Labour Party. There was, for the first time, a working man sitting in the Cabinet.

During this period, the franchise was progressively extended, with important changes in 1867 (which almost doubled the electorate and eliminated the remaining pocket boroughs) and 1884 (when the vote was extended, for the first time, to a large fraction of the working class). Voting became secret in 1872. Universal male franchise came in 1918, along with the vote for married women over thirty, and universal female franchise in 1928.

Beneath these changes lay enormous changes in the interests represented in parliament – reflected in the parties. The first is the decline in the landed interest and its switch from the Whigs to the Conservatives. In the middle of the nineteenth century, the landed interest was still dominant, the Whigs being the party of the very wealthy aristocratic families and the Conservatives the party of the smaller landowners. During the years after 1832, aided by the change in the franchise, this gradually changed. Within the Whig-Liberal Party, the number of MPs with landed interests declined from 321 in 1832, to 197 in 1868 to 30 in 1900. In the Tory-Conservative Party the peak was 301 in 1841 (up from 123 in 1832), 185 in 1868 and 150 in 1900.[6] The proportionate decline is shown in Table 5.1: from 34 per cent to 16 per cent of MPs interests.

Table 5.1 Interests represented in Parliament (1868-1900)

	1868	1874	1880	1885	1886	1892	1895	1900
Land and farming	34	31	27	18	19	17	17	16
Armed services	10	9	8	6	6	5	6	7
Manufacturing and transport	22	24	25	27	26	26	25	26
Finance	14	15	17	18	18	19	19	18
Merchants	6	6	6	7	6	6	6	6
Newspaper proprietors	0	0	1	2	1	2	2	2
Lawyers	8	9	9	10	11	12	12	10
Men of letters and academics	3	3	4	6	5	6	6	6
Journalists	0	0	1	1	2	2	2	2
Other Professions	2	3	2	5	4	4	4	5
Working men	0	0	0	1	1	1	1	1

Source: Calculated from data in Thomas (1939), pp. 14-17. This table gives the number of MPs with a particular interest as a percentage of the total number of interests. Though it is hopefully a reasonable proxy, it is does not represent the percentage of MPs because MPs might have more than one interest. Unfortunately, Thomas provides few details about how the figures were obtained and they should be treated with extreme care.

6 Thomas (1939), pp. 4-5, 14-15.

Table 5.1 also shows other interests represented in Parliament. Manufacturing and financial interests rose during the 1870s, thereafter remaining fairly constant. The rising class was not the manufacturers, but the professions. Adding together the four categories of profession shown in Table 5.1 we obtain a rise from 13 per cent in 1868 to 23 per cent to 1900. This is part of the phenomenon that has been given the label 'The rise of professional society'.[7] Lawyers were, perhaps inevitably the largest professional group though much larger proportional rises came with journalists (up from zero to 32 between 1868 and 1900) and 'Men of letters and academics' (up from 38 to 72 in the same period, peaking at 81 in 1892).

Given its significance for economists who entered Parliament, it is worth noting an important change in the role of professional people between the eras before and after the watershed of the 1832 Reform Act. Before 1832, wealthy businessmen and professionals could easily find their way into Parliament. A well known example (not typical of economists in this respect) is David Ricardo. Another is Joseph Hume.[8] Trained as a doctor, he entered the army as a surgeon and made his fortune in India. On his return, he purchased his parliamentary seat from the Duke of Cumberland for £10,000. He expected to be MP for life, so when he failed to get re-elected, he sued and received £1,000 in compensation.[9] In contrast, after 1832, elections were more frequently contested and opportunities to enter through patronage were fewer: entering Parliament became more difficult and it was more unusual for an MP to represent a constituency that he had never visited prior to the election day.

As significant as the overall numbers are the differences in the way various interests were represented between parties. The big change was the consolidation of the Conservative Party as the party of the propertied class. Whereas in the first half of the century, the large landowners had been Whigs, by its end, they were predominantly conservative. This is shown in Tables 5.2 and 5.3, which presents the same information in two ways. The main data is the number of MPs within each party with an interest in land, finance or manufacturing. In Table 5.2 this is expressed as a percentage of all MPs with the same interest. In 1868, 47.4 per cent of MPs with a landed interest were Liberal, a proportion that fell to 13.8 per cent by 1900. In contrast the number of MPs with landed interests who were conservative rose from 44.5 per cent to 69.1 per cent. The change in allegiance of those with financial interest was similar, though more dramatic: by 1900, 65.1 per cent of MPs with a financial interest were conservative, and only 17 per cent were liberal. Table 5.3 shows the situation within each party: by 1900 only 9 per cent of liberal MPs had an interest in land and 12 per cent an interest in finance; in contrast, over 20 per cent of Conservatives had an interest in each of these. This parallel reflects the alliance between the landed interests, finance and empire that Cain and Hopkins (1993) have called 'gentlemanly capitalism'.

7 Perkin (2002).

8 Hume was still an MP after 1848, so is mentioned below.

9 Rutherford (2004), p. 568.

Table 5.2 Distribution of economic interests across the main parties (1868-1900)

	Liberal		Conservative	
	1868	1900	1868	1900
Land	47.4	13.8	44.5	69.1
Finance	69.6	17.0	23.7	65.1
Manufacturing	65.8	35.0	25.5	49.0
Total	59.6	25.3	31.9	53.6

Source: As Table 5.1. Each figure gives the number of MPs with a particular interest as a percentage of all MPs with that interest. The last row gives the relative size of the two parties, as measured by interests declared (which because of multiple interests is not the same as number of MPs).

Table 5.3 Distribution of economic interest within each of the main parties (1868-1900)

	Liberal		Conservative	
	1868	1900	1868	1900
Land	26.9	9.0	47.3	21.2
Finance	16.6	12.0	10.5	21.6
Manufacturing	24.8	36.5	17.9	24.2

Source: As Table 5.1. Each figure gives the number of MPs with a particular interest as a percentage of all interests within the corresponding party.

The declining representation of landed and financial interest in the Liberal Party was reflected in a rise in the number of professional men, shown in Table 5.4. Professionals were more numerous amongst the Liberals than the Conservatives. The difference was particularly marked for journalists, men of letters and academics. Though not shown here, these categories of professional men were also important in the Irish Nationalist Party.

As this account of the political changes makes clear, the decisive political issues of the period were economic or had a major economic dimension. The political structure that emerged around 1870 was the direct result of the conservative split over the Corn Laws and protection. Thirty years later, Joseph Chamberlain's attempt to use imperial preference (and hence protection) to promote the empire aroused similar passions and was one of the factors that led to the return of the reforming liberal government of 1906. Alongside trade policy in importance came Ireland, the second defining issue for British politics, that in the 1880s broke up the liberal coalition that had formed after the repeal of the Corn Laws. Though attention is often focused on the religious dimension of the Irish problem, its economic dimension was fundamental. The majority of the Irish people were not only Catholic, but poor; the reason they were so poor was the system of land tenure, the result of British occupation. Though part of the United Kingdom, and represented in the Parliament, Ireland's economic and social structure was that of a colony. The economic problem was both a problem of economic development and a problem of the distribution of wealth, in which measures to promote development directly challenged the property rights of wealthy landowners, often resident in England and with voice in Parliament.

Table 5.4 Professionals in Parliament, 1868-1900

	Liberal		Conservative	
	1868	1900	1868	1900
Lawyers	9.2	12.0	5.1	8.8
Men of letters and academics	4.2	9.3	1.0	3.5
Journalists	0.0	3.0	0.0	1.3
Other[10]	2.5	4.5	1.3	4.4
Total	15.9	28.8	7.4	18.0

Source: As Table 5.1. Each figure gives the number of MPs with a particular interest as a percentage of all MPs with that interest. The last row gives the relative size of the two parties, as measured by interests declared (which because of multiple interests is not the same as number of MPs).

For the other major economic issues, it is possible to turn to royal commissions that were convened during the period. There was a royal commission (1885) on the depression that affected wide sections of industry and was particularly severe in agriculture in the late 1870s and throughout the 1880s. It was during this period that the problem of unemployment came to be seen as such, rather than as a problem of indigence.[11] The problem of depression spilled over into other areas of concern. Long term depression merged into the problem of Britain's industrial decline relative to the United States and Germany. Clearly, depression could be used as justification for protection, especially in a world where Britain moved further towards free trade than did its rivals. Unemployment was intimately involved with problems of poverty that were increasingly scrutinised in the period around 1900, when its relation with labour market structures were investigated by the Webbs, Llewellyn-Smith, William Beveridge and the Royal Commission on the Poor Laws (1909).[12] Depression also fuelled debate over the monetary system, for the period was largely one of falling prices; depression was blamed on falling prices which in turn was blamed, by some, on the failure of the money supply to

10 Includes doctors of medicine and architects and others.

11 Harris (1972); Hobson (1896) was the first to use the word 'unemployment'.

12 This activity had direct legislative consequences in the establishment of labour exchanges and other measures of social reform under the Liberal government.

keep pace with demand. Silver and bimetallism were thus on the agenda. There was even an international conference convened on the subject.

Other economic issues included the finance of local government, for the late Victorian age was one when local authorities were active in improving living conditions, local achievements being reflected in the civic architecture in cities such as Birmingham, Manchester and Leeds. Changing social conditions raised the question of poverty among the elderly, water supply, sanitation and a host of other problems. There were royal commissions on many of these. Education, inadequate even by the standards of continental Europe, was in part an economic issue given that the provision of compulsory education meant either working with or replacing the numerous voluntary bodies that were responsible for schools. As with Ireland, however, the economic issues were clouded by religion. Finally, there was the problem of India, which started the period run by the East India Company and ended it being considered the jewel in Victoria's imperial crown. Empire raised questions of war (the Crimea, Afghanistan, the Sudan, and against the Boers), there being significant opposition to all of these.

Who were the economists who entered Parliament?

The difficulties involved in establishing who counts as an economist during this period are well known and are extensively discussed elsewhere. The absence of clear-cut criteria means that there is the danger of circular reasoning – drawing certain conclusions about economists and then adjusting the definition of an economist so as to make it true. One way to avoid that problem is to accept the judgement of a third party about who was and who was not an economist. In this spirit, we take an economist to be someone whose biography appears in the recently published *Biographical Dictionary of British Economists*. Donald Rutherford's criteria for inclusion in this dictionary are broadly similar to those adopted by Fetter in his study of the classical period; the main one is that the person concerned should have published something significant on economics.[13] This is, of course, at the margin, a highly ambiguous criterion, for economic writing shades into the political. Most readers will probably think that if Rutherford has erred, it is on the side of being too inclusive.[14] For example, Charles Bradlaugh is well known, but as a free-thinker and political campaigner, not as an economist; however, even though his writings failed to make much impression on those usually considered economists, he published several works on economic questions. Robert Lowe wrote very little on economics but his critique of relativism and his views about economics being complete around 1870 are well known that he is included. Given that all economist-MPs are identified, readers who question the inclusion of

13 Rutherford (2004), pp. vii-viii.

14 The dictionary covers 600 economists, from the middle ages to those who died only recently. No living economists are included.

particular individuals can easily make the necessary adjustment to what follows. As regards omissions, the main problem is the spate of literature published on protection, free trade and tariff reform around 1900. Some of the authors of this literature (for example, Arthur Balfour, who became Prime Minister) are not included.[15]

Figures 5.1 and 5.2 summarise information about the 25 economists who entered Parliament between 1848 and 1920. Further details are provided in the Appendix. Figure 5.1 shows the periods for which each was in Parliament.[16] Figure 5.2 shows the number of economists sitting in Parliament in each year.[17] Several things are worth noting about these numbers. The first is that they are much lower than for the 'classical' period, covered by Fetter. Fetter had 62 economist-MPs in an 88-year period; we have 25 in a 72-year period. If we subtract those who retired before 1868, the end of Fetter's period, the contrast is even stronger: it becomes 17 economist-MPs in a 52-year period. Thus Figure 5.2 shows a decline in the number of economists in Parliament from around 6 to 8 in the period up to 1886, to only one in the period 1896 to 1909 (Bartley up to 1906, and Snowden thereafter). There was then a slight rise to 1918 but the total was never more than three. Of these, with the exception of John Stuart Mill and Richard Cobden, who belong very much to the classical era, few are major figures. The only ones to appear in standard histories of economics are John Bright (as an associate of Cobden's during his youth), James Thorold Rogers (arguably a historian as much as an economist), and William Hewins (important in the early history of the LSE and in the controversy over tariff reform). Prominent theorists are, Mill apart, conspicuous by their absence.

The dominant political allegiance of economists is clear: the list includes 13 Whigs and Liberals as well as three Radicals to only 6 Conservatives and Liberal-Unionists. They represented constituencies from many parts of Britain.[18] The Appendix also provides limited information on these economist-MPs' backgrounds.[19]

The first category is those who entered Parliament before 1848, plus John Stuart Mill who, though he entered Parliament later, was very much a contemporary

15 Including these would slightly alter the statistics. However, excluding these MPs is justified in that, unlike the situation before 1848, they were clearly differentiated from those known as economists. Again readers who are not convinced should allow for this when interpreting the figures on numbers of economist MPs.

16 Where people were MPs for discontinuous periods, they are listed twice. Service as an MP is shown as continuous even where someone changed constituencies (details are given in the Appendix).

17 This graph does not take account of when someone entered or left Parliament during the year. If an economist retired in a particular year, and another economist was elected, it would show as two MPs for that year, even though there was never more than one at any time. This explains some of the spikes in the graph.

18 It is tempting to say 'all parts' but there is none from Wales.

19 Father's occupation is included as a conventional indicator of social class. The column labelled 'Economics' indicates the broad fields on which they wrote, and in some cases their claim to be considered an economist.

Figure 5.1 Economists in Parliament (1848-1920)

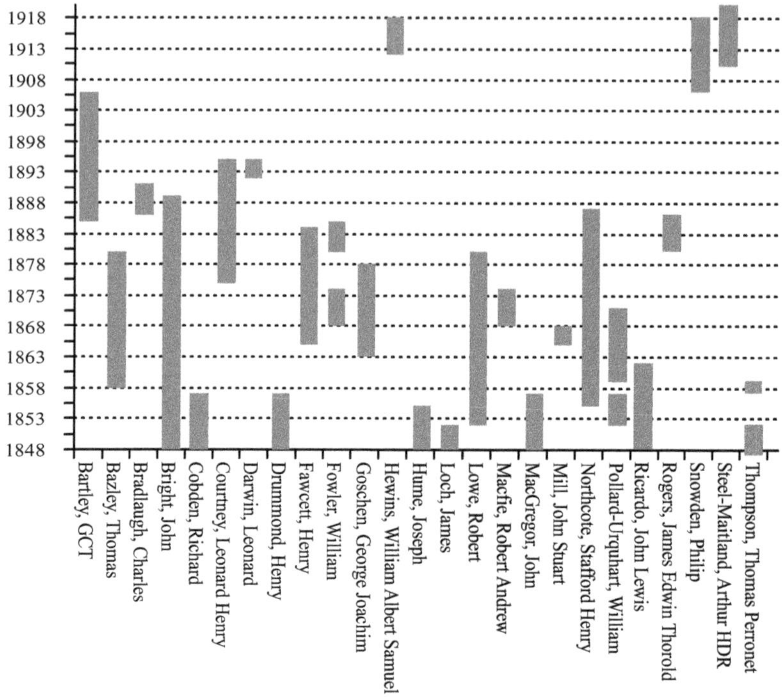

Source: Rutherford (2004).

Figure 5.2 Number of economists in Parliament (1848-1920)

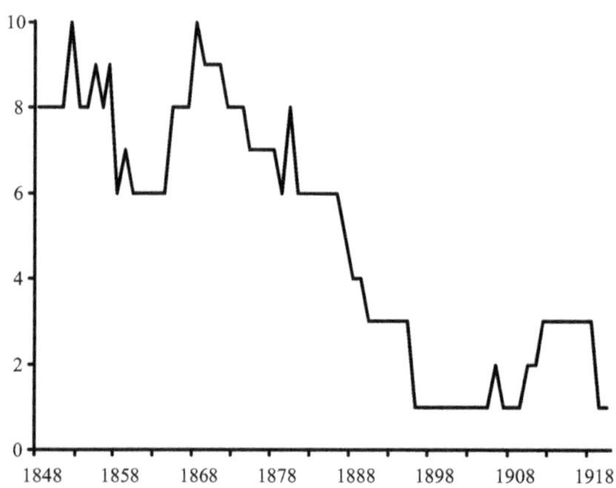

Source: Rutherford (2004).

of this group. These belong to the age of classical economics, documented by Fetter. Apart from Perronet Thompson and Joseph Hume, they had no higher education. Henry Drummond, who later founded the Drummond chair of political economy, spent two years at Oxford but did not take a degree. Their backgrounds and their extra-parliamentary careers were varied. Two came into Parliament via the army. They were generally Radicals, and were uniformly free traders.[20] Most of their economic writings were on free trade and currency, the burning political issues of these years of the Anti Corn Law League, of which Cobden and Bright were the most renowned spokesmen. The Corn Laws did not just raise the price of bread: they were seen as legislation that benefited a privileged minority, one of the hallmarks of the old corruption. The case against the Corn Laws was moral and even religious as much as economic.[21] In Cobden's hands, free trade became a crusade for peace, offering an alternative to the traditional 'great power' diplomacy personified by Palmerston. Bright was the only one to become a government minister, though Richard Cobden had responsibility for the negotiations that led to the Cobden-Chevalier Treaty (negotiated with his friend and fellow-economist, Michel Chevalier) establishing free trade between Britain and France in 1860.[22] On his death he was venerated as a national statesman, on a level with Peel. The defence of free trade came to be known as 'Cobdenism'. Though his parliamentary career lasted longer, Henry Fawcett also falls into this category of classical-economic radicalism, where radicalism included parliamentary reform and free trade.

We then have the twelve economists (plus Mill and Fawcett) who entered Parliament during the five decades from 1850 to 1900. Of this group, all eight had a university education, though the most commonly studied subjects were mathematics, followed by classics (economics not being available at that time). They were overwhelmingly Liberals, the exceptions being Stafford Northcote and George Bartley; Leonard Darwin (son of Charles) was a Liberal-Unionist. Of those whose fathers' occupations are known, five were professionals (clergy, writers, civil servants and journalists), four were from industry and finance, and one was son of a Baronet.[23] In contrast with the classical period, three of those in parliament during this period were professors (Fawcett, Courtney and Thorold Rogers) and another (Lowe) briefly followed an academic path before turning to the law and then to journalism.[24] Lowe had previously served in the Australian legislature

20 Other radical causes included electoral reform and religious toleration.

21 See Howe (1997).

22 The Treaty contained a critical most-favoured nation clause. After 1860, France entered into a series of further treaties with other European countries, and due to this clause, these countries had to reduce their tariffs on British goods. Britain could therefore have unilateral free trade as well as benefiting from bilateral bargaining over tariffs.

23 A minor position in the aristocracy. It is not an occupation but indicates social status.

24 Courtney is also notable for having written over three *thousand* newspaper articles between 1865 and 1881, when he was the leader writer for *The Times*.

(1843-1850). Almost half were academics or writers, with no significant business interests. Only three had active business interests.

The main interests within economics were free trade, land reform (important in India and Ireland, where it was indissolubly linked to the problem of poverty) and currency were still the main economic interests of this group. William Pollard-Urquhart and Courtney recognised that free trade implied the need for alternative sources of tax revenue, and investigated direct taxation. Robert Macfie applied free trade to inventions, arguing that patents and authors' copyright, which gave them monopoly privileges, should be limited. Writings on currency moved on from the issues dominant in the middle of the century to cover bimetallism, Leonard Courtney (an admirer of William Jennings Bryan's views on silver) and Leonard Darwin supporting it, and Robert Macfie opposing it. Thorold Rogers was, of course, well known as a historian and for his work with Henry Newmarch on the history of prices. Robert Lowe saw liberalism as involving much more than free trade, being the principle that no class should be subservient to another. He became renowned for claiming, on the centenary of the *Wealth of Nations*, that the great work of political economy had been done,[25] and he was fiercely critical of John Kells Ingram's Comteist claim that economics should become part of the general science of sociology: sociology did not yet exist and economics should stand or fall according to the laws passed in its name.[26]

This group had a number of achievements outside Parliament to their credit. Thomas Bazley was the first large manufacturer to institute the practice, which became the norm, of paying wages on Fridays rather than Saturdays, as had previously been usual. Bradlaugh was responsible for changing the laws of evidence, so that those who refused to swear an oath on the bible could still give evidence in court. George Bartley founded the National Penny Bank to encourage small savers, an institution that by 1911 had attracted savings from 22 million depositors.

The final group of three economists entered Parliament during the last liberal government. Philip Snowden was the son of a weaver who came up through the Independent Labour Party and went on to a distinguished ministerial career in the interwar labour and coalition governments. His writings were on socialism, having something in common with Marx, but more strongly influenced by Fabian socialism. Arthur Steel-Maitland and William Hewins were Conservatives (once we enter the twentieth century, there were no longer any liberal economists in Parliament). Hewins, an economic historian, was a supporter of protection and became secretary of Joseph Chamberlain's Tariff Commission, and in addition to holding a chair at King's College London, was founding director of the London School of Economics.

---

25 See Hutchison (1953), p. 3.
26 See Rutherford (2004), p. 698; Hutchison (1953), pp. 1-5.

Economists' activities in Parliament

The British political system is such that achievements in Parliament are hard to distinguish from politicians' activities as government ministers. A successful parliamentary career is generally, though by no means always, associated with rising to ministerial office – ideally to the Cabinet or to be Prime Minister, from which position more can be achieved than can be achieved from the back benches.[27] In seeking economists' influence in Parliament it is, therefore, appropriate to cover not just their activity as private members, but also their careers as ministers. Those who held government office included Bright, Lowe, Northcote, Fawcett, Goschen, Courtney, Snowden and Steel-Maitland.

Bright's reputation had been established outside Parliament but after the repeal of the Corn Laws he continued to advocate radical causes in Parliament. On the main political issue, Ireland, Bright took the position that the causes rather than the consequences of unrest should be tackled, proposing various measures of land reform and religious equality (disestablishment of the Irish Church). He was among the small minority who opposed George Grey's Bill introducing the poorly-defined offence of sedition. In 1849, a speech on land reform established his reputation as a parliamentary orator, receiving applause from both parties and being praised by Disraeli.[28] He continued to work on Ireland but did not abandon other radical causes. He continued to press for free trade, agitating against suggestions that Lord Derby's government might reintroduce protection. When Cobden was in Paris negotiating with Chevalier, Bright was his voice in Parliament. He argued for religious equality and together with Cobden he sought financial and electoral reform. Through investigating a proposal to encourage the supply of cotton from India, he discovered maladminstration in the East India Company and he argued against the renewal of its charter. India should be governed by a government department and a series of reforms implemented. His popularity (and Cobden's) plummeted when they criticised Palmerston for declaring war on Russia in 1854. He was even burnt in effigy. In the late 1850s, Bright was amongst those agitating for further extension of the franchise and when he realised that the House of Lords was going to be a persistent barrier to reform, he denounced 'the modern peerage, bred in the slime and corruption of the rotten borough system'.[29] During the American Civil War, Bright was instrumental in helping defeat a proposal to recognise the Confederacy (favoured by many as free traders and the source of the cotton that British spinners, including Bright himself, needed). During this period he drew apart from Cobden who did not share his passion for electoral reform.

27 The 'front benches' cover government ministers on one side, and their opposition counterparts who hold no formal office (though the Leader of the Opposition has become a salaried position). The back benchers are thus those who are not the official spokesmen for the main parties.

28 This is drawn from a DNB article by someone identified only as I. S. L.

29 Quoted in DNB entry.

When Lowe and other Whigs opposed Gladstone's electoral Reform Bill in 1866, it was Bright who described them as refugees going into the cave of Adullam.

Bright achieved influence outside government, with Cobden, through his opposition to the Corn Laws and their support for free trade. He did not achieve government office until Gladstone's first government, when he became President of the Board of Trade. As a Quaker, he was one of the first nonconformists to sit in the Cabinet. In 1871 he opposed his own government's Education Act, on the grounds that it encouraged denominationalism. In Gladstone's second administration he was Chancellor of the Duchy of Lancaster but in 1886 he was offered no position, having become disillusioned with Gladstone. When the Liberal-Unionists split, Bright joined them, in loyalty to his fellow Birmingham MP and radical, Joseph Chamberlain.

Whereas Bright stood squarely in the radical section of what became the Liberal Party, Lowe came from the Whig side. On entering Parliament he was actively involved in debates in the House and quickly achieved office, under Palmerston as President of the Board of Trade and Paymaster General (1855-1858). His liberalism found expression in his putting through the Joint Stock Companies Act (1856), ending a situation where the only way to form a company, without a special Act of Parliament, was through a small partnership with unlimited liability. He moved on to be Vice President of the Board of Education (1859-1864) where he sought to link school grants to children's performance in arithmetic, reading and writing (a measure in the spirit of Adam Smith's attitude towards education). He then became one of the Adullamites, opposing extension of the franchise, but returned to office under Gladstone (1868-1873) as Chancellor of the Exchequer. His budgets cut taxes substantially. In 1871 he failed to implement Jevons' idea of a tax on matches. He then became Home Secretary for a year, the last office he held. On retirement from the Commons, he went to the House of Lords.[30]

Amongst those who never held office, the MPs who most clearly ranked alongside those who did were Cobden and Mill, both radicals and close associates of Bright. In the debates over parliamentary reform that led, tortuously, to the 1867 Reform Act, Mill was considered the leading radical alongside Bright, arguing vigorously for female suffrage. In the public mind, Mill was associated above all with votes for women, cartoons in *Punch* showing him as holding the cup of logic in his hand; Bright was shown sometimes as a bear chained to Mill, and as a boxer fighting the aristocracy, supported by Mill, cup of logic in hand. The second of these is reproduced as Figure 5.3.

Fawcett was a friend and close colleague of Mill and shared his radical commitment. He went so far as to criticise Gladstone's first government, of which he was officially a supporter, for its failure to carry through its programme. The 1871 Education Act, for example fell short of the goal of universal compulsory education. He developed interests in preserving common land in the face of attempts to

30 The article in Rutherford (2004) on which this paragraph is based is by John Maloney.

bring in enclosure legislation and in the problems of India. In opposition he became reconciled to his party and in 1880 accepted the post of Postmaster General. Like his radical colleagues, he argued against several military and imperial ventures.[31]

Figure 5.3 Parliamentary Gladiators: Salisbury, Disraeli, Lowe, Bright and Mill

Source: *Punch* 2 February 1867; Mill offering the cup of logic to Bright; Lowe tending the suit of armour; Disraeli sharpening the sword, assisted by Salisbury.

Northcote had been Private Secretary to Gladstone (then a Tory) in the early 1840s and under Gladstone's influence became committed to free trade, despite remaining a conservative. He first achieved office as Secretary of State for India (1867-8) the main economic measure he introduced being financial decentralisation. In Disraeli's first majority administration, he became Chancellor of the Exchequer, where he sought to reduce the National Debt by setting up a sinking fund of £28 million to cover interest payments. He tried to reduce taxes and to balance the budget, but failed in the latter aim, for deficits continued to rise. In the 1880s, when the 'fair trade' movement began, Northcote opposed it. In 1885, at the age of

31 This draws mostly on the DNB article by 'L. S.' (perhaps Leslie Stephen).

67, he became First Lord of the Treasury,[32] and a year later Foreign Secretary, but had agreed to resign by the time of his death in 1887.[33]

Goschen espoused several radical causes, such as the secret ballot, abolition of tithes (taxes for the church), disestablishment of the Irish church, and opposing the religious test to get into Oxford and Cambridge. However, he opposed the foreign policy ideas of Cobden and Bright, favouring a tougher approach. He became Vice President of the Board of Trade under Lord Russell (1865-6) and joined the Cabinet in 1866 as Chancellor of the Duchy of Lancaster. He was active in debates over parliamentary reform. In Gladstone's administration he was President of the Poor Law Board (1868-1871) and then First Lord of the Admiralty. Later in his career he became involved in foreign affairs. Disraeli appointed him (he was not a conservative, but party lines were much less rigid than they have since become) to report on Egypt's financial situation in 1876, and helped renegotiate Anglo-French control over Egypt's finances. He later spent time in Constantinople, helping enforce the provisions of the Treaty of Berlin concerning the frontiers of Greece and Montenegro.

Leonard Courtney served in Gladstone's second government as Under-Secretary of State for the Home Office (1880-1881), and the Colonial Office (1881-1882). He was Financial Secretary to the Treasury from 1882-1884, but resigned from that position in order to oppose the government's extension of the franchise. After Gladstone's conversion to Home Rule, Courtney joined the Liberal-Unionists, claiming Ireland was unfit to govern itself. Over the remaining years of his parliamentary career, Courtney opposed the government's imperialistic ventures in Africa, from Egypt to South Africa and was a leading 'pro-Boer' MP. After his defeat in 1906, he went to the Lords, where he spoke against rearmament, and blamed the First World War on diplomatic failures.

Of those who failed to achieve ministerial office during this period, various causes were supported. Robert Macfie agitated for free trade in inventions, and an alternative to patents (which created monopolies) as a way of supporting inventors. He was, however, conservative in his support of the empire. Thorold Rogers, who had worked with Cobden and Bright in the 1860s, made few contributions to debates, though was responsible for a resolution that local property taxes be divided between owner and occupier. He helped the passage of the Civil Disabilities Relief Act (1870), taking advantage of it by being the first to resign from Holy Orders.

Snowden, though he entered Parliament in 1906, provides a bridge to the subsequent era. A working man, invalided out of the Civil Service through a cycling

---

32 First Lord of the Treasury is the title usually held by the Prime Minister. However, as the Prime Minister, Lord Salisbury, was in the Lords, the titles were split. The rationale for this was that the Commons were responsible for financial matters. Salisbury was also Foreign Secretary.

33 The article from Rutherford (2004) from which this paragraph, and the ones on Goschen and Courtney are taken are all by Marjorie Bloy.

accident, he became interested in socialism and joined the Independent Labour Party in 1894, becoming its national Chairman from 1903-1906. During his back-bench parliamentary career, from 1906-1918 (liberal and then coalition governments) he was an effective speaker (once a means had been worked out for him to catch the attention of the Speaker, a task made difficult by his physical disability). He established a reputation on the questions of drink and the national finances, and was reputed to have influenced David Lloyd George's radical budget of 1909. He consistently opposed the First World War, working to support conscientious objectors and to associate the ILP with opposition to the war. He achieved office in the labour governments of 1924 and 1929-1931 as Chancellor of the Exchequer. Though outside Parliament he had sought to make socialism 'a gospel of love not hate',[34] in Parliament he held a comparatively traditional position, based on the nineteenth-century liberal notions of sound money, balanced budgets and free trade.[35]

The remaining two economists to enter Parliament before 1920 were Steel-Maitland and Hewins. Steel-Maitland had previously been secretary to Austen Chamberlin when he was Chancellor of the Exchequer, and he entered government during WW1, from 1915-1919 holding a series of junior posts as Parliamentary Under-Secretary in the Colonial Office and then the Foreign Office, and Parliamentary Secretary to the Board of Trade, where he was head of the Department of Overseas Trade. His achieved cabinet rank as minister of labour under Balfour (1924-1929). In Parliament, Hewins spoke 'frequently and passionately' about tariff reform, and was rewarded with the post of Under Secretary of State for the Colonies, from 1917-1918.

The careers of these economists are very much reflections of the liberal era in British politics. Party loyalties were loose, and even where there was no split, it was not uncommon for MPs to take positions at variance with those of their parties. MPs might have to resign from government to oppose government policy but their career was not thereby ended. There were important differences between parties, but MPs were part of a common social setting (it is with some justification that the House of Commons has been described as the best gentleman's club in London). It would be going too far to claim that these economists were successful because of their economic expertise, but there was an element of that. Of the non-academics, Lowe mixed with economists and was appointed to the Board of Trade because of his knowledge of economic questions. However, these men advanced as much because of their political skills and their administrative abilities as for any technical economic knowledge.[36] This outline of their careers makes the point that

34 DNB entry on Snowden.

35 This paragraph is based on the DNB entry by R.C.K. Ensor and the article in Rutherford (2004) by Noel Thompson. The latter contains a useful short discussion of Snowden's success or failure as Chancellor (which lies outside the scope of this paper).

36 The same was largely true of the Civil Servants. There may have been distinguished economists working in the Civil Service (for example, James and John Stuart Mill, and John Maynard Keynes) and later on may have had to pass examinations in economics

this group of economists, even though they include three Chancellors of the Exchequer, did not base their careers on economics alone. Those who perhaps came closest, Lowe and Northcote, are those who are closest to the classical era. Even Mill was known primarily as a supporter of votes for women and as the intellectual amongst the Radicals (as in Figure 5.3). Though academic economics was becoming more professional, no formal training was required to acquire a reputation as an economist (opportunities to obtain such training were limited). For most of the questions where economics issues were involved, the problems were practical rather than theoretical, combining the economics with the political, and the type of knowledge represented by John Stuart Mill's *Principles* was sufficient. Economists blended into the educated elite and came to exert an influence on areas that had nothing to do with economics.

Conclusions

The period from the repeal of the Corn Laws to WW1 saw the extension of the franchise and many of the features associated with the liberal era in European history. Britain became more democratic and the State became increasingly involved in economic life. However, the period when economists played their major role in Parliament, introducing liberal economic ideas (notably free trade) came earlier, in the less democratic age when patronage and the political power of the old landed aristocracy were still very strong. It has been argued that this made it easier for professionals to enter Parliament, for they could find a patron to put them there, or buy a seat with their own wealth. This meant that, paradoxically, parliamentary reform made it harder for professional men to become MPs. However, there is little evidence that this explains the fall in the number of economists in Parliament in the second half of the century. Ricardo was notorious for having purchased his seat, but most of the classical economists in Parliament did not enter this way.

In the first half of the century, 'free trade' was a popular cause, associated with the radical fight against monopoly and the 'old corruption'. Economists such as Ricardo and Mill associated free trade with growth. However, this was not the only case for free trade. Another view, widely held amongst liberal Tories, was that free trade meant getting rid of the artificial props that got in the way of God's providential order. The case for *laissez-faire* was moral as much as economic. From this perspective, free trade led not to growth but to stability and morality; evangelical

(as was Keynes) but they were not employed specifically as economists. A Chief Economic Adviser to the Government was established after 1918 but he played a minor role. The provision of economic advice to the government was largely informal, as was possible in a society where the ruling elite formed part of a single social group. Though its antecedents can be traced to the Economic Advisory Council in the 1930s and the Second-World-War Economic Section of the Treasury, The Government Economic Service was not established till the 1960s. See Coats (1993), p. 520.

religion was more important than secular political economy.[37] From the 1950s this evangelical case for *laissez-faire* began to be displaced by the secular one emphasising growth. At the same time, there was an expansion of State activity: working conditions were regulated; measures were taken to improve urban living conditions and the provision of basic education. However, in the public mind, supported by politicians such as Lowe and Gladstone, whose economic outlook was still in the classical mould, economics was associated with *laissez-faire*. Economists (Walter Bagehot, William Stanley Jevons, Arnold Toynbee and Henry Sidgwick and even John Elliot Cairnes) were seeking to distance themselves from this position whilst avoiding any association with socialism.[38] The environment in which economists could prosper in Parliament as they had done earlier in the century no longer existed.

The answer might also lie on the supply side. The major universities, Oxford and Cambridge, the ones likely to train those who were going to advance furthest in British society, were not turning out large numbers of economists. One has only to think of Alfred Marshall's complaints about how few and how poor were the men who were coming to him through the moral sciences tripos, the only way one could study economics at Cambridge before 1903. The situation at Oxford was not much more likely to train high-flying economists, though it is noteworthy that two of the economist MPs during this period were eminent economists from Oxford: Thorold Rogers and Hewins. With the establishment of the London School of Economics (1895) and the Cambridge economics tripos (1903) the situation began to change, but by the time the effects were felt, the liberal age, as defined here, was ending.

It is also correct to argue that there were ample opportunities for economists to enter into public debate without entering Parliament.[39] Recall Marshall's involvement with to the royal commissions on the aged poor, on depression of trade, on gold and silver, on labour, and on local government finance; or the work of Beatrice and Sidney Webb and their contemporaries. These opportunities were, of course there before 1848.[40] However, in an age when the scientific status of economics was under strong criticism on account of its association with dogmatic *laissez-faire*, and economists such as Marshall were struggling to re-establish its scientific credentials by avoiding unnecessary controversy, this route of offering carefully considered 'scientific' advice may have been much more attractive than becoming involved in Parliament. The centrality of economic questions, on which passions ran high, to the politics of this period – the only other issue of comparable importance was Ireland, and that had a major economic dimension – may have been another reason why it would have been hard to be a professional economist in Parliament.

---

37 Howe (1997), pp. 8-9. See Hilton (1988).
38 See Hutchison (1953), pp. 8-12.
39 Fetter (1980), p. 7.
40 E.g. Senior, Chadwick and McCulloch.

Another possibility is that economists' involvement in Parliament declined because of the changes that took place in the nature of economic theory. Economics clearly did change very significantly in the second half of the nineteenth century. Whether or not one accepts the idea of a 'marginal revolution' around 1870, with all that the word revolution implies, there was increased emphasis on individual behaviour and, though only a minority of economists engaged in it until perhaps the 1950s, mathematical modelling of that behaviour. This has led Fetter to conclude that the reason why economists no longer chose Parliament as the means to make their voice heard was that they were increasingly 'discussing what private business, administrative bodies of the Bank of England should do, not what Parliament should do or stop doing'.[41] By the end of the classical period, he argues, the broad objectives of the classical economists had been achieved.

However, this is hardly a satisfactory explanation. There is a strong sense in which those economists who served in Parliament represented the old, pre-professional approach to economics, reminiscent of the classical era, in contrast with the newer ways of doing economics in the universities (think of Marshall or Francis Edgeworth, as extreme examples). Lowe's remark about the great work of political economy having been done came after observing that contemporary controversies in the subject 'although they offer a capital exercise for the logical faculties, are not of the same thrilling importance as those of earlier days'.[42] A gulf was opening up between academic economists and those working in business and government.[43] However, the role of the State was increasing, and it is arguable that more formal economics was required to take policy advice beyond what someone trained in Mill's *Principles* alone could provide. The tariff and tax reform were keenly debated issues throughout the period. Designing a tax system and even setting tax rates were both tasks undertaken in the House of Commons.[44] Regulation of industry was increasing; the State was becoming more involved in education, labour and in many other areas in which modern economics might have had something to contribute. Bimetallism was an issue that called for technical expertise. Indeed, the fact that royal commissions regularly called upon economist witnesses suggests that their views were sought.

Perhaps what needs to be explained is not the decline of economists in Parliament during the liberal era (after 1848) but the unusual circumstances that led to the profusion of economist-MPs during the period of classical economics. Adam Smith's work, as interpreted by the classical economists, chimed with political and religious arguments for free trade and *laissez-faire*. The Philosophic Radicals,

41 Ibid.

42 Hutchison (1953), p. 3.

43 As evidence that this was happening by 1885, Hutchison (1953, p. 2) quotes a remark by Henry Sidgwick on how bankers knew no political economy – 'they [the bankers at the Political Economy Club] read Mill some time ago, and look at him from time to time on Sundays.'

44 Deliberately put this way because the convention was that the Lords did not reject money bills.

inspired by Jeremy Bentham, were making the case for rational reform to make government more efficient. There were strong interests favouring radical, reforming positions for which classical economics could provide a rationale. As the liberal era progressed, these exceptional circumstances disappeared.

References

Cain, P.J. and Hopkins, A.G. (1993), *British Imperialism*, 2 vols, Longman, London.

Coats, A.W. Bob (1993), 'Britain: the Rise of the Specialists', in A.W.B. Coats, *The Sociology and Professionalization of Economics: British and American Economic Essays*, **2**, Routledge, London.

Dictionary of National Biography (1997), CD-ROM edition, Oxford University Press, Oxford.

Fetter, F.W. (1980), *The Economist in Parliament, 1780-1868*, Duke University Press, Durham, NC.

Harris, J. (1972), *Unemployment and Politics, 1886-1914*, Oxford University Press, Oxford.

Hilton, B. (1988), *The Age of Atonement: the Influence of Evangelicalism on Social and Economic Thought, 1795-1865*, Clarendon Press, Oxford.

Hobson, J.A. (1992[1896]), *The Problem of the Unemployed*, Routledge and Thoemmes Press, London and Bristol.

Howe, A. (1997), *Free Trade and Liberal England, 1846-1946*, Clarendon Press, Oxford.

Hutchison, T.W. (1953), *A Review of Economic Doctrines, 1870-1929*, Clarendon Press, Oxford.

Perkin, H. (2002), *The Rise of Professional Society*, second edition, Routledge, London.

Rubinstein, W.D. (1987), *Elites and the Wealthy in Modern British History: Essays in Social and Economic History*, Harvester Press, Brighton.

Rubinstein, W.D. (1998), *Britain's Century: A Political and Social History 1815-1905*, Arnold, London.

Rutherford, D. (2004) (ed.), *Biographical Dictionary of British Economists*, Thoemmes Continuum, Bristol.

Smith, A. (1976[1776]), *An Inquiry into the Nature and Causes of the Wealth of Nations*, Clarendon Press, Oxford.

Thomas, J.A. (1939), *The House of Commons, 1832-1901*, University of Wales Press Board, Cardiff.

Appendix

Table 5.5 Economists' Parliamentary careers and backgrounds*

Name and life	MP	Party	Constituency	Father's occupation	Higher education	Career/ Interests	Economics	Other comments
Hume, Joseph 1777-1855	1818-1830 1837-1837; 1837-1841; 1841-1855	Radical	Aberdeen; Middlesex; Kilkenny; Montrose	Ship-master	Aberdeen (Medicine)	Surgeon and Army administrator	Labour; currency; savings	Method for drying gunpowder; leader of Radical party
Loch, James 1780-1855	1827-1830; 1830-1852	Whig	St Germains; Wick	Lawyer	Unknown	Lawyer and Estate Manager	Scottish trade and industry	
Thompson, Thomas Perronet 1783-1869	1835-1837; 1847-1852; 1857-1859	Radical	Hull, Bradford	Merchant and Banker	Cambr. (Maths)	Army, Journalist and Newspaper proprietor	Rent, Corn Laws, Currency	Philosophic radical
Cobden, Richard 1804-1865	1841-1857	Radical	Stockport; West Riding	Small farmer	–	Cotton	Free trade	Anti Corn Law League; Cobden-Chevalier Treaty
Ricardo, John Lewis 1812-1862	1841-1862	Liberal	Stoke on Trent	Financier	Unknown	Finance, Railways, Telegraphs	Opponent of intellectual property	Free trade; abolition of State tolls on Elbe
Bright, John 1811-1889	1843-; 1847-1857; 1857-1889	Radical /Liberal	Durham, Manchester, Birmingham	Book-keeper	–	Cotton	Free trade	Anti Corn Law League; Ministerial career (see text)
MacGregor, John 1797-1857	1845-?1853	Whig	Glasgow		–	Historian and statistician	Commercial statistics; Britain and American legislation	Free trade

Name and life	MP	Party	Constituency	Father's occupation	Higher education	Career/ Interests	Economics	Other comments
Drummond, Henry 1786-1860	1847-1857	Cons.	West Surrey	Banker	Oxford (no degree)	Banker	Currency; Corn Laws	Active in debates on Divorce Bill (1857); Religious enthusiast; Founded Drummond Chair, Oxford
Pollard-Urquhart, William 1815-1871	1852-1857; 1859-1871	Liberal	Westmeath		Cambr. (Maths)	Writer	Agricultural distress; taxation; land credit; currency	Advocacy of direct taxation
Lowe, Robert 1811-1892	1852-1880	Liberal	Kidderminster	Clergyman	Oxford (Classics and Maths)	Academic, Lawyer, Journalist	Anti-relativist; economics as complete	Ministerial career
Northcote, Stafford Henry 1811-1887	1855-1858; 1858-1866; 1866-1887?	Cons.	Derby; Stamford; North Devon	Baronet	Oxford (Maths and classics)	Lawyer, Civil Servant	History of Navigation Laws; finance	Secretary to the Great Exhibition (1851) Ministerial career
Bazley, Thomas 1797-1885	1858-1880	Liberal	Manchester	Cotton manufacturer then journalist	–	Cotton	Cotton industry; education; free trade	Payment of wages on Fridays (not Saturdays)
Goschen, George Joachim 1831-1907	1863-1878	Liberal	City of London	Merchant	Oxford (Classics)	Merchant and Director of Bank of England	Currency and international finance	Ministerial career
Fawcett, Henry 1833-1884	1865-1874; 1874-1884	Liberal	Brighton; Hackney	Draper	Cambr. (Maths)	Academic; Professor, Cambridge (1863-84)	Textbook; labour; poverty; Indian finance	Reform Bill (1867); religious tests; factory acts to agricultural labourers
Mill, John Stuart 1806-1873	1865-1868	Radical	Westminster	Journalist and Civil Servant	–	Civil Servant	Too well known to require listing	Franchise for women; Philosophic radical

Name and life	MP	Party	Constituency	Father's occupation	Higher education	Career/ Interests	Economics	Other comments
Macfie, Robert Andrew 1811-1893	1868-1874		Leith Burghs	Sugar refiner	Edinburgh	Sugar refiner	Free trade in inventions – limitation of patents and authors' copyright; empire and trade	Free trade in inventions
Fowler, William 1828-1905	1868-1874; 1880-1885	Liberal	Cambridge		University College London (Classics and Maths)	Lawyer and businessman	Land reform; currency and finance (against bimetallism); crisis of 1866	
Courtney, Leonard Henry 1832-1918	1875-1885	Liberal	Liskeard	Banker	Cambr. (Maths)	Journalist and Academic Professor, UCL (1872-5)	Bimetallism	Front bencher; Resigned over failure to get proportional representation; anti Boer War; argued for peace in WWI
Rogers, James Edwin Thorold 1823-1890	1880-1885; 1885-1886	Liberal	Southwark; Bermondsey		Oxford (lit hum)	Academic, Professor, Kings College London (1859-90)	History of prices; economic history	Clerical Disabilities Relief Act
Bradlaugh, Charles 1833-1891	1880(6)-1891**	Radical	Northampton	Clerk to Solicitor	–	Journalist and Newspaper Proprietor	Land reform; inheritance; wage deregulation	Freethinker; responsible for change in laws of evidence
Bartley, George C.T. 1842-1910	1885-1906	Cons.	North Islington	Civil Servant	–	Education (examiner)	Education; poverty; savings	National Penny Bank (1875); voted against free education bill 1891

Name and life	MP	Party	Constituency	Father's occupation	Higher education	Career/ Interests	Economics	Other comments
Darwin, Leonard 1850-1943	1892-1895	Liberal-Unionist	Lichfield	Naturalist	Royal Military Academy at Woolwich	Army	Bimetallism; municipal trade (public choice); Eugenics	President of Royal Geographical Society; President of Eugenics Society
Snowden, Philip 1864-1937	1906-1918; 1922-	Labour	Blackburn	Weaver	–	Junior civil service clerk; ILP activist	Evolutionary view of socialism	Ministerial career
Steel-Maitland, Arthur H.D.R. 1876-1935	1910-1929; 1929-1935	Cons.	Birmingham; Tamworth	Army	Oxford (Classics)	Politician	Poverty and US policy (New Deal)	Ministerial career
Hewins, William Albert Samuel 1865-1931	1912-1918	Cons.	Hereford City	Merchant	Oxford (Maths)	Academic; Professor, Kings College London (1897-1903)	Economic history	Secretary of Tariff Commission; Director of LSE (1895-1903)

Notes:

* Sorted by date of first entering Parliament.

** Bradlaugh was an atheist who refused to swear an oath and sought the right to affirm. He was elected in 1880 and in repeated elections over the next few years, but could not take his seat till 1886.

Chapter 6

French Economists in Parliament from the Second Republic to the Outbreak of the Great Crisis (1848-1929)

Yves Breton

Introduction

The French economists examined in this chapter include only those Members of Parliament who published on the subject of economics. Based on this selection criterion, a list of forty-one figures has been drawn up, covering the period under consideration. While names of certain members of parliament who were not professional economists do appear on the list, for example the chartered engineer and mathematician Charles Dupin, the historian Adolphe Thiers and the philosopher Jules Simon, these remain exceptions. The overwhelming majority of the forty-one figures were professional economists. Their date of birth and death are cited in parentheses together with the first citation of their name, in order to highlight this information. The period examined begins on 25 February 1848, the date of the proclamation of the Second Republic, and terminates on 27 July 1929, the day of the resignation of Raymond Poincaré from his position as head of the government, an office he had held for three years.

The aim of this chapter is to outline the main economic and social debates that took place within the political institutions of the period in question, as well as the positions adopted by the economists and the role they played. But an analysis of their individual contributions to parliamentary discussion without regard for the overall economic, political and intellectual framework would be meaningless. It is therefore imperative first to present the economic and political background, followed by essential information concerning the diffusion of political economy and the social and professional characteristics of the economists investigated here. These different aspects are addressed in the context of the three significant moments of the period: the Second Republic (25 February 1848-1 December 1852), the Second Empire (2 December 1852-3 September 1870) and the first sixty years of the Third Republic (4 September 1870-27 July 1929).

The Second Republic

On 22 February 1848 street demonstrations broke out in Paris. On the following day, king Louis-Philippe dismissed minister Guizot and summoned Adolphe Thiers (1797-1877) for consultations, to little avail. Despite the lack of positive results, on 24 February, with riots still raging in the capital, a provisional government was set up at the Hôtel de Ville. The Second Republic was proclaimed the very next day.

The opening months of the Second Republic: 25 February to 9 December 1848

Bowing to pressure from the workers, the provisional government set up a Government Commission for the Working Classes, better known as the Luxemburg Commission (28 February 1848). The Commission recognised universal suffrage (2 March), freedom of the press and of association, as well as the principle of the abolition of slavery in the French colonies (4 March). In order to address the banking and monetary crisis, discount banks (7 March) and 100 franc banknotes were created, and the forced circulation of banknotes was established (15 March). 'Socialist' economists were widely represented in the provisional government. Louis Blanc (1811-1882),[1] a member of the provisional government, presided over the Luxemburg Commission, which also included the socialist economists Victor Considérant (1808-1893), Constantin Pecqueur (1801-1887) and François Vidal (1812-1872). Liberal economists, on the other hand, did not enjoy such a favourable position. Louis Wolowski (1810-1876) was very isolated in the anti-socialist struggle he was spearheading within the Commission. Michel Chevalier (1806-1879) was excluded from the Council of State. The Chair of Political Economy at the Collège de France which he had held since 1840 was suppressed by Hippolyte Carnot, the minister of education (7 April).

Six liberal economists were elected[2] to the Constituent Assembly (23 April 1848).[3] Bastiat was very active within his Finance Committee and Félix de Parieu was the *rapporteur* entrusted with reporting on several parliamentary commissions. Three socialist economists were elected,[4] to whom should be added a member of the moderate Left: Jules Simon (1814-1896). Charles Dupin (1784-1873) was the

1 His work *L'Organisation du travail* published in 1839 was reprinted in several editions before the 1848 Revolution.

2 F. Bastiat (1801-1850), L. Faucher (1803-1854), F. de Parieu (1815-1893), L. Reybaud (1799-1879), P.H. Sainte-Beuve (1819-1855), L. Wolowski.

3 The Assembly numbered 500 Moderate Republicans, a minority of about 290 right wing members and 90 or so Republicans.

4 L. Blanc, the Fouriérist, V. Considérant and the 'Christian socialist' F. de Lamennais (1782-1854). They would later be joined by two socialist economists: P. Leroux (1797-1871), P.-J. Proudhon (1809-1865) and the conservative economist A. Thiers (1797-1877), all three of whom were elected in the by-elections of 4 June 1848. Thiers was the head of the Order Party which grouped together the moderate Republicans, Bonapartists, Orléanists and Legitimists.

only protectionist economist to be elected.[5] The Constituent Assembly elected an Executive Committee (10 May 1848) composed of moderate politicians, and this Assembly replaced the provisional government. Blanc thereby found himself relegated to a minor position, an effect which lay behind the occupation of the premises of the Constituent Assembly (15 May). The following day, the Luxemburg Commission was suppressed. The dissolution of the National Workshops (21 June) resulted in the Paris insurrection of 23 June, which continued for three days until it was harshly repressed by the troops of General Cavaignac. 'Through the Grace of God', Bastiat wrote at the beginning of July 1848, 'the cause of order and civilisation has carried the day'.

The Assembly then struck back at the press by re-establishing the fiscal stamp and deposit (Act of 11 July), and then at the clubs (Act of 28 July), accusing them of being tools manipulated by revolutionary propaganda. It authorised the government to take action against left-wing politicians (L. Blanc, Marc Caussidière, etc.) on the charge that they had been part of the 15 May demonstrations (Act of 26 August 1848). The chair of political economy of the Collège de France was restored (14 November 1848).[6]

The constitutional project stipulated that the President of the Republic was to be elected by universal suffrage for four years. He would not be immediately eligible to stand for re-election. Passed on 4 November 1848 by 793 votes against 30,[7] the Constitution was solemnly promulgated on 21 November 1848.

Economic and social questions

The provisional government recognised the right to work (Decree of 25 February 1848). National Workshops were set up. On 20 May, Count Falloux demanded their immediate dissolution, submitting a written report outlining his request drafted on behalf of the Labour Committee of the Constituent Assembly. A counter-attack was launched by Considérant, who suggested the creation of a committee to listen to a proclamation that he had drawn up together with Louis Blanc and which had been signed by Simon and another sixty or so representatives. Massively rejected, Considérant's proclamation underlined that 'the Assembly wishes to enshrine, by all possible and practical means, the right to live through work enjoyed by all men born into this world; that it seeks to develop, by subsidies and encouragements of all kinds, this great principle of association, destined to

---

5 See Dupin (1827). Obtaining admission to and graduating from the École Polytechnique as top of his class (1801-1803), Dupin rapidly acquired great scientific acclaim which earned him membership of the Academy of Sciences as early as 1818. He entered the Académie des Sciences Morales et Politiques in 1832, the year of the re-founding of this learned society.

6 The liberal economist Claude-Marie Raudot (1801-1879) was elected (26 November 1848).

7 The socialist parliamentary economists, including Proudhon, voted against the proposal. The other parliamentary economists voted in favour.

freely unite all interests, all rights'. The proposal to embody the right to work in the preamble of the constitution was likewise rejected (596 votes against 187). Numerous members of the Constituent Assembly had probably read the hostile articles against the right to work published by the liberal economists in the *Journal des débats*, the *Revue des deux mondes*[8] and also in their own review: the *Journal des économistes*, founded at the end of 1841.

Except for the ban on *marchandage* (Decree of 2 March 1848),[9] the labour legislation drawn up by Louis Blanc and his friends in the Luxemburg Commission was challenged. In the aftermath of a sharp clash between Leroux and the liberal parliamentary economists who were led by Faucher, the 2 March 1848 Decree limiting the working day to 10 hours (Paris) and 11 hours (Province) was repealed. The maximum duration of the working day was now set at 12 hours (Act of 9 September 1848).

In order to compensate for suppression of the *octroi* and of the salt tax (29 February 1848), the so-called '45 centimes' levy was introduced (16 March 1848).[10] The tax on drinks was restored (21 June) as soon as the conservative forces returned to power. In addition, these forces rejected the proposal to impose an income tax put forward by Proudhon when he addressed the finance committee of the Assembly (July 1848).[11] Thiers underlined the inexactness of the data contained in this project, pointing out that its application would result in economic ruin. On 27 July, he launched a further attack, which led to the Assembly's near unanimous adoption (with the exclusion of only two votes)[12] of the following agenda: 'Considering that the proposal by citizen Proudhon is an abhorrent attack on the principles of public morals, that it violates the right of property, that it encourages betrayal and treachery, that it takes advantage of the very worst passions; considering, moreover, that the speaker has slandered the February 1848 revolution, claiming to turn it into an accomplice of the theories he has developed, it will be struck off the agenda'.

The establishment of the Second Republic: 10 December 1848 to 1 December 1851

General Cavaignac – elected to the head of the executive (28 June 1848) for services rendered during the Paris insurrection – Louis Napoléon Bonaparte and several others stood for the 10 December 1848 presidential elections. Bonaparte

8 Faucher published an article in the *Revue des deux mondes* (15 April 1848) arguing against the ideas of Blanc on the right to work and the social workshops. In this context one may also cite Chevalier who, between 21 March and 2 June 1848, published a series of thirteen letters in *Journal des débats*, dealing with the organisation of labour. The letters were subsequently gathered together in a book.

9 This term referred to a workforce recruited by intermediaries.

10 Direct taxation was increased by 45 per cent on each franc levied.

11 This required owners to agree grant a discount on tenancies and farm rents for three years.

12 Among which that of Proudhon.

was supported by Thiers and Faucher.[13] The other non socialist parliamentary economists supported Cavaignac. Immediately after his electoral victory, Bonaparte summoned former royalist 'notables' in order to set up his first Cabinet. Odilon Barrot assumed the presidency and Count Falloux was entrusted with the Ministry of State Education and Religious Worship. Bonaparte then called two liberal economists to be members of his government: Hippolyte Passy (1793-1880) and Faucher. The former was nominated finance minister by virtue of his financial background,[14] and held this office until 30 October 1849.[15] The latter was made head of the Interior Ministry, where he engaged in a policy of harsh repression. In May 1849 he was forced to resign for having posted in the various departments the names of the representatives who, on 7 May 1849, had demonstrated their opposition to Oudinot's first attack against republican Rome.

On 13 May 1849, the Constituent Assembly was replaced by a Legislative Assembly with more right-wing leanings, which was elected for three years, and in which the party in favour of order held a majority. The economists of the Constituent Assembly were re-elected, with the exception of Simon, who did not stand for election this time, and Blanc and Proudhon, who had gone into exile abroad. Considérant did enter the Assembly but held his seat for only a short period.[16] Félicité de Lamennais, Pierre Leroux and Martin Nadaud (1815-1898) were elected for the 'Montagne'.

Bonaparte's real concerns did not appear until after he had set up his second ministerial Cabinet (31 October 1849). One of his major aims was to regain control over the educational system. To this end, he enlisted the support of F. de Parieu, minister of State education and religious worship,[17] who prescribed the adoption of texts on primary and secondary education drawn up by Count Falloux.[18] The Primary Education Act (11 January 1850) granted prefects the possibility of dismissing instructors whose thoughts and beliefs were 'bad'. The vote on secondary education (15 March 1850) stirred considerable controversy among the body of State teachers, particularly as it placed university chancellors and departmental academic councils under the authority of the clergy and the bishops. The two Acts were voted by the non socialist parliamentary economists including Charles Dupin, while the members of parliament of the *Montagne* cast their votes against these Acts. Bonaparte's second major concern was to contain the opposition and above all the opposition of the *Montagne*, which was shown to have strong support on the occasion of the by-elections on 10 March 1850.[19] The former secretary of the

13 In the case of Thiers, for opportunistic reasons.

14 H. Passy was at the head of the Finance Ministry from 12 May 1839 to 1 March 1840.

15 He would later preside over the budget committee of the Legislative Assembly until the *coup d'état* of 2 December 1851.

16 Compelled to leave the country, he did not return to France until 1869.

17 A position he held until 24 June 1851.

18 This work was carried out between 20 October 1848 and 30 October 1849.

19 These were by-elections held to fill the 21 seats of the *Montagnards* who had been forced out (demonstration of 13 June 1849).

Luxemburg Commission, François Vidal, was among the members elected as part of the opposition. In order to keep the opposition in check, several Acts were voted or prolonged: the Acts on the Press (8 June 1850) and on Clubs (16 July 1850).[20] It was now stipulated that three years of residence in the same location constituted a prerequisite for the right to vote (Act of 31 May 1850), a move that resulted in a roughly one-third reduction of the electoral body. A further concern – and by no means the least important – underlying Bonaparte's plan of action was the question of his re-election. As early as May 1851 he called for a modification of Article 45 of the Constitution according to which the President could not stand for immediate re-election. With this aim in mind Faucher, once again interior minister (10 April 1851), invited the General Councils to request a revision of the constitution, but despite his efforts the revision debated in the Assembly (July 1851) mustered no more than 446 votes in favour versus 278 against, i.e. two-thirds of the ballots cast. Crucially, Article 111 of the constitution stated that a three-quarters majority was required. At the beginning of October 1851, Bonaparte took up a position against the Act of 31 May 1850 that Faucher had defended when he was vice-president of the Legislative Assembly.[21] Having thus been rebuffed, Faucher resigned once more (26 October 1851).

Economic and social questions

The overwhelming power of the Party of Order within the Legislative Assembly was not totally extraneous to the absence of major legislative changes and the sluggish nature of its debates.

Hippolyte Passy merely demanded that the tax on salt be restored. This demand was favourably received by the Assembly and was passed on 27 December 1848. The only parliamentary economists to vote against the measure were Simon and the socialist parliamentary economists. Passy's successor as finance minister, Achille Fould, was likewise faced with difficulties pertaining to the budget and thus proposed restoration of the tax on drinks previously suppressed by the Constituent Assembly (16 May 1849). His proposal was voted into Law by the Legislative Assembly (2 December 1849).

The conclusions contained in the report on the agricultural colonies in Algeria, presented by the liberal economist Louis Reybaud, were approved by the Legislative Assembly without in-depth debate.

The question of the workers was raised by Nadaud in January 1850. Nadaud cited the non parliamentary liberal economist Adolphe Blanqui, who gave a grimly realistic description of the difficult living conditions of the working class.[22] His

20 With the approval of all the liberal parliamentary economists and also of Thiers.

21 Bonaparte renewed his intention of repealing this Law in a speech delivered to the Assembly (4 November 1851). This did not prevent the Assembly from throwing out this abrogation (session dated 13 November 1851).

22 See Blanqui (1849).

intervention sparked a heated difference of opinion among these present at the parliamentary session, so that it became necessary for the interior minister to call members to order, as he wished to avoid initiating a genuine debate on this topic.

The speech by Bastiat in favour of the freedom of coalition (November 1849) and the statement by Sainte-Beuve in praise of free trade (27 June 1851) had little effect despite support by the liberal parliamentary economists. Thiers and – albeit to a lesser extent – Charles Dupin acted as spokesmen for those who opposed free trade.

The end of the Second Republic: from 2 December 1851 to 1 December 1852

During the hours leading up to the *coup d'état* of 2 December 1851, Bonaparte neutralised the important members of the opposition. Thiers and Nadaud were arrested.[23] By 21 December 1851 Bonaparte was in a position to organise a referendum, the subject of which was incorporated into his 2 December proclamation: 'The people of France wish to maintain the authority of L.N. Bonaparte and delegate to him the powers necessary to set up a constitution on the bases proposed in this proclamation'. The constitution written down after the referendum was promulgated on 11 January 1852. From that time on, Bonaparte wielded extensive powers: elected for ten years, he was empowered to take the initiative of law-making single-handedly, sign treaties (commercial treaties and so forth), and by virtue of Article 3 he 'governed through the means of the ministers, the Council of State, the Senate and the Legislative Body'.

The Council of State examined all proposals for new laws before submitting them as a Bill to the Legislative Body. The councillors of State, numbering between 40 and 50, were nominated – and equally, their nomination could be rescinded – by the President. The senators, numbering a maximum of 150, were nominated for life or by right (cardinals, field marshals, admirals) and interpreted or completed the Constitution through the *sénatus-consultes*, thereby ensuring that laws voted by the Legislative Body conformed to the Constitution. The Legislative Body itself was elected for a six-year term, but performed only a secondary role as it had no right of initiative. The fairly limited presence of the opposition as members of this body (elections dated 29 February 1852) can be explained by the system of 'official candidature'.[24] The presidential Decree issued on 17 February 1852 reinforced the antidemocratic character of the regime by allowing suspension of newspapers; furthermore, if a presumed offence in the press were reiterated, the paper could be totally suppressed.

---

23 Both of them were forced into exile. Thiers was allowed to return to France in August 1852, but he played no part in political activity until 1863. Nadaud did not come back to France until 1870.

24 In this framework, the interior minister was invited to mention to the President the names of men who enjoyed considerable public esteem for their dedication and their worthy actions: landowners, paternalistic employers, etc. We may cite Ch. de Wendel and E. Schneider, director of Creusot.

The majority of parliamentary economists manifested their opposition by retreating to private life (Thiers, H. Passy, Raudot, Sainte-Beuve, Wolowski, Lamennais, Vidal) or by rejecting their nomination to the Advisory Committee that had been created shortly after the *coup d'état* (Faucher, Reybaud). To these should be added the name of Simon, while Leroux had sought refuge abroad. Only Dupin, F. de Parieu and Chevalier sided with Bonaparte,[25] the second by accepting his nomination to the Advisory Committee and the third by publicly avowing his support.[26] Charles Dupin was nominated senator, on 25 January 1852. F. de Parieu was nominated president of the finance sector of the Council of State; Chevalier became part of the section dealing with public works, agriculture and trade. Chevalier's support, which triggered considerable tension in relations with members of the very liberal Société d'Economie Politique, is not altogether surprising. In effect he shared the ideas of Bonaparte presented in his *Extinction du paupérisme* (1844) and further described in his famous speech in Bordeaux (9 October 1852). In his small pamphlet – *Extinction du paupérisme* – of which 'the only aim is the wellbeing of the working class', Bonaparte promised the creation of a vast programme of public works as well as economic and social reform. 'I seek to win over to the cause of religion, morals and a comfortable life' – thus he spoke in Bordeaux – 'that portion of the population which … barely has any knowledge of the precepts of Christ; which … can scarcely enjoy the products of basic necessity. We have vast tracts of uncultivated land that needs to be tilled, roads to be opened up, ports to be dug, canals to be made ready for navigation, our railway network to be completed'. This speech, with its Saint-Simonian overtones, was naturally highly appealing to such former disciples of Saint-Simon as Chevalier, Fould and the Pereire brothers.[27]

Economic and social questions

The government's first major concern was to overcome the crisis into which the country had been plunged. According to economists and financial consultants close to Bonaparte (Chevalier, Fould, the Pereire brothers, etc.), the situation could be improved only by developing infrastructures and by using the tool of credit.

Steps taken to develop the rail network would, it was argued, facilitate trade and commercial exchange and give a decisive boost to the iron, mechanical and coal industries. The government therefore set about putting such measures in place. The concession for the Paris-Lyon rail company was awarded to a financial consortium dominated by the Pereires and the Rothschilds (5 January 1852). The concession of the Railway of the North was prolonged for 99 years (19 February 1852) in return for a commitment that parts of the rail network would be extended. The

---

25 Proudhon endeavoured to explain and justify the *coup d'état* in the work he wrote while in prison (Proudhon, 1852).

26 See Walch (1975), p. 71.

27 Émile (1800-1875) and Isaac (1806-1800).

prolongation considerably lightened the annual charges on the loan and made it possible to lower tariffs significantly. Exploitation of the resources consisting of the network of railways, roads, ports and canals required a radical transformation of the manner of financing, and the expected need for substantial investment made it necessary to resort to credit.

A number of initiatives were undertaken in this framework. For example, a convention drawn up on 3 February 1852 extended the Bank of France's privilege of issue to 1867; the Bank, for its part, was required to accept the principle of advances on railway securities and was obliged to decrease its bank rate from four to three per cent. A further measure was the creation, in November and December 1852, of two banks, the Crédit Mobilier and the Crédit Foncier. Fould[28] and the Pereire brothers took part in the Crédit Mobilier operation, while the Crédit Foncier was the result of the fusion of the Banque Foncière de Paris, founded on 28 March 1852, with another two analogous establishments. During the latter operation, Wolowski was compelled to play a backstage role compared to his brother-in-law Faucher, due to the fact that Wolowski himself had been so bold as to express his opposition to the *coup d'état.* The policy of easy credit was justified by the theory of productive expenditure, a theory that was defended by Bonaparte himself[29] and likewise by his two collaborators Persigny[30] and Haussmann.[31]

According to this theory, investment expenditure expanded and increased revenues so successfully that repayment of debts which initially seemed colossal became absolutely effortless. This policy caused considerable apprehension in the sphere of orthodox finance (A. Fould, P. Magne),[32] which began to launch a scare campaign warning of the risk of bankruptcy.

The only social measure enacted during this period was the Decree of 26 March 1852, which specified that a mutual assistance society had the right to enjoy certain advantages whenever it included several non-worker honorary members or whenever – bowing to the dictates of security – its president was nominated by the ruling powers.

The Second Empire

The Second Empire officially began on 2 December 1852 after the restoration of 'imperial dignity' approved by the plebiscite of 21 November 1852. It is generally distinguished into the 'authoritarian' period (2 December 1852-1859)[33] and the

---

28 He was finance minister (30 October 1849-25 January 1852) with the exception of two brief interruptions in 1851.

29 See Bonaparte (1844).

30 Interior minister from 1851 to 1854 and then from 1860 to 1863.

31 Prefect of the Seine for seventeen years (1853-1869).

32 Finance ministers between 31 October 1849 and 1870.

33 His authoritarian character was accentuated by the *sénatus-consulte* of 25 December 1852 and by the Law on General Security (19 February 1858). The first text stipulated

'liberal' period (1860-3 September 1870). This distinction is of interest here as it had a number of economic effects, with a more rapid period of growth in the former stage than in the latter.

The authoritarian Empire: 2 December 1852 to the end of 1859

The themes addressed by Bonaparte (the Bordeaux speech) were favourably taken up by Frédéric Le Play (1806-1882), who believed that support for the Empire would safeguard France from violence and anarchy.[34] Nominated member, in 1853, of the sub-committee entrusted with preparing the 1855 Universal Paris Exhibition,[35] he rose to its head a few months later, and as a result of his successful leadership he was nominated Councillor of State at the end of 1855. In the same year, the Academy of Science awarded due recognition to *Les Ouvriers européens* (1855). The Société d'Economie Sociale that Le Play created in 1856 benefited from the moral and financial support of the Emperor, and also featured the presence of former Saint-Simonians – Arlès-Dufour, Émile Pereire, Chevalier – but also of the protectionist Dupin, inasmuch as the objectives of these latter figures had a number of points in common with those of the Society: 'to found a progressive future for the working classes on conscientious study of their past and present condition. To ensure that prosperity is attainable by the less well-off classes and staple necessities attainable by the poorest classes. To elevate the people towards God through wellbeing and gratitude'.

At the same time, the government maintained strict control over the different means of expression available to liberal economists. Such was the case of the *Journal des économistes*, threatened with sanctions on numerous occasions: in April 1854, in September 1855 and in March 1857. Obliged to keep careful watch over their statements, the liberal economists also faced severe difficulties in their teaching activities. The chair of economics and rural legislation of the Agronomic Institute of Versailles, held by Léonce de Lavergne (1809-1880) since the time of its creation in 1850, was suppressed after the *coup d'état*. Lavergne would not regain his post until 1876!

---

that the Emperor was to authorise all works of public utility by decree. He was to preside over the Senate and the Council of State when he judged it to be desirable. He had the right to modify customs tariffs. The second text, voted following the Orsini attempt (14 January 1858), stripped those at whom it was aimed of all legal guarantees.

34 This did not prevent him from making bitter observations about the corruption of certain high-ranking officials.

35 Within this sub-committee, Chevalier was the head of the domestic economy committee. Engaged as an advisor consulted by the Emperor on economic questions, he withdrew from his teaching position at the Collège de France in 1852. He was replaced until 1866 by the liberal economist Henri Baudrillart. Dupin was one of the main *rapporteurs* of this exhibition.

Economic and social questions

In his *Examen du système commercial connu sous le nom de système protecteur* (1852), Chevalier criticised the protectionist speech delivered by Thiers to the Legislative Assembly on 27 June 1851. By allowing ironworks to 'impose leonine bargains on the railway companies', he argued, protectionism was an obstacle to the development of the railways.[36] At the same time, however, he feared that an overhasty opening up of the frontiers could jeopardise the French economy, and it was not until the end of the 1855 Universal Exhibition of Paris that he began to mitigate his attitude somewhat, conceding that the time to open up France's frontiers had arrived because the exhibition had made it clear that France no longer lagged so severely behind England. The emperor, on the other hand, was more cautious, as he had to contend with the hostility of the Legislative Body towards the proposals for partial liberalisation of trade that he put forward at three different moments: 1853, 1856 and 1859. This accounts for his reluctance to brutally impose free trade despite possessing sweeping powers (art. 6 of the Constitution of 14 January 1852; art. 3 of the *sénatus-consulte* of 25 December 1852), despite enjoying considerable support and despite his free-trade convictions.

With regard to the question of the deregulation of bakeries, the emperor exercised great caution in addressing this issue, since it could easily trigger unrest among the general public. Before reaching a definitive decision, he entrusted Le Play with carrying out several in-depth investigations, which were conducted in London, Brussels and Paris.[37] Only after their completion did Le Play propose deregulation.

Chevalier introduced a number of proposals for reorganisation of the Bank of issue and of the banking system in the *Journal des débats* (15 October and 8 November 1855). His aim was to give the Bank of France the possibility of extending its credit operations by authorising it to mobilise its entire capital. During the second semester of 1857, in a crisis context, the councillors of State held a debate on the Bill concerning renewal of the Bank of France's privilege of issue up to 1897. Interestingly, those who took a stand on this issue – notably Félix de Parieu – more or less totally disregarded the proposals put forward two years earlier by Chevalier. To the latter's great chagrin, they insisted only on the need to renew the privilege of issue: 'A great establishment like the Bank of France … cannot enjoy the full extent of its credit unless it has the certainty of a fairly long future'.[38] The privilege of issue was duly voted by the Legislative Body on 9 June 1857, with 225 votes in favour and 15 against.

The question of the freedom to draw up a will was another question that occupied a central role in Le Play's thought. In his view, the disorganisation of the

---

36 See Chevalier (1855).
37 See Le Play (1857, 1858, 1860).
38 These motives were published in *Le Moniteur* – the official newspaper of the era – of 16 and 17 May 1857.

French family and the falling birth rate was to be attributed to the laws on succession enshrined in the Civil Code. His proposal was that these laws should be replaced by the freedom to draw up one's own will, thereby enabling the father of the family to choose whichever one of his children he deemed to be most fit to succeed him. Thanks to the support of Morny, Le Play had the opportunity to illustrate his system to the Emperor and to the members of the Emperor's Private Council.

The liberal Empire: 1860 to 3 September 1870

A series of decrees and of *sénatus-consultes* liberalised the Empire. It became possible to publish detailed reports in the press providing information on debates held within the Legislative Body and the Senate (Decree of 24 November 1860). The Legislative Body had extensive opportunity to discuss amendments including those rejected by the Council of State (*sénatus-consulte* of 18 July 1866). 116 members of parliament (6 July 1869) expressed the hope that the Empire could be transformed into a parliamentary regime, and their hope was partly satisfied (*sénatus-consulte* of 8 September 1869). Furthermore, the Legislative Body was granted authority to introduce Bills and the right to vote a parliamentary agenda for daily discussion. As regards the Senate, it was transformed into a second legislative house (*sénatus-consulte* of 20 April 1870). All these reforms were triumphantly endorsed by a plebiscite (8 May 1870); meanwhile, the liberalisation of the regime translated into a reinforcement of the opposition: 32 members of parliament in May 1863 and almost 75 in May 1869, out of a total of little less than 300 members.

With the exception of Dupin, who was isolated on account of his protectionist ideas, the economists who had espoused the cause of the Empire continued to enjoy the support of Louis Napoléon Bonaparte. Chevalier was appointed to the Senate (16 March 1860) by virtue of his contribution to the establishment of free-trade. Nominated head of the French delegation to the Universal Exhibition of London in 1862, he belonged to the so-called Royal Palace Group that launched the idea of sending a delegation from the working class. Le Play was given the task of organising the French section and drawing up the general report. The Emperor encouraged him to publish his works[39] and nominated him General Commissioner of the 1867 Universal Exhibition of Paris.[40] A gallery was made available to him at the Exhibition, which he used as a showcase for presenting firms that had been instrumental in assuring the material, moral and intellectual wellbeing of their workers or had succeeded in creating an atmosphere of harmony between the workers and their employers. The perfect organisation of the Exhibition, its twelve million visitors and good financial outcome increased the stature and acclaim of Le Play. He entered the Senate in December 1867. F. de Parieu assumed important functions within the Council of State: Vice-president (1865) and President (July

39 Le Play (1864).

40 Michel Chevalier was the President of the international jury.

1869). He was raised to the rank of minister entrusted with the presidency of this Council once Émile Ollivier had inaugurated his Ministry (2 January 1870). Finally, Napoleon III supported the candidacy of the Pereire brothers in the 1863 legislative elections.

The Emperor's relations with the liberal economists improved after the signing of the 1860 free trade treaty agreement. Obviously, there was now one less reason for them to oppose him. The Emperor, for his part, sought their support in order to defend his treaty. The case of Frédéric Passy (1822-1912), who preached the good tidings of free trade in the framework of lectures and free courses held in the major provincial cities, is exemplary.[41] Building on this new situation, the liberal economists began to demand the creation of chairs of political economy, lest their newfound freedom should at some point come under threat once more. But they obtained only one chair, set up experimentally at the Faculty of Law in Paris (1864). It was awarded to a faithful of the imperial regime: Anselme Batbie (1828-1887).[42] Students rapidly became disillusioned with his approach, based as it was on an apology of government policy. Jules Simon, elected member of parliament for the opposition in 1863 and 1869, was not openly antagonistic to the government even though his works portrayed a grim picture of social reality.[43] No such accommodating attitude was shown by either Thiers or Léon Say (1826-1896).[44] The former, elected to Parliament in 1863 and 1869, unceasingly criticised government policy. As for the latter, Napoléon III appreciated neither his writings[45] nor his connections with republican circles. A wealth of documentation pertaining to this man of finance, so closely linked to the Rothschilds and to the *Journal des débats*, subsequently formed the background to Jules Ferry's novel *Comptes fantastiques d'Haussmann* (1868).

Economic and social questions

The cautiousness of the 1850s was replaced by genuine liberal audacity. Accompanied by the apostle of free trade, Richard Cobden, Chevalier submitted to Napoléon III a series of propositions drawn up in England in great secrecy towards the end of 1859. France was represented by Chevalier and Eugène Rouher.[46] Cobden himself was accompanied by important political figures. The Emperor accepted the propositions (letter dated 5 January 1860 addressed to Achille Fould, minister of State, and reproduced in the *Moniteur* dated 15 January 1860). The Franco-English free-trade treaty was then signed (23 January 1860). Stipulated to hold for a duration of ten years, the treaty suppressed all prohibitions, taxes on raw materials and on the majority of foodstuffs; in addition, it established *ad valorem* rights that were not to

41 See Passy (1862).
42 He held the chair until 1873.
43 See Simon (1863, 1866, 1867).
44 The grandson of J.-B. Say.
45 Say (1865, 1866).
46 Incumbent minister of agriculture, trade and public works.

exceed 30 per cent on coal and manufactured articles. The treaty was supported by liberal economists and the Pereire brothers. During a session of the Senate on 11 May 1866, Chevalier took up a position hostile to the demand for protection that was being voiced by farmers.[47] In a speech delivered during that same session, Dupin criticised 'the partisans of free-trade, so haughty, so triumphant'! The prime butt of his criticism, in this context, was no less than Chevalier himself. Thiers likewise missed no opportunity to criticise the 1860 treaty and all the other free-trade treaties signed by France, but his protectionism was rejected by Simon in a fine speech delivered on 20 January 1870 to the Legislative Body.[48]

The poor wheat harvest in 1861 had the effect of preventing the deregulation of bakeries. In early 1863, the subject was discussed once again within the Council of State in the presence of Napoléon III, whose final lingering hesitations were dispelled by the arguments of Le Play, Rouher and Baroche.[49] The date of deregulation (Decree issued 22 June 1863) was carefully chosen to coincide with a period when the extension of the rail network was beginning to noticeably reduce local shortages and price fluctuations.

The great novelty of this period was the possibility of talking freely of the right of coalition. The *rapporteur* on the Bill (19 February 1864) was Ollivier, who had been nominated by Morny, the President of the Legislative Body. This was the first time since 1852 that a Republican had assumed such momentous responsibility. Simon was one of the six members of the committee entrusted with assisting him. The Bill was adopted by 221 votes against 36 (2 May 1864), and its conformity to the constitution was recognised by the Senate (64 votes against 13). It was then definitively adopted on 25 May 1864. Particularly interesting is the observation that the members of parliament who supported the Bill, first and foremost Ollivier – whose educational background and training was that of a jurist – buttressed their position by constant appeal to arguments taken from liberal economic doctrine.[50]

The senators debated the 'petition of Sieur Furet concerning the Bank of France and the Bank of Savoy', condemning the increase in the bank rate imposed by the Bank of France. The petition was massively rejected by the senators: 83 votes against, only 2 in favour, including the ballot cast by Chevalier. In order to understand Chevalier's vote, it should be recalled that he was hostile to the Bank of France's monopoly over issue, admiring instead countries like Scotland and the United States where fiduciary issue was a privilege open to numerous banking institutions. His monetary conceptions were very close to the ideas espoused by the Pereire brothers, with whom he maintained close links in the framework of the railways and the bank (Crédit Mobilier).

Frédéric Le Play did not succeed in convincing a majority of politicians that his ideas on the family and on the rights of succession were well founded. His

47 *Annales du Sénat et du Corps Législatif*, 1866, **5**, pp. 140-1.
48 *Annales du Sénat et du Corps Législatif*, 1870, **1**, pp. 242-60.
49 He was then minister without portfolio presiding over the council of State.
50 *Annales du Sénat et du Corps Législatif*, 1864, *Annexes*, **2**, pp. 133-51.

proposal which tended towards 'extension of the rights attributed to the father of the family', submitted in 1865 by a group of members of the Legislative Body, gathered no more than 42 votes in favour. In 1867 and in 1870 the Legislative Body and the Senate once again rejected the proposal of freedom to draw up one's own will.

The Third Republic

Barely two months after the triumphant plebiscite of 8 May 1870, the Second Empire was starting to crumble. In the wake of the hostile reception awarded to certain diplomatic overtures pertaining to the throne of Spain, Ollivier declared war on Prussia (19 July 1870). Only one senator voted against this move, namely Chevalier, while Thiers and Simon likewise expressed their opposition, within the Legislative Body. As soon as the hostilities began, the situation developed in a manner extremely adverse to France: the Emperor was taken prisoner at Sedan (2 September 1870). Two days later, the Third Republic was proclaimed at the Hôtel de Ville of Paris,[51] and a government of national defence was set up.

The founding of the Republic: 4 September 1870 to 30 January 1879

Faced with a desperate military situation, the government signed the armistice (28 January 1871). Upon the request of the Prussians, a National Assembly was elected (8 February 1871). Eight economists,[52] of whom only one – Louis Passy (1830-1913) – has not been mentioned previously here, were elected in this Assembly dominated by the monarchists. Thiers, elected 'chief of the executive power of the Republic' (17 February 1871) negotiated the Treaty of Frankfurt (10 May 1871) in which France was obliged to cede Alsace and part of Lorraine as well as pay the victors an indemnity of 5 billion francs. But these negotiations with Bismarck were seen as a betrayal by the members of the Paris Commune, whose rebellion was brutally repressed (the week of bloodshed, 22-28 May 1871). By declaring himself in favour of a 'conservative republic' (13 November 1872), Thiers was effectively in breach of the Bordeaux pact of 10 March 1871, according to the terms of which he had undertaken to remain neutral in the debate, as he had to address the question of the fate of the regime. Finding himself in the minority within the National Assembly,[53] he resigned on 24 May 1873, thereby also precipitating the fall of

51 Chevalier, Dupin and Le Play withdrew to private life.

52 Three belonged to the Centre Right and the royalist majority: A. Batbie, L. de Lavergne and L. Passy. Three were part of the Centre Left: A. Thiers, L. Say and L. Wolowski. L. Blanc, who had returned to France after the fall of the Second Empire, sat on the Extreme Left and presided over the Republican Union. J. Simon occupied a position on the Left.

53 Batbie, de Lavergne and Passy declared themselves in favour of the dismissal of Thiers; Say and Simon were against this.

Léon Say,[54] who had been his finance minister since 7 December 1872. On 4 July 1873, Say was elected *rapporteur* of the budget committee.

Thiers was replaced by a monarchist, Field-Marshal de Mac-Mahon. These developments ushered in a period of instability. After the ousting of minister de Broglie (16 May 1874), the ministries were generally never held by the same figure (Cissey, Buffet, Dufaure, Simon) for longer than a year, although this instability did not involve either the Finance Ministry or the Undersecretary of the Finance Ministry, which were headed for slightly more than two years by Say and Louis Passy (10 March 1875-16 May 1877). As the hope of restoring the monarchy was fading on account of Count de Chambord's refusal to return to France without unfurling the white flag (August-October 1873), Léonce de Lavergne and fifty or so monarchist members of parliament ended up accepting the Republic. His group[55] thereby permitted the adoption of the constitutional laws passed in February 1875 (organisation of the Senate, organisation of the public powers) and July 1875 (relations among the public powers).

Henceforth, the President was to be elected for a seven-year term by the two Houses jointly. The Senate was to be elected for nine years, while the Lower House was to be elected by universal suffrage for four years. De Lavergne, Simon and Wolowski[56] were elected in the first elections (10 December 1875) which had been called in order to choose the 75 names who were to be nominated as life senators. Batbie, Joseph Garnier (1813-1881), Say and de Parieu[57] entered the Senate on the occasion of the second round of elections (30 January 1876). Following these elections, the monarchists enjoyed a slight majority in the Senate. In contrast, the outcome of the legislative elections (February-March 1876) resulted in a republican majority. Thiers, Blanc, Albert de Mun (1841-1914), L. Passy and Nadaud were elected. Of these figures, the first two now exerted only a negligible influence on political affairs, while de Mun, a member of the Catholic far-right, played no further role as his election was invalidated in 1878.

After obtaining authorisation from the Senate,[58] Mac-Mahon dissolved the Lower House (June 1877) in the hope of having a royalist majority elected. To his regret, the legislative (October 1877)[59] and senatorial (January 1879)[60] elections

54 Say, like Thiers, of whom he was a faithful ally, was favourable to the establishment of a conservative Republic.

55 This group included 54 members of parliament, half of whom belonged to the Centre-Left and the other half to the Centre-Right.

56 Wolowski died on 14 August 1876.

57 Charles Renouard (1791-1878) entered the Senate on 24 November 1876 following a by-election. He took up a placed as part of the Centre-Left formation. Garnier, who was in poor health, took very little part in the works of the Senate.

58 Renouard, de Lavergne and Say voted against the dissolution of the Lower House. Batbie and de Parieu voted in favour of the dissolution.

59 Blanc, Passy and Nadaud were re-elected. Thiers died on 3 September 1877.

60 Batbie was re-elected.

resulted in a republican majority. Given that the restoration of the monarchy was impossible, Mac-Mahon resigned on 30 January 1879.

Prompted by a number of intellectuals,[61] representatives of business circles and the world of finance,[62] the École Libre des Sciences Politiques was created in 1872. A product of the aftermath of the 1870-71 defeat, its main aim was to train elites that would be capable of challenging and competing with the Prussian elites, and endow these French elites with the necessary background to enter the civil service competition that selected officials for the great State institutions. As political economy had been part of the syllabus for this competition since 1870, the School necessarily had to teach this subject. Its growing popularity among students raised some concern among the twelve law faculties whose student numbers had shown only sluggish growth. The teaching of political economy was not included in these faculties until 1877 (Decree issued in March 1877), that is to say one year after the victory of the Republicans in the legislative elections. It was introduced as a course to be held in the second year of the *licence* in law, and was at first taught by holders of a doctorate or *agrégation* in law. The doctorate in political economy and the *agrégation* 'with mention of economic science' were set up considerably later, in 1895 and 1896 respectively. The type of political economy taught in these faculties and at the École Libre des Sciences Politiques was mainly liberal.[63]

During this same period social Catholicism also attracted considerable interest. In 1871, its two major representatives, Albert de Mun and René de la Tour du Pin, founded the Catholic Worker Circles, which were associations of workers and labourers gathered together under the leadership of a Catholic bourgeois elite whose goal was to prepare Catholics to engage in trade union struggles. Their journal – *L'Association catholique* (1876) – became a tribune for de Mun. Le Play no longer benefited from favourable endorsement by the governmental powers, and his social economy failed to be presented at the Universal Exhibition that opened in Paris in May 1878.

Economic and social questions

By the end of the Franco-Prussian War, France was crippled by a heavy weight of debt, estimated by the budget committee of the National Assembly as amounting to roughly 15 billion francs, of which five billion were owed to Prussia alone as a war indemnity. How should these vast sums be reimbursed?

According to Lavergne and Wolowski, what was needed was to carry out a comprehensive refounding of the fiscal system by modelling it on the American and English systems (session of 22 December 1871 at the National Assembly).

---

61 Prominent among whom were Hippolyte Taine and Émile Boutmy.

62 We may cite Say and H. Germain, the founder of Crédit Lyonnais. Wolowski was on the list of share-holders-founders of the École.

63 The chair of economics of Ecole Nationale des Ponts et Chaussées had been held from 1846 on by the liberal Garnier.

Lavergne suggested the establishment of a direct tax on landed property and personal property. Wolowski, on the other hand, put forward the idea of a system similar to English income-tax, which would apply to all incomes and would be a light and proportional rate. Both of these conceptions were sharply contested by Thiers, who felt that the declaration of incomes harboured a risk of fiscal inquisition and 'socialist' danger. He thus sternly reminded all those who considered an income tax as the tax of the future that on no account would he tolerate its introduction in France! He was followed in this attitude by Say, who opposed Maurice Rouvier's income tax project (December 1875). In the eyes of both Thiers and Say, the tax should restrict itself to balancing budget expenditure: it could not be expected to redress social inequalities.

What Thiers believed was that the granting of loans and a slight modification of taxation would suffice to service the country's debts. The loans of June 1871 and July 1872 proved extremely successful by virtue of the support of the *Haute Banque*, which was the great beneficiary of these loans. Indirect taxes on objects and on luxury activities, together with customs tariffs (July 1872) underwent a slight increase. Say, entrusted by Thiers with the Finance Ministry (7 December 1872), shared the point of view championed by the latter, and it was under Say's responsibility[64] as finance minister that the country was restored to financial viability. His determination to provide solid roots for the Republic led him to stray momentarily from the liberal credo in the difficult economic climate of the closing days of this period. Indeed, Say was actually responsible for the financial aspects of the Freycinet plan conceived shortly after the republican victory (February-March 1876) by the minister of public works.[65] This plan, designed to construct 16,000 kilometres of rail track and to develop the canals and ports was, in Say's view, the only means to give a boost to the economy without resorting to protectionism. Thus with the prudence and talent for spotting the right moment that was characteristic of a great financier very closely linked to the interests of the Rothschilds, he conceived a brilliant idea in order to finance the plan (6 billion francs over ten years): the issuing of government stock at three per cent whenever the circumstances were such that financing was needed, and amortisement to extend over 75 years. Implementation of the plan began in May 1878. Yet this move does not imply that Say had converted to State interventionism. The new lines were to be exploited by private companies under State guarantee, and not bought out or controlled by the State as urged instead by Gambetta.

The scant attention paid to social aspects in this period was not unrelated to the sorry state of the workers' movement, which had been crushed during the Commune. Even the prohibition on the International Association of Labourers (Act of 14 March 1872)[66] failed to stir an outcry. The only social law passed at that time

---

64 He was many times finance minister: 7 December 1872-24 May 1873, 10 March 1875-16 May 1877, 13 December 1877-28 December 1879.

65 See Gonjo (1972).

66 L. Blanc voted against this Law.

(19 May 1874) was the work of the Moral Order, which sought to mitigate the most blatant abuses of the liberal regime. It forbade child labour, prohibiting the employment of those under the age of 12; those older than 12 were not to be employed in factories or workshops for longer than 12 hours in a day. Night labour was forbidden for girls below the age of majority and for boys under 16.

Wolowski fought against the increase in customs tariffs (July 1872) that arose due to Thiers' vigorously protectionist beliefs. In fact, Wolowski had already made a speech in the National Assembly (1 February 1872) to defend the 1860 free-trade treaty, which was under renewed threat from another Bill.

The Republic confronted with crises: 31 January 1879 to 22 May 1898

No sooner had a colonial policy been devised in the early 1880s in order to give some satisfaction to wounded national pride that had been so profoundly humiliated during the 1870 defeat than France entered into one of the bleakest economic periods of its history. The deterioration of the economic set-up followed closely after the collapse of the Union Générale (19 January 1882),[67] which cast doubt on the Freycinet plan. France's economic growth declined so dramatically that by the end of the period in question the country had fallen back to fourth place in world ranking, behind England, Germany and the United States, after ranking not far short of first position at the end of the Second Empire.[68] Unemployment was rife, social conflict (Decazeville, 1886, Paris, 1888) and violence (Fourmies, 1 May 1891) proliferated. Widespread corruption and the emergence of anarchism during the second decade aggravated the general tension. Between 1885 and 1889, victims of the economic crisis and opponents of the republican government joined forces under the banner of the Boulangiste movement;[69] February 1889 then saw the eruption of the Panama affair, the greatest political-financial scandal of the third Republic. Almost 800,000 subscribers were damaged by the insolvency of the company which had been in charge of building the canal. By the time of the 1893 elections, the scandal resulted in massive abstention from voting, so that a major change-over of elected members of parliament ensued. Out of the 317 Republicans – Opportunists and Progressives – elected, 190 were new arrivals in Parliament. Support for the Monarchic Party and the Bonapartists also waned, as the Catholics, spurred by Pope Leo XIII, rallied round the Republic. Thus overall, these elections signalled the advancement of Socialism.

The Liberal School now had a new weekly magazine – *Le Monde économique* – founded in 1891 by Paul Beauregard (1853-1919), who had held a professorship at the Faculty of Law in Paris since 1881 and was the author of the widely known text *Éléments d'économie politique* (1889). Among the few opponents of the Liberal School in the Law Faculties, one may cite Paul Cauwès (Paris) and

67 A commercial bank of Lyon.
68 See Breton, Broder and Lutfalla (1997).
69 Inspired by General Boulanger, minister of war between 7 January 1886 and 30 May 1887.

Charles Gide (Montpellier). In his *Précis du cours d'économie politique* (1879), Cauwès defended the view that the State must not be subject in all circumstances to free-trade dogma, above all when it is a question of defending national labour. Nor should the State be indifferent to social problems. Gide's work *Principes d'économie politique* (1884, 1898, 6th edn) criticised liberal ideas on competition and wages. The *Revue d'économie politique* (1887), in which Gide was one of the leading figures, gave free rein to a number of different streams of thought such as cooperativism, national economy, State socialism, and so forth. Le Play's School also boasted a review – *La Réforme sociale* (1881) – and its own followers. One of the latter, Émile Cheysson, held the first chair of social economy set up in 1893 by Count de Chambrun in the École Libre des Sciences Politiques. Social Catholicism also continued to gain ground, while two other new positions appeared for the first time on the scene during this period: Marxism and Solidarism. The programme of the French Workers' Party created in Marseille (October 1879) was drawn up jointly with Marx himself. The position denominated Solidarism espoused by Léon Bourgeois (1851-1924) was presented in the form of articles in *La Nouvelle Revue* (1896) and subsequently taken up again in *Solidarité*.[70] The solidarism that formed the core of the programme designed by the Radical Party towards the end of the period in question stood in opposition both to individualism and also to collectivism.

The liberal economists were present to a lesser extent in political institutions than had been the case earlier. They could boast only two ministers: Say, entrusted with finance at the beginning of the period[71] and Yves Guyot (1843-1928) who was placed in charge of public works (22 February 1889-18 February 1892). At the beginning of 1879 they numbered no more than four in the Senate: Batbie, de Parieu, Simon and Say, and by the end of the period there were none left at all. In 1889 Say left the Senate and moved to the Lower House, where, likewise, there were now no more than two or three liberal economists: in 1881, Louis Passy and his nephew, Frédéric Passy; in 1885, they were joined by Guyot;[72] in 1889, Guyot, L. Passy and Say. The two latter figures were re-elected in 1893. The social Catholic de Mun was repeatedly re-elected to the Lower House from 1881 onwards. The Marxist Jules Guesde (1845-1922) entered the Lower House (1893-1898). The solidarist Bourgeois was elected to the Lower House for the Radical Party in 1888, being nominated Undersecretary of State for the Interior Ministry in May 1888, several times minister and head of government (1 November 1895-23 April 1896).

---

70 Bourgeois (1897).

71 From 30 January 1879 to 28 December 1879 and from 30 January 1882 to 7 August 1882, i.e. slightly more than seventeen months versus fifty-six months during the previous period.

72 A member of the Budget Committee in 1886, Guyot was elected general *rapporteur* of this committee on 4 November 1888. More concerned with the social question than the liberal economists were, Fernand Faure (1853-1929), professor of political economy, was elected to the Lower House in 1885. He was immediately elected *rapporteur* of the budget committee.

Economic and social questions

The liberals continued to oppose the introduction of an income tax. Guyot regarded it as tyrannical inasmuch as it was levied on persons rather than on things (November 1886). He recommended instead that a tax on capital should be adopted. Frédéric Passy and Say also attacked the notion of a tax on income, but adduced old arguments.[73] The tax should have the purpose of assuring the functioning of the general services of the State; in no way should it act as a tool for equalising fortunes, nor should it pave the way to fiscal inquisition. These arguments were exploited by the senators at the point when they ousted minister Bourgeois (23 October 1896)[74] who, desiring to enact a policy of solidarity,[75] had integrated the income tax in his programme at the moment when he had set up his Ministry in late October 1895.

The negotiations conducted by Say – who had been nominated ambassador to London (24 April-24 May 1880)[76] – with the aim of prolonging the 1860 free-trade treaty, did not result in any significant outcome. This failure was attributed to the French protectionists. Customs tariffs were slightly increased on certain manufactured articles following the intervention by Jules Méline, vice-president of the customs committee and closely linked to the Vosges weavers (May 1882). Méline, nominated to the Ministry of Agriculture in June 1884, vigorously defended agricultural protectionism on the basis of the enormous difficulties faced by farmers and peasants.[77] His arguments succeeded in obtaining a vote in favour of an excise of 3 francs per hectolitre of imported wheat (28 March 1885). This excise was raised to 5 francs in 1887 despite the protests by F. Passy. As for Say, he was equally unsuccessful with regard to the double tariff (Act of 11 January 1892), and was unable to avert its promulgation. The first maximal tariff was applicable to all countries, while the second, minimal (15 to 30 per cent), was to be negotiated after setting up special conventions with a given State. Protectionism was reinforced by the 1897 Act, the so-called 'Padlock' Act, which gave the executive the power to modify excises on cereals, wine and meat in cases of agricultural surplus production. The authors of these laws drew their inspiration from the theory of compensatory duties presented by Paul Cauwès in his writings.[78]

It is worth underlining that the boost of colonisation at the beginning of the 1880s lay at the origin of the violent disputes in Parliament, which pitted the critics

73 See respectively F. Passy (1889) and Say (1889), 3rd lecture.

74 This policy was criticised by Say in a speech to the House (session dated 21 March 1896).

75 The theory of the quasi-social contract embodied in this policy shows the debt of the privileged classes with respect to the dispossessed. This programme also provided for workers' pensions.

76 On 25 May, he was elected President of the Senate.

77 Due to falling prices from 1873 onwards (revolution in the sphere of transport, increased competition, etc).

78 As the economic advisor of Méline, head of government (29 April 1896-1 November 1898), Cauwès set up the Société d'Économie Politique Nationale (December 1897). Méline was its honorary president.

of colonisation (Guyot, F. Passy, de Mun, etc.) against the staunch supporters of the colonial undertaking (Say and others).

At the beginning of the period, the Conservative Republicans' social programme restricted itself to enlightening workers on their duties, leaving them to be masters of their own destinies and organising social relations exclusively for the freedom of forming and joining trade unions. One should therefore hardly be surprised by the suppression of the obligation of maintaining Sunday as a rest day (Act of 12 July 1880), nor by the acceptance of trade associations (Act of 21 March 1884). The Conservative Republicans were as hostile as the liberal economists to State intervention in the labour sphere. The ultra-liberal Guyot, for instance, criticised a Bill presented to the House in 1888 designed to regulate child labour, the employment of girls under the age of majority and of women as factory workers. F. Passy was not altogether adverse to setting a legal limitation on their working hours, but warned against an excess of regulations introduced as a pretext to eliminate all abuses (June 1888). He proposed a series of amendments to the 'dangerous' Bill concerning responsibility in cases of accidents to workers in the workplace (June and July 1888). De Mun, on the other hand, espousing a more 'social' outlook, declared himself in favour of labour regulations in manufactures and expressed the hope that the principle of professional risk would replace the theory of criminal responsibility in the field of accidents in the workplace. Furthermore, he called for the five-day week to be applied to all workers.

The decline of the influence of liberal economists in governmental and parliamentary circles is illustrated by the creation of the Higher Council of Labour (Decree of 27 January 1891) and the Labour Office (Act of 21 July 1891), and by the reorganisation, in 1892, of the Office of Labour Inspection. The two abovementioned Bills were finally voted into law (Acts of 2 November 1892 and 9 April 1898).[79] In the case of the first Act concerning the working hours of women and children,[80] what proved decisive was the stand taken by Simon in that bastion of conservatism that was the Senate (July 1891). He countered the arguments of those who criticised State intervention by pointing out that a reduction in working hours was hardly likely to come as the result of an agreement between employers and workers, since neither of these two parties believed they had any interest in such a move. As regards the second Act, the employer was to pay the worker a lump sum compensation in the case of an accident in the workplace.[81] The governmental programme of Bourgeois's Ministry (1 November 1895) sought to introduce legislation on workers' pensions, but this proposal failed to take into account the hostility of the Senate and the House. Only partial results were obtained in the field of workers' retirement schemes.[82]

79 One may also cite the Act of 1893 on hygiene and job safety for workers.

80 It improved the Law of 19 May 1874. See *supra*.

81 Elected to the House in May 1898, Beauregard underlined the drawbacks of this Law (Beauregard, 1898b).

82 The first collective convention between factory owners and strikers was formulated in

The failure by the Republic to achieve any major breakthroughs in the social domain led to widespread disillusionment among the working classes. The workers were increasingly attracted by political movements that dealt specifically with their problems: working hours, pensions, insurance schemes, etc. The leader of the French Workers' Party, Guesde, pleaded this cause unceasingly during the 1893-1898 government. To regain consensus among the workers, the Republic found itself having to endeavour to demonstrate that not all the social forces of the country were – as had transpired in the Panama scandal – 'in the service and under the orders of high finance'.[83]

The Radical Republic: 22 May 1898 to 2 August 1914[84]

While growth appeared to be strengthening,[85] a number of severe problems loomed on the horizon: political problems – the Dreyfus affair,[86] antagonistic relations between the Catholic Church and the State, etc. – as well as social problems. The Socialists broke off relations with the Radicals. This split became more pronounced after the victory of the Radicals and the Socialist-Radicals in the 1906 elections and the nomination of the radical Clemenceau to the position of head of government (25 October 1906-24 July 1909). Clemenceau violently repressed the strikes of blue-collar and white-collar workers and the demonstrations mounted by the southern grape growers. His successor, the independent socialist[87] Aristide Briand (24 July 1909-2 March 1911), adopted a different line and tried to work towards a compromise. With this aim in mind, he championed the creation of a Committee for Social Democracy led by Léon Parsons and Étienne Antonelli (1879-1971). The Lower House that ensued from the May 1910 elections had to contend with rising tension on the international scene. The Act that extended military service to three years (7 August 1913) was greeted with pronounced dissatisfaction by the Left, especially since the Left had been unable to persuade Parliament to vote the Income Tax Act. The parties of the Left emerged victorious from the May 1914 elections after waging a campaign against the Military Service Act and in favour of a tax on incomes.

Against this backdrop, the Liberal School boosted its position within the École Libre des Sciences Politiques, while maintaining its presence in its traditional strongholds. The chartered engineer-economist Clément Colson and Beauregard held teaching positions in this subject, the former starting from 1905 and the latter

---

the mines (Arras convention, 1891). The Act of 29 June 1894 set up pensions for the benefit of the miners.

83 In the words of the socialist Alexandre Millerand.

84 The eve of Germany's declaration of war on France.

85 Production increased by an average of 1.8 per cent a year until WW1.

86 Captain Dreyfus was wrongly accused of treason on suspicion of working for the Germans.

87 He refused to join the French Section of the Socialist International (SFIO) founded in April 1905.

from 1910. The election of Colson to the Académie des Sciences Morales et Politiques in 1910 was not totally unrelated to his great *Cours d'économie politique* (1901-1907).[88] This notwithstanding, the domination of the Liberal School did not preclude the expression of other schools of thought. From 1898 on, Gide held a course in comparative social economy funded by the Count de Chambrun in the framework of the doctorate at the Faculty of Law in Paris.[89] He taught the same course two years later at the École Nationale des Ponts et Chaussées. From 1895 onwards, Cauwès resumed his teaching position at the Faculty of Law in Paris. The solidarist doctrine upheld by Bourgeois achieved considerable acclaim[90] despite its juridical and philosophical fragility.[91] Finally, it is worth citing Adolphe Landry (1874-1956) and his critique of individual property, which he put forward in his graduation thesis that bore a most deceptive title – *L'utilité sociale de la propriété individuelle* (1901) – and in his remarkable *Manuel d'économique* (1908).

The presence of liberal economists within political institutions continued to wane. They could muster no more than two in the Lower House: Louis Passy and Beauregard.[92] They sat side by side with de Mun,[93] Guesde, re-elected in May 1906, and Landry, a member of the Radical Party, elected in May 1910. The latter sat on several committees (taxation, trade, etc.), and was re-elected on 26 April 1914. Bourgeois was a member of parliament (1898-1905) and later senator (1905-1914). He was the only 'heterodox' figure on whom ministerial functions were conferred.[94]

Economic and social questions

At the heart of the Radical Party's programme stood the vexed question of income tax, hotly contested by the wealthy classes and by those who regarded it as an attempt on individual freedom. This was the case of Beauregard, for instance: 'A

88 See Zouboulakis (1998).
89 See Pénin (1997), p. 81.
90 According to Gide, this was attributable to the author's 'elevated situation' and the 'opportune moment of its appearance'.
91 See Bourgeois (1902).
92 L. Passy died on 31 July 1913. Beauregard belonged to the group of progressive republicans who were moderate conservatives. In August 1902, he took part in the foundation of the Ligue de la Liberté de l'Enseignement which criticised the Law of 1 July 1901 on associations: 'They are exploiting the 1901 Law to strangle the freedom of teaching while proclaiming their respect for it' (Beauregard, 1903, p. 73).
93 He opposed the Dreyfus supporters who had regrouped in the Ligue des Droits de l'Homme by joining the Ligue de la Patrie Française. He worked actively against the anticlerical policy of Waldeck-Rousseau and Combes which ultimately led to the Law enacting the separation between Church and State (9 December 1905). He died on 6 October 1914.
94 He was minister of labour and of social insurance in the first Raymond Poincaré Cabinet (14 January 1912-17 January 1913).

tax on global revenue will never be a tax forming part of a regime of freedom, for the independence enjoyed by individuals of the State disappears as soon as each one finds himself classified in public registers according to the degree of wealth he possesses'.[95] These clashes account for the extreme caution displayed by the leaders of the Radical Party. Thus Joseph Caillaux,[96] minister of finance in the Waldeck-Rousseau government (22 June 1899-6 June 1902), relinquished the idea of proposing such a measure, fearing he would not obtain a majority if it were put to the vote. The radical Émile Combes, head of government (6 June 1902-19 January 1905), warned that it was necessary to 'act cautiously in this domain so as not to cause alarm among interests' (12 June 1902). The Income Tax Bill submitted in late 1904 by his finance minister, Maurice Rouvier, was rejected. It was not until the Caillaux Bill, tabled on 7 February 1907, that the Lower House actually passed the Law with a strong majority (9 March 1909). However, the House knew full well that the Senate was going to reject it! Some months later Landry, who had just recently entered the Lower House (May 1910), made his own attempt to persuade the government to submit a Bill for a progressive and global tax on income and capital.[97] The bewildering array of Bills and proposals can be explained by the State's need to procure new resources to finance the rising expenditure (social solidarity, military expenses, etc.), but it was not until the international situation began to crumble that a tax of this kind was voted into Law (15 July 1914).[98] Paul Leroy-Beaulieu eloquently reflected the state of mind of liberal economists when he stated in an article that the new tax was 'as catastrophic as the repeal of the Edict of Nantes'!

Genuine progress was recorded in the domain of the institutions[99] and social legislation: an eight-hour day for postal workers (Act of 30 March 1900), an eight-hour day in the mines (Act of 29 June 1905), an obligatory weekly 24-hour rest period (Act of 13 July 1906). Many members of parliament were hostile to these laws, as their effect was to decrease the nation's power by imposing constraints on the will of the individual. Beauregard approved the Act of 14 July 1905 which placed an obligation on the State, the *départéments* and the municipalities to provide welfare and care for those over the age of 70, for the infirm and those suffering from incurable diseases.[100] In contrast, he opposed the Act of 5 April

95 Beauregard (1898a), p. 770.

96 L. Say, a friend of his father's, assisted him in an advisory capacity and in 1887 he intervened in his favour to recommend him to the jury presiding over the competition for Finance Inspector. Caillaux came second in 1888; in 1890, he became Finance Inspector.

97 Landry was well aware that a decrease in marginal utility can justify a progressive income tax. Beauregard never ceased to oppose the progressive income tax in his *Éléments d'économie politique*.

98 The Senate would eventually pass it in 1916.

99 Reorganisation of the Higher Labour Council (Decree of 1 September 1899), reinforcement of labour inspections by recruiting a greater number of inspectors, creation of a Ministry Labour and Social Insurance (1906).

100 Beauregard (1906), p. i.

1910 on worker and peasant pensions, arguing that they would be partly funded through social security contributions by employers and thus would have the effect of increasing production costs. Guesde likewise cast his vote against this Bill, but for a different set of reasons. In his view, the pensions were insufficient, and moreover, he felt that the age at which workers and peasants became eligible to receive their pensions was far too advanced: at the age of 65, many of them were already no longer of this world. The Act of 5 April 1910 was in effect nothing short of a 'law for the deceased'.

Concern over the general status of the French population was by no means a new phenomenon. It appeared as early as the beginning of the 1850s,[101] and intensified towards the turn of the century and in the first few years of the twentieth century, when the death rate exceeded the birth rate, as occurred in 1890-1892, 1895 as well as 1907 and 1911. The alarm reached a peak when the 1913 figures for the German and French populations were published: 39.8 million French citizens, 66 million Germans. Politicians, however, took little heed of this matter until the beginning of the twentieth century, when they created a non-parliamentary Committee on depopulation (Decree of 21 June 1902) and a sub-committee entrusted with the task of studying measures to increase the birth rate.[102] The Committee achieved only negligible results. Its activities were brought to a close mainly because its deliberations apparently bolstered the arguments of those who claimed to see a link between the decline in religious belief and the falling birth rate. It was therefore implausible, the Committee concluded, to expect a growth in the level of population. Furthermore, the call for a population increase was a risky proposition because it could arouse mistrust among the parties of the Left and Extreme Left. These parties, who held a majority in the Lower House, might begin to suspect ulterior motives – for instance, that the underlying aim was to create an abundant labour force in order to decrease the relative power of wages or set up the right circumstances to usher in the army. Landry was the only parliamentary economist to champion the fight against the falling birth rate. In 1912, he was nominated administrator of the National Alliance for the Growth of the French Population. He founded a 'group for the defence of large families', and this group, active within the Lower House, contributed to the passing of the Law on Assistance to such families (1913). But his Bill demanding that the wage increase for postal workers, already allocated within the budget, should be destined exclusively to providing a rise in wages for workers with dependant children was rejected. He also urged that part of the product deriving from the income tax should be utilised to encourage the birth rate and that the size of families should be taken into consideration in fixing the level of this tax.[103]

Beauregard was very isolated in the Lower House when he criticised the Act of 29 March 1910 which raised general and minimum customs duties. This Act

---

101 See Charbit (1981).
102 F. Faure, Y. Guyot and Ch. Gide were members of this sub-committee.
103 See Landry and Nogaro (1914), pp. 140-1.

reinforced protectionism and endowed the government with weapons to ensure more rigorous application of the principle of reciprocity and of compensatory duties.

The War and the inter-war period (3 August 1914 to 27 July 1929)

The overall feeling was that the war Germany declared on France (3 August 1914) would be short-lasting. But by the time several months had gone by, the fact that it had even lasted so long was a cause for general surprise and consternation. France faced the need to produce, or procure, the provision of fresh supplies, equipment and material necessary for the military forces and the civilian population. It was imperative to find some means of financing the war effort and at the same time to ensure the presence of a sufficient workforce to operate the factories and carry out essential agricultural tasks. The State thus increased the level of intervention in order to respond to these multiple demands: requisitioning of wheat, flour and coal (Act of 16 October 1915); taxation of certain prices (Act of 20 April 1916). When Clemenceau came to power (16 November 1917-18 January 1920), the government increasingly took on the characteristics of a planned economy: the merchant navy was placed under the control of the government (December 1917); generalised rationing was introduced; exchange controls were set up (April 1918). At the end of hostilities (11 November 1918), a heavy toll had been taken both on the human plane[104] and in material and financial terms. The State was severely in debt to the Bank of France, England and the United States. Foreign possessions had been decimated. People on a fixed income were penalised by the almost threefold increase in retail prices between 1913 and 1918.

In the jubilation of victory, a right-wing majority denominated 'National Bloc' was elected (November 1919). It immediately had to grapple with the difficulties linked to the peace settlement, the reconstruction of the economy and a wave of strikes (railway workers, miners) during the first semester of 1920. The birth of the Communist Party (December 1920),[105] the difficulties faced by the franc on the exchange market and the continuing price rises all represented further elements causing general uncertainty. The disastrous state of the public finances induced the Poincaré government (15 January 1922-8 June 1924) to increase taxation by 20 per cent (24 February 1924). The Party of the Right, weakened by the hardships and sacrifices it had been compelled to impose, lost the elections to the Cartel of left-wing groups. The government set up by the radical Édouard Herriot (15 June 1924) had to wrestle with the same financial difficulties, accentuated by the recognition of the USSR (29 October 1924), which led the banks to refuse to renew the treasury bonds that had been underwritten. The ousting of Herriot (10 April 1925)

104 Losses numbered 1.4 million men, without counting the fall in the birth rate. There were also 740,000 war invalids.

105 J. Guesde refused to enter into this party, which sprang from the split in the Socialist Party at the Congress of Tours.

ushered in a period of ministerial instability, to which a solution was found by the formation of a Cabinet of National Union (23 July 1926) headed by Raymond Poincaré and representing all the parties with the exception of the Communists and the Socialists.[106] Confidence began to rise, and capital flowed back into France. In the April 1928 elections, the Cartel was defeated by the moderates. Despite all the monetary and financial difficulties, the economy experienced strong growth, so that by 1922 the national revenue had returned to 1913 levels and continued to increase by five per cent a year until 1929.

Colson's presence made itself felt more and more in the Grandes Écoles of chartered engineers.[107] The classical liberalism built up by Henri Truchy in his *Cours d'économie politique* (1920), which formed part of his academic activities at the Faculty of Law in Paris, was representative of the approach taught in such Faculties. However, innovative courses were also held by various figures: for example Antonelli, who taught at Lyon from 1919 to 1924. His *Principes*[108] were concerned mainly with application of the mathematical method to political economy, in a Walrasian perspective. Another such figure was that of Albert Aftalion, who in 1923 was appointed to the chair of statistics at the Faculty of Law in Paris,[109] where he successfully introduced the new statistical methods.[110] Adopting this framework, he demonstrated that important economic truths can be discovered by analysing and carefully comparing statistical data, a position that was shared by Charles Rist and Bertrand Nogaro (1880-1950) of the Faculty of Law in Paris.[111]

The death of Beauregard (22 March 1919) marked the end of the presence of liberal economists in the political institutions. Bourgeois was entrusted with high-ranking functions: minister until 1917 and President of the Senate (1920-1923). Landry and Nogaro were appointed as ministers of education, but for too short a space of time to undertake any effective action. Faure, the only economist in the Senate, was a member of the Finance Committee during his six years of office as senator (1924-1929). Guesde and Landry were elected to the Lower House (elections of 16 November 1919). The former died on 28 July 1922. The latter, re-elected in all the legislative elections, was a member of the Finance Committee and continued to wage his battle in favour of large families. Antonelli and Nogaro entered the Lower House in May 1924 as members of the Cartel of left-wing groups.[112] Both were re-elected in April 1928. Inasmuch as they sat on the Finance Committee, they concerned themselves with monetary questions. In addition, Antonelli specialised in social questions, and served two terms on the Social

106 The Poincaré government lasted until 27 July 1929.

107 In 1914 he was nominated to the École Polytechnique and in 1919 to the École des Mines of Paris.

108 See Antonelli (1914).

109 Previously occupied by Fernand Faure.

110 See Aftalion (1928).

111 Nogaro was appointed to the Law Faculty in Paris in 1921.

112 The former was a member of the Socialist Party, the latter a member of the Radical-Socialist Party.

Assurance and Providence Committee that was entrusted with drawing up and amending the subsequent Bills. During his term of office on the Committee he published a number of reports.

Economic and social questions

During the postwar period, political leaders cherished a dream – but they were not alone in this, as the entire weight of public opinion was solidly behind them – of restoring the prewar value of the franc. Therefore, there was no plan for devaluation of the currency. Yet the franc remained extremely fragile. It staggered from one crisis to another: March 1919, end 1923-March 1924, spring 1925, April-May 1926. But it was not until this last crisis that the minister of finance entrusted a panel of experts composed of bankers, industrialists and two professors from Faculties of Law, Gaston Jèze and Charles Rist,[113] with drawing up a plan for the strengthening of the franc. In the report it submitted in early July 1926, the panel demanded a reduction in State expenditure, an increase in taxation levels, conversion of the floating debt into redeemable bonds and an easing of taxation on stocks and shares. The fall of the Briand-Caillaux Cabinet triggered by Herriot (16-17 July 1926) and the extremely short-lived duration of the Herriot Cabinet[114] resulted in intense speculation against the franc. The appointment of Poincaré as head of the government (23 July 1926) and his commitment to balance the budget succeeded in stemming the onslaught against the currency.[115] The price of sterling and of the dollar expressed in francs had dropped by half (December 1926) as compared to the peak recorded some six months earlier (23 July 1926).

The revalorisers and the stabilisers stood in sharp opposition to one another. The former cherished the hope of re-establishing the franc/gold parity existing before the World War, a position naturally shared by bankers and persons of private means, and supported by the conservative press as well as numerous liberal economists. 'Quite apart from its injustice', wrote one such economist, Camille Perreau of the Faculty of Law in Paris, 'devaluation would have the drawback of drastically and perhaps irremediably shaking public confidence in the security of fiduciary circulation and would, henceforth, be seriously detrimental to the credit of the Bank of France and the credit of the State'.[116] The latter view had considerable backing among industrial sectors that looked towards the export trade, and was championed by economists who gravitated around the *Revue d'économie politique* (Gide, Rist, etc.).[117] Their convictions were reinforced by the negative effects of stabilisation of the pound and its pre-war parity with the dollar (1925) on

113 Nominated deputy governor of the Bank of France by Caillaux, and finance minister since 24 June 1926.

114 The Herriot government lasted no more than two days: the 20 and 21 July 1926.

115 The value of the currency was swayed above all by factors of collective psychology (Aftalion, 1927).

116 Perreau (1925), p. 408.

117 Nogaro espoused the position of the stabilisers (Nogaro, 1922).

the British economy: widespread unemployment and social unrest. In his decision to devaluate the franc, Raymond Poincaré was not insensitive to the arguments put forward by Gide.[118] The new official value of the franc (Monetary Law dated 24-25 June 1928) corresponded to the parity it had achieved on 23 December 1926 (65,5 mg of gold), i.e. a four-fifths cut in comparison to the Germinal franc. This amputation represented the price of the war.

Worried by the upsurge of a revolutionary wave about to sweep across Europe, Clemenceau sought to alleviate social unrest by proposing the adoption of the eight-hour day. Tabled a few weeks before the 1919 Mayday celebrations, his proposal was put to the vote and passed (Act of 23 April 1919). Despite the ban on demonstrations, the trade unions mobilised their troops on the issue of the manner in which the new Law was to be implemented. Crowds flocked to the 1st May demonstration and violent scuffles broke out. After the eight-hour working day had been voted into Law and the principle of collective agreements had been recognised (Act of 25 March 1919), no further important social measure was taken for another nine years, before the Social Insurance Act passed on 5 April 1928. The speech presenting this Bill to the Lower House was delivered by Antonelli, who forcefully and resolutely refuted the arguments adduced by those who opposed the project. Faithful to his Proudhonian inspiration, he conceived a decentralised system on the model of mutualism. But this proposal incurred the wrath of the Chambers of Commerce, employers and the liberal economists:[119] firstly because it substituted the principle of State intervention for the free action and responsibility of the individuals involved, and secondly because it increased production costs.[120] The law, dubbed 'the Mad Law' by conservative circles, was not implemented, on account of this opposition. It thus proved necessary to vote another Act, passed on 30 April 1930.

Conclusion

The above developments show the extreme disparity of the political influence of the forty-one parliamentary economists discussed in this chapter. Many among them played only a minor role in the political framework; frequently, their parliamentary activity went no further than casting their vote. Others, on the other hand, played a more prominent role by virtue of their personal acclaim or their institutional position.[121] In this context, one may cite, in alphabetical order, Antonelli, Blanc, Bourgeois, Chevalier, Faucher, de Parieu, Say, Simon, Thiers, etc. Finally, there are some figures whose influence is easily identifiable. This is the case, for instance, of

118 See Miquel (1989), p. 627.
119 But also of farmers and the body of medical doctors.
120 See *Journal des économistes*, Oct. 1928, pp. 216-17; Hubert (1928).
121 President of the Republic, head of government, minister (finance, interior, education), *rapporteur*, member of committees (finance, budget), etc.

Lavergne, whose stance with regard to the future of the French Monarchy led to the adoption of the 1875 constitutional laws and the establishment of the Third Republic. Similarly, in 1893 Yves Guyot was instrumental in the rejection of a Bill supported by Guesde, demanding the suppression of the employment agencies.[122] But above and beyond the disparity of political influence of the parliamentary economists, a number of general conclusions can be drawn from the developments outlined in this chapter.

Liberal political economy continued to form the main thrust in the approach to the teaching of economics that was predominant in France throughout most of the period. The teaching of economics was provided by the Faculties of Law (Decree of March 1876), by the *grandes écoles d'ingénieur* (creation of chairs), as also in independent courses and lectures. This notwithstanding, the influence of liberal political economy on government policies was extremely variable. Until the late 1870s, it remained particularly strong with the exception of the two months after the February 1848 Revolution and the authoritarian period of the Second Empire. Its influence subsequently diminished until the appointment of Raymond Poincaré to the position of head of government on 23 July 1926.

The extent to which governmental economic policy was effectively influenced by liberal political economy fluctuated according to the political situation (democratic regime, authoritarian regime) and the economic climate in the country at large. By the same token, the stronger or weaker presence of liberal economists within political institutions varied in relation to these factors. The presence of liberal economists in Parliament (Constituent Assembly, later the Legislative Assembly) was strongest at the beginning of the period considered here. Almost non-existent during the Second Empire, their presence rose significantly again during the first decade of the Third Republic, only to decline constantly thereafter. After the death of Beauregard, on 22 March 1919, liberal economists no longer figured among the members of parliamentary assemblies or within the governments. Finally, the appearance of new doctrinal streams of thought such as the national economy, solidarism or mutualism, which provided political leaders with fresh inspiration for principles underlying their action, was not extraneous to the relative decline of the influence of liberal political economy.

References

Primary sources

Aftalion, A. (1913), *Les crises périodiques de surproduction*, 2 Vols, M. Rivière, Paris.
Aftalion, A. (1927), *Monnaie, prix et change, expériences récentes et théorie*, Sirey, Paris.
Aftalion, A. (1928), *Cours de statistique*, Puf, Paris.

---

122 See Guyot (1910), p. 172.

Antonelli, É. (1911), *La Démocratie sociale devant les idées présentes*, M. Rivière, Paris.
Antonelli, É. (1912), *Les actions de travail dans les sociétés anonymes à participation ouvrière*, Preface by A. Briand, Alcan, Paris.
Antonelli, É. (1914), *Principes d'économie pure*, M. Rivière, Paris.
Antonelli, É. (1928), *Guide pratique des assurances sociales. Commentaire et texte complet de la loi du 5 avril 1928*, Payot, Paris.
Beauregard, P. (1889), *Éléments d'économie politique*, A. Picard et Kaan, Paris.
Beauregard, P. (1898a), 'L'impôt sur le revenu', *Le Monde économique*, 18 June, pp. 769-70.
Beauregard, P. (1898b), 'La loi sur les accidents du travail', *Le Monde économique*, 9 July, pp. 33-5.
Beauregard, P. (1903), *Brochure relative à l'Assemblée générale de la Ligue de la liberté d'enseignement*, Au siège de la Ligue de la Liberté de l'Enseignement, Paris.
Beauregard, P. (1906), 'Préface', in A. Revillon, *L'assistance aux vieillards, infirmes et incurables, en France – La loi du 14 juillet 1905*, Sirey, Paris.
Blanqui, A. (1849), *Des classes ouvrières en France pendant l'année 1848*, Paguerre, Paris.
Bonaparte, L.N. (1844), *Extinction du paupérisme*, Paguerre, Paris.
Bourgeois, L. (1896), *Solidarité*, A. Colin, Paris.
Bourgeois, L. (1902), *Essai d'une philosophie de la solidarité, conférences et discussions présidées par MM. Bourgeois, Alfred Croiset, École des hautes études sociales, 1901-1902*, Alcan, Paris.
Chevalier, M. (1842-1850), *Cours d'économie politique*, 3 Vols, Capelle, Paris.
Chevalier, M. (1852), *Examen du système commercial connu sous le nom de système protecteur*, Guillaumin, Paris.
Chevalier, M. (1855), *Cours d'économie politique*, **1**, 2nd edition, Capelle, Paris.
Colson, C. (1901-1907), *Cours d'économie politique*, 7 Vols, Gauthier-Villars, Paris.
Dupin, Ch. (1827), *Forces productives et commerciales de la France*, Bachelier, Paris.
Ferry, J. (1868), *Comptes fantastiques d'Haussmann*, Le Chevalier, Paris.
Guesde, J. (1905), *Le collectivisme au Collège de France*, G. Bellais, Paris.
Guyot, Y. (1910), 'Du rôle politique des économistes', *Journal des économistes*, May, pp. 161-76.
Hubert, R. (1928), 'La loi sur les assurances sociales et ses diverses répercussions', *Journal des économistes*, Oct., pp. 117-33; Nov., pp. 261-79.
Landry, A. (1901), *L'Utilité sociale de la propriété individuelle. Étude d'économie politique*, Société nouvelle de librairie et d'édition, Paris.
Landry, A. (1908), *Manuel d'économique. A l'usage des Facultés de droit*, V. Giard et E. Brière, Paris.
Landry, A. and Nogaro, B. (1914), *La crise des finances publiques en France, en Angleterre, en Allemagne*, Alcan, Paris.
Le Play, F. (1855), *Les Ouvriers européens, études sur les travaux, la vie domestique et la condition morale des populations ouvrières de l'Europe*, Imprimerie Impériale, Paris.
Le Play, F. (1857), *Rapport à son excellence M. le ministre de l'agriculture, du commerce et des travaux publics, sur la Boulangerie de Paris, Conseil d'État, N° 686, 12 mars 1857*, Imprimerie Impériale, Paris.
Le Play, F. (1858), *Question de la Boulangerie du département de la Seine, 1er rapport, Conseil d'État, Annexe au N° 686, 23 janvier 1858*, Imprimerie Impériale, Paris.
Le Play, F. (1860), *Question de la Boulangerie du département de la Seine, 2ème rapport, Conseil d'État, N° 1143*, Imprimerie Impériale, Paris.
Le Play, F. (1864), *De la réforme sociale en Europe déduite de l'observation des peuples européens*, 2 Vols, H. Plon, Paris.
Mun, A. de (1885), *La question ouvrière*, J. Lecoffre, Paris.

Mun, A. de (1908), *Ma vocation sociale, souvenirs de la fondation de l'œuvre des cercles catholiques d'ouvriers, 1871-1875*, P. Lethilleux, Paris.
Mun, A. de (1914), *La question sociale, sa solution corporative*, Action populaire, Bibliothèque syndicale, Reims.
Nadaud, M. (1873), *Histoire des classes ouvrières en Angleterre*, Preface by L. Blanc, E. Lachaud, Paris.
Nogaro, B. (1922), *La stabilisation des changes*, Imprimerie Georges Cadet, Paris.
Passy, F. (1862), *Leçons d'économie politique faites à Montpellier*, 2 Vols, 2nd edition, Guillaumin, Paris.
Passy, F. (1889), 'L'impôt progressif sur le revenu', *Extrait du Journal officiel.*
Pereire, É. and I. (1866), *Enquête sur la Banque de France*, Imprimerie de P. Dupont, Paris.
Perreau, C. (1925), *Cours d'économie politique*, **1**, 3rd edn, Librairie générale de droit et de jurisprudence, Paris.
Proudhon, P.-J. (1852), *La Révolution sociale démontrée par le Coup d'État du 2 décembre*, Garnier frères, Paris.
Rist, Ch. (1924), *La déflation en pratique (Angleterre, Etats-Unis, France, Tchéco-Slovaquie)*, M. Giard, Paris.
Say, L. (1865), *La Ville de Paris et le Crédit Foncier; Observations sur le système financier de Mr le préfet de la Seine*, Dentu, Paris.
Say, L. (1866), *Examen critique de la situation financière de la ville de Paris*, Dentu, Paris.
Say, L. (1886), *Les Solutions démocratiques de la question des impôts, conférences faites à l'École des Sciences Politiques*, Guillaumin, Paris.
Simon, J. (1863), *L'ouvrière*, L. Hachette, Paris.
Simon, J. (1866), *Le travail*, A. Lacroix, Paris.
Simon, J. (1867), *L'ouvrier de huit ans*, A. Lacroix, Paris.
Thiers, A. (1848), *De la propriété*, Paulin, Paris.
Truchy, H. (1920), *Cours d'économie politique*, 2 Vols, Sirey, Paris.

Secondary sources

Breton, Y. and Lutfalla, M. (1991) (eds), *L'économie politique en France au 19ème siècle*, Economica, Paris.
Breton, Y., Broder, A. and Lutfalla, M. (1997) (eds), *La longue stagnation en France, L'autre grande dépression, 1873-1897*, Economica, Paris.
Charbit, Y. (1981), 'Du malthusianisme au populationnisme, Les Économistes français et la population 1840-1870', *Travaux et documents. Cahiers*, **90**, Ined-Puf, Paris.
Gonjo, Y. (1972), 'Le "plan Freycinet", 1878-1882: un aspect de la "grande dépression économique en France"', *Revue historique*, **503**(July-September), pp. 49-86.
Le Van-Lemesle, L. (2004), *Le juste ou le riche. L'enseignement de l'économie politique, 1815-1950*, Comité pour l'histoire économique et financière de la France, Paris.
Luciani, J. (1992) (ed.), *Histoire de l'Office du travail (1890-1914)*, Syros, Paris.
Miquel, P. (1989), *La troisième République*, Fayard, Paris.
Mothier, J.-Y. and George, J. (1994), *La plus longue des républiques, 1870-1940*, Fayard, Paris.
Pénin, M. (1997), *Charles Gide (1847-1932). L'esprit critique*, L'Harmattan, Paris.
Pirou, G. (1930), *Les doctrines économiques en France depuis 1870*, 2nd edn, Armand Colin, Paris.
Walch, J. (1975), *Michel Chevalier, Économiste saint-simonien*, J. Vrin, Paris.
Wrigth, V. (1972), *Le Conseil d'État sous le Second Empire*, Presses de la Fondation nationale des sciences politiques, Paris.

Zouboulakis, M. (1998), 'Clément Colson (1853-1939): A Liberal Serving the Public Interest' in W.J. Samuels (ed.), *European Economists of the Early 20th Century*, **1**, *Studies of Neglected Thinkers of Belgium, France, The Netherlands and Scandinavia*, Edward Elgar, Cheltenham, pp. 29-45.

Chapter 7

German Economists in Parliament (1848-1918)

Harald Hagemann and Matthias Rösch

The Frankfurt National Assembly of 1848-1849

The revolution of 1848-1849 which started in early March 1848 predominantly in Baden belongs to the highlights and turning points of German history. For a while a constitutional compromise was adopted: the monarchs remained but the Cabinets they appointed governed in agreement with the Parliaments. The predominantly liberal ministers sought to achieve reforms and the maintenance of law and order alike. The decentralised revolution aimed at the foundation of a German national State and a German Parliament. The 574 delegates of the 'Pre-Parliament' who met in the Frankfurter Paulskirche from 31 March to 3 April mainly came from the Southwest. They were already split into a liberal centre and a democratic left, and the latter into a moderate left around Robert Blum and a radical left led by Friedrich Hecker and Gustav von Struve favouring a 'second revolution'.

The 812 members of the Frankfurt National Assembly who had their constitutional meeting at 18 May 1848 represented an intellectual elite of Germany. They were elected by 'equal and universal suffrage' (i.e. on average about 80 per cent of males were allowed to vote of whom between 40 and 75 per cent participated in the elections) and majority rule. At a time when the genesis of political parties was at a very early stage the indirect vote, in particular, favoured the election of notabilities. Among the members of parliament three-quarters had a university degree, whereas only four were craftsmen, one was a small farmer, and no member elected from among the workers. Professors, advocates, judges/public prosecutors and higher-ranked members of the civil service each contributed groups of about one hundred members.[1] The Frankfurt National Assembly was a civil servants' and jurists' Parliament, sometimes also called a '*Professorenparlament*'. About ten per cent of the members were noblemen. It was symbolic that Heinrich von Gagern and Professor Ernst Moritz Arndt became the first Presidents of the Assembly. The elected members also included the leading economists Bruno Hildebrand and

1 See Wollstein (1999), p. 17. On the dominance of members of parliament with legal training see also Siemann (1976), pp. 308ff.

Friedrich Benedict Wilhelm von Hermann. Johann Heinrich von Thünen (1783-1850) had participated in the special meeting of the Landtag in Schwerin, Mecklenburg and was elected as a substitute for the National Assembly but finally decided not to travel to Frankfurt on account of poor health.[2]

What was the overall outcome of the elections to the Frankfurt National Assembly? Due to the general and indirect elections and the majority rule, ultra-conservatives, i.e. supporters of a Metternich-style system, and socialist revolutionaries alike were mainly absent. The political groups were structured into *Fraktionen*, i.e. parliamentary parties, which were named after the hotels or restaurants where they met (see Appendix).[3] The seats on the right of the Paulskirchen Parliament were taken by the members of the Café Milani, a group of moderate conservatives who came mainly from Prussia, Bavaria and Austria, with strong Christian and federalist orientations, and favoured agreements with the monarchs and existing governments. The Casino and its split-off the Pariser Hof comprised the liberal right, the greatest group of parliamentarians who mainly came from the Southwest, the bourgeoisie from the Rhineland and from the professorship in North Germany. They regarded themselves as the only 'true realists', opposed to all varieties of utopians. Favouring a constitutional monarchy, they were determined adversaries of radical democratic and egalitarian tendencies on the left. Among the members of the Casino were Friedrich Christoph Dahlmann (1785-1860) and many other prominent professors such as Georg Beseler, Johann Gustav Droysen and Karl Theodor Welcker who all were members of the most important Constitutional Committee. Although they all favoured liberal principles, the members of this group were emotionally against radical politicisation. With regard to the constitution, emphasis was more on participation in the institutions of a strong State than on defending liberal rights against the government. As the strongest group the Casino left its mark on the debates and decisions in the National Assembly.

The liberal left consisted of the Württemberger Hof and the related splinter group the Augsburger Hof. Their members came mainly from small and medium States. In contrast to the liberal right and inspired by the ideas of a classless society of early liberalism they emphasised people's sovereignty more strongly and aimed to grant the monarch only the right to a suspensive veto. A prominent member was Robert von Mohl (1799-1875) from Wurttemberg who in 1845 had developed the idea of the model of parliamentarianism, in which the government is carried by the trust and majority in the Parliament, and he had also fought for this idea in the Constitutional Committee. The controversial question of whether a unified Germany should consist of a *großdeutsche Lösung* (greater German solution) with Austria or a *kleindeutsche Lösung* (smaller German solution) without Austria became a dominant issue in national politics, extending across constitutional dividing lines in autumn 1848. This led to a regrouping of parliamentary parties in

2 See Hippauf (2000).
3 See Wollstein (1999) and Nipperdey (1983), pp. 611-12.

which the Westendhall (on the left) and the Augsburger Hof (on the right) separated from the Württemberger Hof whose remaining members favoured the greater Germany including Austria. The most important group of the democratic left was the Deutscher Hof, the party of the eminent Robert Blum (1807-1848), who also represented this group in the Constitutional Committee. He became the martyr of the liberal-democratic revolution when the more radical revolution in 'red Vienna' was overpowered by counterrevolutionary troops led by General Windischgrätz. In heavy fightings more than two thousand people were killed. These events in which the reactionary forces emerged victorious also marked the beginning of the end of the Frankfurt National Assembly. Sent to Vienna as a member of the delegation of the democratic left, Blum was arrested by the Emperor's troops and executed on 9 November. This intentional and provocative denial of the immunity of a parliamentarian, who throughout his life had always been an enemy of violence and had favoured political compromise, not only demonstrated the powerlessness of the Paulskirche but was also rightly recognised in Germany as Habsburg Austria's turning away from a common German and liberal concern.

Whereas the Deutscher Hof at the beginning numbered about 100 parliamentary members, later 60, the Donnersberg group was the most radical group favouring a greater and democratic Germany, to be achieved if necessary by revolutionary means. The about 40 members of this party of revolutionary republicans basically came from the democratic strongholds of Baden – where Friedrich Hecker (1811-1881) and Gustav von Struve (1805-1870) had failed to execute a 'second revolution' in March-April 1848 – Hesse and Saxony. In the autumn of 1848, however, the hour of the reactionary counterrevolution struck, first in Austria, then in Prussia, with the consequence of driving back the achievements of the 'March revolution' and eroding the influence of the Frankfurt National Assembly until spring 1849. In March 1849 the new constitution was passed: it was *kleindeutsch* (without Austria) and remarkably democratic and modern. However, when Frankfurt was beleaguered by Prussian-led troops the remaining members of the first German Parliament decided on 30 May 1849 to move to Stuttgart, the capital of Wurttemberg, the only Kingdom in the Deutscher Bund which had recognised the new constitution. But as early as 6 June, the solemn beginning of the Stuttgart Rump Parliament, a conflict with the government of Wurttemberg arose which finally stopped further sessions by armed force on 18 June.[4] This signified the definitive end of the Frankfurt National Assembly.

Economists in the Paulskirche and in the Economic Committee

The heyday of the Frankfurt National Assembly lasted only for the short period from May to September 1848. During that time the Paulskirche faced two major tasks: the founding of a new unified German State and the passing of a new consti-

4 For detailed information on the Stuttgart Rump Parliament see Weiß (1999).

tution establishing unity and liberty alike. These months of awakening were a period of engaged debates and hard work in committees where professional experts and members with excellent rhetorical skills played a decisive role. In the following we concentrate on economists who were members of parliament and are listed in Table 7.1.

Table 7.1 Economists in the Frankfurt National Assembly

Name	Electoral district	Membership			
		Pre-Parliament	National Assembly	Economic Committee	Stuttgart Rump Parliament 1849
Backhaus, Hermann	Waldeck		X		
Fallati, Johannes	Nagold		X	X	
Hermann, Friedrich von	München		X	X	
Hildebrand, Bruno	Marburg	X	X	X	X
Höfken, Gustav	Dortmund		X		
Lette, Wilhelm A.	Nauen		X	X	
Makowiczka, Franz	Saaz		X	X	
Mohl, Moritz	Heidenheim	X	X	X	X
Mohl, Robert von	Mergentheim	X	X		
Stahl, Friedrich W.	Ellingen		X	X	
Tellkampf, Johann L.	Schweidnitz		X		

Source: The table is based on data from Koch (1989) and Schwarz (1965).

Robert von Mohl was professor of public law at the first special faculty for *Staatswirtschaft* (State Economy) which had been founded by Friedrich List at the University of Tübingen in 1817. The faculty became the first institutional realisation of the special blend of German economics which included the consideration of historical, sociological and legal aspects. In 1844 Robert von Mohl became the founding editor of the oldest surviving and highly acknowledged scholarly journal in the German language area, characteristically named the *Zeitschrift für die gesamte Staatswissenschaft*.[5] In 1860 Albert Schäffle (1831-1903) took over editorial responsibility when he was appointed Professor of Economics at the University of Tübingen. Schäffle, who was also a member of the Second Chamber of Wurttemberg from 1861 to 1865 and of the Customs Parliament in 1868, retained the editorship of the journal even in his years in Vienna, where he was appointed professor at the University in 1868. Subsequently, in another turbulent period at the end of the French-German War, he became Austrian minister of trade for a few months in 1871. After another reactionary backlash he returned to Stuttgart, maintaining the editorship of the journal until his death.

Like Hildebrand and his elder brother, Moritz Mohl (1802-1888) had already been a member of the Pre-Parliament. After having studied State sciences in Tübingen and agriculture at the newly founded (in 1818) Academy in Hohenheim, Stuttgart, he participated in various trade negotiations as, for example, envoy of Wurttemberg in the Berlin negotiations which led to the foundation of a Prussian-German *Zollverein* (customs union). Although he did not embark on an academic career Moritz Mohl published various economic papers and pamphlets and stood out in the Economic Committee particularly for his stand on the elimination of guild coercion. While not a member of any of the parliamentary groups discussed before, he voted with the democratic left. He was considered as the 'most diligent'[6] member of the Economic Committee, disposed 'to talk on everything'.[7]

The increasing importance of economic matters was reflected in the fact that the Committee for Work, Industry and Trade – termed the Economic Committee – had been founded upon the initiative of Hildebrand even before the National Assembly passed standing orders.[8] Friedrich Ludwig von Rönne, the former President of the Prussian Trade Office with extensive experience on practical issues of customs policies, became the first chairman of the Economic Committee which finally had 38 members, most of whom were adequately qualified. The most influential and active member was Bruno Hildebrand (1812-1878), besides Wilhelm Roscher (1817-1894) and Karl Knies (1821-1898) one of the founders of the older Historical School. After studies at the universities in Leipzig and Breslau Hildebrand had become professor of State Sciences at the University of Marburg in liberal Hesse in 1841. He had always been an activist in the liberal and patriotic movement and clashed with the authorities even before the revolutionary period, particularly after he had been elected Prorector of his university in 1845. His main work *Die Nationalökonomie der Gegenwart und Zukunft* (The Economics of the Present and the Future), in which he launched attacks against Adam Smith and classical economics, was published in the very same year of the 1848 revolution. As the representative of the electoral district of Marburg, Hildebrand was elected a

5 Since 1986 the new name is *Journal of Institutional and Theoretical Economics*. For further details see Hagemann (1991).

6 Klaßen (1984), p. 89.

7 Conze and Zorn (1992), p. 31.

8 See Albrecht (1914), p. 8.

deputy of the Frankfurt National Assembly and became a member of the Economic Committee from its foundation up to the end of the Stuttgart Rump Parliament. As a member of the Westendhall group he belonged to the moderate wing of the democratic left.

Very soon after its foundation the Economic Committee found itself facing a great number of topics to debate and an even greater number of petitions. As early as in the second session seven subcommittees were founded to facilitate work. The members could volunteer for active participation in more than one subcommittee. The following list of the subcommittees is a good indicator of the main economic issues forming the focus of the Paulskirchen Parliament.[9] The number in brackets refers to the members engaged in the various subcommittees:

1. Agriculture and Forestry (5);
2. Industry and Mining (6);
3. Trade, Sea Traffic and Customs Regulation (13);
4. Internal Communication, Postal and Railway System, Canals and Internal Customs (9);
5. Money, Credit and Banking (7);
6. Mint, Weights and Measures (4);
7. General Working Conditions, Emigration, Settling Down and Freedom of Movement (15).

It soon became clear that the 'social question' was a major concern for most members. Bernhard Eisenstuck, the later Chairman of the Economic Committee, even emphasised that 'the efforts of the Parliament only centre around two questions: the making of the constitution … and the social appeasement of the *Vaterland*'.[10] Bruno Hildebrand soon became the chairman of this most important seventh subcommittee. Like the Verein für Sozialpolitik later founded in 1872,[11] of which he became a founding member, Hildebrand was opposed both to the *laissez-faire* positions of the Manchester school as well as to the revolutionary ideas of Marxism. In 1848 he stood up for the principles of the liberal revolution, as a member of the Frankfurt National Assembly as well as a deputy for Bockenheim in the Diet of the electorate of Hesse (*Kurhessen*) where he made the application to deny the government the required finances which were unconstitutional. This caused him the loss of his professorship in the restoration period, and Hildebrand emigrated to Switzerland to escape being arrested.

In Switzerland, where he later became an honorary citizen, Hildebrand was awarded a professorship for State sciences at the University of Zurich and also became director of a railway company. In 1856 he obtained an appointment in Berne where he founded the Swiss Statistical Office. More than a decade after his

9 For a more detailed analysis see Conze and Zorn (1992).
10 Quotation after Conze and Zorn (1992), p. 27.
11 See Hagemann (2001).

emigration Hildebrand came to terms with German constitutional reality and accepted an offer from the University of Jena in 1861. He initiated the foundation of the Statistical Office of the united Thuringian states in 1864. The previous year had seen the publication of the first issue of the new journal *Jahrbücher für Nationalökonomie und Statistik*, of which Hildebrand was the founding editor until his death in 1879, when he was succeeded by his son-in-law Johannes Conrad. The evolution of statistics into a modern and important subject was a widespread phenomenon in the mid-nineteenth century. The use of more sophisticated statistical techniques achieved increasing significance: to use data purely for descriptive or illustrative purposes was no longer adequate. Displaying hostility to British classical economics and the treatment of economic laws as epistemologically analogous to physical laws, Hildebrand was an early advocate and spearhead of this movement. However, he never published the second volume of his main work with the treatment of the 'historical method' which he had announced in 1848.[12]

Karl Knies (1821-1898), who later had a profound influence on Max Weber, had been a student in his home town Marburg where he was appointed university lecturer after completing his dissertation. Under the influence of his mentor Hildebrand Knies also became a progressive liberal who sought to address the economic and social problems of his time. The restoration caused a break in his academic career. Knies emigrated to Switzerland from 1852-1855 where he became a teacher in Schaffhausen. In that period he published his programmatic treatment *Political Economy from the Viewpoint of the Historical Method* (1853), which gives a good insight into the ideas of the older Historical School. In 1855 Knies was appointed professor at the University of Freiburg in liberal Baden. Although a protestant from Hesse he was elected deputy in the Diet and became involved in the education reform. In 1865 he moved to the University of Heidelberg, where Friedrich von Wieser, Eugen von Böhm-Bawerk, but also many Americans like John Bates Clark, Richard T. Ely, the founder of the American Economic Association, and Edwin R.A. Seligman, were among his students, and where he taught until death.

Friedrich Benedict Wilhelm von Hermann (1795-1868) was the most outstanding economic theoretician in the Frankfurt National Assembly. Hermann had made his reputation with the book *Staatswirthschaftliche Untersuchungen* (1832), which was published in the very same year in which he was promoted to a full professorship at the University of Munich, where he had held a special professorship for technology and political economy since 1827. With his *opus magnum* Hermann laid the foundations for a German brand of classical economics on which later work by Thünen and Hans von Mangoldt was built. He was one of the first authors who attempted to use the classical principle of extensively and intensively decreasing marginal returns as an explanation of all forms of income within an analysis of the short run, i.e. with a given amount and structure of the capital stock.

12 For a detailed assessment of Hildebrand's achievements as an economist, including his stages theory, see Schefold (2004), pp. 377-99.

He regarded all economic variables as the outcome of the forces of supply and demand and placed the analysis of the factors lying behind it into the centre of his investigations. It is therefore no surprise that Alfred Marshall later praised 'the brilliant genius of Hermann'[13] and quoted him frequently in his own *Principles of Economics.* Schumpeter also admired Hermann's analytical capabilities and judgements and stressed that Hermann's work should not be discounted since 'he stands out for lack of competition'.[14] In 1839 Hermann became the founding director of the Bavarian Statistical Bureau.

Having been main advisor on economic and social questions to Maximilian II of Bavaria, Hermann represented the electoral district of Munich in the Frankfurt National Assembly. In the Paulskirchen Parliament he was a member of the group Württemberger Hof, the left wing of the liberal centre which favoured the 'greater German solution'. This was the dominant position in the Paulskirche in summer 1848, when a Law was passed and the popular Habsburg prince Erzherzog Johann, who had been delegated the regency in Austria on 15 June, was elected *Reichsverweser* by the Frankfurt National Assembly on 28 June, by 436 against only 112 votes. On 13 July Erzherzog Johann nominated prince Karl zu Leiningen, a leading German 'Whig' and half-brother of Queen Victoria, as Prime Minister, who formed a Cabinet with ministers mainly from the right wing of the liberal centre but also some members from the left centre. After the events in Vienna a few months later the 'greater German solution' was more or less dead and the 'smaller German solution' began to dominate, as reflected in the splitting off of the Württemberger Hof into three equally numerous groups, with the Westendhall on the left and the Augsburger Hof on the right, both favouring the 'smaller German solution'.

With all his practical experience on customs matters and the other issues, Hermann became the Chairman of the third Subcommittee on Trade, Sea Traffic and Customs Regulation. Here he was able to use his enormous analytical talents and statistical knowledge. Hermann was a dedicated liberal in the best sense of the classical tradition, who advocated a constitution which recognised the sovereignty of the people and the abolition of nobility by birth. This caused him some temporary problems in the restoration period after the end of the Frankfurt National Assembly, compelling him to relinquish the Ministry in Bavaria. However, his advice was soon badly missed by the King and in 1850 Hermann was reappointed to the Bavarian civil service. Hermann, who always had favoured federalist structures and the greater German solution including Austria, also became a member of

13 Marshall (1961), p. 768.

14 Schumpeter (1954), p. 503. For a modern assessment of Hermann's theoretical achievements, particularly his contributions to the theory of capital, profits and relative prices, see Kurz (1998). Kurz emphasises that Hermann's writings reflect 'a period of transition from classical to marginalist economics and one in which the 'social question' became ever more pressing. On the one hand Hermann contributed to the development of the classical theory of value and distribution, and on the other he prepared the ground for the replacement of that theory by marginal productivity theory', Kurz (1998), p. 119.

the Bavarian Parliament from 1849 to 1855. Among his students were Georg Friedrich Knapp and Lujo Brentano, who also had been heavily influenced by the anti-Prussian tradition of Southern Germany, and later held a chair at the University of Munich for a prolonged period.

Johannes Fallati, professor of new history and statistics at the University of Tübingen and co-editor of the *Zeitschrift für die gesamte Staatswissenschaft* from 1844 until his death in 1855, was the chairman of the fourth subcommittee. In August 1848 Fallati became Undersecretary in the Trade Ministry. Like Hermann he first was a member of the Württemberger Hof before he shifted to the Augsburger Hof in the separation of December 1848. The importance of the (free) trade debate is signalled by the high number of members of the Economic Committee who signed in for the third and fourth subcommittees. In the debates on protective tariffs the followers of Friedrich List achieved a majority. The deputy Ernst von Merck estimated that 22 of the originally 30 members of the Economic Committee favoured the levying of tariffs for the protection of the domestic economy, among them Fallati, Hermann, Hildebrand and Moritz Mohl. This reflected the reservations against free trade ideas in Southern Germany according to the position expressed in the policy of the *Zollverein* (Customs Union), which favoured liberal principles but had been established in 1834 under Prussian leadership.[15] Later, following the entry of several new members and the departure from the committee of some defenders of protective tariffs, the ratio changed and the adherents of free trade and those of protective tariffs were temporarily equally strong.[16]

Nevertheless, in the third subcommittee there had always been a strong current favouring free trade, which showed the limits of the power and influence of the chairman Hildebrand. A central role in these free trade activities was played by Wilhelm-Adolf Lette (1799-1868), a member of the Casino group who had studied philosophy and law but, without any academic position, published on economic issues. Lette was an activist in the German free trade movement which sprang up in opposition after the raising of the first protective tariff on pig iron in 1844 had led to major controversies within the German Zollverein. Lette later became the first chairman of the permanent delegation of the Congress of German Economists from its foundation in 1858 until his death in 1868. However, even deputies, particularly from Southern Germany, who favoured protective tariffs, such as the leader of the 'Greater Germans' von Hermann, favoured the customs union with Austria.[17]

A member of the Economic Committee and its Secretary was Franz Makowiczka (1811-1890). He was an activist in the Württemberger Hof and was forced to resign from his professorship at the University of Cracow which he had held since 1846. From 1849-1851 he edited the German newspaper of Bohemia in Prague before the Austrian government kicked him out of this position too. In 1852 he

15 See Conze and Zorn (1992), p. 31.
16 See Albrecht (1914), p. 13.
17 Ibid., p. 26.

became professor of State sciences and public finance at the University of Erlangen, a position which he kept until his death. From 1869-1873 he was a member of the Second Chamber in Bavaria and leader of the Liberal Party.

Members of parliament, however not of the Economic Committee, were also Hermann Backhaus (1817-1901), Johann Wilhelm Gustav Höfken (1811-1889) and Louis Tellkampf. All three belonged to the Württemberger Hof. Tellkampf, who had earlier taught in the Unites States, was professor of State sciences at the University of Breslau from 1846 until his death in 1876. Backhaus, who came from Hesse and had obtained his PhD at the University of Jena in 1840, was a member of the Committee for International Law and later, from 1872 until his death, Professor of Agricultural Economics at the University of Kiel. Höfken had written on scientific and political issues for various German newspapers. He became *Privatdocent* for social economics at the University of Heidelberg and was a member of the Frankfurt National Assembly from May to September 1848, where he was active as a member and reporter of the Committee for International Law and Policy. Höfken moved to Vienna in the following year, where he embarked on a career in the Trade Ministry, was ennobled ('von Hattingsheim') in 1867 and became one of the cofounders of the Kreditanstalt in 1885.

Economists in the Reichstag (1867-1918)

As the result of the 1866 Prussian-Austrian War the Deutsche Bund of 1815 was blown apart, not by the national movement but by the antagonism of its two leading powers. One outcome of the resulting new order was the foundation of the Norddeutsche Bund with Prussia as the hegemonial power which had annexed Hanover, Hesse, Nassau and Frankfurt, the formerly independent city of the Paulskirchen Parliament which was now humiliated and obliged to pay contributions. Thus the smaller German solution (without Austria) materialised, and was completed by the addition of the southern German states when the Deutsches Reich was founded after the French-German War of 1870-1871. Bismarck's policy of combining Prussia's hegemony with the federal principle was reflected in the constitution of the Norddeutsche Bund with a *Bundesrat* as the central agency, whose Presidency was managed by the Chancellor directly appointed by the Prussian King, and the *Reichstag*, a new Parliament elected in secret ballots and on the basis of universal and direct elections. However, the Parliament was limited to a legislative function. From 1871 (1874) the Reichstag had 382 (397) deputies who were elected for three years, and for five years from 1890 onwards.

Until the end of Imperial Germany in 1918, several economists became members of the Reichstag (see Table 7.2). However, their role never was as important again as in the Frankfurt National Assembly of 1848-1849. Characteristically the new Reichstag also was located in Berlin, the capital of Prussia which became the capital of Germany in 1871. For lack of space some cases are selected and discussed in greater detail.

Table 7.2 Economists in the Reichstag (1867-1918)

Name	Membership	Parliamentary Party	Electoral district
Arnold, Wilhelm	1881-1883 (Death)	K	Kassel
Bamberger, Ludwig	1868-1893	NL/LV/DFrP	Mainz
Baumstark, Eduard	1867	NM	Stralsund
Bernstein, Eduard	1902-1907	SPD	Breslau
	1912-1918	SPD/USPD	Breslau
	1920-1928	USPD/SPD	Potsdam
Braun, Karl	1867-1871	NL	Wiesbaden
	1871-1874	NL	Reuß younger line
	1874-1884	NL/LV	Liegnitz
	1884-1887	DFrP	Saxony
Lette, Wilhelm A.	1867	NL	Frankfurt/Oder
	1867-1868 (Death)	NL	Waldeck-Pyrmont
Michaelis, Otto	1867	NL	Stettin
Mohl, Moriz	1871-1874	NM	Wurttemberg
Mohl, Robert von	1874-1875 (Death)	NL	Baden
Naumann, Friedrich	1907-1912	FrVp	Heilbronn
	1913-1918	DFVp	Waldeck-Pyrmont
	1919 (Death)	DDP	Berlin
Oppenheim, Heinrich B.	1874-1877	NL	Reuß older line
Prince-Smith, John	1871-1873/4	NL	Anhalt-Zerbst
Richter, Eugen	1867	F	Erfurt
	1871-1874	F	Schwarzburg-Rudolstadt
	1874-1906 (Death)	F/DFrP/FrVp	Arnsberg
Schulze-Delitzsch, Hermann	1867-1874	F	Berlin
	1874-1883 (Death)	F	Wiesbaden
Schulze-Gaevernitz, Gerhart von	1912-1918	DFVp	Baden
	1919-1920	DDP	Baden
Seelig, Wilhelm	1871-1874	F	Kiel
	1890-1893	DFrP	Kiel
Tellkampf, Johann L.	1871-1876 (Death)	NL	Liegnitz

List of abbreviations: NM: no membership in parliamentary parties; DDP: Deutsche Demokratische Partei (German Democratic Party); DFrP: Deutsche Freisinnige Partei (German Liberal Party); DFVp: Deutsche Fortschrittliche Volkspartei (German Progressive People's Party); F: Fortschrittspartei (Progressive Party); FrVp: Freisinnige Volkspartei (Liberal People's Party); K: Konservative Partei (Conservative Party); LV: Liberale Vereinigung (Liberal Association); NL: Nationalliberale Partei (National Liberal Party); SPD: Sozialdemokratische Partei Deutschlands (Social Democratic Party); USPD: Unabhängige Sozialdemokratische Partei Deutschlands (Independent Social Democratic Party).

A very interesting and important case is Ludwig Bamberger (1823-1899) who had been a young revolutionary in his home town of Mainz in 1848-1849, where he edited the *Mainzer Zeitung*. He had been elected a member of the Paulskirchen Parliament in a by-election in 1849 and he commanded a military revolutionary unit of volunteers from Rhinehesse in Kirchheimbonlanden during the *Pfälzer Erhebung* (Palatinate revolt) in May-June 1849. Due to the latter activities Bamberger, who first emigrated to Switzerland, was sentenced to death for *Hochverrat* (high treason) by a court in Zweibrücken in 1851.[18] After periods in Zurich, Geneva, Bern, London, Antwerp, Rotterdam and Brussels, Bamberger entered into the management of his uncle's bank, Bischoffsheim & Goldschmidt in Paris, where he embarked on a successful career as a banker. Bamberger underwent a transition from a revolutionary democrat to a liberal but never bourgeois citizen, who came back to Germany in 1866 and achieved a long-term career as a member of parliament. In 1867 he was elected as the Mainz delegate to the Customs Parliament and shortly afterwards became a member of the Reichstag. Bamberger associated himself with the National Liberal Party, in those years allied with Bismarck. At the end of the French-German War Bamberger became a close financial advisor of Bismarck, for some time becoming a rival of Gerson Bleichröder, thus provoking metaphors like the 'red' and the 'white revolutionary'.

Most important was Bamberger's decisive role in the foundation process of the first monetary union in Germany and the Reichsbank.[19] During the nineteenth century the monetary system in Germany was characterised by a confusing diversity. The splitting of the monetary system in the post-Napoleonic Deutscher Bund led to a conflict between the opposing interests of advocates and adversaries of the political unification movement, who clashed on the battlefield of currency policy. The rivalry between Prussia and Austria was reflected in the coexistence of the Taler, adopted also by most states in the Prussian-dominated north, and the Gulden, adopted also by most states in the sphere of Austrian influence in the South. Although both currencies were silver-based, the confusing diversity was exacerbated by the fact that a certain amount of silver was fixed at 14 Taler in Prussia but 24.5 Gulden in Austria. Moreover the situation was further aggravated in that one Taler was worth 30 Groschen in Prussia, with 12 Pfennigs as one Groschen, whereas in Saxony one Groschen was worth 10 Pfennigs, and in Mecklenburg, for example, one Taler was equivalent to 48 Schillings. At the central banking place Frankfurt, which belonged to the Gulden area, bills could be paid in emergency cases by French francs but not by Prussian Taler, which created competitive disadvantages for Prussian merchants while not worrying Austrian diplomats. The time was certainly ripe for a major currency reform after the foundation of the German Reich, and Bamberger became the most active and enthusiastic proponent. In June 1871 a committee of the Reichstag voted for a standard of currency with a decimal subdivision as the first step. The introduction of the Mark, having the equivalent of 100 Pfennigs, became a major programmatic issue of the National

---

18 For greater details on Bamberger's life and achievements see the biography by Koehler (1999).

19 See also Häuser (1998) and James (1998).

Liberal Party. The next steps were the *Gesetz zur Ausprägung von Goldmünzen*, the Law for the stamping of gold coins, launched by the Reichstag in December 1871, and the *Münzgesetz* (Coinage Law) from July 1873. A transformation to the gold standard was associated with the new currency, although silver Taler coins remained in circulation even until 1907. The realignment rates were 3 Marks for one Taler and 1.71 Marks for one Gulden.

The transformation to the gold standard did not necessarily imply the establishment of a central bank. However, debates on the foundation of the Reichsbank ran through the whole year 1874 against the background of massive outflows of gold after the *Gründerkrise* had taken grip of the German economy. In the decisive debates in November 1874 Ludwig Bamberger took the initiative and presented a new Bank Bill in which emphasis concerning the main function of the central bank was placed on being the lender of last resort and not on currency stability, which should be guaranteed by the gold standard. On 30 January 1875 the Reichstag voted with great majority for the foundation of the Reichsbank. In March 1875 the Kaiser signed the bills and on 1 January 1876 the Reichsbank started work. Of the 32 banks of issue in the Deutsches Reich twelve then gave back their concessions immediately, most importantly the Preußische Bank which was merged in the Reichsbank. Over time the number of remaining banks of issue besides the Reichsbank continued to decrease. By the end of the Wilhelminian era only those in Saxony, Bavaria, Baden and Wurttemberg remained. Like the Bank of England the Reichsbank was a privately owned institution which, due to Bamberger's design, was remarkably independent from direct political interference by the government. Interestingly, this relative independence in the highly authoritarian period after 1879 was not only emphasised by genuine liberals but later more and more also by social democrats who were excluded from power in the Wilhelminian system.

In the first elections to the Reichstag after unification in 1871 the National Liberal Party won 125 out of 382 seats (1874: 155, 1877: 128). Together with the Deutsche Fortschrittspartei the two liberal parties had a majority of 53 per cent. However, in the wake of the six years of recession that had started in 1873 Bismarck reoriented his trade policy. Whereas in spring 1862 Prussia had entered into a trade agreement with France and thereby approached the free trade policies of the Western powers that had signed the Cobden-Chevalier treaty in 1860, clearly distancing itself from the more protective policies of Austria, Bismarck now gave in to the mounting pressures of industrialists and farmers and began his *Schutzzollpolitik* in 1878. This caused a major crisis in the National Liberal Party, leading to a secession of a group including Bamberger in 1880 who did not follow Bismarck's reorientation in contrast to the party majority and upheld the principles of free trade. In 1884 Bamberger and the other secessionists united with the Progressive Party to form the Deutsche Freisinnige Partei. The alliance later split over a conflict on the military budget in 1893.

As in other countries conflicts and controversies on trade issues characterised debates in Parliament and among economists in nineteenth-century Germany. The introduction of protective tariffs on pig iron in 1844 had provoked a reaction and led to the genesis of the free trade movement in Germany in which John Prince-Smith (1809-1874), a naturalised Prussian citizen who had come from England in 1831, played an instrumental role. Influenced by Richard Cobden and John Bright who had founded the Anti-Corn-Law League in England in 1838 (and were successful with the repeal of the Corn Laws in 1846) and Frédéric Bastiat, who had constituted an Association of Free Trade in Paris in 1846, Prince-Smith started an initiative to found a German Free Trade Union. After a preparatory gathering in December 1846 some 200 businessmen, journalists and economists subsequently met in the Berlin Stock Exchange in March 1847 and founded the Deutscher Freihandelsverein. Similar associations were soon founded in Hamburg, Stettin, Breslau and other, predominantly Prussian and seacoast cities, whereas in Southern Germany greater reservations to free trade views persisted, with even many of the leading political liberals following protectionist tendencies. Prince-Smith was also the head of the German delegation to the famous Free Trade congress that met in Brussels in 1847.

In 1848 Prince-Smith travelled to Frankfurt, together with his friend and fellow free-trader Julius Faucher (1820-1878), to influence the members of the Paulskirchen Parliament, particularly those of the Economic Committee, in the direction of Manchester liberalism. The result was not overwhelming. Prince-Smith had greater success as a teacher at the Free Trade School which he founded and where he became the mentor of many later important economic journalists such as Julius Faucher, Max Wirth, Otto Michaelis and Otto Wolff. Like Prince-Smith, Faucher and Michaelis also became members of the Prussian Parliament in the 1860s (see Table 7.3). Michaelis was also a short-term member of the Reichstag, and soon became responsible for finance, trade and traffic affairs in the newly founded Reichskanzleramt (Chancellor's Office). As a member of the Reichstag, shortly before his death on 3 February 1874 Prince-Smith witnessed his greatest triumph. With the elimination of tariffs on the import of pig iron and the last tariffs for exports, the free trade movement in Germany was at its peak. However, with the setting in of a prolonged and deep recession in the very same year the influence of liberal economic ideas soon started to wane.[20]

From 1860 until his death Prince-Smith had also been the Chairman of the Volkswirtschaftliche Gesellschaft, i.e. the Economic Society which was one of the followers of the Free Trade Union. As a deputy of the Prussian Parliament from 1861 to 1866 he was not particularly active and attended only those sessions in which economic issues were at the centre. He remained aloof from the intense constitutional controversies between the liberals and Bismarck, which had led to the formation of the Progressive Party in 1861, and did not stand for re-election in 1866. He was much more active as a contributor to the *Vierteljahresschrift für Volkswirtschaft, Politik und Kulturgeschichte*, a quarterly journal for economics,

20 On Prince-Smith see the biography by Otto Wolff (1880).

Table 7.3 Economists in the Prussian Parliament

Name	Membership	Parliamentary party	Electoral district
Braun, Karl	1867-1870	NL	Wiesbaden 2
	1870-1879	NL	Breslau 7
Degenkolb, Carl G.	1852-1855	Linke	Merseburg 8
Faucher, Julius	1862-1866	F	Merseburg 3
	1867-1868	F	Cologne 5
	1868-1870	NL	Cologne 5
Lette, Wilhelm A.	1852-1855	Linke	Merseburg 8
	1855-1858	Linke	Frankfurt 3
	1859	?	Frankfurt 3
	1860-1861	von Vincke	Frankfurt 3
	1862	Rechte (Grabow)	Frankfurt 3
	1862	NM	Frankfurt 3
	1863	FPV	Frankfurt 3
	1863-1866	Linkes Zentrum	Frankfurt 3
	1866-1868 (Death)	NL	Frankfurt 3
Michaelis, Otto	1862-1866	F	Stettin 1
	1866-1867	NL	Stettin 3
Nasse, Erwin	1869-1879	FK	Koblenz 4
Prince-Smith, John	1861-1866	F	Stettin 2
Richter, Eugen	1869-1870	F	Frankfurt 3
	1870-1879	F	Arnsberg 4
	1879-1882	F	Berlin 4
	1882-1885	F	Arnsberg 4
	1886-1893	DFrP	Arnsberg 4
	1894-1898	FrVp	Berlin 2
	1899-1905	FrVp	Arnsberg 4
Riedel, Adolf F.J.	1849-1852	Rechte	Potsdam 7
	1852-1855	Linke	Berlin 2
	1859-1861	von Vincke	Berlin 2
Rodbertus, Johann K.	1849	Linke	Berlin 2
Schulze-Delitzsch,	1849	Linke	Merseburg
Hermann	1861-1872	F	Berlin 3
Seelig, Wilhelm	1873-1893	DFrP	Kiel
Tellkampf, Johann L.	1849-1852	Linke	Breslau 7
Wagner, Adolph	1882-1885	K	Potsdam 6

List of abbreviations: NM: no membership in parliamentary parties; DFrP: Deutschfreisinnige Partei (German Liberal Party); F: Fortschrittspartei (Progressive Party); FPV: Freier Parlamentarischer Verein (Free Parliamentary Association); FK: Freikonservative Partei (Liberal Conservative Party); FrVp: Freisinnige Volkspartei (Liberal People's Party); K: Konservative Partei (Conservative Party); Linke (Left); Linkes Zentrum (Left Centre); NL: Nationalliberale Partei (National Liberal Party); Rechte (Right); von Vincke.

Source: The table is based on data from Haunfelder (1994) and Mann (1988).

policy and cultural history that was edited by his closest associate Julius Faucher from its foundation in 1863 to 1875, and which should be regarded as the central scientific journal of the German free trade movement. Prince-Smith also succeeded Wilhelm-Adolf Lette from 1868-1874 as the chairman of the permanent delegation of the Congress of German Economists which had been founded in 1858 as the first scholarly association of German economists. Although the Congress advocated free trade, the members varied in their views and could not overall be reduced to holding radical and simplified positions of Manchester liberalism.[21] Nevertheless the Congress found itself embroiled in a complex and antagonistic relationship with the Verein für Sozialpolitik from 1872 to its end in 1885. The Verein had been founded as a reaction to the social question and in opposition to both the revolutionary ideas of Marxism and *laissez-faire* positions of the Manchester School as they were shared by several members of the Congress, who were ignorant of the poverty and problems brought about by the growing industrialisation process in Germany. It was a leading congressman, the journalist Heinrich Bernhard Oppenheim (1819-1880), who had launched the attack against the group of professors founding the Verein für Sozialpolitik and coined the term *Kathedersozialisten* (socialists of the chair) in December 1871. Interestingly in 1848 Oppenheim himself had been an active radical democrat (whose attempt to become a deputy in the Frankfurt National Assembly failed), even supporting ultraleft activities of Struve in Baden. As a *Privatdocent* at the University of Heidelberg in the 1840s Oppenheim with his radical-democratic views strongly influenced his young student Bamberger, who three decades later in 1876 followed his former master in heavily attacking the chair socialists in a famous speech in the Reichstag.

On the other hand, it was the long-time chairman (1874-1890) of the Verein für Sozialpolitik Erwin Nasse (1829-1890), Professor of economics at the University of Bonn since 1860, also a member in the Prussian Parliament from 1869-1879, who, in contrast to his successor (1890-1917) Gustav Schmoller, stood firm in his free trade views after Bismarck's reorientation of trade policy towards protective tariffs which caused a major crisis within the Verein in 1879.[22]

A life-long advocate of free trade was also Lujo Brentano (1844-1931), the leader of the left within the Verein, who was an ardent proponent of the establishment of trade unions to improve the conditions of the working class and thereby to solve the social question within the framework of a capitalist economic system. Brentano was convinced that the German economy required free trade because it had developed into an industrial economy for which it was important to supply cheap food for the workers and the rapidly growing population and to generate export markets for industrial products. The protective tariffs would benefit agriculture and heavy industries but would imply substantial competitive disadvantages for the manufacturing and consumption-goods industries. He also pointed to the enormous

---

21 See Hentschel (1975) for a differentiated treatment of the German free traders and the Economic Congress.

22 See Hagemann (2001) for greater details.

increase of wealth in Britain after the abolition of the Corn Laws and free trade as a means to secure peace in the world.[23] Although he was highly political,[24] Brentano, who was born into a well-known Catholic patrician family with strong anti-Prussian sentiments, did not follow a political career in Imperial Germany. When the government of the new Weimar Republic considered appointing him as the ambassador to the United States Brentano declined because of his advanced age.

An economist who had received his basic training from Karl Heinrich Rau was Eugen Richter (1838-1906). Richter first was a free-lance author and then became one of the first professional politicians in Germany. He was a committed free trader and a convinced and very active member of the Congress of German Economists. In 1867 he became a member of the Reichstag and shortly afterwards of the Prussian Parliament, and remained a member of both houses until his death. Richter was a leader of the liberal left strongly opposed to Bismarck's policies as well as to Marxist tendencies among the social democrats. In 1874 he became the chairman of the Progressive Party and after the unification with the secessionists from the National Liberal Party – who opposed Bismarck's protectionist policies – the chairman of the new Deutsche Freisinnige Partei. Whereas both groups of the new political party agreed on combating Bismarck's social and trade policies, on military issues they held different views. These led to a split in 1893 when the secessionists from the National Liberal Party voted in favour of Chancellor Caprivi's Military Bill comprising a greater increase of the budget. Upon petition by the chairman the advocates of Caprivi's Bill, including Bamberger, were excluded from the Liberal Party. They founded a new Free Parliamentary Association, whereas the remaining part led by Richter now changed its name to the Freisinnige Volkspartei (Liberal People's Party).

A close associate of Richter in the fight for free trade in the Reichstag and in the Prussian Parliament over many years was Karl Braun (1822-1893), who succeeded Prince-Smith as the chairman of the permanent delegation of the Congress in 1874, until the end of this association in 1885. Besides Lette, Rudolf von Bennigsen (1824-1902), the later long-time chairman of the National Liberal Party, Schulze-Delitzsch, Hopf and Pickford, Braun had already been one of the first six elected members to that delegation in 1858. Having been a liberal activist in 1848-1849 he lost his accreditation at the courts of justice during the restoration period in Hesse-Nassau and became a politician. He was President of the Parliament in Hesse-Nassau until the annexation by Prussia in 1866. As a committed free trader he was among the secessionists from the National Liberal Party.

One of the very few professors of economics in the Reichstag and the Prussian Parliament was Wilhelm Seelig (1821-1906).[25] Seelig, a specialist on agricultural and customs policy, came from Göttingen, where he had written a doctoral disser-

23 See Brentano (1931), pp. 271-5.

24 He repeatedly was involved in conflicts with industrialists at meetings of the Verein because of his favouring of the organised coalition of workers.

25 See Biesenbach (1969), pp. 104-7 and Pusback (1988), pp. 334-8.

tation on Colbert's financial system in 1844 and obtained his habilitation a year later, subsequently obtaining an appointment at the University of Freiburg in 1853 to succeed Peter Mischler. The latter had moved to the Charles University in Prague, where he exerted a stronger influence on his famous student Carl Menger. After only one year Seelig accepted the offer from the University of Kiel, mainly for political reasons because he hoped to avoid the appointment of another 'pro-Danish' professor. There he stayed as a professor of economics, public finance and statistics for half-a-century. Interestingly, Karl Knies who had been placed *primo loco* ahead of Seelig by the philosophical faculty of Freiburg University in 1853, but had not been appointed by the Ministry in Baden during the restoration period when he was in his Swiss exile, became Seelig's successor in 1855.

A short-term member of the newly constituted Norddeutscher Reichstag in 1867 was Eduard Baumstark (1807-1889), from 1829-1838 *Privatdocent* at the University of Heidelberg, where he had been influenced by Rau, and since 1838 Professor of Economics at the University of Greifswald. In contrast, a politically far more active figure, maintaining his political commitment for a considerably longer period, was Hermann Schulze-Delitzsch (1808-1883), who had already become a member of the Prussian Parliament in 1849 and again from 1861-1872. Always an activist of the liberal left, Schulze-Delitzsch was one of the most decisive opponents of Bismarck and one of the co-founders of the Progressive Party in 1861. From 1867 until his death in 1883 he was also a member of the Reichstag. Together with Bennigsen he was one of the main founders of the Deutscher Nationalverein in 1859. For Schulze-Delitzsch the liberal ideas of Bastiat and others were compatible with the ideas and praxis of social reforms. He was an outstanding member of the Congress from the very beginning. However, when the Verein für Sozialpolitik was founded in 1872, Schulze-Delitzsch, who belonged to the small minority that saw Manchester liberalism as in crisis, and who, like Schmoller, Brentano and Wagner, recognised the need for a more ethical science and for social reforms, eventually left the Congress. A charismatic speaker and a man of practical reform more than of deeper theoretical analysis, he is best remembered today as the founder of the *Genossenschaftsbewegung* (cooperatives movement). As early as 1849 he had founded the first association of shoemakers and joiners in his home town Delitzsch in Saxony. As a liberal he consistently favoured competition balanced by solidarity and mutual liability within the voluntary activities of a group, with the State as guarantor of the rule of law but not as the supplier of financial means. Here as on other issues Schulze-Delitzsch clashed with Ferdinand Lassalle, who claimed financial support from the State for his productive associations. Lassalle also attacked Schulze-Delitzsch on the issue of the latter's aim of forming a liberal workers movement, in a biting and witty pamphlet *Herr Bastiat-Schulze von Delitzsch* (1864), which however became obsolete with the foundation and growth of the trade unions. Like his contemporary Friedrich Wilhelm Raiffeisen, who founded the rural cooperative banks, Schulze-Delitzsch can be seen as an idealist reformer and educator who endeavoured to strengthen the forces of self-help within free associations of producers and consumers.

Bismarck's reorientation of trade policy, his introduction of the socialist laws (1878-1890) and the reactionary tendencies in the Wilhelminian era (1888-1918) did not provide fertile soil for the activities of economists, of mainly liberal conviction, in Parliament. Indeed their number was quite limited, and their degree of activities by no means matched that of 1848-1849 or the early and mid-1870s after unification. The hegemony of protectionist policies and the illiberal climate in the political sphere in general led many economists into opposition and/or a retreat from engagement in Parliament. It also contributed to the dissolution of the Congress of German Economists in 1885, and to a longer crisis within the Verein für Sozialpolitik after the controversies on trade policy at the 1879 meeting. Within the Verein it marked the beginning of a long period of social-conservative dominance until a new generation took centre stage in the 1890s, with Max Weber and his younger brother Alfred, Werner Sombart and Friedrich Naumann as their most brilliant minds. They had noted that the Verein had only very little influence on Bismarck's great projects of social legislation, the introduction of accident, health and old-age insurance in 1884 and 1889, with which he sought to pacify the workers in the period of the anti-socialist laws. Having realised that the central authorities of Imperial Germany were not willing to undertake liberal reforms, to devise a fundamental solution for the social question and to overcome the disintegration of society, they were less inclined to make political compromises than older numbers such as the chairman Schmoller or Wagner. On the other hand, led by Max Weber, although themselves holding a strong political commitment they insisted much more strongly on the separation of value judgments from scientific analysis. Such differences led to a major controversy at the 1905 conference when Naumann, supported by his friend Weber, attacked Schmoller because of his illusions on the role of the State, thus triggering the subsequent *Werturteilsstreit*, a fundamental debate about normative judgments which persisted until the beginning of WW1.[26]

Friedrich Naumann (1860-1919) was a protestant theologian and pastor from Saxony who first associated with the Christian-socialist movement in 1890 and became a full-time publicist and politician in 1894.[27] In 1896 he founded the Nationalsozialer Verein (NSV), a political party by which he endeavoured to attract the industrial workers away from the social democrats by playing the national card. However, the attempt failed and the NSV basically attracted only young people from the liberal bourgeoisie and was not successful at elections. This episode came to an end when Naumann dissolved the NSV, after which most former members joined the Freisinnige Volkspartei (Liberal People's Party) in 1903. Naumann, who first became a member of the Reichstag in 1907, now played a key role in unifying the different groups of the liberal left. In 1910 the Free Parliamentary Association and the Liberal People's Party, the two groups which had split in 1893, united with the third party of the liberal left, the Deutsche

26 See Hagemann (2001), pp. 164-7.

27 On Naumann see Heuss (1937) for a more detailed description.

Volkspartei, to form the new Fortschrittliche Volkspartei (Progressive People's Party). Two years later the new party formed an alliance with the Social Democratic Party for the elections to the Reichstag. This reform alliance, which had been long desired by Naumann who favoured the change of the German constitution to a parliamentary monarchy, was so successful in the elections that the social democrats for the first time won the relatively highest number of seats (110). After the end of WW1 Naumann became a member of the Constitutional Committee in the National Assembly and was instrumental in anchoring human rights in the constitution of the Weimar Republic. He became the first chairman of the new party of the liberal left, the Deutsche Demokratische Partei (DDP), which together with the Social Democratic Party (SPD) and the Catholic Zentrumspartei formed the 'Weimar coalition' and the first government of the new republic. Naumann was the founder of modern organised liberalism in Germany. Although a theologian by professional training, who was attacked by Schmoller as 'pastor Naumann' in the 1905 controversy at the meeting of the Verein für Sozialpolitik, thereby calling his ability to argue on economic issues into question, Naumann – who in his political, economic and social thought was deeply influenced by Marx and particularly his close friend Max Weber – wrote a very successful book entitled *Neudeutsche Wirtschaftspolitik* (1902). In this book, which by 1911 had appeared in no fewer than thirteen editions, he conceptualised the programme on society and economy of the liberal left, in which he favoured an 'Industrial Parliamentarianism' with freedom of development of the trade unions. Throughout his life Naumann was a passionate patriot who also actively worked towards a reconciliation between the Christian Churches and the social democrats. With the support of the liberal and socially engaged industrialist Robert Bosch he founded the School for Citizens in Berlin in 1917, which became the Hochschule für Politik in 1920.

The Progressive People's Party, the new united party of the liberal left, included 42 members who became members of the Reichstag in 1912, among whom mention should be made of Gerhard von Schulze-Gävernitz (1864-1943) whose social-liberal views had been strongly shaped by his teacher Brentano.[28] Schulze-Gävernitz, who had obtained his habilitation with Roscher in Leipzig in 1890, had taught in Freiburg since the winter semester 1893-94, continuing from 1896 until his retirement in 1923 as full professor of economics. He shared the political and social views held by Max Weber, who was his colleague in Freiburg from 1893-1897, and by Naumann. Even more intensely than Weber, Schulze-Gävernitz supported a concept of modernisation of society, combining the affirmation of modern capitalism with the acceptance of trade unions and social democracy as stabilising forces of the system, making the German economy stronger to compete on the world level. This concept of modernisation was endangered by tendencies of liberal imperialism which brought Germany into conflict with Britain, whose economy, parliamentarianism and successful imperialistic world policy acted as a

28 For a more detailed analysis of Schulze-Gävernitz's political activities in Wilhelminiam Germany see Krüger (1983).

form of role model. Schulze-Gävernitz was a *politischer Nationalökonom* in the full sense of the three elements included. His dispute with Marxism and the Historical School alike from a neo-Kantian perspective was typical of the search for a new theoretical paradigm by some of the young social scientists of the time. In contrast to the period of half a century earlier, he was one of the very few economists inclined to follow a political career. Schumpeter's assessment of Schulze-Gävernitz is well balanced: 'So far as technical economics is concerned, this Freiburg professor can hardly be called an economist at all. But he was more a genuine social philosopher, almost what I like to call a social theologian, and at the same time a political observer who did not lack realism'.[29]

In the second half of the nineteenth century the German economy experienced a rapid process of industrialisation with a strong and pervasive State intervention. During that period the SPD became the largest and most important Marxist Party, exerting great influence, ideologically and practically, on the international development of the socialist movement. Despite discrimination concerning the division of electoral districts, the socialist laws, and so forth, the number of seats in the Reichstag grew steadily from 2 in 1873 to 110 in 1912. From 1902 onwards, when he first was elected to the Reichstag (with some interruptions until 1928) Eduard Bernstein (1850-1932) was among them. He was even named in Mark Blaug's list of one hundred *Great Economists before Keynes*.[30] Influenced by the opposition of Bebel, Liebknecht and others against the French-German War and by Marx's study of the Paris Commune, in 1871 Bernstein – who originally had been a bank clerk – became a socialist who was a delegate when the Social Democratic Worker's Party united with Lassalle's General Union of German Workers in Gotha in 1875. Thereafter he became a leading theoretician and publicist of the socialist movement. During the socialist laws he was in exile in Switzerland from where, due to Bismarck's intervention, he was forced to emigrate further to England in 1888. There he became a close friend of Friedrich Engels, who made him his literary executor jointly with August Bebel, and established close relationships with the Fabians. It was not until 1901 that Bernstein was allowed to return to Germany. At that time the revisionism controversy was fully under way. Against the background of rapid economic growth in the United States and Western Europe, and based on his observations of the discrepancies of these developments with orthodox Marxist doctrines such as the pauperisation thesis, an intensifying class conflict and the economic collapse theory of the demise of capitalism, Bernstein had begun to challenge these doctrines and to revise Marxist theories in a series of articles in the socialist theoretical journal *Die Neue Zeit* (edited by Karl Kautsky) between 1896 and 1898 and in a subsequent book on the premises of socialism and the tasks of social democracy.[31] This brought him into a fierce conflict with the guardians of the Holy Grail of Marxist orthodoxy, in particular Kautsky and his associate Rosa

29 Schumpeter (1954), p. 853.
30 See Blaug (1986), pp. 22-3.
31 See Bernstein (1899).

Luxemburg (1870-1919), one of the first women to acquire a PhD in economics from the University of Zurich in 1898. In 1903 the SPD officially condemned Bernstein's revisionist views. It was not until 1959, with the Godesberg programme, that the SPD officially abandoned the last Marxist doctrines and thereby finally accepted some of Bernstein's main ideas. Despite official condemnation, however, Bernstein exerted increasing influence on many of his contemporaries, for example also in the social sciences where Max Weber took up Bernstein's views on the changing class structure. Despite many accusations of being a 'reactionary', Bernstein voted against the war credits from 1915 onwards and joined the left-wing Independent Social Democratic Party of Germany (USPD) in 1917. He became Assistant Secretary to the Treasury in the short coalition government of SPD and USPD at the end of WW1 in 1918-1919. After rejoining the SPD he became increasingly disappointed with the weak response of the SPD against reactionary nationalist attacks in the young Weimar Republic.

With very few exceptions, such as Schulze-Gävernitz, the reactionary climate in the Wilhelminian era did not attract German academics to parliamentary activities, and even less so economists, who were mainly liberals of a different blend, in contrast to the climate of awakening in 1848-1849 and partly also for a short period after unification in the 1870s, when the influence of the National Liberals was at its peak. Some were also active in the regional Parliaments, of which the Prussian Parliament was by far the most important one. However, these politically committed activities were in strong decline after the late 1870s, as can be seen from Table 7.3.

In addition to some of the economists already discussed, the most prominent professors of economics included Carl Friedrich Wilhelm Launhardt (1832-1918), Gustav von Schmoller (1838-1917), and Adolph Wagner (1835-1917) as members in the Prussian Upper House (see Table 7.4), mainly as representatives of their respective universities. This Second Chamber in Prussia was comprised of noblemen and outstanding citizens who were directly nominated by the Prussian King.

Table 7.4 Economists in the Prussian Upper House

Name	Membership	Representative
Baumstark, Eduard	1859-1889 (Death)	University of Greifswald
Eiselen, Johann Friedrich Gottfried	1862-?	University of Halle
Launhardt, Carl Friedrich Wilhelm	1898-1918 (Death)	Technical University of Hanover
Nasse, Erwin	1889-1890 (Death)	University of Bonn
Schmoller, Gustav von	1889-1917 (Death)	University of Berlin
Tellkampf, Johann Ludwig	1855-1876 (Death)	University of Breslau
Wagner, Adolph	1910-1917 (Death)	Nominated directly by the King

Source: The table is based on data from David (1911).

Launhardt hardly ever left his home town Hanover, where he made his career as an engineer specialised in highway, railroad and bridge construction. In 1871 he became Professor at the Polytechnique (and Director from 1875), which became the Technical University of Hanover. After becoming the first Rector of this university from 1880 to 1886, Launhardt was appointed a life-long member of the Prussian Upper House in 1898. Using geometry and calculus and the analysis of networks, he made seminal contributions to the theory of freight tariffs, the optimal direction and density of highways and the theory of industrial location. In contrast to the other economists examined here, he was not directly involved in the political sphere.

Whereas Schmoller was the leader of the centre and was the chairman of the Verein für Sozialpolitik from 1890 until his death, Wagner was a leading member of the right, who as a long-time enemy of Brentano often allied himself with the industrialists. Having been a student of Rau, Wagner subsequently became professor at the Trade Academy in Vienna (1858), and the universities of Dorpat (1863), today's Tartu in Estonia, Freiburg (1868) and from 1870 onwards in Berlin, a position he held for 46 years. His most important contributions were in the field of public finance, where he made his name by stating a historical 'law of growing State activities' (Wagner's law). Scientifically, Wagner sought to steer a middle course between the historical school and a more theoretically oriented approach. Politically he was distant from liberal views. A member of the Conservative Party during his years in the Prussian Parliament from 1882-1885, he held very strong State socialist beliefs (favouring progressive income taxation, wealth, inheritance, luxury and capital gains taxes) so that the term 'socialist of the chair' is more appropriate for Wagner than for any of the other figures mentioned so far. However, he was unsuccessful in seeking to exert a stronger influence of his ideas within the Verein für Sozialpolitik, of which he had been one of the main founders. He therefore basically refrained from public activities in the Verein but remained present in the standing committee, where he gave the cooptation procedure of new members a more conservative bias. Wagner shared the deep scepticism of contemporary German conservatism with regard to the development of the capitalist economy and was also not immune from anti-Semitism. He went so far as to dub Bismarck and Emperor Wilhelm I 'State socialists'. In a speech to the Prussian Upper House in 1913 he stated: 'I have been annexed and owe it to Bismarck that I have become Prussian, and that fact I always have thought to be the greatest'.[32] It is difficult to imagine a leading professor of economics expressing Wagnerian ideas of the dominance of the State (and the execution of distributive justice by the administration) against liberalism and methodological individualism in a German Parliament today.

32 See Lindenlaub (1967), **1**, p. 156.

References

Albrecht, P. (1914), *Die volkswirtschaftlichen und sozialen Fragen in der Frankfurter National-Versammlung*, Thiele, Halle.

Bernstein, E. (1899), *Die Voraussetzungen des Sozialismus und die Aufgaben der Sozialdemokratie*, J.H.W. Dietz, Stuttgart. English edition: *Evolutionary Socialism*, Huebsch, New York.

Best, H. and Weege, W. (1998), *Biographisches Handbuch der Abgeordneten der Frankfurter Nationalversammlung 1848/49*, Droste, Düsseldorf.

Biesenbach, F. (1969), *Die Entwicklung der Nationalökonomie an der Universität Freiburg i. Br. 1768-1896. Eine dogmengeschichtliche Analyse*, Eberhard Albert Universitätsbuchhandlung, Freiburg im Breisgau.

Blaug, M. (1986), *Great Economists before Keynes. An Introduction to the Lives and Works of One Hundred Great Economists of the Past*, Wheatsheaf, Brighton.

Bohnert, D. (1980), *Die Behandlung der sozialen Frage in den Debatten der Frankfurter Nationalversammlung 1848/49*, Heilbronn.

Brentano, L. (1931), *Mein Leben im Kampf um die soziale Entwicklung Deutschlands*, Eugen Diederichs Verlag, Jena.

Conze, W. and Zorn, W. (1992) (eds), 'Die Protokolle des Volkswirtschaftlichen Ausschusses der deutschen Nationalversammlung 1848/49. Mit ausgewählten Petitionen', in *Forschungen zur deutschen Sozialgeschichte*, **6**, Boldt, Boppard am Rhein.

David, E. (1911), *Handbuch für das Preußische Herrenhaus*, Heymanns, Berlin.

Eatwell, J., Milgate, M., and Newman, P. (1987) (eds), *The New Palgrave. A dictionary of economics*, Macmillan, London.

Freitag, S. (1998) (ed.), *Die Achtundvierziger. Lebensbilder aus der deutschen Revolution 1848/49*, Beck, München.

Häuser, K. (1998), 'Dogmengeschichtliche Betrachtungen zur deutschen Währungsunion von 1871-1876', in E.W. Streissler (ed.), *Studien zur Entwicklung der ökonomischen Theorie XVII. Die Umsetzung wirtschaftspolitischer Grundkonzeptionen in die kontinentaleuropäische Praxis des 19. und 20. Jahrhunderts*, Part II, Duncker & Humblot, Berlin, pp. 67-94.

Hagemann, H. (1991), 'Learned Journals and the Professionalization of Economics: The German Language Area', *Economic Notes*, **20**, pp. 33-57.

Hagemann, H. (2001), 'The Verein für Sozialpolitik from its Foundation until World War I', in M.M. Augello and M.E.L. Guidi (eds), *The Spread of Political Economy and the Professionalisation of Economists. Economic Societies in Europe, America and Japan in the Nineteenth Century*, Routledge, London.

Haunfelder, B. (1994), *Biographisches Handbuch für das Preußische Abgeordnetenhaus 1849-1867*, Droste, Düsseldorf.

Hentschel, V. (1975), *Die deutschen Freihändler und der volkswirtschaftliche Kongreß 1858 bis 1885*, Ernst Klett, Stuttgart.

Hermann, F.B.W. von (1832), *Staatswirthschaftliche Untersuchungen*, Anton Weber, München.

Heuss, T. (1937), *Friedrich Naumann. Der Mann, das Werk, die Zeit*, Deutsche Verlags-Anstalt, Stuttgart.

Hildebrand, B. (1848), *Die Nationalökonomie der Gegenwart und Zukunft*, Rütten, Frankfurt am Main.

Hippauf, R. (2000), *Johann Heinrich von Thünen. Ein Lebensbild*, Hinstorff, Rostock.

James, H. (1998), 'Die Reichsbank 1876 bis 1945', in Deutsche Bundesbank (ed.), *Fünfzig Jahre Deutsche Mark. Notenbank und Währung in Deutschland seit 1948*, C.H. Beck, München, pp. 29-89.

Jansen, C. (2000), *Einheit, Macht und Freiheit. Die Paulskirchenlinke und die deutsche Politik in der nachrevolutionären Epoche 1849-1867*, Droste, Düsseldorf.

Klaßen, K. (1984), *Mitverwaltung und Mitverantwortung in der frühen Industrie. Die Mitbestimmungsdiskussion in der Paulskirche*, Peter Lang, Frankfurt am Main.

Knies, K. (1853), *Die politische Oekonomie vom geschichtlichen Standpuncte*, Schwetschke, Braunschweig.

Koch, R. (1989) (ed.), *Die Frankfurter Nationalversammlung 1848/49. Ein Handlexikon der Abgeordneten der deutschen verfassungsgebenden Reichs-Versammlung*, Kunz, Kelkheim.

Koehler, B. (1999), *Ludwig Bamberger. Revolutionär und Bankier*, Deutsche Verlags-Anstalt, Stuttgart.

Krüger, D. (1983), *Nationalökonomen im wilhelminischen Deutschland*, Vandenhoeck & Ruprecht, Göttingen.

Kurz, H.D. (1998), 'Friedrich Benedict Wilhelm Hermann on Capital and Profits', *The European Journal of the History of Economic Thought*, **5**, pp. 85-119.

Lassalle, F (1864), *Herr Bastiat-Schulze von Delitzsch, der ökonomische Julian, oder: Kapital und Arbeit*, Schlingmann, Berlin.

Lindenlaub, D. (1967) *Richtungskämpfe im Verein für Sozialpolitik. Wissenschaft und Politik im Kaiserreich vornehmlich vom Beginn des 'Neuen Kurses' bis zum Ausbruch des Ersten Weltkriegs (1890-1914)*, 2 Vols, Franz Steiner Verlag, Wiesbaden.

Mann, B. (1988), *Biographisches Handbuch für das Preußische Abgeordnetenhaus 1867-1918*, Droste, Düsseldorf.

Marshall, A. (1961[1890]), *Principles of Economics*, ninth (variorum) edition, Macmillan, London.

Naumann, F. (1902), *Neudeutsche Wirtschaftspolitik*, Buchverlag der 'Hilfe', Berlin.

Nipperdey, T. (1983), *Deutsche Geschichte 1800-1866. Bürgerwelt und starker Staat*, C.H. Beck, München.

Pusback, B. (1988), 'Die Kameral- und Staatswissenschaften an der Universität Kiel bis zum Ende des 19. Jahrhunderts', in N. Waszek (ed.), *Die Institutionalisierung der Nationalökonomie an deutschen Universitäten*, Scripta Mercaturae Verlag, St. Katharinen, pp. 302-53.

Schefold, R. (2004), *Beiträge zur ökonomischen Dogmengeschichte*, Verlag Wirtschaft und Finanzen, Düsseldorf.

Schultz, F. (1950), 'Professoren im Paulskirchen-Parlament', in *Männer und Ideen der achtundvierziger Bewegung, Frankfurter Universitätsreden*, **2**, Klostermann, Frankfurt am Main.

Schumpeter, J.A. (1954), *History of Economic Analysis*, Allen and Unwin, London.

Schwarz, M. (1965), *MdR. Biographisches Handbuch der Reichstage*, Verlag für Literatur und Zeitgeschehen, Hannover.

Siemann, W. (1976), *Die Frankfurter Nationalversammlung 1848/49 zwischen demokratischem Liberalismus und konservativer Reform. Die Bedeutung der Juristendominanz in den Verfassungsverhandlungen des Paulskirchenparlaments*, Peter Lang, Frankfurt am Main.

Spenkuch, H. (1998), *Das Preußische Herrenhaus. Adel und Bürgertum in der Ersten Kammer des Landtages 1854-1918*, Droste, Düsseldorf.

Weiß, B. (1999), *Das Stuttgarter Rumpfparlament 1849. Das Tagebuch von Emil Adolph Roßmäßler und das Selbstverständnis der Abgeordneten*, Klett-Cotta, Stuttgart.

Winkel, H. (1977), *Die deutsche Nationalökonomie im 19. Jahrhundert*, Wissenschaftliche Buchgesellschaft, Darmstadt.

Wolff, O. (1880), 'John Prince-Smith: Eine Lebensskizze', in J. Prince-Smith, *Gesammelte Schriften III*, edited by Karl Braun, Herbig, Berlin, pp. 209-398.

Wollstein, G. (1999), 'Vorparlament und Paulskirche', in *Revolution von 1848, Informationen zur politischen Bildung*, **265**, pp. 14-24.

Appendix

Table 7.5 Parliamentary groups in the Frankfurt National Assembly

General orientation	DEMOCRATIC LEFT				LIBERAL CENTRE					CONSERVATIVE RIGHT
Wings	Ultraleft	Moderate Left			Left Centre			Right Centre		Protestants, Conservatives
Parliamentary party	Donnersberg	Deutscher Hof	Nürnberger Hof (Splinter group separated from the Deutscher Hof in Oct. 1848)	Westendhall (Splinter group separated from the Deutscher and Württemberger Hof in Sep. 1848)	Württemberger Hof	Augsburger Hof (Splinter group separated from the Württemberger Hof in Dec. 1848)	Landsberg (Separation of Casino and Württemberger Hof)	Casino	Pariser Hof (Splinter group separated from the Casino)	Café Milani
Political goals	Greater and Democratic Germany (achieved by revolution)	Unity of Germany without Austria ("Kleindeutsches Erbkaisertum") Parliamentary and democratic Republic			Majority in favour of a Greater Germany	Unity of Germany without Austria	Democratic monarchy; Prussian leadership	Majority in favour of Prussian leadership	Greater Germany	Integrity of the individual monarchies but in a federal system
					Parliamentary Monarchy			Strong central power with people's representation restricted to legislative assemblies		
Share	5%	15%			13%			34%		6%

Source: Wollstein (1999) and own modifications.

Note: The sum of the shares does not amount to 100 per cent since many members of parliament did not belong to any group.

Chapter 8

Economists and Political Economy in the Italian Parliament from the Unification to the Rise of the Fascism (1861-1922)

Massimo M. Augello and Marco E.L. Guidi*

Introduction

This chapter is largely based on the results of collective research on 'The Economists in the Italian Parliament, 1861-1922', supported by the Italian Ministry of University and Scientific Research for the years 2000-2002. This research has examined both the activities of the most eminent economists who became members of parliament in the period extending from the political unification of the country to the rise of the fascist regime,[1] and the main economic debates that marked the life of this institution, reflecting the dramatic problems that arose in an age of transition from an agriculturally-based country to an industrial society.[2] In another paper[3] we have attempted a quantitative analysis of the activities of the most numerous and significant subset of parliamentary economists, the thirty members who taught political economy or other economic subjects in the universities and in the new schools of advanced economic studies that were created after 1868. The aim of the cited quantitative analysis was to highlight the social and professional identity of the economists involved in politics, and to bring to light some characteristics of their political activity that help to understand how they viewed their intellectual activity and their scientific mission. The present study, in contrast, adopts a more qualitative approach. It examines the participation of a broader group of economists in parliamentary activities, focusing on their role in debates and in law making, their contribution to policy making, and the role that political economy had in parliamentary debates.

The choice of the period examined hardly requires any justification. Most of the liberal revolutions of 1848-1849 ended in tragedy for those who hoped for

* The authors are grateful to Roger Backhouse for his comments on an earlier draft of this chapters. Usual disclaimers apply.

1 See Augello and Guidi (2003).

2 See Augello and Guidi (2002).

3 Augello and Guidi (2005).

unification and liberalisation. Both in the regions of northern Italy under the rule of the Austrian crown and in the Kingdom of the Two Sicilies, the restoration of official authority was accompanied by a repression that obliged the majority of liberal intellectuals, among whom there were many economists, to fly to Piedmont, the only area in which a liberal constitution was conserved. Some economists participated in the short-lived parliaments and governments created in 1848 and 1849: Francesco Ferrara was a member of the Sicilian Parliament and a component of the unfortunate deputation that was sent to Turin to ask King Carlo Alberto to allow his son Amedeo to accept the crown of Sicily;[4] Pellegrino Rossi was prime minister of the Roman Republic, where he was murdered in troubled circumstances at the opening of the Chamber of Deputies on 15 November 1849;[5] Pietro Torrigiani participated in the provisional government of the Duchy of Parma, offering the local troops to Carlo Alberto during the siege of the Austrian fortress of Peschiera;[6] finally, some Neapolitan economists, like Antonio Ciccone and Antonio Scialoja, took part in the liberal revolution of 1848, becoming members of parliament. After escaping to Turin, Scialoja was vice-minister in the Sardinian government in 1859-1860.[7] But these were isolated experiences, which cannot be compared with the continuous and qualified presence of a wide number of economists in national Parliament after 1861.

A second parallel reason for the choice of the period between 1861 and 1922 is that after unification the process of academic institutionalisation of political economy was radically accelerated, fostering the spread of economic studies in Italy and the professionalisation of economists. This in turn had an important feedback in the prestige economists enjoyed in the political life of the country.

This chapter is divided into four clearly defined sections. The first section outlines the political situation of Italy in the so called 'liberal age' and reviews the general state of economic studies in this period; the second section discusses the definition of 'economist' and examines the social and professional characteristics of economists in Parliament; a third section studies the nature of the economists' contribution to parliamentary and government activities, the intellectual and political role they played, and the relationship between their scientific activities and their political commitments; finally, the last section discusses the contribution that political economy gave to parliamentary debates and policy orientations, and *vice versa* the stimuli that economists' political activities gave to the evolution of economics in Italy in the liberal period.

---

4 See Faucci (1995), pp. 66-74.
5 See Ledermann (1929).
6 See Augello (2003), p. 82.
7 See Gioli (2003), p. 2.

The 'liberal age' and the growth of economic studies

Historians usually refer to the period of Italian history between 1861 and 1922 as the 'liberal age'. After the military conquest of the Kingdom of the Two Sicilies in 1860 by a semi-official army led by Giuseppe Garibaldi, the new Kingdom of Italy was proclaimed in 1861. An institutional setting based on constitutional monarchy and on a parliament elected under limited suffrage was extended to the whole country, on the basis of the liberal constitution conceded by Carlo Alberto of Savoy, which the Kingdom of Sardinia had enjoyed since 1848. To mark the continuity with the past and the leading role of the House of Savoy in unification of the country, the first King of Italy retained the epithet of 'the second' instead of adopting the more obvious title of Vittorio Emanuele I. The parliaments elected after the unification also conserved the numbering dating from the 'Albertine' constitution, and after a short transitory term in 1860 (seventh Parliament), the first national assembly elected in 1861 was called 'eighth Parliament'. Unfortunately, the Prime Minister who had been the craftsman of the unification, Camillo Benso, count of Cavour, died immediately after proclamation of the Kingdom of Italy. Two regions were still excluded from the newly created Italian Kingdom: the Venetian area, dominated by the Austro-Hungarian Monarchy until 1866 (Trento and Trieste were annexed only after WW1), and Rome, which was conquered only on 20 September 1870 and soon thereafter became the capital of Italy.[8]

The Italian Parliament was divided into two houses: the Chamber of Deputies, which was elected for five years, and the Senate, whose members were appointed for life by the Crown, following a complicated system of representation that mirrored the composition of the national elite. Until the reform of 1882, the franchise was limited to those who were literate and paid a tax of 40 liras per annum, featuring less than eight per cent of the adult population.[9] But in 1882 the suffrage was radically extended, the requirement now being limited to completion of the first two years of primary school or payment of a tax of 19.80 liras. The electorate rose as a consequence to 6.9 per cent of the population (a quarter of male adults) and a great number of middlemen entered Parliament. Universal male suffrage was introduced in 1911, while women had to wait until 1946 to have access to a polling station.

Immediately after unification, the cabinets appointed by the Crown, with the help of Parliament, engaged first in a strategy of 'State building' and then in a huge effort of 'nation building', which aimed at the unification of cultural and legal traditions and at the economic and social modernisation of the country. From an economic point of view, in 1861 Italy was an agricultural country.[10] In Lombardy,

---

8 For a synthesis in English on this period see the recently updated Mack Smith (1997). A recent outlook, in Italian, is Sabbatucci and Vidotto (1995, 1999).

9 Some professional groups had the suffrage independently of their income. These included university professors, civil servants and graduates. See Mastropaolo (2002).

10 For a synthesis on the economic condition of Italy in the liberal age see Castronovo (1995), chapters 1-3, and Zamagni (1993), part 1.

Piedmont and in the Venetian area a developed agriculture based on silk production, rice and farming profited from integration with rural manufactures and a network of rich commercial towns, whereas in central and southern Italy, but also in various areas of the North, the persistence of outdated systems of tenancy was one of the main causes of the immobilism and poverty that prevailed there. In order to promote the development of the country, the right wing ministries in power between 1861 and 1876 focused on normative and administrative unification, infrastructures, schooling and free trade, whereas the left wing cabinets that succeeded them after the so-called 'Parliamentary Revolution' of 1876 adopted a more interventionist strategy – especially after the adoption of the protectionist 'general tariff' of 1887 – in order to promote the industrialisation of the country. By the end of the nineteenth century the typical contradictions of modernisation had already exploded. The northern part of Italy was rapidly industrialised, whereas the ancient kingdom of Naples sank into an aggravated state of backwardness. Trade unionism and socialist ideas spread among the working classes, and a Socialist Party was created in 1892. Although the Vatican *non-expedit* of January 1868 obliged Catholics not to engage in politics, a Catholic movement rapidly developed in civil society. The cabinets headed or manoeuvred by Giovanni Giolitti tried to solve the contradictions of the country with a strategy of 'government by administration' and conciliation with the Socialist Party and the labour movement.[11] However, during the first decade of the twentieth century the newly created organisations of landowners and manufacturers embraced a more and more intransigent attitude toward the working class. After WW1, these tensions exploded and culminated in the *coup d'état* orchestrated by Benito Mussolini in October 1922, which marked the rise of the fascist regime.

The period under review was also decisive for the institutionalisation of political economy. After the Restoration, the reactionary governments of the Italian regional states had seriously restricted the teaching of economics at university, considering it a vehicle of liberal and democratic ideas. But following the unification of Italy in 1861 chairs of political economy were introduced in the majority of law faculties.[12] In 1876, the new university regulations added the teaching of statistics, while public finance was established as a compulsory course in the academic year 1885-1886, following a period in which it already existed as an optional course. In the generality of cases, both these specialities were taught by economists. Likewise in the eighties, the teaching of economic disciplines was introduced in the two Higher Schools of Commerce that were created in Genoa and Bari, similar to the first institution of this kind which had been founded in Venice in 1868.[13] This expansion multiplied

11 See Pombeni (2002).

12 See Augello and Giva (1988).

13 The Higher Schools of Commerce (Scuole Superiori di Commercio) were of a university level. Other institutions of this kind were created in Milan (Commercial Luigi Bocconi University, a private institution founded in 1902), Rome (1905), Turin (1911) and Trieste (1918). They were subsequently transformed into Faculties of Economics. Another similar institution was the Higher School of Social Sciences (Scuola Superiore di

the opportunities for economists to obtain a university position. The number of academic economists rose from 8 in 1860 to 26 in 1880, and to 41 in 1890, a figure that remained approximately stable for the rest of the liberal period.[14] The academic recruitment, based on the instrument of 'free lectureship' of which we will speak later, functioned as a mechanism of co-optation into the scientific community of economists, while the birth of the first Institutes of Economics at the universities of Pisa, Siena and Turin[15] and the institution of grants and prizes, coupled with increasing opportunities to go abroad for post-graduate studies in economics, favoured a more specialist training of the younger generation.

These phenomena corresponded to the spread of economic studies in Italy. A large number of economic textbooks were published, and a host of journals specialised in economic and social sciences emerged out of an already lively production of learned and scientific periodicals, promoting the debate on political economy and the spread of economic ideas within public opinion.[16] Political economy was also popularised through dictionaries and encyclopaedias. The Genoan economist Gerolamo Boccardo published a *Dizionario della economia politica e del commercio* (1857-1861; 2nd edition: 1875-1877; 3rd revised edition: 1881-1882) and was the editor of an important universal encyclopaedia.[17] Finally, the institution of economic associations, often of a practical and political orientation, stimulated the debate on economic theory between opposed schools of thought and fostered the institutionalisation of political economy in the university system.[18] A consequence of this intense activity was the rapid assimilation of the international economic debate: the empirical methodology of the historical school was largely accepted from the mid-1860s onwards, while marginalism penetrated at the end of the eighties and became the orthodox approach by the end of the first decade of the twentieth century.[19]

Scienze Sociali) of Florence, established in 1875, and later transformed into a Faculty of Political Sciences. This picture can be completed with the establishment of the first Higher Schools of Agriculture in Milan (1870) and Portici, near Naples (1872), followed by Perugia in 1895, where the teaching of political economy was introduced for limited periods. See Augello and Guidi (1988).

14 See Augello and Guidi (2005).

15 A Historical and Legal Seminar was established at the University of Pisa in 1876, and a Legal Circle was created at the University of Siena in 1880. Both had an economic section. The Institute for Practical Exercises in Political and Legal Sciences of Turin University was founded in 1881. Its 'class' of economics was transformed in 1893 into an autonomous Workshop of Political Economy. These institutes had been the creation of some of the most representative economists of the second half of the nineteenth century, who saw in them a centre for the training of the younger generation of economists: Giuseppe Toniolo in Pisa, Achille Loria and later Augusto Graziani in Siena, Salvatore Cognetti de Martiis in Turin.

16 See Augello and Guidi (1996).

17 See Guidi (1994); Augello and Guidi (2001c).

18 See Augello and Guidi (2001b).

19 See Buchanan (1960); Barucci (1972, 2003).

Italian economists in the liberal age: social and intellectual characteristics

Before undertaking a detailed analysis of the role that the economists exerted in the Italian Parliament, it may be useful to discuss the definition of 'economist' which seems to be the best suited to the context of mid nineteenth-century Italy. This task is far from being easy, since the social and intellectual features of the economists dramatically evolved during the period under review.

A further complication is represented by the fact that, as shown by the papers contained in Augello and Guidi (2002), references to political economy and its principles were very frequent in parliamentary debates, although sometimes they were only instrumental. One of the most widely represented groups in Parliament was that of jurists and lawyers. Among them, those who had graduated in law after 1861 had attended regular courses in political economy, while the next generation had been trained in statistics and public finance as well. The learned journals they read and the juridical encyclopaedias they consulted were rich in articles on economic topics. But even those of the earlier Risorgimento generation who entered Parliament after the unification of Italy had received some economic training. For example, the group of Neapolitan jurists of which Pasquale Stanislao Mancini was an eminent representative had studied political economy in the private schools of law that were set up in Naples in the 1830s and 1840s for the training of young candidates to legal professions,[20] and political economy had also been present in the curriculum of legal studies at Turin University since the 1840s.

A similar familiarity with political economy was also widespread among those protagonists of unification and of the political life of the liberal age, who strictly speaking cannot be considered economists. Noteworthy names include Camillo Benso count of Cavour,[21] Marco Minghetti, Quintino Sella, and Sidney Sonnino,[22] all of them prime ministers, and Stefano Jacini, who was the president of the parliamentary committee for the agricultural inquiry (1877-1881).[23] Political economy was part of the private education these descendants of noble and wealthy families had received in their youth. Moreover, the network created by economic associations, academies, journals, newspapers, and publishing houses generated an ongoing debate concerning the economic problems of the country, in which the arguments of political economy were clearly echoed.

The case of the representatives of agricultural, industrial and banking interests who were present in Parliament was similar. The examples of Alessandro Rossi and Giuseppe Colombo,[24] who represented the industrial interest in the Senate from 1886 to the first decade of the twentieth century, were the most significant. Unlike the majority of politicians, whose background was based on law and humanities,

20 See Di Battista (1983), pp. 94-8.
21 See Romeo (1984), pp. 279-97.
22 See, respectively, Gherardi (2003), Are (1974b), Haywood (1999) and Carlucci (2002).
23 See Caracciolo (1958); Guidi (2002).
24 See, respectively, Are (1974b) and Lacaita (1985).

these members of the northern bourgeoisie had received a technical and scientific training associated with economic instruction. This peculiarity was responsible for the early attention these figures paid to the currents of industrialist and protectionist economics that emerged in the central decades of the nineteenth century.

Therefore, political economy was present in parliamentary debates even independently of the presence of a specialised group of experts. But one might ask whether such a specialised figure truly existed in post-1861 Italy and was present in Parliament.

There are two kinds of criteria that can be employed to answer these questions. We might classify them as 'objective' and 'subjective' respectively. The most important objective criteria are those of *authorship* and *profession*. The former was certainly the most obvious for contemporary observers, especially at the beginnings of the liberal age, since publishing books and articles on economic topics with sufficient continuity was considered to signal a vocation for this subject. However, it would be difficult to make a sharp distinction between economists and non-economists on the basis of a rigorous criterion of authorship. On the one hand, a large number of politicians, industrialists and agriculturists involved in policy making published economic pamphlets and articles, often hosted by learned and economic journals. The question is whether these works should be considered as evidence of scientific proficiency in political economy, or occasional tracts of a political and practical nature. On the other hand, many scholarly economic authors never dealt with theoretical matters, preferring to focus on applied issues which were, nevertheless, considered part of the science of political economy – education, poor laws, population, colonies, and emigration. Moreover, in some cases their 'scientific' activity was concentrated in a single period of their life, either before or after their political career.

The criterion of authorship is therefore ambiguous when employed in isolation. However, it may prove useful in association with other criteria, often of a more subjective nature. For example, a single book published by Marco Minghetti (1859) earned him an undisputed *reputation* of being an economist. Minghetti (1818-1886) was one of the political leaders of the Right Party, which held the majority in the Chamber of Deputies from 1860 to 1876. He was the minister of internal affairs in the first national Cabinet headed by Cavour in 1860, and was elected to Parliament in the same year. He was later minister of finances and of agriculture, industry and trade, and was twice appointed Prime Minister (1863-1864 and 1873-1876). A similar case was that of Luigi Luzzatti (1841-1927), who became professor of constitutional law at the University of Padua in 1863 and was elected to the House of Deputies in 1870, where he remained until 1921, after which he was appointed to a seat in the Senate. He was repeatedly minister of 'agriculture, industry and trade', of the treasury, of finances, and of 'mail and telegraph'. Finally he was Prime Minister from 1910 to 1911. Luzzatti's works on various topics of political economy, and his militancy in the cooperative movement and in the development of technical and commercial education, were the basis for his reputation as an economist, which was sanctioned in 1895 when he was awarded a lectureship in political economy at the University of Perugia for some years, while continuing to teach constitutional law at the University of Rome.[25]

A second objective criterion is that of *profession*. In mid nineteenth-century Italy, the fact of regularly lecturing in economics in some university, with or without tenure, was already a distinctive mark of the economist's identity. However, this criterion may be also confusing, at a time in which the demand for economists was at times higher than the supply due to the rapid academic institutionalisation of economics, as demonstrated by the number of courses of political economy, public finance and statistics that were entrusted to professors of law and (to a lesser extent) philosophy, sometimes for long periods. On the one hand, however, the major authors of contributions to economics sooner or later became professors of economics. On the other hand, the fact of being tenured in economics produced many disciplinary conversions, when this was not the outcome of spontaneous evolution. Lastly, the development of economic teaching and research at university level undoubtedly made the new generations of economists recruited in the 1880s and after more professional from the point of view of training,[26] 'specialisation' and 'persistence'.[27]

As a matter of fact, the evolution of the institutionalisation of economics during the liberal age produced an increasing professionalisation of academic economists. Augello,[28] analysing the 50 scholars who taught with continuity political economy from 1861 to 1900, identifies some generational differences following two criteria. The first is the period of training, which allows identification of three 'generations':

1. those who graduated before 1861, most of them in law;[29] only a minority of these economists attended a regular course in political economy during their university studies;
2. those who graduated between 1861 and 1876, all of them in law; these economists had more opportunities to learn some rudiments of economics during their training, since political economy was compulsory in law faculties;
3. those who graduated after 1876; among these, the majority graduated in law faculties, where they could attend lectures in political economy, statistics and, especially after 1886, public finance, while others graduated in the Higher Schools of Commerce, where they also attended courses of economic history, business administration, banking and finance. In addition, some went abroad for post-graduate studies in economics.

A second criterion is provided by the period of recruitment; this criterion identifies two generations:

25 See Petrovich (2003).
26 See Coats (1991).
27 See Stigler (1965).
28 See Augello (1992).
29 Exceptions are Francesco Ferrara and Vittorio Ellena, who had no graduation.

1. those who obtained a professorship before 1876; these economists worked in an academic environment in which political economy was considered an appendix to law studies;
2. those who became professors after 1876; these economists benefited from an organisation of law studies in which economics had a wider scope, along with administrative and political studies, while some of them pioneered economic teaching in the Higher Schools of Commerce created in this period.

Following the first of these criteria, we can observe that the first generation had less intensive training and specialisation in economics than the two others. Post-graduate studies were a rarity, and periods abroad for specialisation were unknown. The traditional channel of specialisation was the so-called 'free lectureship'. In order to be granted the title of 'free lecturer', young scholars were required to write a memoir on some scientific topic under the supervision of a titular professor. They then submitted their work to a jury of a university. This title allowed them to give a series of non-compulsory lectures within the main university courses, and gradually became a prerequisite for access to tenure. However, this channel of specialisation concerned only a minority of economists. Moreover, almost one half of them started their academic career by teaching non-economic subjects, and continued lecturing on such topics even after they were tenured in political economy. The average age at which tenure in economics was obtained was over forty. Moreover, none of these economists started their active life as a lecturer or professor of economics. Some were employed in the civil service, others were politicians, and others were lawyers, physicians and journalists. For only a minority did their active working life begin with a lectureship or professorship, albeit in legal topics. Finally, some economists of this first generation abandoned their academic position to undertake other activities, especially in the political field.

Turning to the two generations that graduated after 1861, the professional character of their academic profile became more evident, especially for the third generation. The proportion of those graduated in law grew in the second generation, while the third generation was divided into those who graduated in law and those with a diploma from a Higher School of Commerce. The data concerning postgraduate studies are also significant. The new university regulations issued after the unification of Italy progressively transformed the title of 'free lecturer' into a necessary prerequisite for annual lectureships and tenures. This novelty explains why a majority of economists obtained this title. The somewhat infrequent cases of economists who had the opportunity to acquire specialised training abroad are also situated in these cohorts. Moreover, those who started their academic career with non-economic lectureships sank to zero in the third generation, and additional non-economic lectureships became a rarity. The average age upon obtaining the first lectureship or tenure decreased to thirty for the second generation and to an even younger age for the third generation. As to pre- and post-academic activities, the second generation was still largely characterised by a professional non-academic start and by some cases of abandonment, while one half of the third generation started as a lecturer or professor of economics, and none of this generation abandoned his tenure before retiring. In conclusion, it seems clear that the professionalisation of economics received a strong impulse from the institutionalisation of political economy in post-unification Italy, and by the end of the nineteenth century a figure of professional academic economist had definitively emerged.

Overall, the criterion of profession allowed us to identify no less than thirty academic economists who obtained a seat in Parliament between 1860 and 1922.[30] Cross-examination of the literature published by these authors confirms that all of them had sufficient expertise in economic science.[31]

This conclusion does not imply that the academic position was the only feature that distinguished an economist from a non-economist. The vantage point of parliamentary activities reveals the existence of another important road leading to specialised and 'professional' economics, that of the civil service, especially in the economic departments of the administration. Many talented young men, often with low levels of education, were recruited to the legislative and statistical services, where they received massive 'on the spot' training in economics and statistics. This was partially a necessity for the young structures of the Italian State. But it was also the result of the enlightened vision of some influential figures, like Luigi Luzzatti, who was the most powerful politician in the ministry of agriculture, industry and trade, and Cesare Correnti and Luigi Bodio, who organised the department of statistics as a 'brain trust' at the ministers' service.[32] Some economists who entered Parliament originated from these departments of the administration, for example Vittorio Ellena, Carlo Francesco Ferraris, Agostino Magliani, and Luigi Bodio. It is interesting to observe that Antonio Scialoja – one of the most important economists of the Risorgimento generation who had published a treatise based on Jean-Baptiste Say's doctrines, translated into French in 1844[33] – abandoned his chair of political economy at the University of Turin in 1849 to devote himself to political activities, and was active in post-unification economic departments of the civil service. Scialoja and Luzzatti were appointed in the 1870s to the head of the governmental committee for the 'industrial inquiry', which prepared the ground for the protectionist and industrialist turn of 1878 and 1887.[34]

Other brilliant economists – like Rodolfo Benini, Augusto Bosco, Enrico Raseri, Bonaldo Stringher, and Carlo Schanzer – were totally or partially trained in the statistical services of the department of agriculture, industry and trade. Although they did not enter Parliament, they played a major role in the special committees

30 See Augello and Guidi (2005), which considers also those who taught statistics and public finance.

31 See Augello (1989, 1994).

32 See Marucco (1996), pp. 39-72; Melis (1996), pp. 108-13, 160-6, 203-16; Favero (2001); Soresina (2001).

33 See Scialoja (1840).

34 See Are (1965); Prodi (1966).

and councils which were created in the last decades of the nineteenth century. Many of them also became professors of economics in universities, while others, like Ellena (a future member of parliament), taught political economy in the special technical schools of agriculture created by the ministry of agriculture, industry and trade. The education they received determined a special vocation of these economists both as scholars and as politicians. As scientists, they made important contributions to empirical and statistical studies, while as members of parliament, ministers and members of governmental committees, they conceived of their political activity as a strictly technical service, inspired by values of loyalty and objectivity, and oriented to functions of expert information and backstage influence.

Finally, there were some protagonists of the scientific and political debate who, beyond authorship of important contributions to political economy, could boast of other entitlements to the qualification of economist. For example, Fedele Lampertico, although he never became professor, held a regular public course on political economy at the Accademia Olimpica of Vicenza from 1863 to 1866. The preparatory materials for these lectures were later gathered together and published in a bulky treatise entitled *L'economia dei popoli e degli stati* (1874-1884), which Francesco Ferrara[35] – the main representative of *laissez-faire* classical political economy – ironically defined 'the Gospel of Lombard-Venetian economists, and Fedele Lampertico their Messiah'. In fact, Lampertico played a major role in the launching of the new 'school' of economic thought based in the universities of Pavia (Lombardy) and Padua (Venetian region), which imported into Italy the modern quantitative approach to statistics and the empirical methodology of the German Historical School. He was the signatory – with Antonio Scialoja, Luigi Cossa and Luigi Luzzatti – of the 'Circular of Padua' (11 September 1874), which announced that a conference would be held in Milan and summoned all economists who subscribed to these methodological guidelines and were favourable to State intervention in social affairs and to the protection of national industry. The Milan conference created the Associazione per il Progresso degli Studi Economici, which actively promoted these policy objectives for more than a decade. But Lampertico was also a key figure in the academic institutionalisation of economics. As a lifelong and very influential member of the Higher Council of Public Education, he was frequently present on the boards of examiners for the recruitment of university professors of economics. One of the reasons why he never became a professor himself was probably that he reputed his condition of 'perpetual examiner' incompatible with the role of applicant.

Another uncommon personage was Count Giovanni Arrivabene, who was a senator from 1860 to 1881. He came from a career as a journalist and writer on various subjects of political economy. For his liberal ideas, he became an exile and settled in Brussels, where he founded in 1855 – with Gustave de Molinari and Charles Le Hardy de Beaulieu – the Société Belge d'Economie Politique of which

35 Ferrara (1874), p. 1009.

he was elected president. Five years later, when the Società di Economia Politica was created in Turin, Arrivabene was elected its president.[36]

As this short review shows, there were many entitlements that can legitimately be invoked for the definition of an economist. But textual analysis reveals that an ongoing effort of definition (and self-definition) regarding the nature and role of economists was an essential element of the discourse on political economy in the nineteenth and early twentieth century. Therefore, another manner of identifying economists in the liberal age might consist in appealing to some 'subjective' or 'discursive' criteria emerging from textual sources such as biographies, memoirs, obituaries, correspondences, and parliamentary reports.

The main criteria emerging from the economic debate are those of self-awareness or self-definition, behaviour, and recognition or reputation. To begin with, those who consciously adopted a scientific and scholarly approach to economic policy defined themselves as 'economists' and emphasised their competence in the field of economics while presenting their opinions in Parliament and in the press. Such an attitude was closely connected with a particular approach to political activities, based on careful examination of facts and statistical evidence, complex deductive reasoning relying on the laws of political economy, and supposed *super partes* attitude in controversial debates. Sometimes these highly competent figures could not conceal their contempt for less learned colleagues who ignored the complex chains of causation and interdependence that bind together economic variables. Finally, public recognition of the economist's status was sometimes bestowed on these experts. At times the economists in Parliament were praised for their doctrinal erudition, and were listened to with attention, as the colleagues of Gerolamo Boccardo and Vittorio Ellena report in their obituaries. On other occasions they were defined as '*sui generis* politicians', as Ghino Valenti wrote in the obituary of Lampertico.[37] However there were also occasions when they encountered the irritation of their parliamentary colleagues, who had little patience with the dogmatism, intransigence and self-conceit the economists revealed in their speeches, the boring details they mentioned, and the lack of flexibility and political wisdom they sometimes demonstrated.

These 'subjective' criteria confirm that the increasing specialisation and academic professionalisation of economists produced a recognisable, albeit variegated, body of experts, whose proficiency and competence was acknowledged by public opinion. Their special attitudes could be distinguished even in their political activities. Although the science of political economy was a more widespread ingredient of political discourse, it was clear to contemporaries that the life of the Italian Parliament was characterised *inter alia* by the presence of a distinct group of 'economists', largely identifiable with the academic profession.

---

36 See Erreygers (2001) and Augello and Guidi (2001b).

37 See Valenti (1907), p. 59.

Representation and policy-making: the role of economists in Parliament

During the liberal age, the presence of economists in Parliament was continuous although variable in its extent. In a House of Deputies composed of 625 members and in a Senate the size of which changed according to the rhythm of appointments, consisting on average of 250 members,[38] they were a trifling minority ranging from no more than ten to fifteen (see Figure 8.1). However, their weight appears more significant compared to that of other academic groups represented in Parliament, and likewise in comparison to the total of academic economists outside Parliament.

Figure 8.1 Number of economists in Parliament per period in which both Houses were in office (1860-1924)

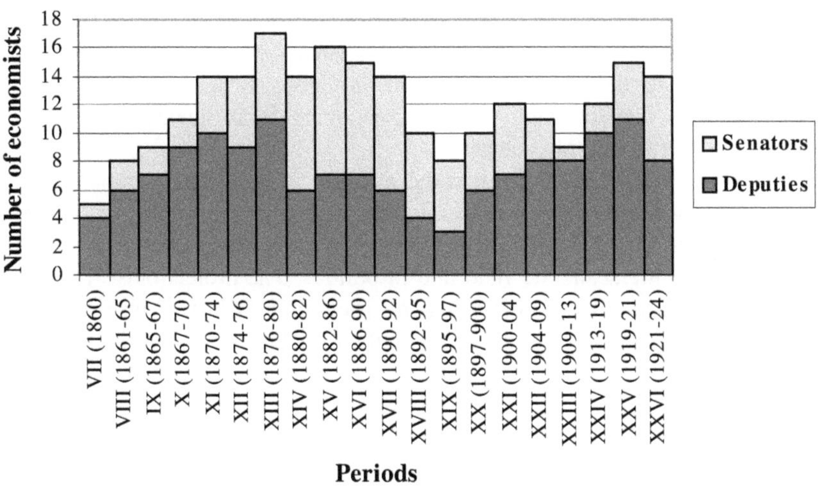

As to the first term of comparison, the evidence collected by Cammarano and Piretti shows that the presence of academics with law degrees ranged from 54 in the period between 1861 and 1882 (i.e. before the first Reform Act) to 34 in the period between 1900 and 1919.[39] As explained above, almost all academic economists had a degree in law, and a rough comparison with the data concerning their presence in Parliament shows that the economists represented 30 to 40 per cent of parliamentary academics with law degrees. These figures were also constantly

38 Members of the House of Deputies were elected every five years or at shorter intervals when Parliament was dissolved by the crown. Senators were nominated by the crown 'without limitation' and were lifelong. As a consequence, the size of the Senate was variable.

39 See Cammarano and Piretti (1996), p. 589, Table 7.

higher than those of academics with degrees in medicine (2 and 3 respectively) and engineering (8 and 4 respectively).[40]

Turning to the weight of parliamentary economists in the scientific community, in Augello and Guidi (2005) we showed that the average percentage of parliamentary economists out of their academic colleagues was as high as 20 per cent, a figure that reveals the profound political commitment of this category of scholars.

Despite a negative trend between 1892 and 1900, the presence of economists in Parliament was not significantly affected by changes in the extension of suffrage. Prior to 1882 university professors were eligible to be elected to the House of Deputies independently of the income qualification that was otherwise indispensable. As a consequence they were largely over-represented in Parliament, and this partially explains the rapid growth in the number of parliamentary economists between 1860 and 1882. After that date, the fall in number of deputies was compensated by new appointments to the Senate, in conformity with a never accomplished constitutional design which aimed at transforming the Upper House into a 'chamber of experts'. An analysis of parliamentary transactions reveals that the economists – with the exception of Ferrara who probably never attended the Senate sessions – took this role very seriously, engaging in an intense activity of bill-drafting and participation in debates.

The 1880s and 1890s were also the eventful years of the Lombard-Venetian group of interventionist economists. Nominations of their members to the Senate were a consequence of the high reputation enjoyed by the leaders of this school of thought both in the academic field and in politics. The protectionist turn fostered by the governments of the Left Wing in office after 1776 was inspired by these economists, although they generally sat on the right benches of Parliament. Among the authors of the 'Circular of Padua', Antonio Scialoja and Fedele Lampertico were nominated in 1862 and 1873 respectively. Luigi Luzzatti succeeded in retaining his seat in the House of Deputies until 1921, when he was appointed senator, and only Luigi Cossa never entered Parliament, although he was a lifelong member of the Higher Council of Public Education. Another economist who was sympathetic to this group was Angelo Messedaglia, who became professor of political economy at the University of Padua in 1858, moving to the University of Rome after his election to the House of Deputies in 1866. In Rome, he played a major role in the development of statistical studies, establishing a close connection between the university and the department of statistics of the civil service directed by Luigi Bodio,[41] who had himself been a professor of political economy at the Venice Higher School of Commerce (directed by Francesco Ferrara) from 1868 to 1872 and became a senator at the end of the century. Messedaglia was appointed senator in 1883, after his defeat in the general election of 1882.

However, senatorial appointments were ecumenically granted to several out-

40 See Augello and Guidi (2003), pp. xxxi-xxxviii, and Augello and Guidi (2005) for a more detailed quantitative account.

41 See Parisi (2003).

standing spokesmen of the *laissez-faire* approach as well. One example is Ferrara, who sat in the House of Deputies between 1867 and 1880, was the minister of finances in the Cabinet headed by Urbano Rattazzi in 1867, and was nominated senator in 1881. Ferrara was the most outstanding Italian economist of the mid-nineteenth century. He was the editor of the first two series of the *Biblioteca dell'economista*, a collection of classical textbooks in 26 volumes (1850-1868), and expounded an original 'cost of reproduction' theory of value, which is generally considered an antecedent of marginalist theory.[42] Gerolamo Boccardo, who was favourable to the classical free-trade approach and continued Ferrara's work as editor of the *Biblioteca dell'economista* (third series, 15 vols, 1876-1900), was also admitted to the Senate in 1877, without previous experience in the House of Deputies.

After 1900 the number of new nominations of economists to the Senate diminished. However, this phenomenon was compensated by a further increase in the number of deputies. The general election of 1900 roughly coincided with the appointment of Giuseppe Zanardelli and Giovanni Giolitti as prime ministers (1901-1903 and 1903-1905 respectively), an event which inaugurated the so-called 'Giolittian age' (1901-1915). The cabinets headed or influenced by Giolitti attempted to introduce the so-called 'government by administration'. Many consultative councils were instituted in technical and economic areas of government, and a host of experts – among whom many economists – became their members. As a consequence, the role of the Senate as a 'chamber of experts' was partially set aside. But, on the other hand, a new generation of pugnacious economists had access to Parliament as representatives of new and more modern parties, such as Radicals, Socialists, and (only at the end of the period) Catholics.

The radical group was an odd assemblage of different factions. Among the economists, it included the Sicilian statistician Napoleone Colajanni,[43] who wavered between protectionism and free-trade and was favourable to State intervention in social policies. Another deputy elected as part of the radical grouping was Francesco Saverio Nitti, who taught public finance at the University of Naples from 1899 and was the editor of the economic journal *La Riforma sociale*.[44] Elected for the first time in 1904, he became minister of agriculture, industry and trade; subsequently, as Prime Minister in 1919-1920, he promoted a massive plan of intervention for development of the metropolitan area of Naples, based on low-cost electric energy supplied by State-owned companies, public housing and fiscal incentives to the industrial plants located in that area. Nitti also sponsored the nationalisation of social insurance with the creation, in 1911, of a monopolistic State-owned company, the INA (National Institute of Insurances).

A very different group of radical economists was that composed by Antonio De Viti de Marco and Maffeo Pantaleoni (with Vilfredo Pareto supporting them from outside Parliament). These economists were the protagonists of the marginalist

42 See Minelli, Guidi and Guccione (2004).
43 See Macchioro (2001) and Bianchi (2003).
44 See Magnani (2003) and Realfonzo, Forges Davanzati and Patalano (2003).

revolution in Italy, whose main contributions to pure economics, public finance and sociology were translated into English and enjoyed some international reputation.[45] During parliamentary debates De Viti and Pantaleoni reported on the policy guidelines discussed within the Association for Economic Liberty,[46] of radical *laissez-faire* tendency, and provided extensive coverage of these themes in the *Giornale degli economisti*, the most influential economic journal of which they were the proprietors and editors, using it as a weapon to spread their liberal ideas.[47]

Among the Socialists, the main representatives were Antonio Graziadei, who was elected in 1910 and was one of the founders of the Communist Party in 1921, Arturo Labriola, elected in 1913, and Achille Loria, who was appointed to the Senate in 1919. The only Catholic elected to the House of Deputies for the Popular Party, of Catholic tendencies, in 1919 was Vincenzo Tangorra, who taught public finance at the University of Pisa.

It therefore seems evident that among experts of an academic and/or scientific level, economists were one of the most widely represented categories in Parliament. Their role was even more considerable within the group of 'technicians' with a natural political vocation, such as those with a training in law. Lastly, their presence in Parliament was considerable even in the Giolittian age, and this may be considered as a sign of the significance they attributed to the legislative power and to parliamentary debates as an arena for the spread of political economy, and as a stepping stone for their engagement in government and in other administrative functions.

Another typical feature of the economists' parliamentary activity in the liberal age was the duration of their presence in Parliament. It is known that before the formation of mass parties a Weberian figure of the professional politician had not yet appeared.[48] However, those who sat in Parliament for prolonged periods have been seen as something similar to 'proto-professional' members of the ruling class.[49] These representatives devoted their whole life to political activities and lost contact with the social and professional milieu from which they originated. The case of economists in Parliament is interesting from this viewpoint (see Figure 8.2). Two well-known figures, Luzzatti and Paolo Boselli (the latter taught public finance at the University of Rome in the 1870s and 1880s and repeatedly held ministerial office, becoming Prime Minister between 1915 and 1917) sat in Parliament for more than fifty years, six others for more than thirty years, and 19, i.e. one half of the total, for more than twenty years. It should also be remembered that the dramatic upheaval marked by the rise of fascism abruptly interrupted the political career of many liberal and socialist economists, who were obliged to resign and in many cases to flee abroad, while the presence of others, especially in the Senate, was only formal.

45 See Asso (2001), Fausto and De Bonis (2003).
46 See Michelini (2000).
47 See Magnani (2003).
48 See Weber (1919); Mosca (1884).
49 See Mastropaolo (1986), pp. 44-5.

Figure 8.2 Number of years in which economists were members of parliament (1860-1923)

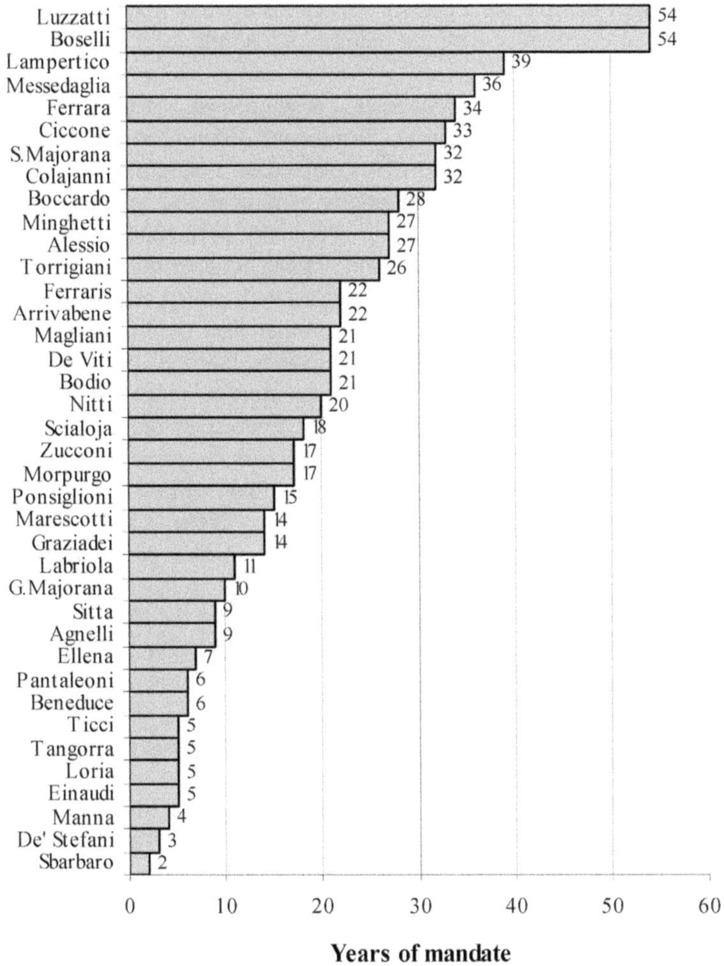

Observing the intense commitment of the economists, it would be tempting to conclude that, for many of them, the access to Parliament represented a radical turn in their intellectual career. The question is whether or not they abandoned their scientific interests when they became 'proto-professional' statesmen. An answer may come from a typology specifically propounded by some political scientists for this period,[50] including three models of representation: *political*, *locally-based* and *interest-based*. The positioning of the economists among these alternatives was not

50 See Martinelli and Zucchini (2001), pp. 817-19.

straightforward. On the one hand, a genuine political vocation was the natural outcome of their legal and economic training. During their studies, they had developed an awareness of the universal character of the law, of the *super partes* function of the State, and of the role the legislator was called upon to play in reforming existing institutions in conformity with the 'natural' economic laws that regulated 'the physiology of civil society'.[51]

On the other hand, however, the economists' consciousness of representing the interests of their electors was less evident. Significant differences can be noted between the generations of the 1860s and 1870s elected by a handful of aristocrats and wealthy people, and the younger generations of radical and socialist economists elected by enlarged or universal suffrage. Yet many economists preferred to regard themselves as 'expert' legislators and policy makers rather than as representatives. Very often, the ground on which they assessed their policy orientations was their belief in the principles of political economy rather than the ultimate will of the people. They participated in parliamentary debates more to persuade their colleagues of the truth of their deductive reasoning, than to reach a reasonable compromise between different interpretations of the interest of the nation. They preferred to draft bills on economic matters and take part in special committees, rather than negotiate with their colleagues. Moreover, their willingness to accept office as ministers or members of administrative boards reflected a view closer to that of the benevolent despot than to the model of the shrewd politician of the liberal age.

As for the other types of representation that were typical of the liberal age, it is interesting to explore the extent to which economists were involved in the representation of local, group or class interests and accepted the typical rules of conduct of nineteenth-century 'leading citizens' (in French: *notables*), developing an extensive network of patronage in their constituencies, or alternatively preferred to become the spokesmen of powerful economic lobbies.

According to Max Weber,[52] the two distinctive features of the nineteenth-century *notable* were *gratuitousness of activities* and *prestige*. The former depended on enjoyment of a private income and leisure and was typical of landed gentry and of professionals like lawyers, who could schedule their professional activities in a manner that allowed them time to devote to politics. Economists, as university professors and sometimes as members of wealthy families, potentially benefited from similar conditions. Moreover, their social prestige was high, despite the young lineage of the science of political economy. It is also worth noting that the economists' behaviour sometimes followed the patterns typical of a *notable*: for instance, the correspondence of Fedele Lampertico[53] and Francesco Ferrara[54] is rich in examples of patronage. The case of Luigi Luzzatti was partially different,

51 The phrase comes from the 'Introduction' to Say (1828-1829).
52 See Weber (1919).
53 See Lampertico (1996-1998).
54 See Ferrara (2002).

because his permanent engagement in government and the civil service prevented him from directly engaging in local systems of patronage. However he acted as a 'mediator' between government and a local network of supporters who in turn possessed their set of patronage connections. Economists also frequently intervened in favour of the interests of their constituency. A typical example was that of the recurring debates on the construction of railways, tunnels and other public works; the debates on tariffs and trade agreements likewise displayed an array of similar examples.

Within this framework, representation of interests took place in two distinct ways. On the one hand, some economists were engaged in projects concerning credit, co-operation or industrialisation, and their parliamentary activity reveals strong support for these interests. The examples of Luzzatti's interventions in favour of co-operative credit, and of the actions undertaken by Boccardo and Boselli to defend the interest of the mercantile marine, can be mentioned here. But on the other hand, economists were also active in fostering the institutionalisation of economics in universities, both at the informal level of under-the-table agreements and recommendations – of which their published and unpublished correspondence furnishes eloquent testimony – and at the official level of legislative initiatives on schooling, university and scientific research. To consider just a few significant instances, in 1872 Antonio Scialoja promoted an official inquiry on secondary and technical education; Lampertico, Luzzatti, with Salvatore Majorana and Emilio Morpurgo, engaged in a series of initiatives in favour of technical education. Moreover, Boccardo, Ferrara, Ferraris, Luzzatti, Majorana, Messedaglia and Nitti were for long periods members of the Higher Council of Public Education, where they had numerous opportunities to defend their interests as academics in general, and as professors of economics in particular. In 1876 Salvatore Majorana, who taught political economy at the University of Catania, introduced a Bill that extended the teaching of political economy to all sections of technical secondary schools. Between 1869 and 1870 Angelo Messedaglia presented a proposal for the creation of an independent curriculum in political and administrative studies within the faculties of law, where economics played a major role. Antonio Ciccone, a Neapolitan economist, participated in 1872 in the foundation of the Higher School of Agriculture in Portici (Naples), and Luzzatti contributed in 1871 to the foundation of the Higher Institute for Forestal Studies in Vallombrosa (Florence). The latter, with Lampertico and Ferrara, was also involved in the founding of the Venice Higher School of Commerce, inaugurated in 1868. We have already mentioned the role played by Correnti, Messedaglia and Bodio in the development of statistical research.

Finally, in their capacity as members of parliament and delegates of government, some economists were instrumental in the foundation of international institutions in which economic research was present, although their efforts were often hindered by frustrating diplomatic negotiations and by discussions on very practical governance problems. The International Institute of Statistics was founded in London in 1885 with the participation of Bodio (as secretary), Boccardo, Ellena,

Ferraris, Lampertico, Luzzatti, Magliani, and Messedaglia. The International Institute of Agriculture (later FAO) was founded in Rome in 1905 thanks to the preparatory work of Pantaleoni and Luzzatti, and to the intense activity of Bodio and De Viti de Marco, and with the participation of other non-parliamentary economists including Umberto Ricci, Pasquale Jannaccone and Giovanni Lorenzoni. Bodio also played an active role in the foundation of the Society of Nations in Geneva after WW1.

This variegated activity differed in many ways from organised lobbying. However, parliamentary economists were certainly decisive for the institutionalisation of economics in the university framework and for the development of economic studies.

In the light of the perspectives outlined above, the question raised earlier as to whether the economists' political activity marked a break in their scientific identity or broadened and enriched their intellectual vocation still awaits an answer.

It cannot be denied that many economists in Parliament were involved in discussions and decisions that bore little relation even to the very broad view of the scope of political economy that was typical of their age. Moreover some elected economists significantly reduced their scientific and publishing activity upon their entry into Parliament. Such was the case, for instance, of Pietro Torrigiani, who was professor of political economy at the Universities of Parma and Pisa, Antonio Ponsiglioni, who taught at the universities of Siena and Genoa, and the above mentioned Salvatore Majorana (Catania).[55]

However, in the central debates on tariffs, trade agreements, the State budget, taxation and public debt, in discussions on the organisation of the banking system, education, or public works, and in debates and inquiries on the condition of agriculture and industry, the voice of economists and the 'economists' approach' always manifested itself. The economists were eager to explain the principles of political economy to those who apparently had no knowledge of the constraints these principles imposed on the action of legislators, and they endeavoured to indicate the incentives and disincentives created by different political arrangements and the re-distributive effects of taxes and tariffs. Some economists specialised in the collection and interpretation of statistical data, using the resulting information to warn their colleagues against measures that ran counter to 'actual facts'. Finally, they made a point of suggesting economic policies that were consistent with the principles of political economy. In all these cases, the economists acted, or claimed to act, as spokesmen of economic science. Was this empty rhetoric, or an elegant way of concealing partisan views? In many cases this was certainly the case, especially when the economists found themselves on both sides of a controversy. However, these attitudes revealed some awareness of the specificities of the economists' intellectual profession, and the extension of their field of action to Parliament and government objectively strengthened their 'partial monopoly' as experts on economic questions.

55 See Augello and Travagliante (2004).

This does not mean that the economists' activity in Parliament always corresponded to this high profile. Once involved in parliamentary life, many of them were constrained to accept approaches to political decisions that contrasted with the principles they had theorised in their university lectures and in the books and articles they had published. Furthermore, it was not infrequent for their approach to depend on the position they occupied in parliamentary dialectic. It was far easier to vindicate the rigorous principles of political economy from the benches of opposition than from those of the majority. This was the case for *laissez-faire* economists like Ferrara, Torrigiani, Manna and Ciccone, who had inspired the economic policy of the Right from 1861 to 1876, whenever the revision of tariffs was debated. The case of De Viti de Marco and Pantaleoni at the beginning of the twentieth century was also interesting. On the one hand, although firmly opposing the 'statalist' and protectionist approach of the majority, they could non refrain from making transactions and compromises with some sectors of Parliament they considered as potential allies, including the Socialists. On the other hand, their exasperated belief in the explanatory and predicting capacity of economics induced them to adopt a rigid and even openly contemptuous attitude *vis-à-vis* the political class. This attitude gradually became the foundation of their political vision, in which a shortcut was created between 'pure' economics and a liberal, anti-interventionist and anti-socialist approach.

However, the economists who were part of the majority and were involved in important legislative and political decisions were likewise often obliged to accept the mechanisms of compromise and mediation between opposed interests that were typical of parliamentary dialectic. Some of them accepted to participate in decisions that conflicted with arguments they had presented in their publications. Others – like Antonio Ciccone – considered these decisions as a tragic betrayal of their inner beliefs. Yet others pragmatically accepted the distance that existed between science and art, while only a few seized the opportunity provided by innovative political decisions to undertake the revision of those principles of political economy that seemed to contradict them. This was the case, for example, of the Lombard-Venetian economists, and of some economists of the younger generation like Francesco Saverio Nitti and Giulio Alessio, who found in legislative activity a stimulus for a deeper analysis of the reasons that justified State intervention in social policies and in the encouragement of national industry. It should also be recalled, as shown above, that the economists often accepted the rules of patronage and mediation of local and economic interests, and defended their interests as academics and scholars.

Despite these difficulties, such ambiguities were probably both a necessity and a mechanism that contributed to strengthening the social identity of economists, who apparently felt a strong need to take an active part in political decisions, and to contribute to the building of the new Italian State and nation. For these figures, the activities of educator, legislator, policy maker and preacher were all essential parts of their scientific mission as economists.

Political economy in Parliament

The unification of Italy and the establishment of a liberal constitution created an arena in which economists could voice the characteristic of political economy as a 'science of the statesman or legislator', establishing the aims and limits of politics and enlightening public opinion and the ruling classes with the systematic insights this science affords into the nature of economic relationships.

Significantly, the new science of political economy inspired by Adam Smith and Jean-Baptiste Say was imported into Italy in a period – that of the Restoration and Risorgimento (1815-1860) – in which the unstable alliance between 'philosophers' and 'legislators' that was typical of the Enlightenment period had been dissolved. While in the United Kingdom David Ricardo sat in Parliament, in Italy the spread of political economy was looked upon with suspicion, since its contents were identified with liberal ideas in politics. Those who cultivated political economy ceased to publicise their ideas on economic policy and confined themselves to learned or technical discussions in scientific academies and 'agrarian' or 'economic' societies. However, as soon as some restrictions on civil liberties began to be lifted, the public dimension of political economy re-emerged with the creation of new debating societies and new journals.

But the national State in 1861 represented a break with the past. A new space – the legislative power – had opened up for expressing both the normative deductions of political economy and its pedagogical and controversial dimension. The 'paper wars' on free trade vs. protectionism, *laissez-faire* vs. interventionism, growth vs. re-distribution, which had characterised economic discourse in the first half of the nineteenth-century in Italy and elsewhere, now entered Parliament and became part of the deliberation process that led to political decisions of strategic importance in the development of the country. For the first time, economists found themselves faced with the task of persuading not only other scholars, but also the ruling class and the representatives of local and economic interests. Significantly, many economists in Parliament systematically published their parliamentary speeches and their opinions on the issues at stake in learned and scientific journals, newspapers, pamphlets and collections. Parliamentary debates thereby became a stepping stone to the enlightenment of public opinion at large. Lastly, parliamentary economists were active in the committees for inquiries on agriculture, industry, tariffs, money circulation, education, and on the conditions of labourers and peasants. The results of these inquiries were frequently disappointing from a methodological viewpoint and also reflected the compromises that had to be established between the requirements of science and those of political wisdom. Nevertheless the role of economists was often significant.

On the whole, the contribution of political economy to important political decisions was significant. Starting with trade regulation, the discussion in May 1861 which eventually led to a reduction of custom tariffs was introduced by Cavour himself, who was the Prime Minister in office. Cavour had a strong economic background, basing his actions on the typical Smithian arguments in favour of free trade.[56] The shift toward protectionism initiated by the general tariff voted in 1878 was the result of the preparatory work of Luzzatti, Scialoja, Lampertico and Ellena, and was presented in Parliament by Agostino Magliani, a statesman with a strong economic background.[57] These economists, with the addition of Angelo Marescotti and Paolo Boselli, followed the evolution of tariffs and trade legislation and agreements until the new general protectionist tariff was approved in 1887. At the end of the liberal age, Giulio Alessio was the inspirer of the 1921 tariff revision.[58] These economists favoured a more industrialist orientation of Italian political economy. Although they did not deny in principle the validity of classical political economy statements on free trade, they developed a series of interesting historical and empirical arguments in favour of protection of infant industries, development of strategic sectors, creation of 'poles' of intensive development, and improvement of social welfare.

In the field of public works, in 1885 Boselli presented a package of interventions in Parliament in favour of the mercantile marine and shipbuilding industry, which represented the first example of industrial policy in the Italian State and paved the way to other interventions in favour of the iron and steel and engineering industry.[59] In contrast, the law that nationalised the railway service, promulgated in 1905, was the result of political compromises unrelated to scientific considerations. However, its author, Carlo Francesco Ferraris, was an economist, and other economists like Giulio Alessio defended it on economic grounds, highlighting the adjustment effects that it could produce on the disequilibria between different areas of the country.[60] Lastly, at the beginning of the twentieth century Francesco Saverio Nitti defended the nationalisation of electric energy as a weapon for the growth of less-developed areas.[61]

Another area of debate was that of public finance. Many important tax reforms were fostered by economists like Ferrara, Minghetti, and Messedaglia, who essentially shared the same orthodox view on budget balance. The same authors were also the protagonists of the measures taken in 1886 for the unification of the land tax and for the institution of a national land register.[62] Moreover, Minghetti, Scialoja, Magliani, Luzzatti and Alberto De' Stefani promoted a series of successive reforms of State accountancy and the public budget.[63] The interesting feature of these debates was the interaction between economic and legal arguments that had been a distinctive characteristic of Italian economic and legal discourse during the eighteenth and nineteenth century. The same association of themes could be perceived in parliamentary debates on the problems of administrative and financial

56 See Bini and Parisi (2002), pp. 11-12.
57 See Magliulo (2002); Guidi (2003); Petrovich (2003); Rancan (2003).
58 See Michelini (2003).
59 See Asso (2003).
60 See Giocoli (2002); Michelini (2003); Tusset (2003).
61 See Patalano (2002); Realfonzo, Forges Davanzati and Patalano (2003).
62 See Parisi (2003).
63 See Faucci (2002).

unification of the country, the regulation of joint-stock companies, intellectual property rights and the military budget.[64]

But perhaps the area in which the 'institutionalist' approach that Italian economists active in the second half of the nineteenth century had inherited from the Italian Enlightenment through the works of Giandomenico Romagnosi and Carlo Cattaneo was that of agriculture. Immediately after unification, the approach to modernisation of the Italian primary sector recommended by liberal economists, and endorsed by the cabinets of the Right, was based on a mixture of free competition and institutional arrangements which favoured the circulation of landed property through the subdivision and privatisation of large estates belonging to the Church and the State, and encouraged investment (long leases, rules of accountancy, irrigation etc.).[65] A typical representative of this orientation was Stefano Jacini, the president of the committee for the agricultural inquiry whose conclusions were published when the new protectionist policy promoted by the Left was already producing its devastating effects on Southern agriculture. The grievances presented at the end of the century by the marginalist economists both in the press and in Parliament were still grounded on defence of the advantages produced by the classical blend of competition, rules and infrastructures.[66]

With regard to monetary policy, although the right-wing majority of the first fifteen years after unification adhered to the classical orthodox view on convertibility, the war against Austria and an international financial crisis obliged the government to decree the forced circulation of paper money in 1866. It was an economist, Antonio Scialoja, who as minister of finances promoted this measure and defended it in Parliament, not without some embarrassment.[67] Other economists of the liberal camp, like Salvatore Majorana and Gerolamo Boccardo, led the attempts to restore convertibility that were undertaken in 1877 and subsequently. In 1880 Magliani, as the minister of finances in office, presented the Bill for the repeal of forced circulation.[68]

Another important event was the debate on the negotiations for the Latin Monetary Union (1865-1894), in which Luzzatti and Ellena were the major architects.[69] The participation of economists in parliamentary debates and special committees was accompanied in this case, as in others, by a wealth of discussions in the specialised press. Almost all economists paid formal homage to monometallist orthodoxy, although they were ready to discuss both political and economic arguments in favour of the gold-silver standard that France had imposed within the Union.

The laws concerning the re-organisation of the issuing and banking system, which culminated in the foundation of the Bank of Italy in 1893, were likewise the

64 See, respectively, Pastorini and Pizzanelli (2002), Teti (2002), Grembi (2002), and Gentilucci (2002).

65 See Lepore (2002); Raffaelli (1997); and Piccioni and Raffaelli (2002).

66 See Guidi (2002).

67 See Gioli (2003), pp. 17-18.

68 See Gioli (2003); La Bruna (2003); Pavanelli (2003); Rancan (2003).

69 See Masini (2002).

result of efforts by economists such as Scialoja, Luzzatti, Minghetti and Boccardo. Nevertheless, the most lively economic debate was aired in the specialised press, where an approach in favour of a plurality of issuing banks – an approach dominated by Ferrara – stood in opposition to the views of the majority of economists, who argued for a central bank on the model of the Bank of England.[70] The debate in Parliament, on the other hand, was dominated by the scandal of the Banca Romana denounced in 1892 by two economists, Colajanni (who was a member of parliament) and Pantaleoni (who was to enter Parliament some years later). The Banca Romana was one of the six issuing banks inherited from the pre-unification period, whose board of directors was accused of having issued two series of banknotes with the same serial numbers. The scandal sprang from the charges brought against the Cabinet led by Giolitti, accused of concealing the truth with legal and illegal means. As a consequence, the debate in Parliament was dominated by moral and political questions and the creation of the Bank of Italy was seen more as a solution to the corruption of the ruling class than as an efficient economic solution to monetary regulation.[71]

A further problem that attracted the attention of Parliament after unification was that of education. Although it was clear that there was a connection between mass literacy, schooling and the expansion of scientific and technical training, on the one hand, and modernisation (or 'civilisation', in Romagnosi's terminology), on the other hand, and although many Italian economists had a clear notion of 'human (or immaterial) capital', the debates on these problems focused more on the cultural and linguistic unification of the country than on economic arguments. The economists who took an active part in them, among whom A. Scialoja, L. Luzzatti, N. Colajanni, and C.F. Ferraris, were no exception to this rule.[72]

Many economists were also seriously engaged in the issuing of laws on social insurance and welfare. The outstanding figure in this area was Luigi Luzzatti, who sponsored laws on social insurance (1898), on the labour of women and children (1902, 1907, 1910), and on public housing (1903).[73] From 1890 onwards Ferraris, acting as ministerial advisor and later as member of parliament, presented a series of bills on compulsory insurance for workers.[74] Nitti and Alessio sponsored the nationalisation of social insurance in 1911. Giulio Alessio promoted a Law on compulsory arbitration in controversies between trade unions and factory owners, although he did not succeed in obtaining its approval in Parliament.[75] This series of

70 See Realfonzo and Ricci (1995).

71 See Giaconi (2002).

72 See Gallifante (2002) and Spalletti (2002). On the notion of 'immaterial capital' in the Italian economic thought of the early nineteenth century see Guidi (2005).

73 See Petrovich (2003).

74 See Tusset (2003).

75 See Michelini (2003) and Realfonzo, Forges Davanzati and Patalano (2003).

efforts represented the logical application of the ideas the 'Lombard-Venetian' group had inherited both from Giandomenico Romagnosi and from German 'chair socialism' on the subject of State intervention in favour of the working class and the poor. It was an approach that was regarded as an instrument for preventing class conflict or the rise of revolutionary socialism, and as a way of securing a harmonious and smooth process of industrialisation. The dramatic issue of emigration was also at the forefront of concern during this era, with Luigi Bodio becoming the key figure of the Giolittian period. In 1901 Bodio sponsored the creation of the General Board on Emigration and remained at its head until 1904. He then headed the parliamentary committee that controlled the action of this board.[76] But even a radical *laissez-faire* economist like Pantaleoni promoted the legal recognition of trade unions, in 1901, as well as the legalisation of strikes, endorsing the action of the Cabinet led by Zanardelli in this circumstance. According to Pantaleoni, the action of trade unions was pro-market, and should not be mistaken for a type of monopolistic intervention.[77]

Debates and law-making on the so-called 'southern question' – i.e. the question of the backwardness and poverty of the regions formerly belonging to the Kingdom of the Two Sicilies – were another example of controversy between the interventionist approach of the 'Lombard-Venetian' economists and the *laissez-faire* approach of marginalist economists. On the one hand, Giuseppe Majorana and Giulio Alessio favoured the introduction of 'special laws' for the development of southern areas suited to specific economic activities, and Nitti – whose industrialist strategy of development dominated parliamentary debate and action in the first decade of the twentieth century – sponsored the Law of 8 July 1904 on the metropolitan area of Naples.[78] But, on the other hand, the question of the development of southern Italy was also kept alive by the lively controversy between these economists and Pantaleoni and De Viti de Marco, who saw in the protectionist tariff on corn and manufactured goods of 1887 – which had provoked retaliations by France and other countries – the main cause underlying the crisis of wine and oil export-led productions in the South.[79] Despite his political and personal affinity with the latter figures, it was Napoleone Colajanni who defended the 1887 tariff, arguing that the main causes of the backwardness of the Mezzogiorno lay in the *latifundium* (badly managed large estates) and the corrupted connexions between Mafia and the State.[80]

These intense activities by economists in Parliament reveal that the majority of them shared a strong propensity to endorse State intervention for the development of the country and for a solution of the 'social question' and the 'southern question'.

76 See Sunna (2002); Soresina (2003).
77 See Bini (2003).
78 See Patalano (2002).
79 See Tortorella Esposito (2002); Zagari (2002); Cardini (2003).
80 See Realfonzo (2002). On the 'moral question' pertaining to the Mafia and public corruption see Forges Davanzati (2002).

This orientation is confirmed by the fact that many economists of the Risorgimento generation (for example Boselli, Ciccone, Marescotti, and Scialoja), who had been educated to the free-trade ideals of classical economics, shifted their allegiance towards interventionist ideas in the late 1870s, in some cases becoming members of the Associazione per il Progresso degli Studi Economici. As argued by Antonio Magliulo (2002) and by Piero Bini and Daniela Parisi (2002), there was a strange paradox in the fact that all these economists, no less than the leaders of the Lombard-Venetian school (Lampertico, and to a lesser extent Luzzatti) never repudiated the classical approach and its *laissez-faire* deductions. On the contrary, they explicitly continued to defend it as the true – albeit abstract – view on economic relationships and economic policy. As a consequence, although they actively sponsored protectionism and the policies in favour of industrialisation, they presented them with tactical and empirical arguments and never formulated a coherent industrialist and interventionist economic theory. As far as social policies were concerned, they were able to claim that the classics of Italian economic thought had largely anticipated the paternalist and redistributive arguments of *Kathedersozialismus*. Only a few economists of the younger generations (like Ellena, Nitti and Alessio) developed interesting arguments in favour of industrialisation and argued for an active role of the State in the economy.

Conversely, among the authors of the opposite field who adhered to *laissez-faire* views, very few, perhaps only Ferrara among those of the classical generation, and Pantaleoni and De Viti de Marco in the marginalist generation, displayed an intransigent attitude *vis-à-vis* government interference in the economic field. Many others, from Minghetti, Boccardo and Magliani to Bodio, actively supported the action of Parliament and government. But the contributions of ideas and stimuli that both Ferrara and marginalist economists furnished to parliamentary debates and legislation from the benches of opposition were also essential for enhancing the theoretical level of discussions and warning against adoption of dangerous and hasty measures.

This does not mean that the voice of political economy was always heeded, or awarded the same attention at all times. In the period dominated by right-wing cabinets (1861-1876) the main policy orientations were consistent with, and based on, the teachings of classical political economy. Not only free-trade, but also the huge investments in education and infrastructures could be justified with classical arguments. Authors like Giandomenico Romagnosi, and later Scialoja and Carlo Cattaneo (who refused an offer of election to the Italian Parliament) had stressed in their work the function of accumulation of knowledge in economic development, and regarded a modern transportation network as a condition for inclusion of the Italian economy in the international division of labour.

In contrast, in the period between 1876 and 1900 dominated by the Left, economic arguments were rarely at the core of debates and decisions on important issues such as tariff regulations, credit, and railways. Even the economists who participated in these debates and sponsored important decisions preferred to avoid technicalities and addressed their colleagues with moral and political arguments.

There are two ways of explaining this change. First, as argued above, the economic arguments in favour of State intervention were generally of an empirical kind, justified as exceptions to the principles of political economy. And second, the enlargement of suffrage after 1882 introduced into Parliament a host of representatives of the middle classes, whose intellectual background was often less qualified than that of their learned colleagues in the elitist parliaments of the 1860s, and whose propensity to represent specific economic and social interests was stronger.

However, a further change took place at the beginning of the twentieth century, in a manner more favourable to political economy. The new policy orientations which aimed to foster the development of southern Italy and the implementation of a modern system of social welfare as well as encouraging a new direction in industrial relations were openly based on sound economic arguments that delved into the notion of effective demand, supply policies, poles of development, etc. On the other side of the political spectrum, the *laissez-faire* opposition rooted its position in the arguments developed by marginalist economists concerning the optimality of free competition. But even in this period, many decisions were taken without considering the arguments of political economy.

Conclusions

In the political background that prevailed in Italy after the unification of the country in 1861, many economists were attracted by the prospect of playing an active role in Parliament and in government. Thirty academic economists and various other experts of political economy were either elected to the House of Deputies or appointed senators. Many of them became ministers both in economic and in non-economic departments, and four were appointed prime ministers. Their political activity was therefore intense and contributed to placing them at the core of the ruling elite.

The analysis attempted in this paper reveals the importance of the economists' political commitment and the place it occupied in their active life. Many elected economists sat in Parliament for more than twenty years. In both houses of Parliament, they often played a technical role, concentrating their efforts on the discussion of economic issues and seizing any opportunity for spreading the principles of political economy and illustrating the limits of a purely political logic. But they did not refrain from meddling with questions of a more political nature, and on occasion did not hesitate to act as *notables*, establishing a network of patronage in their constituencies, or sponsoring powerful economic interests, as well as their 'professional' interest in the institutionalisation of economics. Overall, their political commitment was intense and can be considered a fundamental ingredient of the intellectual mission they aimed to fulfil in the Italian society.

Finally, this analysis of the attention paid to the teachings of economics in parliamentary debates and political decisions highlights not only a number of cases in which economic arguments were endorsed by the political class, but also some

– perhaps many other – circumstances in which they were largely ignored. Conversely, the intense political experience of many Italian economists was probably a consequence of a tradition of thought that emphasised the role of social and political institutions in economic life.

Still to be addressed is the question as to whether the economic debates in Parliament contributed to orienting the evolution of Italian economics in some specific directions. The answer can be only conjectural, although it appears plausible that some features of late nineteenth-century and early twentieth-century Italian economic thought may have been influenced by the stimuli economists received from their institutional experiences. To begin with, consider one of the distinctive features of the Italian school of 'scienza delle finanze', its emphasis on the twofold nature, economic and political, of public finance. Such an awareness of the role of government in determining the distribution of taxation and the weight of public debt may have profited from the daily experience of political mechanisms that many economists acquired in Parliament and in governmental agencies. Second, the interest taken by some Italian economists (Pantaleoni, Pareto, Del Vecchio, etc.) in dynamic analysis as an application of a mixed methodology which combines economics, sociology and political science could be considered as a consequence of their knowledge of political machinery and of its interference in economic phenomena. Third, the shortcuts between pure economic analysis and free-trade policies, typical of the Italian marginalist school, were also a partial result of economists' political engagement and their opposition to the inefficiencies of the Italian State. Finally the high level of statistical studies in Italy between the end of the nineteenth century and the first decades of the twentieth century is also a result of the efforts made by those economists who shared important political responsibilities.

It may be concluded that the ancient propensity of Italian economists to study the interaction between political and social institutions, laws and economic phenomena, which was probably responsible for their desire to play an active role in politics, was in turn strengthened by their political experience.

References

Are, G. (1965), *Il problema dello sviluppo industriale nell'età della Destra*, Nistri-Lischi, Pisa.

Are, G. (1974), *Alle origini dell'Italia industriale*, Guida, Napoli.

Asso, P.F. (2001) (ed.), *From Economists to Economists. The International Spread of Italian Economic Thought, 1750-1950*, Polistampa, Firenze.

Asso, P.F. (2003), 'Intervento pubblico, marina mercantile e politica commerciale nell'azione parlamentare di Paolo Boselli', in Augello and Guidi (2003), pp. 265-87.

Augello, M.M. (1989), 'The Societies of Political Economy in Italy and the Professionalisation of Economists (1860-1900)', *History of Economics Society Bulletin*, **11**(1), pp. 99-112.

Augello, M.M. (1992), 'La nascita di una professione accademica: gli economisti italiani post-unitari (1860-1900). Un'analisi quantitativa', *Quaderni di storia dell'economia politica*, **10**(3), pp. 3-39.

Augello, M.M. (1994), 'L'evoluzione della letteratura economica in Italia: 1861-1900. Un'analisi storico-quantitativa', *Il pensiero economico italiano*, **2**(1), pp. 7-36.

Augello, M.M. (2003), 'Pietro Torrigiani tra economia e politica: tassa sul macinato e corso forzoso', in Augello and Guidi (2003), pp. 81-108.

Augello, M.M., Bianchini, M., Gioli, G. and Roggi, P. (1988) (eds), *Le cattedre di economia in Italia (1700-1900). La nascita di una disciplina 'sospetta'*, Franco Angeli, Milano.

Augello, M.M. and Giva, D. (1988), 'La definitiva istituzionalizzazione accademica dell'economia politica: le università di Padova e di Torino (1860-1900)', in Augello *et al.* (1988), pp. 241-89.

Augello, M.M. and Guidi, M.E.L. (1988), 'I "politecnici del commercio" e la formazione della classe dirigente economica nell'Italia post-unitaria. L'origine delle Scuole Superiori di Commercio e l'insegnamento dell'economia politica (1868-1900)', in Augello *et al.* (1988), pp. 335-84.

Augello, M.M. and Guidi, M.E.L. (1996), 'The Emergence of Economic Periodical Literature in Italy (1750-1900)', *History of Economic Ideas*, **4**(3), pp. 15-62.

Augello, M.M. and Guidi, M.E.L. (2000) (eds), *Associazionismo economico e diffusione dell'economia politica nell'Italia dell'Ottocento. Dalle società economico-agrarie alle associazioni di economisti*, 2 Vols, Franco Angeli, Milano.

Augello, M.M. and Guidi, M.E.L. (2001a) (eds), *The Spread of Political Economy and the Professionalisation of Economists. Economic Societies in Europe, America and Japan in the Nineteenth Century*, Routledge, London.

Augello, M.M. and Guidi, M.E.L. (2001b), 'The Associations of Economists and the Dissemination of Political Economy in Italy', in Augello and Guidi (2001), pp. 70-90.

Augello, M.M. and Guidi, M.E.L. (2001c), 'Gli economisti e le iniziative enciclopediche nell'Italia liberale. Ricognizione e analisi storica', in Roggi (2001), **41**, pp. 257-98.

Augello, M.M. and Guidi, M.E.L. (2002) (eds), *La scienza economica in Parlamento 1861-1922. Una storia dell'economia politica dell'Italia liberale – I*, Franco Angeli, Milano.

Augello, M.M. and Guidi, M.E.L. (2003) (eds), *Gli economisti in Parlamento 1861-1922. Una storia dell'economia politica dell'Italia liberale – II*, Franco Angeli, Milano.

Augello, M.M. and Guidi, M.E.L. (2005), 'The Italian Economists in Parliament from 1860 to 1922: a Quantitative Analysis', *The European Journal of the History of Economic Thought*, **12**(2), pp. 279-319.

Augello, M.M. and Travagliante, P. (2004), 'L'opera di Salvatore Majorana Calatabiano (1825-1896) tra politica ed economia: per una nuova scienza "della conservazione e del perfezionamento sociale"', *Il Pensiero economico italiano*, **12**(1), pp. 7-28.

Barucci, P. (1972), 'The Spread of Marginalism in Italy (1871-1890)', *History of Political Economy*, **4**(Summer), pp. 512-31.

Barucci, P. (2003) (ed.), *Le frontiere dell'economia politica. Gli economisti stranieri in Italia: dai mercantilisti a Keynes*, Polistampa, Firenze.

Bianchi, G. (2003), 'Napoleone Colajanni da liberista circospetto a "protezionista condizionato"', in Augello and Guidi (2003), pp. 439-55.

Bianchini, M. (1996) (ed.), *Political Economy in European Periodicals, 1750-1900*, special issue of *History of Economic Ideas*, **4**(3).

Bini, P. (2003), 'Progetti (e mancate realizzazioni) di economia di mercato in Italia all'inizio del Novecento: Maffeo Pantaleoni in Parlamento (1900-1904)', in Augello and Guidi (2003), pp. 551-72.

Bini, P. and Parisi, D. (2002), 'Sulla via dello sviluppo', in Augello and Guidi (2002), pp. 3-20.

Buchanan, J. (1960), '"La Scienza delle Finanze": The Italian Tradition in Fiscal Theory', in Id., *Fiscal Theory and Political Economy. Selected Essays*, The University of North Carolina Press, Chapel Hill.

Cammarano, F. and Piretti, M.S. (1996), 'I professionisti in Parlamento (1861-1958)', in M. Malatesta (ed.), *Storia d'Italia. Annali*, **10**, *I professionisti*, Einaudi, Torino, pp. 521-89.

Caracciolo, A. (1958), *L'inchiesta agraria Jacini*, Einaudi, Torino.

Cardini, A. (2003), 'De Viti de Marco in Parlamento', in Augello and Guidi (2003), pp. 573-91.

Carlucci, P. (2002), *Il giovane Sonnino fra cultura e politica, 1847-1886*, Archivio Guido Izzi, Roma.

Castronovo, V. (1995), *Storia economica d'Italia. Dall'Ottocento ai giorni nostri*, Einaudi, Torino.

Coats, A.W. Bob (1991), 'Economics as a Profession', in Id., *The Sociology and Professionalization of Economics, British and American Economic Essays*, Routledge, London and New York 1993.

Di Battista, F. (1983), *L'emergenza ottocentesca dell'economia politica a Napoli*, Facoltà di Economia e Commercio, Bari.

Erreygers, G. (2001), 'Economic Associations in Belgium', in Augello and Guidi (2001a), pp. 91-108.

Fausto, D. and De Bonis, V. (2003) (eds), *The Theory of Public Finance in Italy from the Origins to the 1940s*, special issue of *Il Pensiero economico italiano*, **11**(1).

Faucci, R. (1995), *L'economista scomodo. Vita e opere di Francesco Ferrara*, Sellerio, Palermo.

Faucci, R. (2002), 'Contabilità dello Stato e bilancio pubblico in Parlamento (e fuori) nell'Italia liberale', in Augello and Guidi (2002), pp. 341-77.

Favero, G. (2001), *Le misure del Regno. Direzione di statistica e municipi nell'Italia liberale*, Il Poligrafo, Padova.

Ferrara, F. (1874), 'Il germanismo economico in Italia', *Nuova antologia*, August, reprinted in Id., *Opere complete*, **10**, *Saggi, rassegne, memorie economiche e finanziarie*, F. Caffè ed., Associazione Bancaria Italiana, Roma 1972, pp. 555-91.

Ferrara, F. (2002), *Epistolario (1835-1897)*, P.F. Asso ed., in Id., *Opere complete*, **13**, Associazione Bancaria Italiana, Roma.

Forges Davanzati, G. (2002), 'La questione meridionale come questione morale. Etica pubblica e sviluppo economico nel dibattito teorico e politico del primo Novecento', in Augello and Guidi (2002), pp. 395-419.

Gallifante, M.F. (2002), 'L'insegnamento tecnico nella seconda metà dell'Ottocento: aspetti del dibattito prima e dopo l'inchiesta Scialoja sulla istruzione secondaria', in Augello and Guidi (2002), pp. 199-228.

Gentilucci, C.E. (2002), 'Il dibattito in Parlamento sui temi delle spese militari e della guerra nell'ultimo ventennio dello Stato liberale: alcune riflessioni', in Augello and Guidi (2002), pp. 295-315.

Gherardi, R. (2003), 'Politica, scienza e opinione pubblica: il riformismo ben temperato di Marco Minghetti', in Augello and Guidi (2003), pp. 31-51.

Giaconi, D. (2002), 'Dallo scandalo della Banca Romana alla fondazione della Banca d'Italia. Cronologia di "una bancarotta morale immensa"', in Augello and Guidi (2002), pp. 105-22.

Giocoli, N. (2002), 'L'esercizio di Stato delle ferrovie italiane: tra teoria economica e volontà politica', in Augello and Guidi (2002), pp. 45-72.

Gioli, G. (2003), 'Commercio, finanza e istituti di emissione nell'attività parlamentare di Antonio Scialoja', in Augello and Guidi (2003), pp. 1-30.

Grembi, V. (2002), 'La questione della proprietà intellettuale: il contributo degli economisti italiani al dibattito', in Augello and Guidi (2002), pp. 267-94.

Guidi, M.E.L. (1994), '"Economy" and "Political Economy" in Italian Dictionaries and

Encyclopaedias. 1729-1861', in M. Albertone and A. Masoero (eds), *Political Economy and National Realities*, Fondazione Luigi Einaudi, Torino, pp. 147-75.

Guidi, M.E.L. (2002), '"Il sapere e l'esperienza che l'Italia contemporanea è in grado di fornire". L'Inchiesta agraria Jacini tra statistica ed economia agraria', in Augello and Guidi (2002), pp. 531-73.

Guidi, M.E.L. (2003), 'L'ascesa di un tecnico. Vittorio Ellena dal Maic al Parlamento', in Augello and Guidi (2003), pp. 413-38.

Guidi, M.E.L. (2005), 'Division of labour and technical change: the Smithian legacy in Italy from Melchiorre Gioja to Carlo Cattaneo', in M.E.L. Guidi and D. Parisi (eds), *The Changing Firm. Contributions from the History of Economic Thought*, Franco Angeli, Milano.

Haywood, G.A. (1999), *Failure of a Dream. Sydney Sonnino and the Rise and Fall of Liberal Italy 1847-1922*, Fondazione Luigi Einaudi and Leo Olschki, Firenze.

La Bruna, A. (2003), 'Un economista liberal-democratico: Salvatore Majorana Calatabiano tra visione, teoria e politica economica', in Augello and Guidi (2003), pp. 131-57.

Lacaita, G.C. (1985), 'Giuseppe Colombo e le origini dell'Italia industriale', in G. Colombo, *Industria e politica nella storia d'Italia. Scritti scelti: 1861-1916*, Cariplo-Laterza, Milano-Roma-Bari.

Lampertico, F. (1874-1884), *L'economia dei popoli e degli stati*, 5 Vols, Treves, Milano.

Lampertico, F. (1996-1998), *Carteggi e diari 1842-1906*, **1**, *A-E*, E. Franzina ed.; **2**, *F-L*, R. Camurri ed., Marsilio, Venezia.

Ledermann, L. (1929), *Pellegrino Rossi. L'homme et l'économiste, 1787-1848*, Sirey, Paris.

Lepore, G. (2002), 'Il problema della vendita dei beni demaniali nei dibattiti parlamentari del 1861-62', in Augello and Guidi (2002), pp. 575-87.

Macchioro, A. (2001), 'Napoleone Colajanni fra socialismo e protezionismo patrio', *Il Pensiero economico italiano*, **9**(1), pp. 79-140.

Mack Smith, D. (1997), *Modern Italy. A Political History*, Yale University Press, New Haven and London.

Magliulo, A. (2002), 'Il protezionismo dell'Italia liberale. Economia classica e politiche di sviluppo nel dibattito parlamentare sulla tariffa doganale del 1887', in Augello and Guidi (2002), pp. 147-78.

Magnani, I. (2003), *Dibattito tra economisti italiani di fine Ottocento*, Franco Angeli, Milano.

Martinelli, A. and Zucchini, F. (2001), 'Profilo sociale e professionale, livello e tipo di istruzione ed esperienza politica dei deputati italiani: evoluzione e prospettive', in Violante (2001), pp. 817-54.

Marucco, D. (1996), *L'amministrazione della statistica nell'Italia unita*, Laterza, Roma-Bari.

Masini, F. (2002), 'Le differenti fasi di negoziazione dell'Unione Monetaria Latina nel dibattito al Parlamento italiano: 1865-1894', in Augello and Guidi (2002), pp. 123-46.

Mastropaolo, A. (1986), 'Sviluppo politico e parlamento nell'Italia liberale. Un'analisi a partire dai meccanismi della rappresentanza', *Passato e presente*, **12**, pp. 29-91.

Mastropaolo, A. (2001), 'Notabili, clientelismo e trasformismo', in Violante (2001), pp. 773-816.

Mastropaolo, A. (2002), 'La classe politica italiana dall'Unità alla Prima guerra mondiale', *Il Pensiero economico italiano*, **10**(1), pp. 39-50.

Melis, G. (1996), *Storia dell'amministrazione italiana (1861-1993)*, Il Mulino, Bologna.

Michelini, L. (2000), 'Il movimento anti-protezionistico e l'Associazione per la libertà economica', in Augello and Guidi (2000), **2**, pp. 405-33.

Michelini, L. (2003), 'Lo statalismo "radicale" di Giulio Alessio', in Augello and Guidi (2003), pp. 475-502.

Minelli, E., Guidi, M.E.L. and Guccione, A. (2004), 'A Note on Francesco Ferrara's Cost of Reproduction', *Journal of the History of Economic Thought*, **26**(1), pp. 107-14.

Minghetti, M. (1859), *Dell'economia pubblica e delle sue attinenze con la morale e col diritto*, Le Monnier, Firenze.

Mosca, G. (1884), *Sulla teorica dei governi e sul governo parlamentare. Studii storici e sociali*, Tip. dello Statuto, Palermo.

Parisi, D. (2002), 'La questione ferroviaria nel periodo 1865-1876', in Augello and Guidi (2002), pp. 21-43.

Parisi, D. (2003), 'Angelo Messedaglia economista in Parlamento: la statistica come fondamento della ricerca economica e dell'intervento attraverso le istituzioni', in Augello and Guidi (2003), pp. 159-78.

Pastorini, F. and Pizzanelli, G. (2002), 'Il contributo degli economisti alla riforma dell'ordinamento degli enti locali', in Augello and Guidi (2002), pp. 237-66.

Patalano, R. (2002), 'Stato, industrializzazione e questione meridionale: la legge per Napoli: 1901-1904', in Augello and Guidi (2002), pp. 443-81.

Pavanelli, G. (2003), 'Le ragioni del liberismo: commercio estero e finanza pubblica negli interventi parlamentari di Gerolamo Boccardo', in Augello and Guidi (2003), pp. 305-31.

Petrovich, G. (2003), 'Luigi Luzzatti: gli inizi della politica per il "benessere delle classi laboriose"', in Augello and Guidi (2003), pp. 233-64.

Piccioni, L. and Raffaelli, T. (2002), 'Il rinnovamento della legislazione forestale (1905-1915): il contributo di Luzzatti e Nitti', in Augello and Guidi (2002), pp. 589-98.

Pombeni, P. (2002), 'Il governo e l'opinione: la posizione del Parlamento nell'Italia liberale (1860-1914)', *Il Pensiero economico italiano*, **10**(1), pp. 17-38.

Prodi, R. (1966), 'Il protezionismo nella politica e nell'industria italiana dall'unificazione al 1887', *Nuova rivista storica*, **1-2**, pp. 42-86.

Raffaelli, T. (1997), 'Dalla repressione del "danno pubblico" alla produzione del "bene pubblico": cultura economica e politiche forestali (1861-1915)', *Il Pensiero economico italiano*, **5**(2), pp. 41-79.

Rancan, A. (2003), 'Scienza e arte di governo in Agostino Magliani', in Augello and Guidi (2003), pp. 333-63.

Realfonzo, R. (2002), 'Il sottosviluppo del Mezzogiorno tra teoria economica e dibattito politico parlamentare nel primo Novecento', in Augello and Guidi (2002), pp. 381-94.

Realfonzo, R., Forges Davanzati, G. and Patalano, R. (2003), 'Nitti in Parlamento: "democrazia industriale" e programma "radicale" per il Mezzogiorno (1904-1911)', in Augello and Guidi (2003a), pp. 593-613.

Roggi, P. (2001) (ed.), *Le grandi 'voci' nei dizionari specializzati (e non) di economia*, special issue of *Storia del pensiero economico*, **41-42**.

Romeo, R. (1984), *Cavour e il suo tempo (1810-1842)*, Laterza, Roma-Bari.

Sabbatucci, G. and Vidotto, V. (1995) (eds), *Storia d'Italia*, **2**, *Il nuovo Stato e la società civile*, Laterza, Roma-Bari.

Sabbatucci, G. and Vidotto, V. (1999) (eds), *Storia d'Italia*, **3**, *Liberalismo e democrazia*, Laterza, Roma-Bari.

Say, J.-B. (1828-1829), *Cours complet d'économie politique pratique*, 6 Vols, Rapilly, Paris.

Scialoja, A. (1840), *I principj della economia sociale, esposti in ordine ideologico*, Tip. di Gennaro Palma, Napoli.

Scialoja, A. (1844), *Les principes de l'économie sociale exposés selon l'ordre logique des idées*, traduit et annoté par Hip.te Devilliers, Guillaumin, Paris.

Soresina, M. (2001), *Conoscere per amministrare: Luigi Bodio. Statistica, economia e pubblica amministrazione*, Franco Angeli, Milano.

Soresina, M. (2003), 'Dietro le quinte. Bodio, un tecnico al servizio della politica e della pubblica amministrazione', in Augello and Guidi (2003), pp. 503-22.

Spalletti, S. (2002), 'Economisti e istruzione al Parlamento italiano (1859-1912)', in Augello and Guidi (2002), pp. 179-97.

Stigler, G.J. (1965), 'Statistical Studies in the History of Economic Thought', in Id. *Essays in the History of Economics*, The University of Chicago Press, Chicago.

Subacchi, P. (1997) (ed.), *Les associations économiques et groupes de pression en Europe XIXe-XXe siècles*, special issue of *Histoire, économie et société*, **26**(2).

Sunna, C. (2002), 'Emigrazione e questione meridionale. Il dibattito parlamentare sullo sviluppo economico del Mezzogiorno (1861-1910)', in Augello and Guidi (2002), pp. 483-511.

Teti, R. (2002), 'La disciplina delle società anonime attraverso i lavori parlamentari: 1865-1925', in Augello and Guidi (2002), pp. 317-40.

Tortorella Esposito, G. (2002), 'Alle origini della questione meridionale. Gli economisti e la politica economica protezionistica', in Augello and Guidi (2002), pp. 421-41.

Tusset, G. (2003), 'L'economia al servizio dello Stato: Carlo Francesco Ferraris', in Augello and Guidi (2003), pp. 523-50.

Valenti, G. (1907), *Commemorazione del socio Fedele Lampertico*, R. Accademia dei Lincei, Roma.

Violante, L. (2001) (ed.), *Storia d'Italia, Annali*, **17**, *Il Parlamento*, Einaudi, Torino.

Weber, M. (1919), *Politik als Beruf*, Duncker & Humblot, München-Leipzig.

Zagari, E. (2002), 'Il dibattito sulla questione agraria e la questione industriale nel Mezzogiorno: il contributo di Francesco Saverio Nitti', in Augello and Guidi (2002), pp. 513-29.

Zamagni, V, (1993), *Dalla periferia al centro. La seconda rinascita economica dell'Italia 1861-1990*, 2nd edn, Il Mulino, Bologna.

Appendix

Table 8.1 Italian economists in Parliament (1860-1922)

Name and life	Graduation	Career (1)	Deputy (2)	Senator (2)	Alignment (3)	Minister (2)	Higher Councils (2) (4)
Agnelli, Arnaldo 1875-1921	Law	Lecturer of PE	1913-1921	—	Extreme Left	Treasury, War	—
Alessio, Giulio 1853-1940	Law	Professor of PF/PE	1897-*1823*	—	Extreme Left	Agric., Finance, Mail, Justice	—
Arrivabene, Giovanni 1787-1881	—	Landowner	—	1860-1881	Right	—	—
Beneduce, Alberto 1877-1944	Maths	Professor of ST/EP	1919-*1924*	1939-1944	Socialist	Labour	Labour, Education, Statistics, Credit
Boccardo, Gerolamo 1829-1904	Law	Professor of PE/ST/PF	—	1877-1904	Right	—	Education, State
Bodio, Luigi 1840-1920	Law	Professor of PE/ST	—	1900-1920	Right	—	Labour, Statistics, State
Boselli, Paolo 1838-1932	Law	Professor of PF	1870-1821	1921-*1932*	Right	Treasury, Agriculture, Finance, Education. Prime Minister (1915-1917)	Labour, State
Ciccone, Antonio 1808-1893	Medicine	Professor of PE	1861-1870	1870-1893	Right	Agriculture	—
Colajanni, Napoleone 1847-1921	Medicine	Professor of ST	1890-1821	—	Extreme Left	—	—
De Luca, Placido 1802-1861	Law	Professor of PE	1860-1861	—	Right	—	—
De' Stefani, Alberto 1879-1969	Commerce, Law	Professor of PE	1921-*1934*	—	Fascist	Finance	—

Name and life	Graduation	Career (1)	Deputy (2)	Senator (2)	Alignment (3)	Minister (2)	Higher Councils (2) (4)
De Viti de Marco, Antonio 1858-1943	Law	Professor of PE/PF	1901-1921	—	Extreme Left	—	Statistics
Einaudi, Luigi 1874-1961	Law	Professor of PF	—	1919-*1946*	Right	—	—
Ellena, Vittorio 1844-1892	—	Civil servant, Lecturer of PE	1886-1892	—	Centre	Agriculture, Finance	Industry, Labour, Statistics, State
Ferrara, Francesco 1810-1900	—	Professor of PE	1867-1880	1881-1900	Centre	Finance	Education, Accounts
Ferraris, Carlo Francesco 1850-1924	Law	Professor of PF/ST	1886-1887; 1904-1913	1913-*1924*	Centre	Public Works	Education, Agriculture, Labour, Statistics, Administration
Graziadei, Antonio 1873-1853	Law	Professor of PE/PF	1910-*1926*	—	Socialist	—	—
Labriola, Arturo 1873-1959	—	Professor of PE	1913-*1929*	1948-1949	Socialist	Labour	Administration
Lampertico, Fedele 1833-1906	Law	Landowner, local politician	1866-1870	1873-1906	Right	—	Labour, Education
Loria, Achille 1857-1943	Law	Professor of PE/ST	—	1919-*1943*	Socialist	—	—
Luzzatti, Luigi 1841-1927	Law	Professor of CL/PE	1870-1821	1921-*1927*	Right	Agriculture, Finance, Treasury, Internal, Mail. Prime Minister (1910-1911)	Education, Labour
Magliani, Agostino 1824-1891	Law	Civil servant	—	1871-1891	Right	Finance, Treasury	Accounts
Majorana, Giuseppe 1863-1940	Law	Professor of ST/PF/PE	1897-1900; 1904-1909	—	Left	—	—

Name and life	Graduation	Career (1)	Deputy (2)	Senator (2)	Alignment (3)	Minister (2)	Higher Councils (2) (4)
Majorana, Salvatore 1825-1897	Law	Professor of PE/PF	1866-1879	1879-1897	Left	Agriculture	Education
Manna, Giovanni 1813-1865	Law	Professor of PE	—	1862-1865	Right	Finance, Agriculture	—
Marescotti, Angelo 1815-1892	Medicine	Professor of PE	1863-1864; 1881-1882	1883-1892	Right, then Left	—	—
Messedaglia, Angelo 1820-1901	Law	Professor of PE/ST	1866-1884	1884-1901	Centre	—	Education, Statistics
Minghetti, Marco 1818-1886		Landowner	1860-1886	—	Right	Agriculture, Finance, Internal. Prime Minister (1863-1864, 1873-1876)	Labour
Morpurgo, Emilio 1836-1885	Law	Professor of ST	1867-1879; 1882-1885	—	Centre	Agriculture	Agriculture, Statistics, Labour
Nitti, Francesco Saverio 1868-1953	Law	Professor of ST/PF	1904-*1924*	—	Extreme Left	Agriculture, Treasury, Internal, Foreign. Prime Minister (1919-1920)	Education, Labour
Pantaleoni, Maffeo 1857-1924	Law	Professor of PF/PE/ST	1900-1904	1923-1924	Extreme Left	—	Administration
Ponsiglioni, Antonio 1843-1907	Law	Professor of PF/PE/ST	1876-1880; 1890-1892	1901-1907	Left	—	Labour
Sbarbaro, Pietro 1838-1893	Law	Professor of PE	1885-1886	—	Right	—	—
Scialoja, Antonio 1817-1877	Law	Professor of PE	1860-1862	1862-1877	Right	Agricult., Finance, Education	Accounts
Sitta, Pietro 1866-1947	Commerce	Professor of PF/PE/ST	1915-1923	1924-1945	Centre	Agriculture, Mercant. Marine	—
Tangorra, Vincenzo 1866-1922	Commerce; Law	Professor of PF	1919-1924	—	Popular	Treasury	—
Ticci, Torello 1828-1913	Law	Professor of PE/ST	1900-1904	—	Right	—	—

Name and life	Graduation	Career (1)	Deputy (2)	Senator (2)	Alignment (3)	Minister (2)	Higher Councils (2) (4)
Torrigiani, Pietro 1810-1885	Philosophy	Professor of PE	1860-1879	1879-1885	Right		State
Zucconi, Giovanni 1845-1894	Law	Professor of PE/ST	1878-1894	—	Centre	—	—

Sources: *Dizionario biografico degli Italiani*, Istituto dell'Enciclopedia Italiana, Roma 1960-; *Il Parlamento italiano 1861-1988*, Nuova Cei, Milano 1989-; A. Malatesta, *Ministri, deputati, senatori dal 1848 al 1922*, 3 voll., Istituto editoriale italiano Bernardo Carlo Tosi, Milano 1940; *Enciclopedia Italiana*, Istituto dell'Enciclopedia Italiana, Roma 1929-. M.M. Augello, *Data Bank on Italian Economists*, University of Pisa.

Notes:

(1) This column lists as 'professors' all those who taught economics or related topics at least for a part of their life. Of all others, only the main occupation is mentioned. List of acronyms: PE = Political economy; PF = Public finance; ST = Statistics; EP = Economic Policy; CL = Constitutional Law.

(2) This column only accounts for those economists whose political jobs started in the period 1860-1922. Dates in italics indicate periods after 1922. The title of 'minister' also includes vice-ministers.

(3) A system of parties was present only in the House of Deputies. The party affiliation of senators is indicated in italics when known. Right = traditional liberal; Left = State interventionist; Extreme Left = ultra-liberal; Popular = Christian Democratic; Socialist = Socialist Party; Centre = moderate.

(4) This column includes:

- the consultative councils depending from single ministries, denominated 'higher councils'. They are abbreviated as follows: Education = Higher Council of Education (1860-); Agriculture = Higher Council of Agriculture (1868-); Industry = Higher Council of Industry and Commerce (1869); Labour = Consultative Commission on Social Insurance and Labour (1869-1894) – Higher Council of Social Insurance and Labour (1894-1903) – Higher Council of Social Insurance (1903-) – Higher Council of Labour (1903-); Administration = Higher Council of Public Administration (1893-); Statistics = Bureau/Direction of Statistics (1861-) – Board/Higher Council of Statistics (1872-); Credit = Higher Council of Credit (1920-). Collaboration with the Bureau or Direction of Statistics, which was a branch of the civil service, has been considered in the case of those economists (De Viti de Marco and Messedaglia) who contributed to it with a continuative consultative activity.
- the State Council (*Consiglio di Stato*) (1860-) (abbreviated as 'State'), the supreme organ of public administration and administrative justice;
- the Court of Accounts (*Corte dei Conti*) (1860-) (abbreviated as 'Accounts'), the supreme court that watches over the management of public finances.

Chapter 9

Economists in the Greek Parliament (1862-1910): The Men and Their Views on Fiscal and Monetary Policy*

Michalis Psalidopoulos and Adamantios Syrmaloglou

Economy and society in the nineteenth century

Having gained independence in 1830, Greece – the first country in South-eastern Europe to overthrow Ottoman rule – introduced a Parliament as an institution of representative government in 1844. During the years of King Otto's monarchy (1833-1862), the Parliament was a forum for the expression of opinion, enabling the Greek people to voice their desire to promote democracy, to see their country expand territorially (in order to include all Greeks still living under the Ottomans) and develop economically. Three political parties, the 'English', 'French' and 'Russian' Party – their names deriving from their orientation vis-à-vis the great powers that had guaranteed Greek independence – dominated the political scene of the time.[1]

Universal male suffrage was explicitly introduced in the constitution quite early, in 1864,[2] while voting, despite the occasional complaints about the handling of procedures and results,[3] was acknowledged as the democratic means of solving political disputes. The political system remained fragile throughout the nineteenth century.[4] The overthrow of the Ottomans did not bring about the immediate entry of

---

* An earlier version of this paper was presented at the HES conference at Duke University in July 2003. We would like to thank conference participants for their comments, especially Massimo Augello and Marco Guidi. The usual disclaimer applies.

1 For the political scene of the decade 1833-1843 see Petropulos (1968). For a discussion of developments in the Greek economy during this period see Petropulos (1981).

2 See Svolos (1998), p. 83.

3 This topic is discussed in Karanikolas (1963).

4 In this context Koliopoulos and Veremis (2002), p. 51 speak of 'unstable and changing alignments and alliances of politicians around a set of leaders of the same generation which provided the country with governments whose main preoccupation was survival in office'. To its credit, this system did not produce a dictatorship or military governments until the interwar years of the twentieth century.

the Greek State into modernity; instead, traditional, pre-modern patterns of government were abandoned gradually, over several decades.[5] Disputes between the Prime Minister and the King, or failure to pass vital legislation, led to the frequent collapse of governments. Foreign policy issues and the intervention of foreign ambassadors in Greek political life further contributed to the prevailing political instability. Between 1865 and 1910, a total of 54 governments were formed, with an average term in office of about 10 months.[6] Members of parliament were quite outspoken, and the session minutes reveal that many debates led to a synthesis of opinions, the ensuing legislation reflecting the compromises achieved.

With the introduction of a new dynasty in 1864, the importance of Parliament increased, especially after 1874, when the King became obliged to grant the mandate for the formation of government to the political leader whose party held the majority of parliamentary seats. The Parliament constantly strengthened its position in the political system. Newspaper reports kept the public informed of parliamentary debates on a daily basis. It is this period, extending until the inauguration of Eleftherios Venizelos as Prime Minister in 1910, that will constitute the focus of attention in the present paper.

These (approximately) fifty years between 1862 and 1910 coincide with major political and economic developments in the European, and especially the South-European economy and society.[7] As far as the present study is concerned, Greek political life can be divided into four periods of varying duration: one spanning the period between 1862 and 1864, a second between 1864 and 1879, a third one between 1879 and 1893, and a fourth period covering the years 1893-1910.

The first, and shortest one, was the period of the Constitutional Assembly, when Greek parliamentary debates were carried out in the political arena free from foreign interference. During this period, certain intellectuals, university professors and civil servants played an important role in the debates and expressed the needs and aspirations of their constituencies and of Greek citizens as a whole at that time.[8]

The second period is characterised by men such as Alexandros Koumoundouros, Epaminondas Deligiorgis and Thrasyvoulos Zaimis, who served as Prime Ministers and implemented long-awaited economic reforms, for example the land reform of 1871 and the tariff system of 1867. Other important figures in Parliament include Sotirios Sotiropoulos, Efthymios Kehayias, Pavlos Kalligas and Athanasios Petsalis. During this period, according to one estimate, GDP rose by 42 per cent.[9]

The third period starts with the resumption of public lending in foreign markets after a long financial embargo.[10] A two party system became the rule in political life,

5 See Kostis (2002), p. 51.
6 For the 54 governments, which were formed between 1865-1910, see Dakin (1972).
7 On these see Cameron (1993) and Palairet (1997). For the interaction of economic thought and policy in some less developed European countries see the essays in Psalidopoulos and Mata (2002). For aspects of Greek economic and social life see Carabott (1997).
8 For an overview of the parliamentary debates during this period see Grapsas (1948).
9 See Kostelenos (1995).
10 On this see Andreades (1939) and Levandis (1944).

with the moderniser Harilaos Trikoupis and the traditionalist Theodoros Deliyiannis succeeding one another as heads of government. They ruled the country for eight and three years respectively. Other important speakers on economic issues during this period include Athanasios Rontiris, Constantinos Karapanos, Constantinos Konstantopoulos, Athanasios Petimezas and Ioannis Valassopoulos. On the economic front, public lending facilitated the implementation of large-scale infrastructure works. Agriculture received a boost with the incorporation of Thessaly into the Kingdom in 1881, a development that increased Greek territory by 28 per cent and population by 18 per cent. A new tariff system in 1884 stimulated commerce and, as a whole, this period witnessed a 64 per cent rise in GDP.[11]

The fourth period starts with Greek bankruptcy due to an agricultural crisis that led to a severe contraction in public finance at a time of huge loan repayments. The imposition of an International Financial Control over Greek finances followed in 1898, leading to contractionary monetary policy, recession and large-scale emigration. Political figures that dominated in this period were Georgios Theotokis, Dimitrios Gounaris and Anargyros Simopoulos. Despite the deflation, GDP rose by 18 per cent.[12]

The study of nineteenth-century Greek parliamentary debates on economic policy has not attracted the interest of many researchers.[13] Whereas it is true that parliamentary speeches have at times been quoted as evidence of the speakers' credo, such studies have more often than not been conducted in an effort to address other questions and issues of historical inquiry, rather than to shed further light into economic policy as such. Use of such evidence has been made in relation to biographical works and has aimed at identifying the patterns of thought of individual politicians and on certain issues, for example Efthymios Kehayias, Alexandros Koumoundouros and Pavlos Kalligas.[14] Other authors have written on issues of general interest and tried to ascertain how Parliament reached consensus or remained split on a certain course of action,[15] but overall the economic debates in Parliament have not been placed at the centre of scholarly inquiries.

Such debates were however quite frequent in Greek Parliament. Trying to sort out the most important of these is a difficult endeavour. Excluding the annual debate on the new budget and some revealing hints about the conduct of economic policy, brought up at times when government had to survive a vote of confidence, a typology of important debates would include legislation centred around such important economic events as:

---

11 See Kostelenos (1995). It is to be noted however that this rise is not comparable with the growth rate of the former period because of the territorial expansion that took place in 1881.

12 Ibid.

13 For notable exceptions see Perakis (2000) and Stassinopoulos (2000), pp. 155-69.

14 For Kehayias, Koumoundouros and Kalligas see the biographical works of Evlambios (1930-1931); Papathanasopoulos (1993) and Masson-Vincourt (2000) respectively.

15 See Vergopoulos (1978) and Dertilis (1980).

- the distribution of national land to the peasants (1871);
- the imposition of taxation on ploughing animals (1880);
- the incorporation of Thessaly into the Kingdom of Greece and its implications for Greek agriculture (1881);
- the participation of Greece in the Latin Monetary Union (1867 and substantially after 1882);
- the desirability and promotion of industrialisation (1860 and thereafter);
- competition in the banking sector, the licensing of new banking houses (1873), the taxing of banking profits and the proper form of credit desired by the productive sectors of the economy;
- the re-opening of the foreign exchange market (1879);
- the 'modernising' policy of Harilaos Trikoupis, mainly in public works;
- the tariff reform of 1884;
- the 'currant crisis' (1892-1893);
- the bankruptcy of 1893 and the imposition of the International Financial Control in 1898;
- the wave of emigration to the United States after 1900 and its implications for the Greek labour market;
- monetary policy under the supervision of the International Financial Control (1898-1910).

These debates constitute a vast agenda of research that is much broader than the purpose of the present essay. Our task here is relatively humble in scope. In what follows, we will first concentrate on the 'economists' in Greek Parliament, taking their participation in these debates as proof of their belonging to an economic community. We will seek to identify who they were, where they had studied (if they had done so), and to what extent they had been influenced by writers and thinkers known to historians of economics. In the subsequent section, we will offer an overview of the fiscal and monetary problems the Greek Parliament found itself facing over the years. We will further attempt to explore the way Greek Parliament debated on fiscal and, to a lesser extent, on monetary issues. By analysing the discourse of Greek economists in Parliament, we will seek to determine if economic science in its various forms played a significant role in decision making, or not. To put it differently, we will endeavour to determine whether a modern – 'modern' within the framework of the era – discourse on these issues was articulated, or whether traditionalist styles of argumentation led to more 'administrative' approaches in public finance and monetary management. The last section will offer some conclusions.

Economists in Greek Parliament: An overview of the men, their backgrounds and their education

Following Fetter, one can define a parliamentary economist as one who had published something relating to an economic problem, or had simply announced that he considered himself a political economist. Furthermore, a member of parliament who played an important role in the economic controversies of his time can also be said to belong to this category.[16]

Between 1862 and 1910, and according to a sample of 179 parliamentary sessions we examined, a total of 64 economists were active in the Greek Parliament, i.e. they participated in parliamentary deliberations. They are included in the Appendix.[17] The table included there reveals that most economists in Parliament were in fact lawyers by profession. The same table shows that many of the parliamentary economists belonged to other professions, some being professors (19 per cent), bankers and bank employees (14 per cent), civil servants (11 per cent), landowners (8 per cent) and journalists (4 per cent).[18] More than half of our sample of economists, approximately 67 per cent, had studied law either at the University of Athens or abroad. Those who had studied in Greece had attended and passed the courses given by Professor Ioannis Soutsos, the only academic economist holding a full professorship in Greece until the end of the nineteenth century.[19] Soutsos' lectures reveal a liberal who placed great emphasis on institutional reforms needed for the country to enter a sustainable developmental path. Influenced as he was by his Genevan mentor Pellegrino Rossi, he participated actively in public life and wrote articles and pamphlets on issues of economic policy. Without ever becoming a member of parliament himself, he was often referred to in the speeches of his ex-students in Parliament.[20]

Table 9.1 shows that 55 per cent of our economists, 33 in number, had studied abroad, some of them in more than one country.[21]

Here a number of interesting points spring to the eye:

- the greatest proportion of foreign-educated Greek economic members of parliament (19) had studied in France, especially in Paris; economic thought in France in the nineteenth century was characterised by considerable diversity, with the liberal tradition of Say forming the core approach;[22]
- a substantial number (7) had undertaken studies in Italy, with the University of Pisa attracting half of them;[23]

16 Fetter (1980), p. 6. See also Gordon (1976).

17 See Greek Parliament (1986).

18 Speaking of landowners, it should be stressed that, in 1883, 83 per cent of peasants were landless (Petropulos, 1981). Therefore the Greek landowning class was small in numbers and large estates were not the norm. Finally, landowners were politically unimportant at least until 1881.

19 Soutsos was a Professor at the Law, not the Philosophy, school. See Ithakissios (1992).

20 Professor N. Saripolos was also a Rossi student. See Saripolos (1889), p. 32.

21 A word of caution is appropriate here. First, many members of parliament studied according to existing biographical information in more than one country. Their names therefore appear more than once in the table. Second, and more important, we have no definitive information as to how 'serious' their studies were, and if they received a formal degree. In some cases solid proof of scholarly study exists (for example Kalligas, Zographos, Gounarakis), but not in all.

22 See Breton and Lutfalla (1991). See also Schumpeter (1954).

23 On Italian economic thought see Faucci (2000), and on Greek students in Pisa see Sideri

- a great number (13) had studied in Germany, with the universities of Heidelberg and Munich attracting members of parliament who also followed academic careers.

Table 9.1 Greek parliamentary economists who studied abroad

Italy	France (Paris)	Germany	Switzerland	Other
Drosos, D.	Antonopoulos, S.	Antonopoulos, S.	Kartalis, A.	Levidis, D. (Odessa)
Kyriakos, D. (Pisa)	Dragoumis, S.	Eftaxias, A.	Vrailas-Armenis, P. (Geneva)	
Valassopoulos, I. (Pisa)	Kalogeropoulos, N.	Gounarakis, N. (Heidelberg, Munich, Leipzig)		
Valsamakis, N. (Siena)	Karapanos, C.	Gounaris, D.		
Valvis, Z. (Pisa)	Kartalis, A.	Kalligas, P. (Munich, Berlin, Heidelberg)		
Vrailas-Armenis, P. (Bologna)	Kyriakos, D.	Kokkinos, E. (Munich, Göttingen, Heidelberg)		
Zaimis, T.	Merlopoulos, P.	Lomvardos, C. (Munich)		
	Negris, F.	Pylarinos, O.		
	Pesmazoglou, I.	Streit, S.		
	Protopapadakis, P.	Vlachos, A.		
	Pylarinos, O.	Zaimis, A.		
	Rallis, D.	Zaimis, T.		
	Saripolos, N.	Zographos, I. (Heidelberg)		
	Theotokis, G.			
	Trikoupis, H.			
	Valaoritis, S.			
	Valsamakis, N.			
	Vrailas-Armenis, P.			
	Zaimis, A.			

What is important to note is the complete absence of economists in Parliament with a British education. This 'black hole' is of particular importance for economic ideas

(1994). According to this latter source, Greek students constituted an important factor in political life in Pisa during turbulent political times (ibid., p. 9). The university as such stood in the midst of a political upheaval (ibid., p. 124) and Greek students, enjoying privileges due to Italian philhellenism, were able to assist their Italian fellow students in many ways (ibid., pp. 289-303). For the impact of the Risorgimento in Greek irredentist aspirations see Liakos (1985).

in Greece, since it underlines the absence of direct knowledge of the environment in which an important and dominant tradition in economic thought flourished.

As we approach the twentieth century, Table 9.1 reveals a gradual shift in the educational backgrounds of Greek economists who had studied abroad, with Germany strongly competing with France as the chosen scholarly destination.

Table 9.2 includes the names of the nine most widely read economists with foreign education, whereas Table 9.3 reproduces the frequency with which the names of certain foreign economists were mentioned in the speeches of Greek members of parliament.

Table 9.2 Members of parliament with in depth studies abroad

Name	Country
Gounarakis, N.	Germany (Leipzig, Heidelberg, Munich)
Gounaris, D.	Germany
Kalligas, P.	Germany (Munich, Berlin, Heidelberg)
Kokkinos, E.	Germany (Munich, Göttingen, Heidelberg)
Kyriakos, D.	Italy (Pisa), France (Paris)
Pylarinos, O.	France, Germany
Saripolos, N.	France (Paris)
Vrailas-Armenis, P.	Italy (Bologna), Switzerland (Geneva), France (Paris)
Zographos, I.	Germany (Heidelberg)

Table 9.3 Economists quoted by Greek Members of parliament (Sample: 179 sessions)

Jeremy Bentham	10
Michel Chevalier	3
Paul Leroy-Beaulieu	9
John Stuart Mill	10
Robert Peel	2
Pellegrino Rossi	4
Adam Smith	8
Anne-Robert-Jacques Turgot	3

Given the above, it can be said that although many of the 64 parliamentary economists did not have any formal economic training in the modern sense, their literacy in economic issues should not be underestimated. As members of parliament they also had access to the Parliament Library and could thus draw on a variety of sources[24] to expand their knowledge or acquire new, accurate information on economic issues.

24 The Library possessed in 1878 among others 75 volumes of the series *Publicistes et économistes contemporains*, published by Guillaumin in Paris, 35 volumes of the *Annuaire de l'économie politique* of M. Block, the (French) *Journal d'agriculture*, the *Journal des économistes*, *L'Economiste français*, *L'Economista*, the *Edinburgh Review*,

Economics professors who sat in Parliament, like Nikolaos Gounarakis, Aristides Economos and Ioannis Zographos had substantial credentials as economists, but did not play an important role in the debates. One could argue that they influenced Parliament with their academic work and their participation in public life and not through their presence in the chambers.

Aristides Economos was a liberal, a supporter of free trade and consequently an opponent of every kind of government privilege that spoiled competition. He was also in favour of the gold standard and rejected bimetallism as a 'source of confusion' for the market. Through his scientific journal, *Oikonomiki Epitheorissis* (Economic Review), he had the opportunity to diffuse his liberal views and thus create an important forum for the absorption of economic ideas into Greek society.[25] Nikolaos Gounarakis was involved in politics between 1899 and 1906. During this period, he even served as a minister of finance between 16 December 1904 and 9 June 1905. On a theoretical level, he underlined the shortcomings of the classical school, arguing that an economic crisis was an inevitable part of the business cycle. Furthermore, he rejected deflation as a means of curing economic crises and, following the spirit of the times, was amongst those who accepted economic interventionism, albeit under certain conditions. As far as monetary policy is concerned, he was a bimetallist.[26] Ioannis Zographos held a PhD from Heidelberg, where he had studied under Karl Heinrich Rau and had his first treatise in Greek introduced by another prominent German public finance specialist, Lorenz von Stein. He was a follower of the currency school, an advocate of the protection of infant industries and a critical observer of the economic policy in the late nineteenth – early twentieth century.[27]

However, were we challenged to name the most distinguished economist in the Greek Parliament, we would unhesitatingly select Sotirios Sotiropoulos. A member of parliament for approximately 30 consecutive years, Sotirios Sotiropoulos participated actively in debates and deliberations, either as minister of finance or as a member of committees on economic affairs. His theoretical and practical skills were recognised both by his supporters and by his rivals. A specialist in fiscal policy, Sotiropoulos left his mark on matters of taxation, especially on the issue of taxing the net revenue from agricultural production, where he argued that such a tax should be an integral part of any real tax reform that sought to be just and cost effective.[28]

Two other academics, Diomidis Kyriakos and Nikolaos Saripolos, who taught International and Constitutional Law respectively, demonstrated significant competence in economics but nevertheless had a very limited parliamentary activity.

---

the *Journal of the Statistical Society of London* and the *Zeitschrift für die Gesammte Staatswissenschaft* (Philimon, 1878, pp. 46-60).

25 See Psalidopoulos (1996).

26 Psalidopoulos (1989), pp. 145-8.

27 See Zographos (1925-1926).

28 See Sotiropoulos (1861). See also Sotiropoulos (1867).

Finally, special mention should be made of Andreas Syngros and Ioannis Pesmazoglou, two of the well-known late-nineteenth-century bankers of Greek society, who became involved in politics partly with a view to promoting their business interests.[29] The same holds true for Efthymios Kehayias and Pavlos Kalligas, who played a prominent role in economic controversies till the end of the 1880s. In their capacity as governors of the National Bank of Greece (henceforth NBG), they used their parliamentary positions to influence contemporary monetary policy and to defend the Bank's monopoly of issue (see also below).

Historical background on fiscal and monetary policy

The history of the transition of the Greek tax system from the Ottoman times to modernity reflects the shift from tax on items toward tax on income and direct taxes in general.

The introduction of a general income tax was a prolonged process. Although it was implemented in two stages, first in 1909 and then in 1919, it was constantly discussed during the nineteenth century.[30] Equity in taxation had to be reconciled with the insatiable short-term needs of governments eager to expand their sovereignty, by military or diplomatic means, to parts of the declining Ottoman Empire inhabited by Greeks.

An overview of the structure of the tax system in the newly independent Greek State and its capacity to support the government with adequate means reveals the presence of both elements of continuity and change. The new system of taxation was introduced gradually, to substitute the system that had been in place before 1821, the year of the Greek revolution.[31]

Under Ottoman rule, the tax system was based on the following two taxes:[32]

- The capitation tax (*haratschi*): This was the major personal tax to be paid by each adult Christian male. Computation of the population living in a village or area was the responsibility of the ruler, while tax collectors were used to levy actual payment of the tax.
- The tithe (*decati*): This was a tax on production, normally 10 per cent, that could rise to as much as 50 per cent in the case of certain estates.

---

29 In particular, in the 1890s Syngros involved himself in politics in order to found a new banking enterprise. For some notes on this, see his memoirs (Syngros, 1998, **3**, p. 152) and also Aspreas (1923, **2**, p. 194). For Pesmazoglou's banking activity at the dawn of the twentieth century, see Kostis and Tsokopoulos (1988), p. 43 and *passim*. For his parliamentary activity see a critique of *Efimeris ton Syzitiseon tis Voulis* (Official Journal of Parliamentary Debates) of the year 1905 and especially session 35, 30 May 1905.

30 On this see Angelopoulos (1933).

31 See Andreades (1939).

32 Sideris (1931), pp. 356-60. See also McGrew (1985), pp. 35-40.

In addition to these taxes, Christian subjects had to pay a tax in lieu of military service, while certain regions were also burdened by irregular added taxes on locally cultivated products, with the tax burden being determined by the occasional expenditure needs of the Sultan.

During the revolution, the provisional Greek governments abolished the hated capitation tax. The tithe, on the other hand, remained in existence and developed into the most easily available resource for the Greek government to cover its needs. Furthermore, cultivators of former Ottoman holdings that came into the legal possession of the Greek State were not recognised by the latter as owners, and were obliged to pay heavy tenant taxes.[33] Property disputes between the government and the peasants led to numerous land distribution laws (1835, 1855, 1864, 1871).

While successive governments continued to regard agriculture as the most significant tax base, during the period of nineteenth-century development many new taxes were introduced: stamps, taxes on buildings, on movable wealth, on professions, etc.[34] But a number of economists, most notably Professor Ioannis Soutsos, criticised the governments that tended to overtax poor peasants, arguing that such an approach impeded the introduction of agricultural improvements and failed to take into account that certain strata and social classes paid no tax at all. What was needed was the introduction of a modest direct tax, to be paid by every citizen.[35]

The most appropriate form that taxation should take was extensively discussed in Parliament. Eventually, a major step forward was achieved in 1880 with the abolition of the 'hated' tithe and the introduction of a 'tax on ploughing animals'. Nonetheless, revenues from this tax remained small in the following decades, partly because of tax evasion but also because of the government's inability to compute revenues properly.[36] Furthermore the number of ploughing animals dropped by 10,000 between 1882-1903, a sign that peasants had reduced the number of animals they used for agricultural operations in order to avoid tax eligibility.[37] The quest for an appropriate direct taxation remained in the agendas of governments until 1909, when a first form of 'net revenues' (meaning total income) taxation was introduced.

Turning now to the monetary policy, the tasks Parliament had to face in the nineteenth century can be summarised as follows.

In 1833 the currency of the Greek State, the drachma, came into life. It was based on silver and copper. From the very beginning the task of the governments was to enforce the currency as a means of payment in a country where Ottoman, Spanish and other coins were in circulation. This was implemented with the aid of

33 See Mitrofanis (1992).
34 On details see Angelopoulos (1933).
35 Soutsos (1879), pp. 204-23.
36 Petmezas (2003), p. 89.
37 Andreades (1904), p. 12.

the NBG, an institution founded in 1841, as a private bank that also performed the functions of a central bank, since it was the sole note-issuing authority in the Greek dominion. Through careful and conservative steps and by incorporating wealthy merchants and usurers into its body of shareholders, the NBG succeeded over time, and despite initial shortcomings,[38] in imposing the drachma as a means of payment. On the other hand, the NBG attracted heavy criticism because security constraints made it reluctant to grant credits to the country's most important productive sector, agriculture. Furthermore, other banking houses demanded to share the privilege of issuing bank notes, while many intellectuals called for greater competition in the banking sector.

Another major task of monetary policy was to ensure that the drachma remained convertible into other currencies so as to encourage diaspora Greeks and other investors to bring money into the country. Convertibility however, remained an elusive goal. Only between 1842-1848, 1848-1868 and 1870-1877 was the currency convertible. In 1867 Greece joined the bimetallic system of the Latin Monetary Union, but could not meet its requirements in practice, until 1882.[39]

Thus a paradox emerged. During the years of low growth rates, the drachma was convertible, but during the years of greater affluence it was not. This was seen by Greek members of parliament as a negative sign, something that needed to be corrected.

A simple explanation for this state of affairs can be offered in terms of the budget deficits and the political relationship between the NBG and the State. As far as the first point is concerned, Greek governments experienced difficulties in balancing the budget, and after 1879 foreign lending was resumed following a prolonged financial embargo. Initially aimed at financing public works, foreign lending was used in place of ordinary consumption expenditure, especially military expenditure. On the second point, the NBG was, as noted above, a private bank performing two roles: that of a commercial and that of central bank. Parliament discussed this issue above all in 1880, when the extension of the privilege of issuing bank notes was being debated.

Over the years the NBG remained unchallenged in its dominant rule,[40] even though it was criticised for following banking school principles, a doctrine outdated as a monetary policy guide in industrialised Europe. Finally, in 1928 a central bank based on currency school principles was instituted, and a new era of public monetary management came into being.

---

38 See Senior (1859).

39 This topic is discussed in Stassinopoulos (2000).

40 On the history of the NBG see the classic study of Valaoritis (1902).

Discourse on fiscal and monetary policy

Discovering realities, continuing traditions

The Constitutional Assembly of 1862-1864 was dominated by newly elected members of parliament.[41] As the supporters of the enthroned King were now a dwindling minority, the new representatives of the people began to scrutinise the economic administration in order to obtain an accurate picture of Greek finances. Soon, however, it became clear that the national finances were in a poor condition and that demands from various regions of the country for greater expenses to promote their development could not be met.

First of all, even the constitutional assembly could not enforce the collection of overdue and current taxes.[42] Athanasios Petsalis, a prominent speaker, warned the deputies – who sought to circumvent this state of affairs by requesting new loans in order to keep expenditures rolling – that the resources of governments were taxes, not loans. 'The Assembly should not rush and accept the principle of loans, because it could destroy the economy',[43] he stressed, averting a plea for a new loan.

The Parliament was thus forced to devise new taxes. Discussion on the nature of possible new taxes raised such questions as equity, principles and progressiveness of taxation.[44] The assembly debated these issues extensively, but no consensus could be reached. A proposal for raising the tax on professions was met with vociferous objections and struggled to be accepted. Harilaos Souidas argued convincingly that a flat rate profession tax hit Athenian businessmen less than those active in the provinces, as the former enjoyed a bigger turnover.[45] Progressive taxation was required as well as taxation of net income. In a semi-populist outburst, Professor Pavlos Kalligas stated: 'I as a big landowner, do not pay taxes',[46] thus demanding the taxing of landowning income.

This provoked a riposte from Athanasios Rontiris, a supporter of agriculture, who regarded agriculture and the merchant fleet of Greece as the only real industries of the country.[47] Tax was a reward for security ensured by the government, but governments had little regard for the security and well being of peasants. Taxing agriculture leads to a decline in the level of population, he argued; at the same time he rejected demands that privileges be awarded to industry, urging that a

41 See Kitromilides (1988) for a study that focuses on the reception of J.S. Mill's (political) ideas in this Assembly.
42 See the *Official Journal of Parliamentary Debates* (henceforth OJPD), session 50, 14 February 1863, p. 637.
43 Ibid., pp. 637-40.
44 Equity was a major theme in the session 333, 3 October 1864. For the discussion that took place in Britain see the massive volumes edited by O'Brien (1999). See also Sabine (1966) and Shehab (1953). For the Greek case see Dertilis (1993).
45 OJPD, session 73, 23 March 1863, p. 340.
46 Ibid., p. 341.
47 OJPD, session 103, 17 May 1863, p. 733. On Rontiris see also Psalidopoulos (1994).

more rational distribution of the tax burden should be enacted before any consideration of raising the existing taxes.

Alexandros Koumoundouros, in his capacity as a former minister of finance, reminded the assembly: 'We have a deficit here and regardless of how we economise we cannot cover it. Therefore you have to admit the raising of existing taxes'.[48] This inability to reach consensus was not new in Greek politics. Members of parliament were well aware of the challenge and of the escalating proportions of the problem, but simply could not agree as to the most suitable measures to adopt; despite the escalating problems.

As early as 1856, for example, the then minister of finance A. Kondostavlos conceded that 'the tax system is anomalous' and blamed an inefficient administration for 'delays' that resulted in a far lower tax revenue than the projected level.[49]

A. Koumoundouros, speaking in 1857, claimed that the tax system 'contained elements in open contradiction with the principles of our country'.[50] The tax system could be transformed for the better if public land were to be distributed to peasants, after establishment of its true value through a land register. This would enable the government to calculate taxes on a realistic basis and not on arbitrary assumptions. Eight years later Koumoundouros repeated 'The existing tax system is barbarous' and was prompted to ask Parliament once more to consider his land distribution proposals.[51] Koumoundouros was also a pioneer in an active role of government in the development process, admitting that prudent governments limit their public spending with an eye to the limits of national production. On the other hand, deficit spending to construct infrastructural works like public buildings 'is the seed of sure and continuous treasures', a 'positive and untransformable capital'. Therefore, in his view, voices demanding the curtailment of central government action in the economy were wrong. An 'economisation of resources' through less public expenditure cannot lead to higher rates of growth, he added.[52]

These claims were solid, given the almost complete lack of infrastructure. Despite economic progress, for 15 consecutive years starting from 1842 tax receipts remained stable at 14 million drachmas.[53] This was an indication, not only for men like Koumoundouros, that, for political reasons, administrations were soft with local communities and did not extract more revenue from a rising National Income.

Dimitrios Christidis argued in the Assembly for a more liberal approach. 'Do not tell me', he said 'that what is good for the private economy has no application for the public'.[54] Since the delays in the paying of taxes raised the deficit, Christidis

48 OJPD, session 93, 3 May 1863, p. 585.
49 See the *Report on State Budget for the Financial Year of 1856*.
50 See the *Report on State Budget for the Financial Year of 1857*.
51 See the *Report on State Budget for the Financial Year of 1865*. Land distribution proposals materialised finally another six years later, in 1871. See also the views of agricultural expert P. Halikiopoulos (1864), especially pp. 48-57.
52 See the *Parliamentary Speech on State Budget for the Financial Year of 1865*.
53 See the *Report on State Budget for the Financial Year of 1857*.
54 See the *Parliamentary Speech on State Budget for the Financial Year of 1873*.

continued, it was imperative for the country to economise, meaning to cut expenditure. No fundamental differences in economic affairs could be observed between the private and the public sector, and this clearly demonstrated that they should be run on the same principles. 'No two ways to economise exist in the world, as there do not exist two truths for the same thing', he stressed.[55]

Christidis was a supporter of commerce and felt that trade was adversely affected by tax: nations that imposed obstacles to trade for no apparent reason were doomed to backwardness and poverty, he argued.[56] A similar interest-specific approach was articulated when Parliament debated a tax on buildings.[57] Diomidis Kyriakos insisted that such a tax should be rejected, adducing the argument that while elsewhere in Europe the labour class was in a desperate condition and property was in the hands of the wealthy – who could thus well afford to pay – in Greece, on the contrary, the majority of the population owned their own home but such houses were extremely small and run-down, little better than hovels: therefore this tax was unjust, for it fell on the shoulders of the poor.

Efthymios Kehayias countered this view by appealing to a highly authoritative name, Adam Smith, who – in Kehayias's interpretation – believed that this tax burdens the rich,[58] thereby making it appropriate to impose this levy on the wealthy in Greece.

Administering the existing, pleading for reform

In the period 1864-1879 fiscal and monetary policy were frequently discussed yet little breakthrough legislation was enacted, apart from the 1871 land reform.[59] However even this step was not accompanied by an important corollary: a land register. Despite the widespread acceptance of its importance[60] and its necessity as an objective base for computing agricultural income, the land register did not materialise. Administrators blamed this failure on the high cost of this endeavour, whereas in effect many politicians sought to retain their role as intermediaries between taxpayers and the government.

A similar situation can be said to have existed in the banking sector, with many speakers advocating greater competition and the curtailment of the dominance of the NBG, but to little avail. During the spring and summer of 1864 Parliament debated the pros and cons of a land bank proposed by Evangelis Valtatzis and modelled after the French Crédit Mobilier. Earlier (17 May 1863) Athanasios Rontiris had drafted a memorandum suggesting either the creation of an agricultural bank or the creation of a section for agricultural credit within the NBG.

55 Ibid.
56 OJPD, session 128, 1 July 1863, p. 331.
57 OJPD, session 172, 8 November 1863.
58 OJPD, session 192, 16 December 1863.
59 On details see McGrew (1985).
60 Diamantopoulos (1861), p. 7.

Alexandros Koumoundouros led the camp that favoured greater competition, claiming that '[p]rivilege is stagnation', and stressing that '[c]ompetition is the father of life and of the development of man and society'.[61]

Pavlos Kalligas and Efthymios Kehayias, on the other hand, in lengthy speeches (18 and 20 August 1864 respectively), used their expertise to oppose the project. The new bank would also have the privilege to issue land bonds and this, they feared, would raise interest rates. European experience, they pointed out, showed that regulation of the market by intermediaries such as the NBG was more in line with the immediate needs of the Greek economy.[62]

On the fiscal front the balancing of the budget was accepted both by the government and the opposition. The minister of finance Dimitrios Christidis underlined the necessity of a balanced budget, equating it with the country's creditworthiness. He therefore espoused a position typical of a governing politician, by urging Parliament not to fall back on the simplistic slogan 'we do not want more taxes',[63] but instead to engage in constructive cooperation by assisting the implementation of the government's expenditure program.

Budget deficits would not disappear unless new taxes were introduced, contended Sotirios Sotiropoulos, a speaker for the opposition, who countered the above arguments in a manner typical of a politician that does not wield the reins of power. He stressed the need to expand production in order to extract more revenue from a larger income pie. 'The economic condition of nations is not judged on the basis of its debt only', he claimed.[64] Credit plays a role too and credit is given to an expanding economy with a promising future.

The short-term needs of the Greek treasury brought a reshuffling of existing taxes. Kehayias was accused of transforming Parliament into 'a cabinet of taxing laws and decrees'.[65] Currants, silk and other products saw their taxing scales rise from 10 to 15 per cent, without any substantial betterment of Greek finances. Ways therefore to attract foreign capital were sought and tax breaks given to the Italian-owned company in Lavrion on the basis that they acted as a 'bait' for much needed investment into the country.[66] At the same time, the opposition favoured the nationalisation of extracting industries that were characterised as 'national capital'.[67] However, this legislation did not mark a turning point in foreign direct investment and the problem of a change in Greek public finances remained unsolved. By the end of the 1870s parliamentary economists had learned one truth: the taxpayer,

61 OJPD, session 266, 16 May 1864, p. 101.
62 The outcome was that the experiment of the creation of a land bank failed. For a discussion of a renewed, failed, attempt to create a new bank some years later see Dertilis (1980).
63 OJPD, session 72, 24 November 1865, p. 471.
64 Ibid.
65 OJPD, session 75, 27 March 1867, p. 326.
66 OJPD, session 37, 22 February 1871, p. 23.
67 Ibid., p. 26.

especially the peasant, was economically exhausted and taxation was regressive in the sense that many professionals and certain social strata paid no taxes at all.

In 1877, therefore, a profession tax was introduced and Sociétés Anonymes were made to pay a profit tax of a modest 2 per cent. In this connection Harilaos Trikoupis started building up his political profile.

In 1876 Trikoupis stressed that 'it is an economic policy error when we cover with loans the deficits of the regular budget'.[68] Nevertheless, he had an understanding for the needs of government, which should be covered by indirect taxes. Trikoupis declared himself an opponent of progressive taxation, and indicating measures he himself was to adopt a decade later, he pleaded for more protective tariffs, a – new – tax on ploughing animals, which he justified as more in line with a developmentalist agenda needed by the country. Sotiropoulos, who was his main opponent at that time, countered this view on the basis of his experience and knowledge of conditions of the market. 'Old taxes are like old shoes' he said, 'they do not press the feet'.[69] A modest income tax for all would be better instead of the Talmudic Greek tax laws. In Sotiropoulos' view, progressive taxation would be accepted, if combined with a reform that would make the relationship between the taxpayer and the government simpler.[70]

Theodoros Deliyiannis, the other important politician who was destined to enjoy a distinguished political career, also took part in these debates. 'We follow the curing of disease without trying to find the reason of the illness', he claimed, speaking about the financial straits faced by the government.[71]

Epaminondas Deligiorgis lamented the absence of industry that was the sole guarantee for economic progress. The country needed capital and a low cost labour force, but such a development could not take place with heavier taxation. Instead, he continued, what was necessary was to introduce expenditure cuts and proceed to the downsizing of government. This divergence of opinions led the Koumoundouros government to relegate the issue to a bipartisan committee for fear of a loss of votes, as it had only a slim majority in Parliament. Despite the unanimous wish for reforms this bipartisan committee replicated existing recipes. The income tax proposal was withdrawn and with it the pleas for reform.

New perspectives, old problems

In 1879 the pressure to reform the tax system softened somewhat. The Trikoupis era began and coincided with the renewed possibility for Greece to obtain foreign loans. The inclusion of Thessaly in the State shortly thereafter gave new impetus and perspectives for development.

---

68 OJPD, session 18, 27 October 1876, p. 87.

69 OJPD, session 19, 28 October 1876, p. 102.

70 In that connection see also the speeches by Zochios and Petimezas in OJPD, session 20, 29 October 1876 and session 24, 3 November 1876 respectively.

71 OJPD, session 24, 3 November 1876.

Ioannis Valassopoulos was a member of Parliament authorised by the government to submit a new proposal for reform of the tax system and for balancing the budget in 1880. Valassopoulos suggested, as many others had before him, the introduction of an income tax. Citing Soutsos, he pointed to industrialists, traders and bankers who were taxed either not at all, or only minimally. He argued that the tithe was responsible for imports of foreign grain and should be replaced with some other lighter form of taxation. There was a need for the government to improve the country's infrastructure, and Valassopoulos favoured public works and the building of railways as a means to achieve this end.[72]

Thrasyvoulos Zaimis, on the other hand, repeated the classic liberal objections to this developmentalist thinking. New taxes and economies were prerequisites for future growth, while possible foreign loans to cover deficits would be disastrous for the economy. It was therefore indispensable to cut expenditures.

It was at this time that Trikoupis took office. In addition to reintroducing foreign loans, his government enacted three laws of great importance: the substitution of the tithe by the tax on ploughing animals, the renewal of the NBG monopoly on the issue of banknotes and the new tariff system of 1884. Trikoupis' inclination toward taxing ploughing animals was known from the past and it is likely that he aimed to implement a tax reform by changing the pattern of agricultural taxation. Koumoundouros, now his opponent, objected on the basis that if the tithe was too heavy it would be more sensible to lower it, rather than abandon such a solid tax altogether in favour of a brand-new tax that might well bring less revenue than expected.[73]

Aristides Economos, a newly elected member of parliament who boasted a solid economic education, attacked Trikoupis' proposal with eloquence and reasoning. The tax on ploughing animals was unjust because it was not based on net income. Ownership of a ploughing animal revealed nothing about the peasant's income, and merely had the effect of taxing the means of production. 'One day', he said ironically, 'you will tax the scissors of the tailor and the hammer of the labourer'.[74] Predictably, this new legislation aroused considerable controversy and sharp debate; nevertheless, when put to the ballot the Law was successfully voted in Parliament and constituted a first major victory for Trikoupis.[75]

On the question of the renewal of privilege of the NBG, Economos once again expressed the minority position which scathingly opposed the proposal. His argumentation was twofold. On the one hand the NBG had become a part of the State apparatus and was unashamedly exchanging favours with the ruling elite. This explained the low taxes it paid and the fact that the monopoly on issuing banknotes was awarded to the NBG for free. On the other hand, he argued, a monopoly raises prices, in this case interest rates. Greater competition in the banking sector would

---

72 See his report on railways in the Supplement of OJPD on 20 January 1880.

73 OJPD, session 93, 22 March 1880.

74 OJPD, session 100, 1 April 1880, p. 1012.

75 It is worth noticing that during these sessions in Parliament the economist most widely cited was Paul Leroy-Beaulieu.

lead to a better allocation of resources, especially the much needed financing of agricultural improvements.

Trikoupis and his followers gave only scanty consideration to these arguments, convinced as they were that their policy had successfully started out on the road towards bringing prosperity to the nation. From their perspective, the only goal that remained to be achieved was the renewal of currency convertibility. As Trikoupis himself put it on one occasion, 'Capital is concentrating only where the currency has the value that is accepted by the general market of the people and not the one that is determined by law'.[76]

Trikoupis believed that a new foreign loan of 72 million drachmas would be sufficient to defend a convertible currency and that since foreign markets continued to show their faith in the Greek economy no problems would be encountered. His great opponent Deliyiannis agreed with him in the analysis of the negative effects of an unconvertible currency. 'Forced circulation', Deliyiannis asserted, 'is a disease that eats the economic flesh of nations',[77] and it is also an indirect taxation of the people in the sense that there is a differential between the market price of notes that are protected by the forced circulation and the market price of metallic money. But where Deliyiannis differed from Trikoupis was on the question of a balanced budget: in Deliyiannis' view this should be awarded absolute priority in order to defend the convertibility of the currency.

The project launched by Trikoupis led to a policy disaster. Convertibility was introduced in 1885 but it was abandoned after just six months. The 'currant crisis' thereafter and the mounting interest on debt that absorbed half of the yearly public revenue led to default in 1893.[78]

Reckoning

The bankruptcy of the Greek State and defeat in the 1897 war against the Ottomans cast a shadow over the economic achievements of the country and led to introversion and self-criticism, on the economic front as well.

The minister of finance Anargyros Simopoulos openly admitted that implementation of the national aspirations, and military spending in particular, was the underlying cause of the parlous state of public finances.[79] He thus pointed to a number of serious misjudgements: foreign loans were used for military purposes and for public consumption, so that in effect 'The dogma of the balanced budget has been loosened for the benefit of national politics'.[80] Proposals for new taxes, such as those put forward by Sotiropoulos in 1879, Kalligas in 1883 and Karapanos

76 See the *Parliamentary Speech on State Budget for the Financial Year of 1884.*

77 See the *Parliamentary Speech on State Budget for the Financial Year of 1885.*

78 In this connection see the introductory essay to the national budget of 1891 submitted by Karapanos.

79 OJPD, session 68, 1 March 1894, p. 1068.

80 Ibid., p. 1071.

in 1891, had gone unheeded. Similarly, attempts to place emphasis on the development of infrastructure and the need to assist production had been consistently disregarded, with every majority in Parliament opting for the easy solution of loan financing, instead of modernising the tax system and boosting the market economy. The failed attempt by Trikoupis to reinstate currency convertibility in 1885 was also a victim of Greece's national aspirations, according to the interpretation offered by Simopoulos, who claimed to belong to the school of economics that adjusts scientific principles to the special circumstances of the country in question.[81] His overall message was therefore clear: a new era had dawned, requiring the country to restate its priorities, settle its obligations with its creditors and at the same time restore production.

The International Financial Control (henceforth IFC), imposed on Greece after 1898 in order to force the country to repay its creditors, set an institutional framework that produced a deflation with a welcome outcome in the exchange value of the currency. The tax system, however, remained in the jurisdiction of the government and ways to reform it were sought without altering taxes that were allotted to repayment of the foreign debt.

In 1903 Parliament debated the possibility of a tax reform. The tax on ploughing animals was recognised to have been a failure both from an economic point of view, since its revenues were low, as well as from a scientific point of view.[82] Nevertheless, the Parliament decided not to cancel it, because of the government's inability at the time to promote a reformed tax agenda. The manipulation of existing taxation, especially indirect taxation, was therefore continued, combined with an effort to control expenditure and the creation of lotteries and special funds for the benefit of the army and navy.

As the exchange value of the currency steadily improved under the austerity package of the IFC, the necessity of an overall tax reform became unanimous. Athanasios Eftaxias attacked the Parliaments' habit of fixing receipts and expenses but never auditing the administration. Governments were comfortable with such a practice, Eftaxias continued, because they could demand complementary or sudden advances without careful calculation of revenues. This state of affairs should be terminated, he asserted, with an overall attempt to put Greek finances on a new basis.

When Eftaxias introduced the tax on net revenue in 1909, thus opening a new era in Greek taxation, he faced rather mild opposition.

Concluding remarks

In this chapter we have endeavoured to identify the economists in the Greek Parliament among those who spoke on economic issues. We have traced their

81 OJPD, session 69, 2 March 1894, p. 1103.
82 OJPD, Supplement, 2 May 1903, pp. 443-4.

social origin and studies and attempted to determine, by following debates on fiscal and on a lesser extent on monetary policy, the ideas and beliefs they espoused.

The conclusion that springs from this inquiry is that all economists in the Greek Parliament were basically of a liberal persuasion in that they believed in the free enterprise economy. On the other hand, they did not always support a minimal role for government, especially on matters related to national aspirations. This reservation can be explained in a number of ways. Private initiative was weak, and with the exception of Greek ship-owners, it did not operate on a world scale. It was thus the government's duty to control and lead the development process, especially since the nation needed its strength in order to fulfil its irredentist goals. As the minister of finance Miltiades Negrepontis put it in 1920, 'I do not believe that a Greek minister of finance could sacrifice the implementations of a grandiose national policy by hesitating or blushing before an economic problem'.[83]

Effectively, then, economists in the Greek Parliament awarded national aspirations priority over economic policy. Our survey of their views on fiscal policy over a fairly long period reveals that they were hesitant to adopt reforms, afraid to alter the status quo, more inclined to accommodate the tax system instead of reforming it according to a set of principles that would have been more in tune with the modern era.

The 64 parliamentary economists of this study resemble Schumpeter's 'consultant administrators'.[84] Naturally, when he coined this term Schumpeter had the cameralists in mind, a pre-capitalist stratum of civil servants entrusted with laying the bases for decision making by the absolute ruler. By contrast, economists in the Greek Parliament were democratically elected representatives of a capitalist-in-the-making economy in south-eastern Europe. They were mostly practitioners and apparently familiar with the business of governing. Their ideas and activities focused mainly on how the government and economy of the country should be run and especially how the public finances should be managed, albeit in a context wherein the short term always imposed its necessities over the long term. Their legacy should be further explored so as to allow a more comprehensive judgement of their failures and accomplishments.

References

Andreades, A. (1904), *L'impôt direct en Grèce et son évolution*, Giard et Brière, Paris.

Andreades, A. [1925] (1939), 'National Loans and Greek Public Finance', in A. Andreades, *Works*, **2**, pp. 299-575, University of Athens, Athens (in Greek).

Angelopoulos, A. (1933), *Direct Taxation in Greece*, Eleftheroudakis, Athens (in Greek).

Aspreas, G.K. (1923), *A Political History of Modern Greece, 1821-1921*, **1-3**, Athens (in Greek).

Breton, Y. and Lutfalla, M. (1991), *L'économie politique en France au XIXe siècle*, Economica, Paris.

83 See the *Parliamentary Speech on State Budget for the Financial Year of 1920-1921*.
84 Schumpeter (1954), p. 159.

Cameron, R. (1993), *A Concise Economic History of the World*, Oxford University Press, Oxford.

Carabott, P. (1997) (ed.), *Greek Society in the Making, 1863-1913: Realities, Symbols and Visions*, Ashgate, Aldershot.

Dakin, D. (1972), *The Unification of Greece 1770-1923*, Ernest Benn, London.

Dertilis, G.B. (1980), *The Question of Banks 1871-1873*, National Bank of Greece, Athens (in Greek).

Dertilis, G.B. (1993), *Taxes and Power in the Modern Hellenic State*, Alexandria, Athens (in Greek).

Diamantopoulos, A. (1861), *About Changes in Taxes*, To Mellon tis Patridos, Athens (in Greek).

Evlambios, M. (1930-1931), *Efthymios I. Kehayias in the National Bank of Greece and His Parliamentary Activity*, **1-2**, S. Vlastos, Athens (in Greek).

Faucci, R. (2000), *L' economia politica in Italia dal '500 a oggi*, Utet, Torino.

Fetter, F.W. (1980), *The Economist in Parliament: 1780-1868*, Duke University Press, Durham, NC.

Gordon, B. (1976), *Political Economy in Parliament 1819-1823*, Barnes and Noble, New York.

Grapsas, C.M. (1948), *Greek Political Encyclopaedia*, **2**(1), Athens (in Greek).

Greek Parliament (1986), *Record of Representatives, Senators and Deputies*, Athens (in Greek).

Halikiopoulos, P. (1864), *Thoughts on Greece*, M. Georgiadis, Patras (in Greek).

Ithakissios, D. (1992), 'John A. Soutsos (1804-1890): Greece's First Academic Economist', *Quaderni di storia dell economia politica*, **10**(2), pp. 136-48.

Karanikolas, G. (1963), *Illegitimate Elections in Greece 1844-1961*, K. Antoniadis, Athens (in Greek).

Kitromilides, P. (1988), 'European Political Thought in the Making of Greek Liberalism: The Second National Assembly of 1862-1864 and the Reception of John Stuart Mill's Ideas in Greece', *Parliaments, Estates and Representation*, **8**(1), pp. 11-21.

Koliopoulos, J. and Veremis, T. (2002), *Greece: The Modern Sequel. From 1831 to the Present*, Hurst, London.

Kostelenos, G. (1995), *Money and Output in Modern Greece: 1858-1938*, Center of Planning and Economic Research, Athens.

Kostis, K. (2002), 'The Formation of the State in Greece, 1830-1914', in M. Dogo and G. Franzinetti (eds), *Disrupting and Reshaping. Early Stages of Nation-Building in the Balkans*, Longo, Ravenna.

Kostis, K. and Tsokopoulos, V. (1988), *Banks in Greece 1898-1928*, Papazissis, Athens (in Greek).

Levandis, J. (1944), *The Greek Foreign Debt and the Great Powers, 1821-1898*, Columbia University Press, New York.

Liakos, A. (1985), *The Italian Unification and the Great Idea: 1859-1862*, Themelio, Athens (in Greek).

Masson-Vincourt, M. (2000), *Paul Calligas (1814-1896) et la fondation de l'État grec*, L'Harmattan, Paris.

McGrew, W. (1985), *Land and Revolution in Modern Greece, 1800-1881*, Kent University Press, Kent.

Mitrofanis, Y.N. (1992), *Taxation of Primary Production in Greece (1828-1862)*, Unpublished thesis, University of Athens, Department of Political Science and Public Administration (in Greek).

O'Brien, D.P. (1999) (ed.), *The History of Taxation*, **1-8**, Pickering and Chatto, London.

Palairet, M. (1997), *The Balkan Economies, c. 1880-1914: Evolution without Development*, Cambridge University Press, Cambridge.

Papathanasopoulos, K. (1993), *Alexandros Koumoundouros. Comments on a Biography*, S.F. Lenis, Athens (in Greek).

Perakis, M. (2000), 'The Replacement of Tithe by the Tax on Animals Used in Agriculture', in K. Aroni-Tsichli and L. Tricha (eds), *Harilaos Trikoupis and His Era*, Papazissis, Athens (in Greek).

Petmezas, S. (2003), *The Greek Agrarian Economy during the 19th Century. The Peripheral Dimension*, University Press of Crete, Herakleio, Crete (in Greek).

Petropulos, J. (1968), *Politics and Statecraft in the Kingdom of Greece 1833-1843*, **1-2**, Princeton University Press, Princeton, NJ.

Petropulos, J. (1981), 'The Greek Economy during the First Decade of Othonian Rule', *Deltion tis Istirikis kai Ethnologikis Etairias tis Ellados* (Bulletin of Historical and Ethnological Society of Greece), **24**, pp. 142-228.

Philimon, T. (1878), 'Composition of the Library of Parliament 1877-1878', *Parartima tis Efimeris ton Syzitiseon tis Voulis* (Supplement of the Gazette of Parliamentary Debates), 17 October 1878, pp. 46-60 (in Greek).

Psalidopoulos, M. (1989), *The Crisis of 1929 and the Greek Economists. A Contribution to the History of Economic Thought in Inter-war Greece*, Foundation of Research and Education, Commercial Bank of Greece, Athens (in Greek).

Psalidopoulos, M. (1994), 'Encouragement of Industry and Economic Liberalism in 19th-century Greece' in M. Psalidopoulos (ed.), *Essays on Greek Industry in the 19th Century*, ETBA, Athens (in Greek).

Psalidopoulos, M. (1996), 'Aristides Economos and the "Oikonomiki Epitheorissis": the Rise and Fall of an Economic Journal in 19th-century Greece', *History of Economic Ideas*, **4**(3), pp. 149-67.

Psalidopoulos, M. and Mata, M.E. (2002) (eds), *Economic Thought and Policy in Less Developed Europe. The Nineteenth Century*, Routledge, London.

Sabine, B.E.V. (1966), *A History of Income Tax*, George Allen and Unwin, London.

Saripolos, N.I. (1889), *Autobiographical Memoirs*, P. Sakellarios, Athens (in Greek).

Schumpeter, J.A. (1954), *History of Economic Analysis*, Oxford University Press, New York.

Senior, N.W. (1859), *A Journal Kept in Turkey and Greece in the Autumn of 1857 and the Beginning of 1858*, Longman, London.

Shehab, F. (1953), *Progressive Taxation: A Study in the Development of the Progressive Principle in the British Income Tax*, Clarendon Press, Oxford.

Sideri, A. (1994), *Greek Students at the University of Pisa (1806-1861)*, **2**, Historical Archive of Neohellenic Youth and National Foundation of Research, Athens (in Greek).

Sideris, A.D. (1931), 'The Historical Process of Agricultural Taxation', *Archive of Economic and Social Sciences*, **11**(3), pp. 355-412 (in Greek).

Sotiropoulos, S. (1861), *Treatise on Land Taxation in Greece*, D. Mavrommatis, Athens (in Greek).

Sotiropoulos, S. (1867), *Report Concerning the Change of the Tax System*, Athens (in Greek).

Soutsos, I.A. (1879), 'The Tax Bills of 1876', *Oikonomiki Epitheorissis* (Economic Review), **7**, pp. 204-23 (in Greek).

Stassinopoulos, Y. (2000), *Monetary Theory and Policy in 19th-century Greece*, Typothyto, Athens (in Greek).

Svolos, A. (1998 [1972]), 'The Constitutional History of Greece', in L. Axelos (ed.), *The Greek Constitutions 1822-1975/1986*, Stohastis, Athens (in Greek).

Syngros, A. [1908] (1998), *Memoirs*, **1-3**, Hestia, Athens (in Greek).
Valaoritis, J.A. (1902), *History of National Bank of Greece (1842-1902)*, A. Konstandinides, Athens (in Greek).
Vergopoulos, K. (1978), *State and Economic Policy in the 19th Century*, Exantas, Athens (in Greek).
Zographos, I. (1925-1926), *Public Finance Studies*, **1-3**, 2nd edn, Hestia, Athens (in Greek).

Appendix

Table 9.4 Economists in the Greek Parliament (1862-1910)

Name and life	Years in Parliament**	Profession	Studies	Remarks
Adamopoulos, Timoleon ?-?	8	–	Law in Athens	He taught Political Economy as reader at the University of Athens
Angelopoulos, Constantinos 1856-1947	8	Economist, Journalist, Governor of State Audit Council	–	Director of newspaper *Paliggenesia* (Rebirth). Also MP after 1910
Antonopoulos, Spyridon 1823-1891	16	Lawyer	Law in Athens, France and Germany	Supporter of Alexandros Koumoundouros, and of Epaminondas Deligiorgis as well
Avgerinos, Andreas 1820-1896	22	–	–	Minister of Finance, Supporter of Alexandros Koumoundouros (later of Harilaos Trikoupis)
Christidis, Dimitrios * 1795-1879	10	–	–	Minister of Finance, Supporter of Epaminondas Deligiorgis
Deimezis, Spyridon 1829-1892	4	Civil servant, Governor of General Office of the Budget and of State Audit Council	Law in Athens	Minister of Finance
Deligiorgis, Epaminondas * 1829-1879	14	Lawyer	Law in Athens	Distinguished politician, Prime Minister, Minister of Finance
Deliyiannis, Theodoros * 1823-1905	29	Civil servant (until 1862)	Law in Athens	Distinguished politician, Prime Minister, Minister of Finance, Opponent of Harilaos Trikoupis
Drosos, Dimitrios ?-1877	6	Civil servant	Italy	Minister of Finance, Supporter of Epaminondas Deligiorgis

Name and life	Years in Parliament**	Profession	Studies	Remarks
Dragoumis, Stephanos * 1842-1923	23	Judge of the court of appeal	Law in Paris	Minister of Finance, Supporter of Harilaos Trikoupis, Leader of political group in 1906
Economos, Aristides * 1835-1890	3	Judge, Lawyer	Law in Athens	He taught Political Economy as reader at the University of Athens Editor of scientific journal *Oikonomiki Epitheorissis* (Economic Review)
Efmorfopoulos, Leonidas 1811-1896	2	Trader	–	He headed the economic association 'Society for the Freedoms of Trade', 1865-1867
Eftaxias, Athanasios * 1849-1931	14	Landowner	Theology and Law in Athens. Economics and Political Sciences in Germany	Minister of Finance
Gounarakis, Nikolaos * 1853-1932	6	Lawyer, Economist and Professor of Political Economy at University of Athens, National Technical University and Economic University of Athens	Law in Athens, Heidelberg, Munich and Leipzig	Minister of Finance
Gounaris, Dimitrios * 1867-1922	6	Lawyer	Law in Athens and Germany	Distinguished politician, Minister of Finance, Prime Minister after 1910
Halikiopoulos, Panayiotis * ?-1886	4	Lawyer, Journalist	–	Supporter of Thrasyvoulos Zaimis
Haralampis, Dimitrios 1796-1879	2	Secretary-general of Ministry of Interior	–	Minister of Finance

Name and life	Years in Parliament**	Profession	Studies	Remarks
Kalligas, Pavlos * 1814-1896	8	Jurist, Professor of Roman Law at University of Athens, Assistant district attorney (Areopagus), Governor of National Bank of Greece	Law and Philosophy in Munich, Berlin and Heidelberg	Minister of Finance, Attended lectures of Friedrich Karl von Savigny and Eduard Gans
Kalogeropoulos, Nikolaos * 1853-1927	17	Lawyer	Law in Athens. Law and Political Sciences in Paris	Minister of Finance
Karapanos, Constantinos * 1840-1914	26	Bank employee (in his youth), Landowner	Law in Athens. Law and Economics in Paris	Prime Minister, Minister of Finance, Leader of 'Progressive' party (political group)
Kartalis, Antonios 1867-1923	11	Lawyer	Law in Athens, France and Switzerland	Supporter of Georgios Theotokis and later of Dimitrios Gounaris, Also MP after 1910
Kehayias, Efthymios * 1819-1885	12	Accountant, Governor of National Bank of Greece	Secondary education only	Minister of Finance, Influenced by Michel Chevalier
Ketseas, Themistocles 1836-1910	1	Civil servant, Governor of State Audit Council	Law	Minister of Finance
Kokkinos, Emmanouil * 1812-1879	2	Jurist, Professor of Administrative Law at the University of Athens	Law in Athens, Munich, Göttingen and Heidelberg	–
Konstantopoulos, Constantinos * 1832-1910	17	Jurist	Law in Athens	Minister of Finance, Supporter of Alexandros Koumoundouros (later of Theodoros Deliyiannis), Leader of political group in 1890
Koumoundouros, Alexandros * 1815-1883	18	Lawyer, Jurist	Law in Athens	Distinguished politician, Prime Minister, Minister of Finance

Name and life	Years in Parliament**	Profession	Studies	Remarks
Kyriakos, Diomidis * 1811-1904	4	Jurist, Professor of International Law at the University of Athens	Law in Pisa and Paris	–
Levidis, Dimitrios 1808-1893	4	Civil servant	Accountancy in Odessa	Minister of Finance
Lomvardos, Constantinos * 1820-1888	19	Medical practitioner	Medicine in Athens and Munich	Editor of newspaper *Foni tou Ioniou* (Voice of the Ionian), Supporter of Alexandros Koumoundouros and later of Harilaos Trikoupis
Mavromaras, Grigorios * 1833-1907	15	Lawyer	Law in Athens	–
Merlopoulos, Panayiotis 1861-1935	11	Lawyer	Law in Athens, Political Sciences in Paris	Supporter of Dimitrios Rallis (and of Eleftherios Venizelos after 1910), Minister of Finance in 1927
Messinezis, Ioannis 1822-1896	14	Lawyer	Law	–
Negris, Fokion * 1846-1928	11	Mineralogist	Mathematics and Mineralogy in Paris	Minister of Finance
Nikolopoulos, Vassilios 1816-1887	14	Judge	Law in Athens	Minister of Finance
Papamichalopoulos, Nikolaos 1827-1888	25	Landowner	-	Minister of Finance
Pesmazoglou, Ioannis 1857-1906	2	Banker	Economics in Paris	–
Petimezas, Athanasios G. * 1828-1885	18	–	–	Minister of Finance, Supporter of Alexandros Koumoundouros and later of Harilaos Trikoupis

Name and life	Years in Parliament**	Profession	Studies	Remarks
Petimezas, Sotirios N. 1820-1893	15	Army officer	Hellenic Army Academy	–
Petsalis, Athanasios * 1802-1871	5	Landowner, Lawyer	Law in Ionian Academy	–
Protopapadakis, Petros * 1859-1922	6	Engineer, Professor of Engineering at National Technical University of Athens, Hellenic Army Academy and Hellenic Naval Academy	Mathematics in Athens. Mineralogy in Paris	Supporter of Dimitrios Gounaris, Prime Minister and Minister of Finance after 1910
Pylarinos, Othon 1833-1899	1	Professor of Roman Law and of Political Economy at Ionian Academy. Professor at the University of Athens	Law in Athens, France and Germany	–
Rallis, Dimitrios * 1844-1921	28	Lawyer	Law in Athens and Paris	Distinguished politician, Prime Minister, Minister of Finance
Rontiris, Athanasios * 1823-1889	14	Jurist, Professor of Administrative Law at University of Athens	Law in Athens	–
Saravas, Dimitrios 1822-1893	10	Lawyer, Judge of the Supreme Court (Areopagus)	Law	–
Saripolos, Nikolaos * 1817-1887	2	Jurist, Professor of Constitutional and International Law at University of Athens	Law in Paris	Attended lectures of Pellegrino Rossi
Simopoulos, Anargyros * 1833-1908	27	Bank employee	–	Minister of Finance, Supporter of Harilaos Trikoupis (later of Georgios Theotokis)
Simos, Efstathios 1804-1878	3	–	–	Minister of Finance

Name and life	Years in Parliament**	Profession	Studies	Remarks
Skouloudis, Stephanos 1838-1928	16	Banker	Secondary education only	Supporter of Harilaos Trikoupis, Prime Minister after 1910
Sotiropoulos, Sotirios * 1831-1898	30	Civil servant	Law	Minister of Finance, Supporter of Alexandros Koumoundouros, No party affiliation after Koumoundouros' death
Stratos, Nikolaos * 1872-1922	7	Lawyer	Law	Prime Minister after 1910
Streit, Stephanos 1835-1920	1	Jurist, Governor of National Bank, Professor of International Law at University of Athens	Law in Athens and Germany	Minister of Finance
Syngros, Andreas 1830-1899	6	Banker	Secondary education only	–
Theotokis, Georgios * 1843-1916	22	Lawyer	Law and Political sciences in Paris	Distinguished politician, Prime Minister, Minister of Finance
Trikoupis, Harilaos * 1832-1896	26	Ambassador, Diplomat	Law in Athens and Paris	Distinguished politician, Prime Minister, Minister of Finance
Valaoritis, Spyridon 1819-1887	13	Ambassador, Diplomat	Law in Ionian Academy and Paris	Minister of Finance, Supporter of Harilaos Trikoupis, He translated Montesquieu's *Spirit of the Laws*
Valassopoulos, Ioannis * 1820-1888	14	Lawyer	Law in Athens and Pisa	Minister of Finance
Valsamakis, Nikolaos 1834-1912	19	Lawyer, Director of General Credit Bank	Law in Siena and Paris	–
Valvis, Zinovios 1800-1886	5	Jurist, Prosecuting attorney	Law in Pisa	Prime Minister, Minister of Finance
Vlachos, Angelos 1838-1920	2	Civil servant, Journalist	Law in Athens and Germany	Minister of Finance, Supporter of Harilaos Trikoupis

Name and life	Years in Parliament**	Profession	Studies	Remarks
Vrailas-Armenis, Petros 1813-1884	1	Jurist, Ambassador, Professor of Philosophy at Ionian Academy	Law and Philosophy in Bologna, Geneva and Paris	He had intense parliamentary activity at the Ionian Parliament
Yiannopoulos, Panayiotis 1808-1886	2	Landowner	–	Minister of Finance
Zaimis, Alexandros * 1855-1936	18	Lawyer	Law in Athens, Paris and Germany	Prime Minister, Minister of Finance
Zaimis, Thrasyvoulos * 1822-1880	13	Lawyer	Law in Athens and Italy	Prime Minister, Minister of Finance
Zographos, Ioannis 1844-1927	2	Professor of Public Finance at University of Athens, Secretary-general of Ministry of Finance, General commissioner of State Audit Council	Law in Athens and Heidelberg	Student of Karl Heinrich Rau, Supporter of Theodoros Deliyiannis

Notes:
* The most distinguished speakers on economic issues in the Greek Parliament between 1862 and 1910.
** Approximately.

Chapter 10

Economists in the Japanese Diet (1890-1930): The Debate on Adoption of the Gold Standard

Jiro Kumagai

> If the silver [standard] had been so good, Western people susceptible to mercenary benefits would never have discarded it. It is of no use any more to discuss, which is better, gold or silver, at present. Because it is a matter of survival of the fittest... Claiming the silver standard is against the natural reason of the matter. There is no room to doubt about the advantage of adopting the gold standard... Once we adopt the gold standard, we can have the same capital equivalent in value as Western countries, and thereby we will have a ticket to enter the civilised monetary group (Yoshiro Sakatani, chief of the budget bureau of the Ministry of Finance, *Tokyo Keizai Zasshi* [The Tokyo Economist], **866**, 6 March 1897).

The political crisis of 1881 and the opening of the Diet

A petition calling for the establishment of a democratically elected national assembly was presented in 1874 by eight former high ranking officials including Taisuke Itagaki (1837-1919) and Shojiro Goto (1838-1897). Although many of the petitioners were previous members of the Council of State, they were all critical of the oligarchic government mainly composed of the Satsuma-Choshu clan. The petition was ignored, but the popular demand for the opening of a national assembly was gradually mounting in the form of the Movement for Freedom and People's Rights. This movement reached its peak in the so-called political crisis of 1881 (Meiji 14th year), which was caused by a political conflict, focusing on the Japanese constitution, between pro-German and pro-British statesmen. The conflict took a sudden turn in the summer of 1881 with the exposure of what was referred to as 'the problem of disposal of the government-owned property in Hokkaido'. The disclosure of this disposal provoked a nation-wide outcry against the government, and the gathering momentum culminated in the Movement for Freedom and People's Rights.

In order to calm the political turmoil, the government was obliged to promise that prompt measures would be taken to draw up the constitution and open the national Diet. Accordingly, Emperor Meiji proclaimed on 12 October 1881 that the Diet would be opened in 1890.

After this Imperial ordinance, the movement for freedom and people's rights was temporarily exalted, and the Liberal Party and Constitutional Progressive Party were formed. But by the mid-1880s, the movement had begun to decline as a result of a split of opinions among the activists; it was then further undermined by the government's appeasement of some of the leaders and by the ruin of a number of powerful farmers who had formed the nucleus of the movement but now found themselves facing financial disaster due to the fall in the price of rice, as a result of the deflationary policy.

During the first flourish of the movement after the 1881 political crisis, a series of private schools were established in Tokyo. These later became major private universities, such as Senshu (est.1880), Hosei (1880), Meiji (1881), Waseda (1882) and Chuo (1885). The spirit underlying the foundation of these schools was based on liberal ideals of British and French origins, similarly to Yukichi Fukazawa's Keio Gijuku School (1868). The introduction of economic education at the above cited schools was strongly influenced by British classical political economy, although studies were not based on original texts of Adam Smith and / or Ricardo, but rather on commentaries to these works.

Tokyo University itself, the only national university at the time, had been established in 1877 with four faculties (Law, Science, Arts, and Medicine); studies on political economy as well as political sciences were included in the Faculty of Arts. The first teacher of political economy at Tokyo University was E.F. Fenollosa (1853-1908), a young Harvard graduate. He taught principally the economic thought of John Stuart Mill, with certain necessary additions in the form of the thought of Henry Fawcett and the Historical School. This indicated that even Tokyo University was to some extent under the influence of classical economic thought, at least in its early stages. But this liberal background was eliminated following the 1881 political crisis, which marked the turning point at which Japan ceased to model itself upon Britain and began to look towards Germany as the model country. After the crisis, political sciences at Tokyo University attached great importance to German *Staatswissenschaft*, and by the same token economics adhered more closely to *Staatswirtschaft*. Thus graduates of Tokyo University began to flock to German universities, with the result that the approach to social policy which prevailed in German academic circles at the time tended to become predominant in economic studies in Japan. This pro-German tendency gradually penetrated into the private universities, as described below, leading to the establishment of the Japanese Association for Study of Social Policy in 1897 (Kyoto Imperial University was founded as the second imperial university in the same year). The Association maintained its authority as the only nationwide academic society until the early 1920s, when it virtually disintegrated because of the ideological conflict between Marxian and non-Marxian economists.

In the meanwhile, private schools retained British and French studies as their educational approach for quite some time, in rivalry with Tokyo University, which was now dominated by German studies. However, since the private schools were compelled to rely on lecturers from Tokyo University in order to maintain good quality as higher educational institutes, the influence of the German Historical School inevitably penetrated into these schools. Thus in parallel with the downturn of the movement of freedom and people's rights, the liberal tradition of private schools also began to ebb away. It is worth noting, in this context, that the government stipulated 'rules and regulations of special supervision over private law schools' in 1886, and under these regulations private higher educational institutes were subjected to the supervision of the president of Tokyo (Imperial) University.

Following the government's decision to adopt Germany as a model country, Hirobumi Ito (1841-1909), a very influential statesman belonging to the Choshu clique, was sent to Europe from 1882 to 1883 in preparation for drafting a constitution based on the Prussian model. The resulting Great Japanese Imperial Constitution was promulgated in 1889.

The Imperial Diet was then opened on 25 November 1890 in the wake of the Imperial Constitution. But the Diet opened by imperial edict was not constructed to reflect the voice of the populace. Aside from the House of Peers, the qualification as Diet electors was confined to adult males who paid the direct taxes (mainly the land tax in those days) of 15 yen as the minimum requirement. On account of this property qualification, only about one per cent (450,000 males aged over 25) of the entire population was listed in the electoral roll for the House of Representatives. Under this strictly limited electoral system the oligarchy of the Satsuma-Choshu clan, a predominant power in the Meiji Restoration, succeeded in retaining power in the government. Yet the conflict between the oligarchic government and the landed interests represented in the Diet was unavoidable, especially in the early sessions of the Diet.

A brief sketch of the history of the Japanese Diet (1890-1930)

In a speech delivered to the first Diet (December 1890-March 1891), Prime Minister Aritomo Yamagata (1838-1922) stressed the need to ensure military preparedness, in order to face the challenge of Western powers that had been making inroads into the Orient. The following Prime Minister and concurrently finance minister Masayoshi Matsukata (1835-1924), who later played a pivotal role in adoption of the gold standard, delivered almost the same speech in the second Diet.[1]

Their speeches mirrored what had been considered as the foremost national task since the Meiji Restoration (1868), namely the need to build up a rich nation with a strong army. The problem, however, lay in deciding who should bear the cost of this task. In 1890, Japan was still essentially an agricultural country, with the proportion of primary industries of agriculture, forestry and fisheries accounting

1 See *One Hundred-Year History of the Japanese Diet* (1985), pp. 37, 48.

for 70 per cent of the working population and 50 per cent of the net national products, against 10 per cent of manufacturing. The government naturally aimed to impose the burden on land, and thus attempted to increase the land tax. But now that the landed interest was far better represented in the Diet, reflecting the contemporary industrial structure and the franchise, the Diet was characterised in its early session – i.e. from 1890 to the outbreak of the Sino-Japanese War (1894) – by an acrimonious confrontation between people's parties demanding a reduction in land tax to preserve the general population's financial resources, and the oligarchic government clamouring for greater expenditure on armaments (armaments expenditure as a proportion of the 1890 national budget was 27 per cent). Against the government policy of pursuing an expansion of the military budget, people's parties such as the Constitutional Liberal Party and the Constitutional Progressive Party, which were mainly composed of former activists of the Freedom and People's Rights Movement, demanded a large-scale retrenchment of the budget to preserve the financial resources of the population.

This fierce confrontation between the people's parties and the government during the early Diets was in most cases settled by compromises, either by governmental manoeuvres to split the opposition parties or by an intervention of the Emperor in the budget. But the Sino-Japanese War marked a turning point in the conflict within the Diet. The war, followed by Japan's abandonment of its occupation of the Liaotung Peninsula as a result of the intervention of Russia, Germany and France, brought an end to the fierce cleavage between the government and people's parties that had focused on the reduction of land tax versus the strengthening of armaments. There ensued a form of national consensus with regard to the use of national resources for reinforcing military power.

By the ninth Diet (December 1895-March 1896), the people's parties expressed their support for an expansion of expenditure on armaments, and thereafter they gradually became less antagonistic to the increase in land tax. Thus the increase in land tax from 2.5 per cent to 3.3 per cent of land value was implemented in 1900 in concomitance with the increase in taxes on alcohol, income, and others. However, although the land taxes increased, little benefit accrued to the tax revenue, which in fact tended to decline, reflecting the advance of industrialisation; consequently, the fiscal burden fell on industrial and commercial interests as well as on the urban inhabitants. Business leaders such as Eiichi Shibusawa (1840-1931, mentioned below), who organised the League for the Increase of Land Tax, almost simultaneously engaged in activity to promote the formation of the League for the Reform of Election Law, in order for business interests to be reflected in the Diet. As the government was not opposed to limited reform of the electoral system, the minimum property qualification for electors was lowered to payment of direct taxes of 10 yen in 1900. Following this reform, the number of adult male electors increased to 980,000 (about two per cent of the total population). The membership of the House of Representatives also rose from 300 to 369.

The change in the electoral system triggered the reorganisation of political parties. Hirobumi Ito, one of the clan oligarchs, formed a new party in 1900, *Seiyu Kai*

(Political Friend Party), as a product of the coalescence of part of the clan oligarchies with part of the people's parties. With the emergence of this party, though led by peers and bureaucrats, the political history of Japan entered into a new stage, which marked a transition from the stage of confrontation and compromise between clan oligarchies and people's parties to that of rotation of political power between old-type traditional clan oligarchies and *Seiyu Kai*.[2]

The First World War brought about great economic and political change. The value of exports from 1913 to 1919 increased as much as 3.8 times, and imports also showed a 3.1-fold increase. Exports exceeded imports during this period. Japan's foreign credit also exceeded foreign debt, so that Japan was transformed from a debtor country to a creditor country. Industrial expansion was seen not only in light industries, but also in heavy industries, such as electric power, mining, iron and steel, and shipbuilding along with the armaments industry. The agricultural population decreased, and the proportion employed in manufacturing, commerce, and public services rose considerably. This economic growth in turn led to an increase in the proportion of the population employed in manual labour, as well as urban middle classes.

Against the background of this industrialisation and urbanisation, there emerged the so-called *Taisho Seihen* (the political movement demanding universal male suffrage in *Taisho Era*). Three combined political parties, *Kenseikai* (Constitutional Party), *Seiyukai*, and *Kakushinkurabu* (Reformist Club) then overthrew the government led by traditional clan oligarchies in the 1924 general election. Under the new government of these combined parties, adult male suffrage was enacted in 1925, and the first election under the new system was carried out in 1928, when a few Socialists were elected.

Thus the era of 'party politics' came into being in Japan. 'Party politics' is to be understood here as the formation of a government based on a party or parties that obtained a majority in a general election. But this epoch-making parliamentary democracy did not last long. It ended as early as in 1932 amid the great depression, the emergence of militaristic and bureaucratic power in tune with the pursuit of overseas markets, and rampant assassinations of the leaders of political parties.

However, if we were to attribute the cause of the collapse of 'party politics' purely to circumstances arising from the stormy period after the Great Depression, we would lose sight of the characteristics of the history of the Japanese Diet from 1890 to 1945, the year that marked the end of WW2. Even during the days of 'party politics' (1924-1932), the members of the oligarchy retained their bastions of power, such as the House of Peers, the Privy Council, the bureaucracy, and military authority, thus protecting the establishment from the people's parties, and still exerting their influence on the party cabinets. It was virtually impossible for political parties to come to power without some consent from the oligarchic establishment. During the era of government by political parties, no fewer than six presidents of parties took office. But among these, Tsuyoshi Inukai (1855-1932)

---

2 See Masumi (1988), **2**, p. 171; **3**, p. 4.

was probably the only party politician to genuinely deserve this description. Four of the six were former high ranking government officials, while the other remaining figure was an army officer. As for cabinet ministers in this period, almost two-thirds of the members of the cabinets were composed of bureaucrats and/or members of the House of Peers, who furthermore held decisive posts, such as ministers of finance, or foreign, or home affairs.[3]

The picture thereby delineated clearly demonstrates that the bureaucrats exerted their power in conjunction with politicians forming part of the oligarchy, who effectively controlled the formation of cabinets even in the period of party politics. Furthermore, a glance at the list of influential economists involved in the process of policy build-up reveals that they were mainly officials who graduated from Tokyo University, became financial bureaucrats, and completed their careers as imperial nominees to the House of Peers (see Appendix). This tendency can be traced both before and after the Sino-Japanese War (1894-1895), which marked the end of the conflict that raged in the early sessions of the Diet between the oligarchy and the people's parties.

In the following section, I will deal with the parliamentary debate on the adoption of the gold standard in Japan, which took place from 1893 to 1897 just before and after the Sino-Japanese War. The direct participants in the debate were members of the Commission on the Monetary System, and of the House of Representatives and Peers. They attempted, almost for the first time, to apply Western economic theory in order to devise an economic policy for Japan that would enable the country to be included within the circle of advanced countries. It was a decisive moment in modern Japanese history, highlighted by a monumental parliamentary debate. But the debate also ultimately demonstrated the dominant role of government officials belonging to the Finance Ministry, predicting that they would hereafter continue to take the lead in framing economic policy.

The silver standard and the economic development of Japan

Japan originally resolved to implement the gold standard as early as May 1871. The gold one-yen coin at that time contained 1.5 grams of fine gold. But since the Mexican silver dollar was very widely used in the treaty ports during that period, the government was compelled to mint the silver one-yen coin simultaneously. Subsequently, in 1878, Japan adopted a bimetallic standard, issuing a decree which stated that the silver coin was acceptable as legal tender in domestic and foreign trade as well. After the establishment of the Bank of Japan (1882), the regulation of the silver convertible banknote was promulgated in early 1884; in January 1886 the Bank began to issue its one-yen paper currency that was convertible into the silver one-yen coin. The silver standard was thereby virtually established in Japan.

3 Ibid., **3**, pp. 85-6.

But let us glance back a moment. In October 1883 when Japan was preparing for the silver standard, Masayoshi Matsukata, then minister of finance and later a strenuous advocate of the gold standard, advanced the proposal that Japan should adopt a silver standard in line with Asian silver-using countries. He buttressed his opinion by pointing out that even Britain, the richest and strongest country with the gold standard, found it necessary to use silver money in trade with Asian countries. This demonstrated that silver, rather than gold, was appropriate for the real state of Asian trade. Interestingly, Matsukata did not at that time reject the concept of a mechanism of bimetallism to adjust prices, provided it was accepted on a world-wide scale. On the other hand, since he regarded adoption of the bimetallic system on such a scale as unlikely, he concluded that it would be a far wiser choice for Japan to adopt the silver standard.[4]

Just at the point when Japan launched the silver standard, however, the world began to experience a lasting dramatic fall in the value of silver as a result of adoption of the gold standard followed by demonetisation of silver in a string of Western countries. For 12 years from 1886, the year Japan adopted the silver standard, to 1897, the year Japan shifted to the gold standard, the exchange rate of the yen dropped by as much as 41 per cent due to the drastic fall in the price of silver against gold. Consequently Japan as a silver country was in a position to gain great benefit in trade with gold-using countries, in the form of a virtual depreciation of the Japanese currency. The price of imports from gold-using countries in terms of Japanese yen rose and the price of exports to such countries fell conversely. Thus the Japanese silver standard proved to be exerting a substantial power to protect her industries.

Establishment of the Commission on the Monetary System

Japanese industries undoubtedly enjoyed a new opportunity for expansion with each decline in the gold price of silver. But there were also injurious effects to be taken into account.

The minister of finance Kunitake Watanabe (1846-1919), addressing the Diet in November 1893, drew attention to the harmful effects of the depreciation of silver on the national budget. Mentioning the soaring national expenditure in terms of gold due to the fact that the value of silver against gold had almost halved in five years, he stated that the government had already set up a Commission on the Monetary System (abbreviated as the Monetary Commission below) to inquire into the benefits and losses of the current silver standard.[5]

Only a few months prior to this speech by the finance minister, India, one of the largest silver-using countries, suspended the free coinage of silver (June 1893) and moved towards adopting a gold standard. Still earlier, the international monetary

---

4 See Research Bureau of the Bank of Japan (1958), pp. 1044-7.

5 See *One Hundred-Year History of the Japanese Diet* (1985), p. 71.

conference in Brussels (November 1892) had failed to reach agreement on a bimetallic system. In October 1893 the USA abolished the Sherman Act which had obliged the US government to buy a considerable amount of silver, and suspended silver coinage completely. These developments gave rise to an avalanche-like decline in the value of silver and prompted Japan to investigate the situation of the silver standard.

Thus the Monetary Commission was established in October 1893 according to an imperial decree with twenty-two members. The members can be broken down into three groups, similarly to F.W. Fetter's categorisation of parliamentary economists in Britain: first, academic economists, second, bankers and businessmen tackling a particular problem closely associated with their day-to-day experience, and third, those who participated in economic debates linked with economic legislation.[6] Fetter's third category closely resembles the most influential group in the debate analysed in this chapter.

The chairman was Viscount Tateki Tani (1837-1911), and the deputy chairman, Inejiro Tajiri (1850-1923).[7]

The remaining twenty members were composed of government officials, bankers/businessmen, professors of political economy, members of the House of Representatives and Peers, and journalists. Among these, the major figures, who worked as members of the special committees within the Commission and participated in the debate in the tenth Diet (March 1897), were as follows: Yoshiro Sakatani (1863-1941), Juichi Soeda (1864-1929), Ukichi Taguchi (1855-1905), Kenzo Wadagaki (1860-1919), Noburu Kanai (1865-1935), Kokichi Sonoda (1843-1923, president of the Yokohama Specie Bank), and Eiichi Shibusawa.[8]

---

6 See Fetter (1980), pp. 12-13.

7 Tateki Tani was a forceful leader of the House of Pees, and held the Ministry of Agriculture and Trade in the Hirobumi Ito's first Cabinet in 1887. He was an ex-military officer, deeply sympathising with small framers, and organised the League against Land Tax Increase in 1898. He did not express his own opinion on the monetary system in the Commission.

Inejiro Tajiri was vice-minister of the Ministry of Finance. After studying political economy at Yale University, he taught at Tokyo University where Sakatani and Soeda were his disciples. He was one of the founders of Senshu School, later Senshu University.

8 Yoshiro Sakatani was chief of the budget bureau of the Ministry of Finance. After graduating from Tokyo University, he became a financial official and gave full scope to his ability as one of the most trusted disciples of Viscount Matsukata. He taught at several private universities.

Juichi Soeda was counsellor of the Ministry of Finance. After graduation from Tokyo University, he entered the Ministry of Finance, like Soeda, and had an opportunity to study under Alfred Marshall. He was a Japanese correspondent of the *Economic Journal*. He also taught at several private universities.

Ukichi Taguchi was an advocate of *laissez-faire* of the Manchester school, and the founder of *Tokyo Keizai Zasshi* [the Tokyo Economist]. He was a distinguished non-governmental economist along with Fukuzawa in the Meiji era.

The Monetary Commission held its first general meeting on 25 October 1893 and concluded its duties at the seventh general meeting on 5 July 1895. The task of the Commission was to investigate, firstly, the causes behind the recent fluctuation in the value of silver and gold, secondly the effects of the fluctuation of these metals upon the Japanese economy, and thirdly the recommendation of a new monetary system for Japan and the manner of enforcing it, should it prove necessary to change the current silver monetary system. The Commission finally submitted a voluminous report, appendices of which abounded in valuable statistics, and abstracts of books, pamphlets and reports about monetary systems published in not only Japan but also Western countries. In the appreciative words of Takao Tsuchiya (1896-1988), a celebrated economic historian, the report has been 'an everlasting value as one of the most important literature in Japanese monetary history'.[9]

According to the report dated 5 July 1895, the decisive vote on the need to change the current monetary system (silver standard) took place at the sixth general meeting of the Commission held in June 1895. The members present at the meeting numbered fifteen. The outcome of the ballot showed that eight favoured the change, whereas the remaining seven opposed it. Thus the Monetary Commission concluded that it was necessary to change the existing monetary system, although the type of standard to be adopted and the time of its implementation were momentarily shelved.

Three salient points should be borne in mind when analyzing the result of this vote. First, within the majority of eight members, Sakatani alone insisted on immediate adoption of the gold standard, albeit virtually a 'limping gold standard' as shown below, while five other gold monometallists maintained that overhasty implementation would be rash since Japan was still short of gold reserve to enforce the change-over. Secondly, the majority included two bimetallists. Thirdly the minority, just short of one vote against the majority, was made up of six bimetallists and one silver monometallist.

If the count had included two other members who were absent from the sixth general meeting, but submitted their opinion (one in favour of bimetallism and the other a supporter of silver monometallism), the bimetallist camp would have achieved a majority in the Monetary Commission. We can conclude, therefore, that the members who expressed their opinion in or to the Commission were split into

---

Kenzo Wadagaki was professor of Tokyo University. He studied in Germany and Britain after graduating from Tokyo University, and became a supporter of the German historical and social policy school.

Noburu Kanai was a professor of Tokyo University. After graduation from Tokyo school, he studied in Germany and became a central figure of the Japanese Association for the Study of Social Policy.

Eiichi Shibusawa was a key leader of Japanese capitalism in its formative period. He took part in setting up some five hundred companies, and was called 'the patron-saint' of Japanese enterprise. He once taught banking practices at Tokyo University.

9 Research Bureau of the Bank of Japan (1957), **16**, p. 10.

nine bimetallists, six gold monometallists, and two silver monometallists (see Table 10.1).

Table 10.1 Opinions in the Monetary Commission about the monetary system to be adopted

Advocates of the necessity to change the present system		Opponents to the change of the present system
Yoshio Sakatani (G)		Kenzo Wadagaki (B)
Gov. financial official	*Favourable to immediate change*	Prof. at Tokyo University, Historical School
Juichi Soeda (G)		Noburu Kanai (B)
Gov. financial official	Sakatani (G) Shoda (B)	Prof. at Tokyo University, Historical School
Koki Watanabe (G)	Taguchi (B)	Sanae Takada (B)
Ex-pres. of Tokyo Univ., ex-Repr.		Prof. at Waseda University, Repr.
Takashi Masuda (G)		Tokujiro Obata (B)
Mitsui Corp.	*Favourable to*	Prof. at Keio University, Peer
Jun Kawashima (G)	*future change*	Kokichi Sonoda (B)
Ex-counsellor of Fin. Min., Repr.	Soeda (G)	President of Yokohama Specie Bank
Ryoichi Kurihara (G)	Watanabe (G)	Eiichi Shibusawa (B)
Journalist, Repr.	Kawashima (G) Kurihara (G)	Leader of business / banking circle
Heigoro Shoda (B)		* Takashi Hara (B)
Mitsubishi Corp.		Gov. official of Min. of Foreign Affairs
Ukichi Taguchi (B)	*Waiting for a*	Masayasu Hotta (S)
Journalist, Repr.	*better opportunity*	Peer, later Min. of Post & Telecom.
	Masuda (G)	* Seion Wakamiya (S) Gov. official of Min. of Agriculture & Comm.

Source: Research Bureau of the Bank of Japan, *Documentations of Japanese Financial History*, **16**, Tokyo, 1957, pp. 576-80 (in Japanese).

Notes:

- G = advocate of gold standard; B = advocate of bimetallism; S = advocate of silver standard.
- Repr. = member of the House of Representatives; Peer = member of the House of Peers.
- * = absent at the 6th General Meeting; they presented their Opinion to the Commission at a later date.
- Middle column shows the differences of opinions among advocates of change about the appropriate timing for the enforcement of the new system.
- Three other members out of 20 (Koichiro Kawata, Governor of the Bank of Japan, Jinkichi Watanabe, Peer, and Naomasa Maki, ex-Repr.) did not present their opinion.

In the light of this composition of the members' opinions, the remark by Ryoichi Kurihara (1855-1911)[10] in the tenth Diet, in reference to the intentional misunderstanding of the Commission's conclusion by the minister of finance Matsukata and other government officials, appears well founded. Kurihara argued that the majority of the Commission consisted of advocates of the silver standard.[11] In effect, since many of the bimetallists argued that Japan should retain its current silver standard until an international agreement on the bimetallic system could be formulated, Kurihara's comment was highly appropriate.

Opinions on monetary standards in the Monetary Commission

Let us now take a look at three types of opinion expressed in the Monetary Commission: bimetallism, silver metallism, and gold metallism. Consider first the bimetallists. They constituted virtually a majority, although their views were not unanimous as regards the timing of implementation. They came from various different backgrounds, ranging from bankers and businessmen to government officials except for two members of the Ministry of Finance, and remarkably all four academics were on the side of bimetallism. These four scholars evidently reflected the contemporary situation of academic circles, which were under the powerful influence of the German Historical School.[12] But Taguchi advocated bimetallism from a different viewpoint, as he was a supporter of *laissez-faire* in the style of the Manchester School.

Bimetallists

Professor Wadagaki, who did not subscribe to classical orthodox economics, maintained that his viewpoint was similar to that of the German Historical School on this issue. Just as there was no universal economic principle applicable to different times and different places, he argued, so there was no single monetary standard applicable to any country. The criterion of choice between the monometallic or bimetallic system was thus reduced purely to a question of convenience. After illustrating the viewpoint of the German Historical School, he put forward some interesting observations on the changing features of British thought at the end of the nineteenth century. Individualism, he suggested, was gradually losing its influence, and collectivism was gaining support instead. This remarkable transformation of ideas was, in his view, permeating into both academic and political

10 Ryoichi Kurihara was a former activist of the Movement for Freedom and People's Rights as well as a journalist. As a member of the Monetary Commission, he advocated the gold standard, but opposed its immediate adoption. Later he sat on the foundation committee of the Industrial Bank of Japan and the South Manchuria Railroad.

11 *The Proceedings of the House of Representatives of the Imperial Diet* (1980), p. 250.

12 On the predominance of the German Historical School in that period, see Kumagai (2001), pp. 206-11.

circles in Britain. Increasing criticism of the gold standard and emerging support for bimetallism in Britain was nothing but an exact reflection of this gradual shift of perspective and its effects upon the monetary system. An upsurging bimetallism in Britain, therefore, indicated that Britain was now undergoing a transformation of the monetary system in accordance with the general change of ideas. As Wadagaki was convinced that a similar shift was under way in almost all advanced countries, he felt there could be little doubt as to the forthcoming worldwide enforcement of bimetallism.[13]

Professor Noburu Kanai, another enthusiastic advocate of the German Historical School, also emphasised a remarkable rise of bimetallism, both among scholars and in practical circles in Britain and Germany, and asserted that many economists had already accepted the international bimetallic standard as an ideal monetary system. Part of his arguments were based on the claim that advocates of the gold standard exhibited a blind and obsessive faith in the old orthodox school, to the point that they failed to understand how its disciplines interacted with the real affairs of the world. By making use of both gold and silver as legal tender, he contended, it would become possible to control the disastrous fluctuation of prices, since bimetallism would exert a countervailing power to stabilise the fluctuation of the price of both metals. The bimetallic standard, Kanai concluded, was not an impractical fantastic vision as gold monometallists argued.[14] Kanai's criticism of the gold standard and advocacy of bimetallism resulted in his dismissal from the post of counsellor in the Ministry of Finance, which was a stronghold of the gold standard.[15]

Turning now to the business world, the figure of Shibusawa provides a representative opinion in favour of bimetallism. Shibusawa maintained that the fluctuation in the value of gold and silver had brought Japan greater profits rather than losses, inasmuch as it helped to protect Japanese foreign trade against gold-using countries through the rising price of imports from gold-using countries and the falling price of exports to such countries. As a consequence, Japanese industries had experienced notable development because exports increased and imports decreased. Additionally, most of the goods imported from gold-using countries had served to produce Japanese manufactured goods at a reasonable price, which, in turn, contributed to expanding the Japanese market overseas. Therefore, he argued, it was wise to retain the existing monetary system, until such a time as an international bimetallic system had come into effect as a result of successful agreement on bimetallism among Western countries.[16] Thus Shibusawa recommended adoption of the bimetallic system at some future date.[17]

---

13 Research Bureau of the Bank of Japan (1957), **16**, pp. 939-40.

14 Ibid., pp. 941-3.

15 *One Hundred-Year History of Tokyo University* (1986), p. 893.

16 Research Bureau of the Bank of Japan (1957), **16**, pp. 944-6.

17 Shibusawa later changed his mind and became an advocate of the gold standard, admitting that he was genuinely ashamed of the opinions he had previously espoused. See 'A

Among the bimetallists in the Monetary Commission, Taguchi was the most celebrated figure. He had already stated his case for bimetallism as early as 1881,[18] and his journal, *Tokyo Keizai Zasshi* (The Tokyo Economist), consistently reported on the progress of bimetallism and related worldwide monetary issues at the end of the century. When the final report of the Commission on Gold and Silver was published in Britain, his journal published a commentary and showed a favourable attitude towards its minority report that advocated the bimetallic standard.[19] When the Bimetallic League was established in Britain in 1885, the Japanese journal provided coverage of its movement quite deliberately,[20] asserting that the 'bimetallic camp is gaining power at a rapid pace like the rising sun and sweeping away the fortress of gold standard'.[21] But when the international monetary conference held in Brussels in 1892 proved to be a failure, even *Tokyo Keizai Zasshi* was at a loss to find any suitable response, and wrote that the possibility of the bimetallic standard seemed to have 'become extinct now'.[22] Nevertheless, Taguchi and his journal never furled the flag of bimetallism, and still persisted in advocating his approach by stating that 'famous economists, by and large, are bimetallists today'.[23] He sought to buttress his position by claiming that Nicholson, Foxwell, Sidgwick, Wicksteed, and even Marshall should be considered as bimetallists.[24]

Clearly, Taguchi's opinion as regards the Monetary Commission report was backed by his long-standing confidence in bimetallism, which he had held ever since he started his career as a journalist with an academic background.

In the commentary on the Monetary Commission report, Taguchi first argued that the fall of prices in gold standard countries was greater than the rise of prices in silver standard countries. In his view, this demonstrated that the degree of the rise in the price of gold was greater than that of the fall in the price of silver. Therefore silver, subject to less fluctuation in price, could be regarded as more suitable for the standard metal. But this did not mean that the current silver standard was ideal. Indeed, Taguchi was well aware that the price of silver was also subject to change, just as was the case with the price of gold. Therefore neither of the two metals was truly fit to assume the role of an ideal standard. But if a combination of the two metals was adopted, the best monetary standard would be realised.

There were widespread misconceptions with regard to bimetallism, Taguchi continued, and these led to the mistaken belief that bimetallism must necessarily end in an alternative standard. In some cases this would result in a gold standard, at

---

Report on the 20th Anniversary of the Enforcement of the Gold Standard', in Research Bureau of the Bank of Japan (1957), **17**, p. 703.

18 See Taguchi's articles 'Bimetallism is the Best for the Monetary System' and 'On Bimetallism', *Tokyo Keizai Zasshi*, n. 51, 56, 59, 60, from January to April 1881.

19 *Tokyo Keizai Zasshi*, n. 453-454, 19 and 26 January 1889.

20 Ibid., n. 316, 15 May 1886.

21 Ibid., n. 343, 20 November 1896.

22 Ibid., n. 569 and 661, 28 January and 1 February 1893.

23 Ibid., n. 679, 17 February 1893.

24 Ibid., n. 728 and 729, 2 and 9 June 1894.

other times a silver standard, as a consequence of the draining from circulation of a highly appreciated metal, a development which would in turn be brought about by the propensity to hoard the highly valued metal. But let us consider what might ensue if a proper legal ratio of exchange between gold and silver were to be set by an international agreement. In this case, if silver became less valuable than gold in the market in comparison with the legal ratio, debtors would undoubtedly seek the silver coin, i.e. the less valuable metal, to meet their debts. Such a move would certainly increase the demand for silver metal; consequently, other things being equal, the price of silver would increase and eventually return to its previous level of value. On the other hand, were gold to become less valuable, the reverse movement would come into being, and consequently, the price of gold would return to the previous level, just as in the case of silver. Thus, if an international monetary conference should succeed in setting the ratio, bimetallism would never result in an alternative standard. But at this point, a further question springs to mind: could an international agreement on the setting of the ratio actually be maintained amid the fluctuation of two metals in the market? Taguchi was optimistic in this regard, pointing out that the countries of the Latin Monetary Union had never attempted to break their agreement, and had instead directed their efforts to maintaining the exchange ratio of gold and silver since 1865. Therefore the Union would have existed, if the artificial demonetarisation of silver since 1873 (the year Germany enforced the gold standard) had not been enacted.

Referring to the investigation carried out by the director of the American Mint, Taguchi then argued that silver together with gold was indispensable for world trade. According to the investigation, the total amount of gold and silver coins in circulation across the world was equal to 78 hundred million yen, with 39 hundred million yen each for gold and silver respectively.[25] Therefore if most countries adopted the gold standard, world trade would be obliged to conduct business only with gold amounting to 39 hundred million yen, instead of 78 hundred million yen composed of gold and silver as had been the case so far. In Taguchi's opinion, if Japan, Western countries, and India were to present a united front, they would be able to control 32 hundred million yen of gold out of the above mentioned total 39 hundred million yen of gold coins, and 29 hundred million yen of silver out of the total 39 hundred million yen of silver coins. If, furthermore, these countries established an alliance for a bimetallic monetary system in order to set a proper exchange rate for gold and silver, the world exchange rate of the two metals would return to the level prior to 1873. Based upon this estimation, Taguchi proposed that the Japanese government should promptly urge European countries and America to establish a bimetallic monetary agreement.[26]

Another important related issue must be mentioned, namely, the relation between bimetallism and free trade. Since the very beginning of his career, Taguchi

25 These figures are also cited by Shibusawa and Sonoda in the report of the Monetary Commission. See Research Bureau of the Bank of Japan (1957), **16**, pp. 946-7.

26 Ibid., pp. 928-39.

had championed free trade:[27] indeed, he considered the bimetallic monetary system and free trade as inseparable entities, arguing in particular that bimetallism would stabilise prices.[28] At the end of the nineteenth century, opinions on this issue were divided, with some thinkers claiming that they stood in contradiction to each other, while others, including a number of Manchester merchants and manufacturers as well as some City bankers, insisted that this was not the case. Overall, however, bimetallism and free trade were generally regarded as a contradiction in terms.

Taguchi's view was that bimetallism would make prices steadier by lessening the fluctuation in the value of money and in the foreign exchange rate through its adjustment mechanism. Worthy of note, in this regard, is his article commenting on a gathering of the Bimetallic League held in Manchester in April 1988. It was Taguchi's contention that British cotton manufacturers, seeking to recoup the losses they had suffered in the wake of destruction of the stable exchange rate between gold and silver, were aiming to raise general prices by depreciating the value of their currency.[29]

Yet such a move, Taguchi claimed, totally failed to take into account that the purpose of the bimetallic standard lay in stabilising general prices. Taguchi espoused a conception of bimetallism that contrasted with an inflationist point of view: 'Economists in the European gold standard countries advocate the international bimetallic standard for the fear of a further decline of prices. But I commit myself to the international bimetallic standard to avoid the rise of rice price produced by an anticipated further decline of silver price'.[30] As the price of rice formed the general basis for prices in Japan at that time, what Taguchi most greatly feared was that the decline in the price of silver would trigger a rise in general prices driven by an increase in the price of rice. He was convinced that raising prices due to currency depreciation would eventually destroy the economic equilibrium. To avert such a risk and achieve stabilisation of the economy, he believed the most appropriate measure would be the adoption of a bimetallic monetary system. Although this recommendation might seem implausible to staunch advocates of the gold standard, Taguchi remained firmly convinced that the gold standard constituted a system that would destroy the balanced economic order that was essential if free trade was to flourish and produce the greatest benefits of its functioning. Thus

---

27 Taguchi published *Free Trade and Japanese Economy* in 1878 (when he was only 23 years old), and subsequently wrote numerous articles and books arguing the case for free trade.

28 Professor Tamaki's interpretation that bimetallism and free trade are incompatible is not applicable to Taguchi's argument (Tamaki, 1988, p. 236).

29 Taguchi seems to regard British bimetallist manufacturers as leaning towards inflationist tendencies. A typical British inflationist view is observed in the minority report of the *Final Report of Commission on the Depression of Trade* (1886) and the *Final Report of Commission on Gold and Silver* (1888). The minority of both Commissions maintained that a continuous fall of prices was caused by the appreciation of the standard of value (gold), and manufacturing and commercial enterprises would be more greatly stimulated with rising rather than falling prices.

30 *Tokyo Keizai Zasshi*, n. 423, 16 June 1888.

price stabilisation based upon bimetallism and free trade based upon price stabilisation were inseparable in his approach.[31]

Silver monometallists

The majority of bimetallists in the Monetary Commission, except Taguchi himself, supported the continuation of the existing silver standard until such a time as an international agreement on a bimetallic system were brought into effect. In this sense, the bimetallists in the Commission were almost all supporters of the silver standard, as mentioned by Kurihara in the discussion of the Diet (see above). Notable exceptions were Seion Wakamiya (1866-1924) and Viscount Masayasu Hotta (1848-1911), who were genuine silver monometallists. Here we will take a brief look at the opinion of Wakamiya.

Wakamiya, the director of the bureau of commerce and industry in the Ministry of Agriculture and Trade, emphasised Japan's weakness in comparison to Western countries. Therefore the overwhelmingly important market for Japan was likely to be in Asian countries. This consideration led Wakamiya to stress three relevant points. First, if the gold standard were adopted, massive capital from Western gold-using countries would enter Japan and the still feeble Japanese agriculture, industry and commerce would certainly come under the control of Western foreigners, thereby hampering the development of the Japanese economy. Secondly, protective tariffs were indispensable for the economic development of a backward country, if such a country was to gain any benefit from trade with advanced countries. The fact that gold was expensive while silver was cheap would bring about a protective effect on Japan. Thirdly, although it was generally held that 70 per cent of Japanese trade was conducted with Western countries and only 30 per cent with Asian countries, the goods Japan was seeking to develop were manufactured goods, for which the most promising market certainly lay in the Orient, not the West. Western countries, Wakamiya warned, were attempting to extend their exports to the Oriental market, with the consequence of a marked intensification of competition. This meant that it was of paramount importance for Japan to retain the current advantageous monetary system, in order to sustain the Japanese position on Asian markets, especially on the Chinese continent.[32]

31 As for a further explanation of the relation between free trade and the idea of social equilibrium in Taguchi's economic thought, see Kumagai (1998), pp. 32-9.

32 Research Bureau of the Bank of Japan (1957), **16**, pp. 956-7. Consider another example of the silver monometallists' opinion. Kunpei Matsumoto (see Appendix) spoke at the meeting on the monetary standard of the Tokyo Economic Club under the auspices of Taguchi as follows: if we adopt the gold standard, we must lose the present and future benefits in the Chinese Continent we are now enjoying, and China will become our dreadful rival with the advantage of her silver standard (*Tokyo Keizai Zasshi*, n. 867, 13 March 1897).

Gold monometallists

We will now turn to the arguments put forward by the gold monometallists in the Monetary Commission. Soeda's view offers a representative example for discussion here.

Soeda sketched a critical account of the bimetallist and silver monometallist point of view based on his conception that the causes of the depression of European gold standard countries lay not in enforcement of the gold standard, but in increasing production accompanied by decreasing costs, i.e. by the increasing application of scientific knowledge, decreasing freight costs, improved communication facilities, and rising worldwide competition. In this perspective, his view echoed the majority opinion of British gold monometallists in the Commission on the Depression of Trade and Industry and the Commission on Gold and Silver. If the depression of Western countries was attributable to the fall of prices caused by appreciation of the gold currency, Soeda continued, then the price of all goods must have fallen equally. But empirical findings showed a diversified decline in the prices of various goods, suggesting that the monetary system could not be blamed for the difficulties experienced in the West. Soeda also criticised the inflationist view which held that rising prices or depreciating currency brought about national prosperity. On the contrary, he claimed that rising prices hindered a sound and proper development of the society and State, and were incompatible with the enduring prosperity of the nation. He did not deny that Japan had benefited from the depreciation of silver and had thereby enjoyed an increase in exports, prosperity of commerce and industry, increasing employment, and so forth. But this was now offset by rising prices due to the depreciation of silver.[33]

Taguchi and Soeda seem to have shared the emphasis on price stability. They disagreed sharply, however, on other points. Taguchi believed that the quantity of circulating gold was insufficient to maintain world trade, arguing that both silver and gold were required. If the gold standard were not supplemented by silver, the resulting demonetarisation of silver would give rise to a disastrous decline in the price of silver price, thereby inevitably destabilising the price system world-wide. Without silver, therefore, Taguchi contended, it would be impossible to sustain increasing world trade and achieve price stabilisation.

Soeda, on the other hand, broached a number of specific points. He attributed the increase in Japanese exports to gold standard countries to the development of Japanese productive capacity rather than to a decline in the value of silver. Stressing, in particular, that Japan needed to purchase men-of-war, engines, machines, etc. from gold-using countries, with which Japan could achieve an increase in productive capacity as well as military power, he pointed out that the current silver standard would be detrimental to Japan, as under declining silver prices Japan was forced to make almost double payments to Britain for purchase of such goods as compared to twenty years before.

---

33 Research Bureau of the Bank of Japan (1957), **16**, pp. 903-10.

Like Matsukata and Sakatani, Soeda also regarded the gold standard as a benchmark that Japan must reach in order to be classified as an advanced country. Regrettably, however, Japan was not yet sufficiently mature to put the gold standard into practice due to a scarcity of gold reserves. Therefore he concluded that in the immediate future all efforts should be directed to accumulating gold.[34]

Drawing up the Monetary Law

In September 1893, a little before the establishment of the Monetary Commission, Matsukata, who had resigned from office in August 1892 yet exerted a latent power in the Ministry of Finance, gave an informal order to bureaucrats of the Ministry of Finance, including Sakatani and Soeda, to investigate the plan to enforce the gold standard. Matsukata had already come to the conclusion that the time had come to change the monetary system, in consideration of the diminishing benefit from the current silver standard. The soaring prices were apparently offsetting the previous advantages of the system. Sakatani, responding to Matsukata's confidence, drew up four drafts, among which the most significant was the paper entitled 'Draft on the Monetary System', proposing a system whereby gold would be the standard metal and the free coinage of silver would be suspended, but silver coins should be continuously used under the strict supervision of the Ministry of Finance. This was the so-called 'limping gold standard' which aimed to save on the use of gold coins and compensate a shortage of gold reserve with silver coins, under condition of abolishing the free coinage of silver, although unlimited circulation of the existing silver one-yen coin would still be permitted with a fixed exchange rate against the gold coin. This was in fact the idea Sakatani himself advocated in the Monetary Commission.[35]

Just one year later, with the formation of his Cabinet in September 1896, Matsukata formed a project team again inside the Ministry of Finance and instructed them to draw up a definitive plan to enforce the gold standard in order to implement the conclusion of the Monetary Commission. He issued these instructions under the assumption that the Commission had concluded in favour of the gold standard, contrary to the real state of affairs in the Commission, where the bimetallist camp was actually predominant. In January 1897, the team issued a report entitled 'Plan for Enforcement of the Gold Standard'. The plan, although aiming to establish 'a pure gold standard' in the future, proposed a gold standard combined with the use of silver coins as a temporary expedient for the time being. Thus it still retained a hint of the 'limping gold standard', similarly to Sakatani's 'Draft on the Monetary System' submitted earlier. In contrast to this plan, Soeda now presented a different view entitled 'A Proposal regarding the Monetary Bill' which

34 Ibid., p. 910.
35 Ibid., pp. 901-2.

was in sharp contrast to Sakatani's conception. Soeda proposed a pure gold standard in this proposal, asserting that anything short of this would be a travesty of the concept of a true gold standard.[36]

Soeda obviously had changed his mind. Earlier, when he was working for the Monetary Commission, he had embraced the notion, as we saw above, that Japan was not sufficiently mature to adopt a pure gold standard because of a shortage of gold reserve.[37] But now the situation had evolved substantially since Japan, as a result of the victory in the Sino-Japanese War, had acquired a gold indemnity totalling 38.1 million pounds (approximately 381 million yen at the exchange rate of the time). Such a sum was equivalent to about 25 per cent of the Japanese gross national product at that time. Thus the most crucial obstacle to enforcing the gold standard had already been settled in 1897.

As Soeda's idea was now agreeable to Sakatani, they cooperated to draw up the new Monetary Bill on the gold standard, and the draft Bill was submitted for discussion at the Cabinet meeting on 25 February 1897. The government then put the Monetary Bill on the agenda of the tenth Diet (December 1896 to March 1897, but the Bill was discussed in March 1897).

The main points of the Monetary Bill are as follows. The gold yen was established as the unit of value in place of the silver yen and the new gold one-yen coin contained exactly one-half the weight (0.75 grams) of the existing gold coin (1.5 grams). The silver one-yen coin already issued was to be gradually exchanged for the gold coin at the rate of one gold one-yen coin for one silver one-yen coin to avoid any disturbance of prices and existing relations between creditors and debtors. Until completion of the exchange, the silver one-yen coin was to keep its position as legal tender to an unlimited extent at the rate of one silver one-yen coin for one gold one-yen coin. The suspension of circulation of the silver one-yen coin was to be notified six months in advance by Imperial ordinance. Any of these silver coins not presented for exchange within a period of five full years reckoned from the day on which their circulation was suspended was to be regarded thenceforth as silver bullion. The Bill, if passed, was set to come into operation on 1 October 1897 (its enforcement was indeed started on that day).

Debates in the Imperial Diet

The House of Representatives at the time of the tenth Diet consisted of about 160 members of the ruling party led by the Progressive Party, and about 140 members of the opposition mainly composed of the Liberal Party and the National Association. But dissension was rife among the opposition: in addition to the unfriendly

36 See Yamamoto (1994), p. 144.

37 The difference of opinion between Soeda and Sakatani at that time was plainly and fully mentioned in Soeda's speech in 'the 20th anniversary of enforcement of the gold standard'. See Research Bureau of the Bank of Japan (1957), **17**, p. 657.

relation among the opposition parties, the Liberal Party, the key opposition, was itself split and the risk of dissolution of the party appeared imminent. Therefore the opposition could not join forces to discuss the issue of the change of monetary system.[38] Accordingly, an easy passage was expected for the Bill. The majority of the press also stood behind the government. *The Yomiuri Shinbun* (20 March 1897) expressed its approval of the Bill, describing it as a golden opportunity to change the monetary system and predicting that Japan would gain great profit in the international trade based on the new gold standard system. *The Miyako Shinbun* (4 March 1897) also celebrated the anticipated adoption of the new monetary system, seen as identification with the world great powers.

The discussion on the Bill in the first reading in the House of Representatives started on 3 May 1897, and continued on 10 and 11 March.[39] The Bill was carried in the first reading with a vote of 151 to 96 on 11 March. Immediately following this ballot, the second and third readings were held on the same day (11 May), and the Bill was passed with a large majority in the House of Representatives. The House of Lords, on the other hand, debated only for a few hours on 15 and 23 March and approved the Bill. Tokujiro Obata, a professor of Keio University, was virtually the only opponent to the Bill in the House of Peers.[40] The actual number of debating days totalled only five in both Houses. This prompted the members of the opposition to criticise the hasty and unfair procedures rushed through by the government. Ryoichi Kurihara, for example, accused the government of exploiting non-constitutional measures contrary to parliamentary democracy.[41]

Taguchi's *Tokyo Keizai Zasshi* also scathingly criticised the way the Bill was pushed through virtually without discussion: 'The Monetary Bill submitted by the government was rushed through the Diet at full stretch. Western people would

38 *The Yomiuri Shinbun*, 17 and 20 February 1897.

39 Participants in the debate in the House of Representatives, except the members mentioned in the text, were as follows: Jun Kawashima (see Table 10.9 and Appendix), Shigeoka Kungoro (see Appendix), Buei Nakano (see Appendix), Okindo Abe (1845-1920, former financial official, a leading figure of the cement industry), Iwajiro Obata (1858-1936, a director of the Japan Silk Yarn Association), Heitaro Higashio (1851-1919, a veteran politician, president of a railway corp.), Go Arai (1858-1909, Journalist), Tokitoshi Taketomi (see Appendix), Kanichi Otake (1860-1944, veteran politician), Shigehiro Komuro (1858-1908, journalist), Naonosuke Ban (see Appendix), Takeo Ayai (1860-1916). As government delegates, Tajiri, Sakatani, and Shigeyoshi Matsuo (1843-1916, later the governor of the Bank of Japan, member of the House of Peers, 1900-1916). See *The Proceedings of the House of Representatives of the Imperial Diet* (1980), **12**, pp. 246-363.

40 In the House of Peers, Obata advocated bimetallism just as he had done in the Monetary Commission. Obata argued that the majority in the Commission held the opinion that the current silver standard had brought a great deal of benefit to Japan. If the gold standard were adopted, Japan's principal exports like silk and tea would be placed in a less advantageous position than their Chinese competitors in Western markets. See *The Proceedings of the House of Peers of the Imperial Diet* (1980), pp. 365-7.

41 *The Proceedings of the House of Representatives of the Imperial Diet* (1980), p. 250.

praise ironically that splendid parliamentary proceedings under the ingeniously fabricated and unparalleled Japanese constitution'.[42]

These criticisms mirrored, in a sense, people's strong interest in this Bill. Therefore although the outcome was predictable, 'the seats for the public were full to the doors' at the time Matsukata, the Prime Minister and concurrently finance minister, inaugurated the first day for discussion of the Bill on 3 March 1897.[43]

Matsukata, mindful of Japan's above described gain of a huge amount of gold from China as a war indemnity, directed attention carefully to the cardinal point of his speech: 'The present world has discarded silver and is heading apparently for gold'.[44] His long speech concurred in many respects with Soeda's reply as a government delegate to the members of the House, but what is of interest here is to examine Matsukata's comments on the merits of the change in monetary system. Firstly, he argued, a change in prices would be averted because gold as a standard would bring about price stability. Second, exports would be boosted, because trade transactions with many foreign countries would be facilitated by the gold standard. Third, exchange rate fluctuations would be lessened. Fourth, access to the world's great financial markets would be rendered far easier, thereby strengthening Japan's relations with the international financial market and thus enhancing development of the Japanese economy. Furthermore, these gains would translate into notable profit in the sphere of public finance. Thus, the change in the monetary standard was of 'the uppermost importance for national affairs'.[45]

Soeda's reply as a government delegate mirrored his opinion expressed in the report of the Monetary Commission, but it is of interest here to focus on the following specific points. First he stressed the fact that about 80 per cent of Japanese overseas trade was conducted by foreign dealers in the concessions, because Japanese traders lacked the capacity to deal skilfully with the risk of fluctuation in the foreign exchange rate. Therefore unless the risk involved in exchange rate fluctuations could be averted, Japan would be unable to fully develop her own trade potential. Indeed, Soeda commented, many traders in the treaty ports of Yokohama and others were already doing business with gold for the precise purpose of avoiding this risk. In fact it was no exaggeration to say that out of sheer necessity Japan had already become a virtual gold standard country.

Secondly, Soeda expressed an optimistic view as regards economic competition with Western countries, emphasising Japan's advantages as compared to the West: greater geographic proximity to the Chinese market, and second, the presence of abundant coal and lower wages. Given these favourable conditions, Soeda was convinced Japan would be extremely successful in trade competition with Western countries, provided Japan adopted the same monetary system as its competitors.

Thirdly he argued that introduction of the gold standard would enable Japan to

42 *Tokyo Keizai Zasshi*, n. 857, 13 March 1897.
43 See Miyake (1967), p. 110.
44 *The Proceedings of the House of Representatives of the Imperial Diet* (1980), p. 248.
45 Ibid., p. 250.

purchase machinery at lower prices from Western countries, due to appreciation of the Japanese currency. Furthermore, in anticipation of a future decline in the price of silver against gold in the future, Japan could expect to import industrial materials at a lower price from China, India, and other silver-using countries in Asia, thereby reinforcing a more advantageous trade position.

Finally, Soeda highlighted the fact that the Monetary Bill followed the spirit of the report by the Monetary Commission. While not denying that many supporters of the gold standard in the Commission did not approve an immediate adoption of gold standard, he underlined the changed situation – a sufficient gold reserve as a result of the indemnity from China – that now enabled Japan to implement the gold standard.[46]

Against Soeda, Taguchi expounded his bimetallic persuasion. As a former member of the Progress Party, he had now become an independent in the wake of the difference of opinion on finance policy. Although many aspects of Taguchi's speech mirrored the opinions he expressed in the Monetary Commission, there is one interesting criticism which deserves closer examination. It centres on a risk inherent in the Bill. According to Taguchi, the idea inherent in the Bill was an 'unparalleled gold standard' in the world.[47] That is to say, although the Bill was designed to expel all silver coins and change the current Japanese silver standard immediately into the British-like gold standard, such a system, Taguchi contended, would inevitably result in a bimetallic system practiced by only one country, because Japan was committed to the buying and selling of both gold and silver from the whole of the world for the coming five years, according to the Bill's provision (Article 16). Now the question was, would Japan be able to stand the foreigners' recurrent scramble for her gold and silver in response to the change of their relative prices?[48] Kurihara echoed Taguchi's view in stating that on closer inspection the new Bill would usher in a very dangerous bimetallism to be practiced by Japan alone. This was 'a false gold standard in essence'.[49]

Taguchi gave a more detailed explanation of the risk contained in this Bill as follows: if the price of gold were to fall in the world market, gold coins would flow into Japan from overseas to seek the exchange for relatively appreciated Japanese silver coins, and conversely if the price of silver fell in the worldwide market, silver coins would flow into Japan to seek the exchange for relatively appreciated Japanese gold coins. This predicted a scenario in which Japan was likely to be tossed about for the following five years, if this Monetary Bill were to be enacted. Thus 'it is not the time to reform the current monetary system. It is wise and adequate for Japan to wait for the time at which the exchange rate of gold and silver will get stable'.[50] This conclusion of Taguchi's speech suggests an apparent

46 Ibid., pp. 346-50.
47 Ibid., p. 341.
48 Ibid., pp. 342-3.
49 Ibid., p. 362.
50 Ibid., p. 345.

retreat from his argument in the Monetary Commission, in which he insisted that the Japanese government should make an immediate effort to establish an international bimetallic agreement in order to change the current silver monetary system to a bimetallic system. He now realised the inevitability of the adoption of the gold standard in the Diet, based on the relative strength of the government and the opposition, with the government side clearly outnumbering the opposition. Therefore his criticism now focused on the defect inherent in the Bill on the assumption of its anticipated passing in the Diet.

Problems after the promulgation of the Monetary Law

The new Monetary Law came into effect on 1 October 1897. But shortly before its promulgation, a decree issued on 18 September 1897 stipulated that circulation of the silver one-yen coin was to be prohibited starting from 1 April 1898. A decree of 10 June 1898 then stipulated that the exchange period of the silver one-yen coin would run until July 1898, i.e. for a considerably shorter period than originally anticipated. This new measure partly alleviated the apprehension previously expressed by Taguchi and others.

The total amount of silver coins exported from Japan was estimated to be 110 million yen at the time the Monetary Bill was passed in the Diet. The majority of the coins that had been transferred to China were severely disfigured because of their use as silver bullion. Flawless silver coins certainly circulated in Hong Kong and Singapore, but they constituted a fairly small quantity and were made use of as the local currency. As a result, the total amount of silver coins flown into Japan from overseas between 10 October 1897 and 31 July 1898 was approximately 10 million yen out of 110 million yen previously drained from Japan. Thus one of the great difficulties accompanying the enforcement of the gold standard, namely, the backward movement of drained silver to Japan, was concluded without difficulties. Taguchi's apprehension of a rapid influx of silver in pursuit of exchange for gold for five years after enactment of the Bill proved to be unfounded. The gold standard Japan adopted did not plunge into 'an unparalleled bimetallism'. The period of exchange of silver for gold was accomplished in a far speedier manner than Taguchi anticipated. The government's decision to enter the club of advanced Western powers seemed to bring about this speedy transaction, and confuted the apprehension felt by bimetallists and some gold monometallists who were cautious of immediate adoption of the gold standard.

Concluding remarks

Why did Japan discard the silver standard although substantial benefits had been accomplished by the silver currency? Bimetallists and silver monometallists were predominant in business and academic world, and a similar situation was reflected in the opinions of members of the Monetary Commission. Nonetheless the gold standard was enacted in the tenth Diet of 1897.

The most important underlying reason lay in the fact that the falling silver price across the world had evidently adversely affected the Japanese economy. The bimetallists, who frequently adduced arguments taken from bimetallic discussions and bimetallic movements in Western countries, particularly in Britain, claimed that the bimetallic system was far better than the gold standard. But as bimetallists abroad lost momentum faced with the continuing decline in the price of silver, the line of reasoning championed by their Japanese counterparts correspondingly lost persuasiveness.

The most powerful driving force urging adoption of the gold standard came from the Ministry of Finance, especially Matsukata and his officials, i.e., mainly Sakatani and Soeda. They stressed that Japan needed to purchase capital goods and war supplies from Western gold-using countries. The so-called 'Post-war Management' accelerated this tendency which, interpreted in popular terminology, was understood as implying the need to reinforce military power and modernise Japan's economic structure so that the country would be protected against any further humiliation by the Western powers (especially Russia, Germany and France) that had forced Japan to abandon the occupancy of the Liaotung Peninsula after the Sino-Japanese War. For successful achievement of the management, the current silver standard was apparently against Japanese interests, since it would lead Japan into increasing payment for purchases from Western countries, particularly from Britain.

Japan also earnestly aimed to bring in foreign loans with the same monetary system as that which prevailed in Western countries. Foreign loans were expected to invest in the expansion of armaments, the development of heavy industries, enhancement of transportation and communication networks, extension of public education, and so forth. But the most notable occasion for the importation of foreign loans was displayed in the procurement of the war expenditure during the Russo-Japanese War (1904-5). The Japanese government succeeded in raising a public loan of 15.6 hundred million yen to finance the war, of which about 50 per cent (eight hundred million yen, or 82 million pounds) was raised in Britain and the United States.

The above described practical reasons were indisputably connected with the catch-phrase Japan had nurtured since the Meiji Restoration (1868): 'a rich nation and a strong army'. The change-over to the gold standard was regarded as a major requisite in order to enter the civilised club composed of great Western powers. As *The Economist* wrote, Japan moved forwards 'to be regarded as a first-class Power' by means of the transformation of her currency to the same standard of value as other first-class powers.[51] Even most bimetallists or anti-gold monometallists probably found this aspect symbolised by the adoption of the gold standard to be highly persuasive. Thus the devastating decline in the price of silver and a Japanese

51 'The Gold Standard in Japan', *The Economist*, 24 April 1897.

dream cherished ever since the beginning of modernisation, 'a rich nation and a strong army', swept away the anti-gold monometallist idea.

Governmental officials in the Ministry of Finance, in their role as bureaucratic economists, undoubtedly shaped ideas in the background leading up to the parliamentary debate on adoption of the gold standard, leaving the political manoeuvre within and outside the Diet to Matsukata, who was one of the most influential clan oligarchs. This foreshowed the significance of their role in economic debates and policy making for coming decades.

References and selected bibliography

Darwin, M.L. (1898), *Bimetallism; A Summary and Examination of the Arguments for and against a Bimetallic System of Currency*, D. Appleton & Company, New York.

Droppers, D. (1898), 'Monetary Changes in Japan', *Quarterly Journal of Economics*, **12** (January), pp. 153-85.

Fetter, F.W. (1980), *The Economist in Parliament, 1780-1868*, Duke University Press, Durham, NC.

Fraser, A., Mason, R.H.P. and Mitchell, P. (1995), *Japan's Early Parliaments, 1890-1905: Structure, Issues and Trends*, Routledge, London and New York.

Gallarotti, G.M. (1993), 'The Scramble for Gold: Monetary Regime Transformation in the 1870s', in M.D. Bordo and F. Capie (eds), *Monetary Regimes in Transition*, Cambridge University Press, Cambridge, pp. 15-67.

The History of Meiji Finance (1971), ed. by the Compiling Society of the History of Meiji Finance, **2**, Yoshikawa Kobunkan, Tokyo (in Japanese).

Ito, T. (1993), *The Japanese Economy*, The MIT Press, Cambridge, MA, and London.

Kumagai, J. (1998), 'Enlightenment and Economic Thought in Meiji Japan: Yukichi Fukuzawa and Ukichi Taguchi', in S. Sugihara and T. Tanaka (eds), *Economic Thought and Modernization in Japan*, Edward Elgar, Cheltenham and Northampton, pp. 23-43.

Kumagai, J. (2001), 'Orchestrating Economic Ideas: the Formation and Development of Economic Societies in Modern Japan', in M.M. Augello and M.E.L. Guidi (eds), *The Spread of Political Economy and the Professionalisation of Economists. Economic Societies in Europe, America and Japan in the Nineteenth Century*, Routledge, London, pp. 200-15.

Masumi, J. (1988), *The Japanese History of Politics*, 4 Vols, Tokyo University Press, Tokyo (in Japanese).

Miyake, S. (1967), *A Contemporary History,* **3**, Iwanami Shoten, Tokyo (in Japanese).

Nakamura, T. (1985), 'The Adoption of the Gold Standard', in T. Nakamura, *Economy of Meiji and Taisho Era*, Tokyo University Press, Tokyo (in Japanese), pp. 62-77.

Okada, S. (1975), *A Study of the History of Monetary Controversy in Meiji Era*, Chikura Shobo, Tokyo (in Japanese).

One Hundred-Year History of the Japanese Diet (1985), ed. by the Compiling Society of the History of Japanese Diets, **1**, Kokkai Hyakunenshi Kankokai, Tokyo (in Japanese).

One Hundred-Year History of Tokyo University, History of Departments, (1986), ed. by the Publishing Committee of One Hundred Years' History of Tokyo University, **1**, Tokyo University Press, Tokyo (in Japanese).

Ono, K. (2000), 'The Formative Process of the Gold Standard in Japan' in *The Collected Writings of Kazuichiro Ono*, **1**, *Modern Japanese Monetary System and Silver Sphere in the East Asia*, Minerva Shobo, Kyoto (in Japanese), pp. 173-238.

The Proceedings of the House of Representatives of the Imperial Diet (1980), **12**, Tokyo University Press, Tokyo (in Japanese).

The Proceedings of the House of Peers of the Imperial Diet (1980), **12**, Tokyo University Press, Tokyo (in Japanese).

Research Bureau of the Bank of Japan (1957), *Documentations of Japanese Financial History: Meiji and Taisho Period*, **16**, Printing Board of the Finance Ministry, Tokyo (in Japanese).

Research Bureau of the Bank of Japan (1957), *Documentations of Japanese Financial History: Meiji and Taisho Period*, **17**, Printing Board of the Finance Ministry, Tokyo (in Japanese).

Research Bureau of the Bank of Japan (1958), *Documentations of Japanese Financial History: Meiji and Taisho Period*, **4**, Printing Board of the Finance Ministry, Tokyo (in Japanese).

Redich, A. (2000), *Bimetallism: An Economic and Historical Analysis*, Cambridge University Press, Cambridge.

Soyeda [Soeda], J. (1894), 'Letter from Japan: The Depreciation of Silver and the Imperial Commission', *Economic Journal*, **4**(December), pp. 730-32.

Soyeda [Soeda], J. (1895), 'Letter from Japan: The Imperial Commission on the Silver Question in Japan' *Economic Journal*, **5**(December), pp. 662-63.

Soyeda [Soeda], J. (1899), 'Letter from Japan: The Adoption of the Gold Standard', *Economic Journal*, **9**(September), pp. 469-75.

Sugiyama, C. and Mizuta. H. (1988) (eds), *Enlightenment and Beyond: Political Economy Comes to Japan*, Tokyo University Press, Tokyo.

Tamaki, N. (1988), 'Economists in Parliament: The Fall of Bimetallism in Japan', in Sugiyama and Mizuta (1988), pp. 223-36.

Walker, F.A. (1896), *International Bimetallism*, H. Holt, New York; reprint, Augustus M. Kelley, New York 1971.

Wilson, T. (2000), *Battles for the Standard: Bimetallism and the Spread of the Gold Standard in the Nineteenth Century*, Ashgate, Aldershot and Burlington.

Yamamoto, Y. (1994), 'Arguments of the Gold and Silver Standards' in Y. Yamamoto, *From Ryo to Yen: A Study of Monetary Problem of the Late Tokugawa and Early Meiji Era*, Minerva, Kyoto (in Japanese), pp. 113-57.

Appendix

Table 10.2 Economists in the Japanese Diet (1890-1930)

Name and life	Education	Representative	Peer	Remarks
Amano, Tameyuki 1860-1938	Tokyo University	1890-1892	–	Professor at Waseda University. Exponent of J.S. Mill Principles
Ban, Naonosuke * 1862-1937	Dojinsha school, Tokyo	1894-1898	–	Editor of the *Tokyo Economist.* Founder of railway Corps
Hamaguchi, Osachi 1870-1931	Tokyo University	1915-1931	–	As Prime Minister, he enforced the return to gold standard (Jan. 1930)
Hara, Takashi * 1856-1921	Judicial School of Minister of Justice	1902-1921	–	Governmental official of foreign affairs and commerce. Prime Minister (1918-21)
Inoue, Junnosuke 1869-1932	Tokyo Univ. Studies in Britain and Belgium	–	1924-1932	As Finance Minister, he enforced the return to gold standard. (Jan. 1930)
Inoue, Kakugoro 1859-1938	Keio Gijuku School	1890-1924	–	Journalist. Vice-president of Tokyo Chamber of Commerce
Inukai, Tsuyoshi 1855-1932	Keio Gijuku School	1890-1932	–	Editor of a protectionist journal. As Prime Minister, he suspended gold standard (1931)
Kataoka, Naoharu 1859-1934	Normal school, Kochi	1892-1930, with short breaks	1930-1934	President of the Nihon Life Insurance. Finance Minister (1926-27)
Kawashima, Jun * 1847-1911	Studies in Germany	1890-1898	1903-1911	Governmental official of Finance Ministry. Diplomat. President of the Kangyou Bank
Kawata, Koichiro * 1836-1896	–	–	1890-1896	Mitsubishi Corp. Governor of the Bank of Japan
Kega, Kanju 1874-1944	Keio University. Studies in Germany	1917-1920	–	Prof. of the Keio University

Name and life	Education	Representative	Peer	Remarks
Kobayashi, Ushisaburo 1866-1930	Tokyo University	1915-1917	–	Professor of public finance at Senshu University
Kurihara, Ryoichi 1855-1911	Some juku schools in Tokyo	1890-1898	1903-1911	Journalist. Counselor of Ministry of Finance
Maeda, Masana 1850-1921	Studies in France	–	1890-1897, 1904-1921	Governmental official in agriculture
Machida, Chuji 1863-1946	Tokyo University	1912-1920, 1924-1946	–	Founder of the *Oriental Economist*. Minister of Finance (1934-36)
Matsukata, Masayoshi 1835-1924	–	–	1890-1924	Eminent financier. Finance Minister five times. Prime Minister twice
Matsumoto, Kunpei 1870-1944	Studies in USA	1904-1912, 1920-1930	–	Journalist in USA, Japan, and China. Ph D. from Brown University. Writings on economics
Mitsuchi, Chuzo 1871-1948	Higher normal school. Studies in Britain	1908-1942	1946-1947	Finance Minister in the late 1920s. Critical of balanced financial policy
Muto, Sanji 1867-1934	Keio Gijuku School. Studies in USA	1924-1932	–	President of the Kanegafuchi Spinning Corp. Famous for paternal manager
Nakano, Buei * 1848-1918	Domain College in Takamatsu	1890-1903, 1908-1912	–	President of the Kansai Railway. President of Tokyo Chamber of Commerce
Obata, Tokujiro * 1842-1905	Keio Gijuku School	–	1890-1905	President of the Keio University. Translator. of W. Ellice, F. Wayland, etc.
Ogawa, Gotaro 1896-1945	Tokyo Univ. Studies in Germany, Austria, Italy	1917-1920, 1924-1945	–	Professor of public finance at Kyoto University. Vice-minister of Finance Ministry.
Onozuka, Kiheiji 1870-1944	Tokyo University. Studies in Germany, France, Switzerland	–	1898-1915	Professor of Tokyo University. An original member of the Social Policy Association
Ooishi, Masami 1855-1935	Risshisha School, Tosa	1898-1915	–	Minister of Agriculture and Trade (1897)
Sakatani, Yoshiro * 1863-1914	Tokyo University	–	1917-1941	Governmental official of finance. Finance Minister (1906-08)

Name and life	Education	Representative	Peer	Remarks
Seki, Hajime 1873-1935	Tokyo Higher Comm. Studies in Belgium	–	1934-1935	Prof. of Tokyo Higher Commerce. Mayor of Osaka City
Shiba, Shiro 1852-1922	Daigaku Nanko (later Tokyo Univ.). Studies in USA	1892-1917, with short breaks	–	Political novelist. Vice-minister of Agriculture and Commerce. National economist
Shibusawa, Eiichi * 1840-1913	Studies in various European countries	–	1890-1891	Governmental official of finance. Leader of Japanese capitalism
Shigeoka, Kungoro * 1862-1906	Judicial School of Ministry of Justice. Studies in France	1894-1906	–	Judge. Professor at Third Higher School (Kyoto)
Shoda, Kazue 1869-1948	Tokyo University	–	1914-1946	Governmental official of finance. Finance Minister (1916-1918, 1924)
Soeda, Juichi * 1864-1929	Tokyo University. Studies in Britain	–	1925-1929	Governmental official of finance. President of several influential banks
Suzuki, Bunji 1885-1946	Tokyo University	1928-1930, 1936-1942	–	Founder of Friendly Society
Taguchi, Ukichi * 1855-1905	School of translation bureau of Fin. Min.	1894-1905	–	Founder of the *Tokyo Economist*. Advocate of the Manchester school and laissez-faire
Tajiri, Inejiro * 1850-1923	Daigaku Nanko (later Tokyo Univ.). Studies in USA	–	1891-1901, 1908-1923	Vice-minister of Finance. Professor of public finance at Tokyo University
Takada, Sanae * 1860-1938	Tokyo University	1890-1898, 1902-1904	1915-1938	President of Waseda University
Takahashi, Korekiyo 1854-1936	Kaisei School (later Tokyo Univ.). Studies in USA	1924-1928	1905-1924	Prime Minister (1921-1922). As Finance Minister, he suspended gold standard (1931)
Taketomi, Tokitoshi 1855-1938	Daigaku Nanmon (later Tokyo Univ.)	1890-1894, with short breaks	1924-1938	Governmental official of finance. Finance Minister (1914-1916)

Name and life	Education	Representative	Peer	Remarks
Tokutomi, Soho 1863-1957	Doshisha English School	–	1911-1946	Founder of the *Nation's Friend.* Liberal later converted to imperialism
Tomita, Tetsunosuke 1835-1916	Studies in USA	–	1890-1916	Introducer of H.C. Carey and F. List. Governor of the Bank of Japan
Tsuda, Mamichi 1829-1902	Studies in Holland	1890-1894	1896-1903	Professor of Institute of Bakufu. Thinker of Meiji enlightenment
Wakatsuki, Reijiro 1866-1949	Tokyo University	–	1911-1947	Governmental official of finance. Finance Minister several times. Prime Minister (1926-1927, 1931)
Watanabe, Jinkichi * 1856-1925	Training school of banking in Finance Ministry	–	1902-1903	Silk manufacturer and banker. Local leader of business
Watanabe, Koki * 1848-1901	Keio Gijuku School, and others	1892-1894	1897-1901	Governmental official of finance. President of Tokyo University. Governor of Tokyo City
Yamamoto, Tatsuo 1856-1947	Keio University	–	1903-1947	Governor of the Bank of Japan. Minister of Agriculture and Commerce several times

Source: The House of Representatives and Councilors, *Seventy-Year History of the Diet System*, **12** vols (in Japanese), Tokyo, 1960-1963; *List of Members of the House of Representatives*, **11**, 1962 (in Japanese); *List of Members of the House of Peers and Councilors*, **1**, Tokyo, 1960 (in Japanese).

Note: * Member of the Monetary Commission, and / or participant in the debate on the monetary system in the 10th Diet.

Chapter 11

The American Anomaly: Why were there no Economists in the US Congress?

Bradley W. Bateman

Introduction

All across Europe in the nineteenth century, economists ran for and were elected to Parliament. Massimo Augello and Marco Guidi, the editors of this volume, have uncovered a fascinating moment in the history of economic ideas, and the chapters in this volume show the many social, cultural, moral, and intellectual reasons that this incursion of economists into elected office took place. The European economists who were elected to office did not champion only one set of economic ideas, of course, and they were not always successful in their attempts to legislate new rules for their emerging national economies. Still, there is at least some kind of pattern to the ambitions and careers of these European economists; as feudalism faded, and industrialism emerged, these men were interested in helping to define the newly emerging economic order.

Oddly, there is no similar phenomenon in the United States. Not only were economists not elected to office, there was no large scale movement by American economists to seek election to Congress in the nineteenth century. There was only one prominent economist elected to the US Congress then, and he was elected in a special election to fill an empty seat in the lower house. When Amasa Walker was elected to the House of Representatives in 1862 as a Republican, he served three months and three days, from 1 December 1862 until 3 March 1863, when his term expired. Walker had held other, state-level offices in Massachusetts, including the very prestigious position of being a member of the Electoral College, the group that casts the votes that decide who is elected President.[1] But, while he had a political career and served in Congress, it is clear that he was asked to serve in the Congress to fill a need of his party. He did not seek re-election, and, in fact, never held another elected office.[2]

---

1 It is, for instance, the Electoral College that elected George W. Bush as the President in 2000, even though Al Gore had received 500,000 more votes in the popular election.

2 For the best treatment of Walker's career, see Dorfman (1949). Walker was the father of

It is not the case, of course, that American economists were not interested in questions of public policy, or the key debates in Congress. Almost everyone in the United States who was identified as an economist held strong views about the key issues of the day. Throughout the nineteenth century and into the second decade of the twentieth century, the United States did not have a central bank, and for most of this period did not have a uniform national currency. In this environment, Americans debated many questions about currency and the banking system: Who should issue currency? Should the currency be backed by gold? Should it be backed by silver? Should it be backed by both gold and silver? Who should charter banks? How should banking be regulated, if at all?

The only other economic issue that might have generated as much controversy as money and banking was the question of the tariff: Should there be a tariff? Should the tariff be a minimal tariff that would be used to generate revenue for the federal government? Or should there be a protective tariff that would be used to support and encourage domestic manufacturers?

In addition to questions about money, banking, and the tariff, there were a steady stream of questions about the rights of labourers; these questions only intensified after the Civil War (1861-1865) when the second industrial revolution began and vertical integration drastically increased the number of factory workers.

In addition to questions about the rights of white workers, there were also questions about America's black population. Before the Civil War, there was debate about the status of the slaves. After the War, there was debate about the status of the freedmen. Should the freedmen being given land as compensation for their former treatment? Should they be educated by the State? What rights did they have as workers and citizens?

And yet, despite all this debate, and all the many positions taken by economists, there was no widespread movement for economists to enter Congress.

The purpose of this chapter, then, is to explore the question why the situation in the United States was so different from that in Europe. Why were there no economists in Congress?

Institutional background

Perhaps the most obvious place to look for an explanation of the different public role of economists in the United States would be to consider that America has never had a parliamentary system. Unlike the modern European nations, America has always had a system in which the chief executive of the nation, the President, is elected separately from the legislature, the Congress. The President also serves as the head of State in addition to being the chief executive officer; thus, there is no

---

Francis Amasa Walker who became the first president of the American Economic Association and served for many years as the president of the Massachusetts Institute of Technology.

Prime Minister in the United States, and the party that controls the legislature, the Congress, is not necessarily the party that controls the executive. This complicated system (by European standards) means that the party in control of the legislature does not have absolute control over the creation of new laws; although they may write and pass legislation, the Congress cannot necessarily depend on the President to sign the legislation into Law. This inability to guarantee that legislation passed by the Congress will be signed into Law is a part of the 'checks and balances' that were written into the American constitution in the eighteenth century in an attempt to force parties to make compromises and to prevent authoritarian rule.

Perhaps, then, it is simply the fact of the difference in the institutional structure of the legislatures in America and Europe that explains the difference that we are exploring? Perhaps it is the relatively weaker role of the legislature in the United States that explains the lack of interest on the part of economists in serving in Congress? Perhaps the 'inefficiency' of the American system of checks and balances led them not to seek office?

Despite the significant differences in the role and power of the legislature in European nations and in America, it is difficult to imagine *a priori* that these changes can account for the different public role of economists in America. On the one hand, European legislatures make compromises and have their own inefficiencies; not least because of the frequent need to forge coalitions of different parties in order to form a government. On the other hand, whatever the 'inefficiencies' in Congress, it would still be the place that economists would have to become involved if their purpose was to take a personal role in shaping economic legislation. But we do not have to answer this question on *a priori* grounds. If we examine nineteenth-century American economic writings, we do not find any major stream in that literature which complains of the 'inefficiency' of Congress on the grounds of its organisation. Nor are there significant personal testimonies of frustration with the possibility of service in Congress. Thus, we must look elsewhere for an explanation of the absence of economists from direct involvement in the American legislative process.

Another institutional possibility for helping to understand this American anomaly might be to consider the actual relationship between the Presidency and Congress that quickly evolved under the American constitution. Although the system was designed to provide checks and balances between the branches of government, there has been a persistent tendency over time for either the President or the Congress to garner more power.[3] In fact, for much of American history, it has been the President who has wielded the greater power. This would appear to return us to our previous question whether the relative weakness of Congress made service there unattractive. Ironically, however, the one period when Congress wielded greater power than the President was in the decades immediately following the American Civil War, when a President was impeached for the first time (Andrew Johnson in

3 See Sundquist (1981) for an excellent treatment of the changing balance of power between the President and the Congress.

1866) and Congress became the site where the battles of Reconstruction and the political future of the freed slaves were fought.[4] The irony that this period would have been the time of the weak Presidency and a strong Congress is that it was during this same time that the greatest surge in European economists serving in Parliament occurred and when the United States, like Europe, was engaged in the massive dislocations of the second industrial revolution. If ever there was a time when economic transition and changing industrial structure might have drawn economists into service, one would have expected it to have been at this very time when Congress was in the ascendant. But it did not happen. American economists still remained out of Congress, just as they had during the first half of the nineteenth century.

Thus, it does not seem to be either the nature of the American constitution or the particular roles of the Congress and the Presidency that have kept American economists out of the legislature.

The importance of ideas and the unimportance of intellectuals

If the answer to our question does not lie in the structure of American government or the actual ways that power is distributed in the system, perhaps it is best to look for a larger cultural or sociological explanation. In this realm, the first answer to suggest itself would almost certainly be the tradition of American anti-intellectualism. From the earliest days of the republic, in the late eighteenth century, Americans, as a whole, have demonstrated a strong and persistent inclination to disparage academic learning and the life of the mind.[5]

But American anti-intellectualism is an easy concept to misconstrue. Americans in the nineteenth century may not have liked *intellectuals*, but they very much liked *ideas*. Thus, while it seems prudent to acknowledge that anti-intellectualism may well have played a role in making a career in Congress seem undesirable, or unlikely, to early American economists, I would also like to make a counter-point that the strong role played by *ideas* in nineteenth-century America was an inextricable part of the reason why economists did not seek elected office in the legislature. For ironically, while intellectuals were not well-respected in many arenas of American life, the vast majority of the people who were disrespectful of scholarly accomplishment and critical thought were animated by a very well-articulated *idea*, republicanism, and this same idea was also at the heart of the work of American economists of all stripes in the nineteenth century.[6]

In its American form, republicanism had its basis in the idea of free men working in free markets. The traditional, European ideal of republican rule at this time,

---

4 See Foner (1984).

5 The classic treatment of American anti-intellectualism is Hofstadter (1963). A related and revealing study is Hatch (1989).

6 See Cohen (2002); Burke (1995); and Foner (1970).

which could be traced back to antiquity in, for instance, Aristotle's political writings, had envisaged a republic as a *polis* led by an elite. This elite might be defined by birth, by wealth, or by education, but it was not a democratic body in the modern sense. The new form of republicanism that arose in America in the early years of the nation eschewed the idea that the rulers of the republic would come from an elite, and argued instead that the common people would select their own rulers and that these popularly elected leaders would hold authority only insofar as they had the support of the electorate.[7] The American republic was not to have a natural aristocracy; all citizens were to be eligible to be leaders. Citizenship in the republic was, in turn, taken to be based on the ability of each man to work with his own hands and, through the fruits of his own labours, to build enough capital to buy land and establish himself as a landowner and capitalist. Not everyone could *come* into the world as a capitalist, of course, but it was taken as axiomatic that everyone could *become* one.

This belief led to the frequent argument in the American economic literature of the nineteenth century that there was no group that could rightfully be called a labouring class in America; according to this argument, all Americans were producers because all laboured in some way to build their fortune.[8] In this republican schema, the fundamental and very important ideal of *equality* was taken to be a referent of the citizen's *opportunities*, but not to a guarantee of a particular *outcome*. Character, luck, and hard work were all understood to help determine how one came out in life's game, but everyone deserved the right to try to make his own fortune.

The ideas of equality of opportunity and fairness helped to create a culture in which capitalism had a strong social warrant, but a warrant that was qualified in an interesting way: success was respected, but privilege was not. One the one hand, the ideas seemed to speak very clearly to the millions who threw over their lives in Europe or on the eastern seaboard of the United States and pioneered on the western frontier of the new nation. The republican ideal was taught in the small one room school houses in rural New England and the Midwestern prairies not because any central authority dictated that it be taught, but because the pioneers, who controlled the schools themselves, believed in its efficacy and wanted their children to share this belief. On the other hand, the republican ideal offered cold comfort to anyone who did come into the world with the privilege of wealth or position. The republican ideal was clearly pro-business and made capitalism a widely shared ideal among the citizens of the early American republic, but it also served rhetorically as a rallying cry against aristocracy, monopoly, and sinecure.[9]

In other words, the republican ideal helped to propagate a strong belief in *laissez-faire* much like the argument that Adam Smith had made in the *Wealth of Nations*: the nation would prosper if the government stood back and allowed

---

7 See Appleby (1984) for a succinct discussion of the emergence of the new "democratic" republicanism in the United States.

8 See Burke (1995).

9 See Dorfman (1949, p. ix).

people to pursue their own self interest, with the important caveat that to ensure the freedom of opportunity, the government would have to avoid granting monopoly privileges to anyone. And, as in Adam Smith's arguments, all of this was underpinned by a deep belief in the inviolability of labour and the right of each person to the fruits of his own labour.

But if Smith's intuition was widely respected by the economists of nineteenth-century America, their true lode stars were two French economists: Jean-Baptiste Say and Frédéric Bastiat. Say's *Treatise on Political Economy* (1803, trans. 1821) was widely used in American colleges and universities in the first half of the nineteenth century.[10] Bastiat was especially influential among American writers because his *Economic Harmonies* (1850) gave them a rhetoric for arguing that a system of *laissez-faire* could work out in the best interests of everyone.[11] The harmony that Bastiat argued would result from the unfettered market system was seen as much preferable to the class conflict thought to be suggested by Smith's successors in the tradition of English political economy, such as Ricardo. Amasa Walker, who had served three months in Congress, and whose *Science of Wealth* was one of the most popular textbooks in antebellum America, was only one of many American economists who placed Bastiat's harmonies at the centre of his system of analysis.

In the end, then, American economists throughout most of the nineteenth century were dedicated to the same economic ideas as the general populace. As Joseph Dorfman has argued in his masterpiece of American economic ideas, *The Economic Mind in American Civilization*, in the first seven decades of the nineteenth century there was no serious dissent among mainstream American economists about the efficacy of *laissez-faire*, the rights of labour, or the dream of the common man working to become a capitalist.[12] This nexus of ideas also had serious appeal with the voting public. While there were nascent labour unions in this period and intense debate about the national debt and the currency (which had still not been established on a national basis), there was no successful electoral alternative to *laissez-faire* and republicanism.

Ironically, the power of the republican ideal might be most clear in the work of the most well-known and influential American economist of the nineteenth century, Henry Carey. Born the son of Matthew Carey, a well-known and very successful publisher in Philadelphia, Henry Carey followed his father into the family publishing business, where he, too, became quite successful. Carey used his position and influence to publish his opinions on economic issues in a series of books, and he was the first American economist to have a 'school of disciples'. On first sight, it is almost unimaginable that Carey would be a proponent of republicanism,

10 As Burke (1995) notes, Adam Smith took some time to become widely accepted in the United States because his depiction of the clergy as 'unproductive labor' was initially taken as anti-clerical and irreligious by many American readers.

11 Ibid., p. 50.

12 Ibid., pp. 48-9.

or its associated ideals; he was after all, born to wealth, the scion of a large and successful business, and is most famous for his advocacy of a high protective tariff.[13] Thus he seems to be the epitome of an anti-republican, or of a republican in the older European sense.

But while the case for seeing Carey as an elite apologist for economic privilege can easily be made, his writings are all couched in carefully crafted republican rhetoric. His argument that American industry needs to be protected by a tariff is directed with venom against the 'monopolists' in England. The purpose of the tariff, in Carey's mind, is to allow for 'true competition' in the American market, where the interests of the workers and owners, against the British monopolists is repeated *ad nauseam*. Carey never argues for capitalists without insisting that the real purpose of his policies is to protect the American worker. Thus, Carey, the son of privilege whose interests would eventually move beyond publishing to include iron manufacturing, understood that to make his ideas appealing to the larger public, he had to wrap them in the republican rhetoric of the times.[14]

Thus, while the argument that anti-intellectualism may explain why American economists did not serve in Congress is almost certainly an important part of the story, there is more to the story than simple anti-intellectualism. While it is very likely that economists living in an anti-intellectual culture felt unelectable, the reality is more complex. The force of the republican ideal and its corollaries (e.g., *laissez-faire*, respect for labourers, and a general distrust of monopoly and sinecure) provided a popular ideal that permeated the writings of economists on all sides of the major issues. In the main thrust of their ideas, American economists in the nineteenth century were widely in agreement with their fellow citizens about the most desirable type of political economy: free market republicanism.

Even Carey, who advocated a protective tariff, always insisted that his ideas be labelled 'free market' since, he could legitimately point out, he was trying to subvert (British) monopoly power and ensure free competition in *American* markets. In an anti-intellectual culture, economists on both sides of the important contemporary issues agreed with the anti-intellectuals about the most important ideas about the economy. In this sense, economists did not need to run for Congress to see that their larger agenda for the emerging economy was implemented. Any American economist elected to Congress would have been bound to argue for a free market position, but that position was already well-represented in Congress.

Unlike the European case, where economists often represented a uniquely liberal voice in the emerging industrial nations, American economists did not have a special role to play as voices for *laissez-faire* and liberal ideas in their young republic. If elected, they would have had strong disagreements about the best

---

13 Carey advocated a lighter, 'revenue tariff' early in his career but converted to a higher, protective tariff later in his career.

14 Dorfman (1946) notes Carey's tendency to always phrase his arguments in a rhetoric that seems inimicable to his position.

policies to protect competition, such as the size of the tariff, but they virtually all would have agreed on the basic principle of free market capitalism.

The professionalisation of economics

But even if this similarity in cultural/political outlook between American economists and their fellow citizens gives us some insight into the answer to our question about why they did not serve in Congress, it cannot be the only reason that they did not serve in Congress. Another obvious place to look in trying to determine other reasons why the experience of American economists was so different from the experience of their European counterparts would be to consider the differences between the United States and the emerging European democracies in the professionalisation of economists.[15]

One very obvious difference in professionalisation, and one which we should not overlook, is that in many European nations nineteenth-century economists found their professional homes in faculties of law. In many of the European countries discussed in this volume, economics was first taught as an academic discipline in faculties of law and the other chapters detail how the first academic positions for European economists were often in these faculties. As we shall see, this was not the case in America. American economists did not commonly have professional homes in law schools until the second half of the twentieth century, after the 'law and economics' explosion expanded out of its early home at the University of Chicago. Thus, unlike their European counterparts, American economists in nineteenth century were not engaged in their daily professional lives with people who taught and studied law and this may have made them less likely to consider entering the arena of elective politics where they could work to create laws. American economists in the nineteenth century were not in the same position as European economists and so may not have developed the same ambitions.

But if American economists in the nineteenth century were not housed in faculties of law, where were they housed? There is not one answer to this question, and the answer changes as we move through the century.

In the first two decades of the nineteenth century, there were not really any professional economists in America. There had, of course, always been economic debate and public discussion of economic ideas, but the generally accepted date for the beginning of systematic writing on the economy in America is taken to be 1820.[16] But even then, the people who did the writing came from different backgrounds and occupied different professions. Many of the people who were identified as economists in the nineteenth century were journalists; at least one of them

15 See Furner (1976) and Ross (1991) for standard treatments of the professionalisation of American economics. Barber (2003) provides an excellent summary.

16 This is the date given in both Dorfman (1949) and in Conkin (1981).

was an underemployed lawyer; a large number of these early economists were businessmen who wrote pamphlets and opinion pieces for newspapers.

Until late in the century, there were very few economists employed in colleges and universities. Economics was taught almost exclusively as a part of a moral philosophy class (see below), but not as a separate subject that the students could study throughout their undergraduate careers. Perhaps the most common profession for the earliest textbook writers was Protestant minister. This is not as surprising as it may sound. One reason that Protestant ministers wrote about the economy is that the American republican ideal had always been intimately intertwined with Protestantism.[17] From the time that the Puritans had colonised Massachusetts in the early seventeenth century, there had been a strong tendency among Protestants to link personal and political freedom to the Protestant revolution in Europe. The belief that American political freedom was part of a covenant with the Christian God was still widespread in the nineteenth century, and these ministers were merely extending the argument to include commercial freedom with the other freedoms that God granted to Americans.

The two most well-known authors in this Protestant tradition were Francis Wayland and John MacVickar. Wayland, an ordained Baptist minister, was the author of *Elements of Political Economy*, the most widely used textbook in American colleges before the Civil War. His success as a text book writer was also influenced by his second (related) profession as a college president (chancellor). At this time, most American colleges and universities were either affiliated with a Christian church or included Christian topics in their basic curriculum and so the president was often an ordained clergyman. In the last term of each student's undergraduate career, it was the standard practice that he would take a course on moral philosophy from the president of the college and Wayland's book was widely used as the text for this course. The text allowed the president and his students to study the 'harmonies' of a free enterprise economy and so prepare them for entering their post-graduate business careers.

Early American economists like Francis Wayland and Amasa Walker, who had academic appointments, pointed the way toward what would become the standard employment of professional economists only in the last three decades of the nineteenth century; but at the start of the American Civil War (1861), university appointments were still not the norm by any means.

When economics did finally begin to be more widely institutionalised in the American universities at the end of the century, it brought about an unpredictable set of events that only further reduced the likelihood that an economist would serve in Congress. On the surface, it might seem likely that the path to professionalisation in the colleges and universities would lead to more explicit political activity on the European model because the Americans who initially filled these posts were trained in the universities in Germany. The first generation of Americans to earn the German doctorate, such as John Bates Clark, Richard T. Ely, and Simon Nelson

---

17 See Marty (1984) and Hatch (1989).

Patten, travelled to Germany in the 1860s and 1870s for their professional training, and they came home deeply committed to using their knowledge to improve American society. But rather than seeking elective office, most of them spent the early years of their careers struggling to hold on to their new academic posts.

The struggle to find and keep an academic position was dictated by the particular way that they translated their new knowledge into action. Clark, Ely, and Patten all committed themselves to some form of Christian socialism in the early years of their careers. They took the native connection between Christianity and the polity seriously and so turned the traditional 'evangelical *laissez-faire*' argument on its head and produced a rhetoric of a Christian State designed to create justice and opportunity for the working class.[18] But the basic story is incontrovertible; the young economists were put under tremendous pressure by the boards of trustees at their respective universities and by the popular press. In essence, they were forced to choose between staying in academe and teaching or holding onto their advocacy of a nascent labour movement. If they wanted to keep their academic careers, they would have to give up their positions on labour. Some chose to migrate to sociology where their ideas were not considered as dangerous, but those who stayed in economics all gave up their open advocacy of labour rights in the 1880s and 1890s.

The young 'ethical economists' who were disciplined by their university trustees had originally tried to create some leverage for themselves through the creation of the American Economic Association in 1885 under the leadership of Richard T. Ely. But their effort was not enough to protect them. On the one hand, the trustees and university presidents held all the trump cards. There was no tenure in American universities until third decade of the twentieth century, and so academics at this time served at the pleasure of their administrators and governing bodies. On the other hand, several of the AEA's founders, such as J.B. Clark, Patten, and Henry Carter Adams, realised almost immediately that for the organisation to have any leverage they needed to attract the older generation of *laissez-faire* economists to join. Thus, within a few years, the group had dropped the wording in its founding documents about their desire for finding a positive role for the State in helping to manage the economy and opened their doors to economists of all stripes.

It is undeniable that the efforts of the younger economists to attract the older economists, and the willingness of the older economists to join the AEA marked the moment at which modern American economics was finally formed. With each passing year, the organisation would become more and more populated by academic economists, and the group's members had soon set up graduate programs that obviated the need to travel to Germany for doctoral training. But the price for this professionalisation was that the younger economists had become less politically outspoken. And, of course, if they were less political in their academic work, there was no chance that they would become active in electoral politics.

18 See Bateman (1998) and Bateman and Kapstein (1999). The professional fate of these ethical economists has been documented most completely by Mary O. Furner (1975) and, in a somewhat different context, most recently by Nancy Cohen (2002).

Ironically, the nature of republican arguments also changed in the decades after the Civil War as the rapid vertical integration of industry caused a widespread abandonment of the traditional ideal of the small entrepreneur in favour of the new large scale industrial enterprises.[19] But the same people who helped shape the turn in republican thinking were anxious to squash the nascent labour movement and were the same people who used their positions of power to pressure the young economists to change their positions on the rights of labourers.

Thus, despite some change in the republican ideal, and despite the professionalisation of economics in the last three decades of the century, economists found themselves at the end of the nineteenth century in an even more tenuous position than they were earlier in the century. They now had doctoral degrees, a professional organisation, and academic positions, but the process of acquiring all these had involved a trade-off that required that they abandon their original aim of increasing the role of the State in the economy. By the end of the century, *laissez-faire* was as fully regnant as it had been at any time in the nineteenth century. The idea that economists would have been elected to Congress at the end of the nineteenth century was undoubtedly less likely than it would have been in 1820.

Conclusion

The question of the vertical integration of American industry in the last decades of the nineteenth century raises one other possible cause for the absence of economists from the US Congress. It is sometimes argued that the United States did not have a national economy until the end of the nineteenth century. The crux of this argument is that only with the construction of the railroads and the rise of large scale industrial enterprises did America integrate its regions into one economy. It is impossible to know whether this fact contributed to the lack of interest on the part of economists from serving in Congress, but the issue is difficult to disentangle because it is at exactly this time that the young economists such as Ely and Henry Carter Adams were being disciplined into quiescence about the 'labour question' and so there was not a large cadre (any cadre) of likely candidates to run for office at this time. That is to say, while we do not observe any difference in participation rates in Congress before, during, or after the second industrial revolution (there was no participation), and so we might infer that it had no influence on the desire to seek public office among economists, there are also extraneous circumstances that could have caused this outcome.

Thus, we are left with only a few thin reeds upon which to make a serious conjecture about why American economists in the nineteenth century were not interested in serving in the US Congress. Their lack of interest may have been the result of the anti-intellectualism in American culture; they may have seen themselves as unlikely candidates for public office. Their lack of interest may also have been the

19 See Cohen (2002).

result of the particular structure and timing of the professionalisation of economists in the United States; unlike their European counterparts they were not intimately connected with legal education. But perhaps the most likely, and unexpected, cause of their lack of interest may have been that, unlike in Europe, they did not have a unique perspective within their own society about the role of the government in the economy. Much like the rest of their countrymen, American economists held a broadly liberal view that suggested that the State should stand back and let people pursue their own fortunes, acting only to check the formation of monopolies. Because this view was widely held, and because it was well represented in Congress, there was no special need for economists to seek election.

In the end, it may simply be that while American economists enjoyed contributing to specialist debates about questions like the appropriate level of tariffs or the proper treatment of national debt, they did not see the need to enter a larger debate about the shape and structure of the American economy. That argument was already settled and the widely agreed outlook was that apart from its specialist functions in collecting revenue or creating a national currency, the federal government had little active role to play in the American economy.

Postscript

In order to make an argument about why American economists did not serve in Congress, I have talked exclusively about the nineteenth century. My clear intention in this argument is to imply that the forces that kept economists out of Congress up until 1900 continued to keep them out of Congress clear through the interwar period that other papers in this volume cover.

It must be noted, however, that while it is true that economists did not enter Congress in large numbers in the twentieth century, they did find some success in the first two decades of the century during the heyday of the Progressive movement (1904-1918).[20] The conservative political tide of the 1890s finally broke during Theodore Roosevelt's presidency during the first eight years of the new century and there was crush of new laws prohibiting child labour, limiting the work day, and providing unemployment insurance. On the federal level, three important pieces of economic legislation were passed during Woodrow Wilson's presidency (1912-1920), the Federal Reserve Act, the Federal Trade Commission Act, and the Clayton Act. For our purposes, Wilson's presidency is itself worth note because he had studied under Richard T. Ely in the 1880s and because he was the president of Princeton University before he entered electoral politics. Thus, he was not only educated as an economist, but he became the rare academic who was elected to public office.[21]

20 I could find only one economist in Congress in the first four decades of the century, Senator Paul Douglas of Illinois.

21 Wilson remains the only prominent American academic to be elected president, and one

The American story is quite different than the European stories in at least two important regards, however. First, the increase in interest in America in economic legislation to address the changing nature of industrial society came before the war; WW1 caused a political reaction in America against the Progressive movement. Thus, unlike Europe, where socialists were elected in many countries in the immediate aftermath of the war, in America conservative forces took control of the executive and legislature after the war and the period of active reform came to an abrupt end. The second difference is that although there was an increased interest during the Progressive period in addressing questions of the rights of labourers and the nature of competition, this still did not lead to an influx of economists to Congress. Whatever was keeping American economists out of Congress at the end of the nineteenth century seemed to have continued to also keep them out of Congress in the early twentieth century.

References

Appleby, J. (1984), *Capitalism and a New Social Order: The Republican Vision of the 1790's*, New York University Press, New York and London.

Barber, W.J. (2003), 'American Economics to 1900', in W.J. Samuels, J.E. Biddle, and J.B. Davis (eds), *A Companion to the History of Economic Thought*, Blackwell, Oxford, pp. 231-45.

Bastiat, F. (1850), *Harmonies économiques*, Guillaumin, Paris.

Bateman, B.W. (1998), 'Clearing the Ground: The Demise of the Social Gospel Movement and the Rise of Neoclassical Economics', in M. Morgan and M. Rutherford (eds), *From Interwar Pluralism to Postwar Neoclassicism, History of Political Economy*, **30**(Supplement), pp. 29-52.

Bateman, B.W. and Kapstein, E. (1999), 'Between God and The Market: The Religious Roots of the American Economic Association', *Journal of Economic Perspectives*, **13**(4), pp. 248-59.

Burke, M.J. (1995), *The Conundrum of Class: Public Discourse on the Social Order in America*, University of Chicago Press, Chicago.

Cohen, N. (2002), *The Reconstruction of American Liberalism, 1865-1914*, University of North Carolina Press, Chapel Hill.

Conkin, P.K. (1981), *Prophets of Prosperity: America's First Political Economists*, Indiana University Press, Bloomington.

Dorfman, J. (1946), *The Economic Mind in American Civilization: 1606-1865*, **2**, Viking Press, New York.

Dorfman, J. (1949), *The Economic Mind in American Civilization: 1865-1918*, **3**, Viking Press, New York.

Foner, E. (1970), *Free Soil, Free Labor, Free Men: The Ideology of the Republican Party Before the Civil War*, Oxford University Press, Oxford.

---

of the few to enter national level politics. At the end of the twentieth century, Phil Graham (Texas), an economist, and Paul Wellstone (Minnesota), a political scientist, were each elected to the Senate.

Foner, E. (1988), *Reconstruction: America's Unfinished Revolution, 1863-1877*, Harper & Row, New York.

Furner, M.O. (1976), *Advocacy and Objectivity: A Crisis in the Professionalization of American Social Science*, University of Kentucky Press, Lexington.

Hatch, N.O. (1989), *The Democratization of American Christianity*, Yale University Press, New Haven.

Hofstadter, R. (1963), *Anti-Intellectualism in American Life*, Knopf, New York.

Marty, M. (1984), *Pilgrims in their Own Land: 500 Years of American Religion*, Penguin Books, New York.

Ross, D. (1991), *The Origins of American Social Science*, Cambridge University Press, Cambridge.

Say, J.-B. (1803), *Traité d'économie politique*, chez Deterville, Paris (translated by C.R. Prinsep, 1821).

Sundquist, J.L. (1981), *The Decline and Resurgence of Congress*, The Brookings Institution, Washington, DC.

Walker, A. (1866), *The Science of Wealth*, Little, Brown, Boston.

Wayland, F. (1837), *Elements of Political Economy*, Gould, Kendall & Lincoln, Boston.

Index of Names

For Product Safety Concerns and Information please contact our EU
representative GPSR@taylorandfrancis.com
Taylor & Francis Verlag GmbH, Kaufingerstraße 24, 80331 München, Germany

www.ingramcontent.com/pod-product-compliance
Ingram Content Group UK Ltd.
Pitfield, Milton Keynes, MK11 3LW, UK
UKHW020019200926
475702UK00014B/1962
9781138258877